THE CIVILIZATION OF THE AMERICAN INDIAN SERIES

UNIVERSITY OF OKLAHOMA PRESS

THE FIVE CIVILIZED TRIBES

CHEROKEE · CHICKASAW · CHOCTAW · CREEK · SEMINOLE

GRANT FOREMAN

Introductory note by John R. Swanton

Books by Grant Foreman published by
the University of Oklahoma Press

Indian Removal: The Emigration of the Five Civilized Tribes
Advancing the Frontier, 1830–1860
The Five Civilized Tribes
Indians and Pioneers: The Story of the Southwest before 1830
Sequoyah

TO

the memory of

JOHN R. THOMAS

A loyal friend of
the Indian

PREFACE

ONE of the most interesting phases of American history embraces the removal of 60,000 Indians from the southern states and their adaptation to a new home within what is now the State of Oklahoma. These tribes, the Cherokee, Creek, Chickasaw, Choctaw, and Seminole, were distinguished by character and intelligence far above the average aboriginal. From their geographical and historical association with the white man in the South they acquired a measure of his culture as well as of his vices. Through the influence of their leading men they had copied some of the customs and institutions of the whites and four of the tribes crudely modeled their governments on those of the states. Because of their progress and achievements they came to be known as The Five Civilized Tribes.

In proportion as these Indians improved in intelligence and culture, wealth, and enterprise, did the white man covet their country in the South. Individually and in concert, by law and without law, he oppressed these owners of the soil and depredated upon their country until they were driven forth to find a refuge in the wilderness west of the Mississippi River. The story of this tragic enterprise covering the decade 1830–1840, is related by the Author in *Indian Removal* (Norman, 1932). He has treated an earlier phase, the unorganized emigration of a few thousand of these Indians prior to 1830 in *Indians and Pioneers* (New Haven, 1930).

Upon arrival at their destination the immigrants were confronted with the problem of adjusting themselves to a strange country and establishing amicable relations with indigenous wild tribes who were required by the Federal Government to make room for the newcomers. This interesting phase of their history was described by the author in *Advancing the Frontier* (Norman, 1933). Next in order is the account of the rehabilitation and reconstruction of these immigrants after the demoralization and impoverishment caused by their forcible removal. This is the subject of the present volume which covers the three decades from 1830 to the beginning of the Civil War.

The Indians arrived in the West in a state of mixed emotions. The treaties by which they held their homeland had been violated by white men who crowded into their country. New treaties by which they surrendered their lands in the South had been negotiated under the influence of coercion and bribes paid to leading members of the tribes. The journey to their new home was a tragic undertaking characterized by incredible misery, hardship, and suffering; thousands died on the way and the survivors arrived in the West destitute and discouraged. These home-loving, pastoral people, broken in spirit and morale, suspicious of their leaders and bitter at the influences responsible for their unhappy situation were illy prepared to begin life anew in a strange country. The one ray of light and hope was the conviction that at last they were so far removed from the white man that they could look forward to a life free from his devastating blight.

The period under consideration may be regarded as an interlude of peace in the lives of these Indians, a short span reaching from their enforced migration to the devastation of the Civil War; during this period their development and progress were remarkable. Fixed of habit and unused to roving and adaptation to new environments, these simple people found themselves bewildered by strange surroundings and problems of adjustment to unfamiliar conditions and methods of living. The western home of the immigrants was guaranteed to them by solemn assurances in the treaties. This was auspicious but the Government had likewise assured them of its protection in their old homes and they had seen those promises ruthlessly flouted. Suspicion of the government's promise of security inhered in their problems, and rendered difficult their reëstablishment and readjustment, a labor that required faith in the Government, confidence in themselves and their leaders and optimism for the future. But necessity, hope, and resolution came to their aid and they gradually entered into an era of reconstruction and improvement. In spite of tremendous difficulties their progress year after year and their achievements in the field of culture and government have no parallel in the history of our Indians.

GRANT FOREMAN

Muskogee, Oklahoma

CONTENTS

BOOK FIVE / *Cherokee*

ILLUSTRATIONS

INTRODUCTORY NOTE

Few of those old line Americans who look askance, and withal somewhat superciliously, upon the governmental experiments of certain of our younger states realize that such experiments are by no means new to their territory, and that five of a much more unique character were initiated and consummated before the present State of Oklahoma came into existence. These experiments consisted in the organization of as many bodies of American aborigines—the Choctaw, Chickasaw, Creeks, Seminole, and Cherokee—into small red republics, voluntarily set in motion, and maintained with a considerable measure of success for more than half a century. Of course many other Indian tribes within our borders preserved some form of self-government long after intimate white contact, but, for the most part, these were mere continuations of existing forms. In the case of the Five Civilized Tribes we have attempts to cast Indian minds into new collective moulds which were in large measure of white origin and intended to lead the individuals composing them into an independent participation in white culture and white civilization. A comprehensive study of these experiments, while it should not fail to interest the citizen of Oklahoma, has a much wider appeal—to the historian, the sociologist, the economist, the student of law, the student of Christian missions and of religion in its wider aspects, but particularly to the man who is primarily concerned with race relations whether as scientist or as the administrator of some primitive tribe.

The story of the five republics constitutes from many points of view, therefore, a major problem, such as one of our larger foundations might well have been called upon to support if that other and more important question, the selection of a competent investigator, could have been satisfactorily determined upon. For research of this sort requires a rare combination of scholarship, industry, and patience, and the presentation of its results an ability to select and coördinate significant matter and to weave it into a concise, carefully documented pattern through the medium of a lucid style. Above all there must be genuine enthusiasm for the subject in hand without which there is always danger of superficiality, carelessness, or repulsive ponderosity of expression which defeats the purposes of the whole undertaking.

Without the support of any such foundation, Oklahoma and the Five Civilized Tribes are fortunate in having a devoted volunteer to assume the tangible expenses and supply the intangible and invaluable services which this project demands. Dr. Foreman's several publications furnish a reference library on that side of Oklahoma history dealing with the Indian population of the eastern portion of the state which, at a modest estimate, involves three-fifths of her story and will be of permanent value to the citizens of the commonwealth, to all interested in her past and solicitous for her future, and to students of race relations everywhere.

The present volume takes up the narrative where *Advancing the Frontier* left it and carries on the story of native efforts for rehabilitation in a new home, efforts to maintain native control and self-derived culture with due adaptations to alien influences and altered conditions, and to keep open that possibility of leading "the better life" to which all normal humanity so fondly aspires. This work and its predecessors are permanent monuments to the virtues and the strivings, the successes and the failures, of the Indian and supply a record of contacts between Indians and whites with which it will be well for a member of the latter race to make himself familiar even though it contains all too much that he cannot contemplate with racial pride.

JOHN R. SWANTON

BOOK ONE / *Choctaw*

CHAPTER ONE / *Problems of a New Home*

A
s OUR aborigines are disappearing into oblivion a few of them have tenaciously retained a place in the progress and culture of the country. Five great tribes of Indians from time immemorial occupied the land that now comprises most of what are known as the Southern States. At an early day white settlers from the East coveting this beautiful country began pushing their settlements into it. Treaties were negotiated from time to time by which the whites were established in the country of the Indians who were thus subjected to a progressive divestiture of their country and corresponding limiting of their habitable domain. As the movement gathered momentum the resistance of the Indians began to take form and manifested itself by an intelligent demonstration of their rights. But this unequal conflict of interests resulted in the inevitable decision—the subjugation and spoliation of the weaker race of people who were driven from their ancestral domain to find homes in a wilderness region west of the Mississippi River lately acquired from France.

These Indians, the Choctaw, Chickasaw, Cherokee, Creek and Seminole, through their contact with the white settlers and missionaries, the struggle to retain their homes, and their innate intelligence, had acquired the rudiments of the white man's culture and were making amazing progress in civilized ways when this achievement was wrecked by the ruthless expulsion from their homes during the decade following the year 1830. But even after this desolating experience their courage and fortitude and resourcefulness enabled them to mend their broken institutions and renew their progress towards an enlightened and cultured existence.

The Choctaw Nation included a few leading men who entertained advanced ideas on the subject of education and industry long before the tribe emigrated from Mississippi. In 1801 the chiefs of the tribe requested to be furnished agricultural implements, to have a black-smith settled among them, and instructors employed to teach their women to spin and weave; one chief asked for cotton cards, as his people already made cloth; and another complained that a cotton gin which he had applied for the year before, had not been sent to him.[1] Doctor Morse furnishes an interesting picture of the Choctaw people in 1822: Within a few years, he says, they had made great advances in agriculture and other arts of civilized life. They raised corn, pulse, melons, and cotton. In one year they spun and wove 10,000 yards of cotton cloth. An ingenious Choctaw for a series of years raised cotton and with cards and spinning wheels made by him, he spun and wove it, and then made it into clothing. The Choctaw also raised a great many cattle. "They are friendly to travelers, for whose accommodation they have established a number of public inns, which for neatness and ac-commodation actually excell many among the whites."[2]

At this period the Choctaw Indians were coming under the in-fluence of the missionaries to whom they were indebted for much of the progress that characterized their condition. In August, 1818, the American Board of Commissioners for Foreign Missions established a missionary station in the Choctaw Nation, which they named Elliott after the celebrated New England missionary. Rev. Cyrus Byington was one of their earliest missionaries and many years later he wrote an account for the purpose of comparing their early condition with their improved state in 1852:[3]

"There was a period, previous to the time when the missionaries went among them, that the Choctaws used the teeth of beaver, and the outer bark of cane and reed dried hard for knives. They made bags of the bark of trees, twisted and woven by hand. Ropes were made of the bark of trees. Blankets were made of turkey feathers. Fire was formerly produced by friction. Two dried pieces of ash wood were

1   United States Senate *Document* No. 1 page 188, Twenty-third Congress, first session.
2   Rev. Jedidiah Morse, *A Report to the Secretary of War on Indian Affairs*, 183.
3   "Improvements in the Choctaw Nation during the last Fifty Years," in the *New York Evangelist*, copied in the *Indian Advocate*, October, 1852, p. 3.

rubbed rapidly across each other till fire was produced. When they planted corn, it was not secured by any fence, nor was the land plowed —it was dug up with hoes, and planted without rows, or any order. *This labor was performed by the women.* The men were hunters, and followed various amusements, talked, smoked, and danced, and attended councils and feasts, weddings and funerals. The women also attended these.

"When the missionaries arrived in 1818, it was a rare thing to see a Choctaw warrior wear a hat, pantaloons, or shoes. Inquiry was made, and but very few were found who would not get drunk, when whiskey was offered them. In very few houses were there floors, windows, tables, beds or chairs. The principal articles of food were corn, sweet potatoes and beans. A species of hominy called tamfula was prepared from their corn, and served up in an earthen bowl with one spoon in it, made of the buffalo horn or of iron. The men ate first, and by themselves. The women and children ate afterwards. At times they had bear meat, venison, wild turkeys and pork for food.

"But many families suffered much for want of food. Their fields were small and poorly cultivated. There were few among them who could read. . . . . The late Dr. Cornelius passed through the Choctaw Nation in 1817, and preached at the Agency. A white man who attended the meeting has since stated to the writer, that he had then resided among the Choctaws seven years, and during that time had not heard a sermon preached, a prayer offered, or a blessing asked at table. They had at that time no written form of government, no written laws, no trial by jury. The widow had no dowry, and children no inheritance in their father's property."

In another account written by Mr. Byington descriptive of the early condition of the Choctaw people,[4] he said "they were ignorant of religion, and letters. Some eight or ten men had been partially educated, when we came here. They could read and write, and some of them understood figures a little. I do not remember a native Choctaw woman who had learned to read before the missionaries came to the nation. They were a nation of drunkards. Only *one man* was pointed

4 Choctaw Mission, Stockbridge, Eagletown, P. O., Choctaw Nation, March 22, 1849, for the *Boston Alliance and Visitor*, copied in *The Indian Advocate*, July, 1849, p. 4.

out as an exception, when the first missionary came. We found *three* more afterwards.

"They were very indolent, poor, wretched, sickly, and dying very fast. They indulged in gross sensual vices. They were guilty of some destructive crimes such as infanticide and murder. They were given up to believe in witchcraft, which they punished with death. Hundreds have been killed for this belief. They were a very superstitious people; believing in signs, birds, dreams, ghosts, wood-nymphs, conjurors, spectres, and the like. They had been greatly reduced in numbers by the small pox, measles, and other diseases. They had never had a missionary located among them, from the foundation of the Christian Church, that we know of, till Brother Kingsbury came.

"They had been compelled to sell tract after tract of their lands, and were broken hearted. In 1830 their ancient inheritance all went at once. While moving west, hundreds perished on the road, and their property was lost. And thousands have died since. We rarely meet an old man or woman now." The bright side of the picture when Mr. Byington describes the amazing progress and improvement of these people in their western home, will be given in its place.

Soon after the missionary influence began to manifest itself, the chief of the Six Towns division of the Choctaw tribe enacted some wholesome laws, that an early observer believes to have been the first printed laws of the Choctaw people:[5] "Six Towns, Choctaw Nation, October 18, 1822. 'Hoolatohooma (or red fort,) Chief of the Six Towns, to the Society of good people, who send Missionaries to the Choctaws:'

"Brothers:—The first law I have made is, that when my warriors go over the line among the white people and buy whiskey, and bring it into the nation to buy up the blankets and guns and horses of the red people and get them drunk, the whiskey is to be destroyed. The whiskey drinking is wholly cast among my warriors. The Choctaw women have long been in the habit of destroying their infants, when they did not like to provide for them. I have made a law to have them punished, that no more innocent children be destroyed. The Choctaws formerly stole hogs and cattle, and killed them. I have appointed a

5   "First printed Laws known to the Writer," published in *The Choctaw Telegraph*, copied in *The Indian Advocate*, May, 1849, p. 4.

company of faithful warriors, to take every man who steals, and tie him to a tree, and give him thirty-nine lashes.

"It has been the custom of the Choctaws, where there are three or four sisters, and they marry, that they all live together in one house. I do not want it to be so any longer. I have told them to move away from each other and settle by themselves, and work and make fields and raise provisions. The Choctaws have taken each others wives, and ran away with them. We have now made a law, that those who do so shall be whipt thirty-nine lashes. And if a woman runs away from her husband she is to be whipt in the same manner.

"The Choctaws some of them go to Mobile and New Orleans. I have told my warriors to stay home and work; and if they go and do not get back in time to plant their corn, their corn is to be burnt down. The number of men, women, and children in the Six Towns is 2,164.

"I want the good people to send men and women to set up a school in my district. I want them to do it quick. I am growing old. I know not how long I shall live; I want to see the good work before I die. We have always been passed by, and have no one to assist us. Other parts of the nation have schools; we have none. We have made the above laws, because we wish to follow the ways of the white people. We hope they will assist us in getting our children educated. This is the first time I write a letter. Last fall is the first time we make laws. I say no more. I have told my wants. I hope you will not forget me. 'Hoolatahooma'."

This letter, evidently written with the aid of an amanuensis, was regarded by the contributor as having an important connection "with the Mission at Goshen in the old nation and at Wheelock in this land. In looking at the history of the Choctaw Nation it appears that the Rev. Alfred Wright went to Goshen, August 1, 1823, the next year after the above letter was written. In the spring of 1826, Jeremiah Evarts, Esq., from Boston, and Corresponding Secretary of the American Board, in passing by Redforts house, called in to see him; the Rev. C. Kingsbury, Samuel A. Worcester and C. Byington were with him. But the chief was very infirm and made hardly any conversation with his visitors. Not long after, he died. The company pursued their way to Goshen, which place they reached at a late hour in the night."

In 1830 the Choctaw people "were spinning and making their own clothing of good homespun cloth. I have myself bought many yards of cloth from full-blood Indians of their own make." At a recent camp meeting they observed good order and "were dressed many of them in cloth of their own manufacture—all clean and decent."[6]

Before the enactment by Congress in 1830 of the measure known as the Indian Removal Bill, there were about 2,000 Choctaw Indians scattered through Texas, Louisiana, and Arkansas Territory.[7] A treaty had been made with those living in their eastern home in 1820, by which they were given a vast domain west of the Mississippi River, including the southern half of the present State of Oklahoma. The next year George Gray of Natchitoches was appointed agent for the western Choctaw Indians and he established his agency on the Sulphur Fork near Long Prairie. After the Treaty of 1825 Maj. William L. McClellan of Mississippi, formerly of Tennessee was appointed Choctaw agent and he located his agency at the abandoned Fort Smith in 1826. Vain efforts were then made to induce the Choctaw Indians both east and west, to remove to their new country. Finally the Choctaw treaty of September 27, 1830, known as the Treaty of Dancing Rabbit Creek, provided the means for effecting the removal of the tribe from the East. A few emigrated that winter but the movement was organized the next year and by 1833 a majority of the tribe had reached their new home in the West.[8]

Some of the immigrants who arrived in 1832 applied themselves industriously and raised a surplus of corn which they were able to sell to the Government to subsist the arrivals expected the next year. Those who began to make preparations for the future all settled on the river and creek timbered bottom lands, for they had a well-fixed conviction that they could not make a living on the uplands nor could they build homes anywhere but in the timber that provided logs for their houses, and rails for fences. They were making considerable progress in the construction of their homes and little farms when, in the first week in June, 1833, there came one of the greatest floods in the history of the Arkansas River.

"I pause to tell you something of the most awful judgment of God,

6 Ward to Kingsbury, May 7, 1830, *Cherokee Phoenix*, July 24, 1830, p. 2, col. 2.
7 Grant Foreman, *Indians and Pioneers*.
8 *Ibid.*, *Indian Removal*. Several hundred Choctaw emigrants who refused to go to the country intended for them traveled to Texas instead, and it was some years before they joined their tribesmen in the Indian Territory.

on these parts and the Terr. of Ark. in the unparrallelled rise of waters; the week of our return from the Osage tour, the rains set in most powerfully and such was the effect that tho at Union and the Neosho the water did not equal the flood of 1826, yet on the Arkansas it far exceeded that one by 8 or 10 feet at least. Mr. Chouteau lost all his trading houses and all the village, or nearly. The water rose into one corner of Ft. Gibson and from the Creek Nation to the south of the Arkansas immense damage has been sustained, hundreds of families have lost everything—fields, houses, stocks of horses and cattle and even their clothes."[9]

On the Verdigris River, besides Colonel Chouteau's trading houses, the Creek Agency was washed away; at Fort Gibson the bakery, several stables, other small buildings and fences were carried down stream. Colonel Arbuckle wrote: ". . . .on the 4th inst., the Grand River or Ne. o. sho for the first time since this post has been established commenced overflowing its banks in front of this Post, and suddenly rose from eight to ten feet higher than any freshet heretofore known; in consequence of which, the greater part of the public and private corn at this point was destroyed."[10] Since the middle of May rain had fallen, several weeks without intermission ". . . .raising the Arkansas River to such a height as has never been seen by the oldest settlers in that section of country. . . . . Nearly all the people who lived upon the river have been ruined. . . . . on the bottoms near several of the creeks every house has been washed away. . . . all the Fork of the Canadian was inundated. At the latter place a large amount of stock, of almost every kind, was washed away; and it is said that, so powerful was the force of the water, the course of the river at Fort Smith was changed entirely, making its way through the farm of Mr. Alexander, and carrying before it almost his whole property. Mr. John Rogers is said to have lost 1,700 bushels of salt; and his works are destroyed. Mr. Webber is said to have lost in stock etc. at least $3,000, besides a small black boy who was drowned."[11]

Prior to that time the highest stage noted on the Arkansas River

9 Vaill to Greene, July 2, 1833, *Missionary Records*, LXXII No. 102, Harvard-Andover Theological Library.

10 Arbuckle to Jones, June 12, 1833, AGO, OFD, 117 A 33.

11 "Letter from Arkansas Territory," June 25, 1833, in *Cherokee Phoenix* (New Echota, Ga.), September 28, 1833, p. 3, col. 1.

of which there was any record was in 1814, and next to that was the flood of 1823.[12] In 1837, when army officers were seeking an eligible site for the new post that was subsequently located at Fort Smith, they reported that at all other places but two, for a distance of thirty miles up and down the river, the flood of 1833 had overflowed the adjacent land for a depth of from one to twenty-five feet.[13] The flood buried in sand Webbers Falls,[14] that Lieutenant Wilkinson in 1807 reported as being "a fall of nearly seven feet perpendicular."[15] The banks of the Arkansas above the Choctaw agency as far up as Harrold's Bluff or Swallow Rock, after the flood waters receded, were "covered with mud, quicksand, and the carcasses of animals destroyed by the water." Captain McClellan, the Choctaw agent, was for some time engaged in cleaning rifles and drying blankets and clothing that had been covered by water for ten days.[16] The loss suffered by the Indians was excessive from the fact that they had all their improvements in the bottoms where they raised nearly all of their corn.[17]

At Fort Gibson the Grand River was out of its banks for more than a week. Travel to the north and east was arrested for twice as long; the flood aggravated the pest of flies, and travelers were compelled for some time to move only at night.[18] Much sickness followed the flood. "Not a family but more or less sick; the Choctaws dying to an alarming extent. . . . . Near the agency there are 3,000 Indians and within the hearing of a gun from this spot 100 have died within five weeks."[19]

In spite of the floods, however, in the autumn of 1833 the more provident Choctaw Indians had a surplus of 40,000 bushels of corn, which the Government purchased to apply on the allowance of the emigrants who were to come the next year. But that did not appease the hunger of a class of earlier arrivals who had consumed their year's

12   *Arkansas Gazette*, June 10, 1833.
13   *American State Papers*, "Military Affairs," VII, 980.
14   *Memoirs of Narcissa Owen*, 43.
15   Elliott Coues, *The Expedition of Zebulon Montgomery Pike*, II, 415.
16   *Document*, II, 845.
17   *Ibid.*, 531.
18   *Ibid.*, 924
19   Armstrong to Herring, September 20, 1833, OIA "Choctaw Agency." "One hundred died last month from various diseases" (Rains to Gibson, September 12, 1833, *Document*, I, 851).

allowance of rations and so had no further demands on the Government. Many of those who were not incapacitated by sickness were engaged in maintaining the strife they had brought from the East. Bitter contention over the selection of chiefs and animosity towards the authority that had caused their removal as well as against the members of the tribe who had acquiesced in it, supplemented other agencies in distracting many of them from the occupation of making homes and farms. Farming was neglected by many, and the next year there was much distress from lack of food and want of means to purchase it.

A majority of the Choctaw tribe being now in the West, Armstrong was given instructions in April, 1833, to carry out the terms of the treaty. Two public blacksmiths had been working for a year and he was instructed to engage a third. A mill-wright was to be employed at not to exceed $600 annually, and the Indians were to be directed to locate their little water mills "upon durable streams, and at good sites. . . . conveniently situated for those who have work to be done, and equitably with respect to the different districts." Ten thousand dollars was appropriated to erect a council house for the nation, a house for the chief of each of the three districts, and a church for each district to be used as a schoolhouse until others were built. Armstrong was directed to determine the plans for the buildings, and let contracts for their construction. Rev. Mr. Stirman had been engaged as a teacher and Armstrong directed him to "repair to Colonel Folsom's settlement, where I believe the anxiety of the Indians for a school is so great that they will erect a temporary schoolhouse."

In the midst of internal strife and jealousy, Agent Armstrong in December, at Doaksville, advised the Choctaw people to organize their government and take over the regulation of their internal affairs that had been exercised by the war department. They accordingly appointed the first of February, 1834, to meet at Turnbull's on the Kiamichi River, half way between the Red and Arkansas rivers to hold their first general council and form a constitution. The meeting was attended by representatives from only part of the tribe, others refusing to participate in it. A constitution was prepared and adopted by representatives of Nitakechi's district,[20] but the people of Pushmataha District without taking the trouble to participate in the adoption of a

20   This district was called Apuckshunnubbee or Oklafaliah (Oklafalaya).

constitution or set up any laws, undertook to select a chief for the whole tribe.

This aggravated the bitter feeling in the tribe and Superintendent Armstrong informed the Indians that he would not recognize chiefs selected in that manner and advised them to begin again, call all their chiefs and ninety-nine treaty captains into council and set up their government before electing officers and injecting politics in their business.

There were only two of the old chiefs in the West, Mushulatubbe and Nitakechi. Greenwood Leflore having abandoned his tribe on removal, remained in Mississippi to enjoy the prosperity that had accrued to him by that event. Red River (Apuckshunubbee or Oakla-faliah) District which included most of his followers, thus being without a chief, on July 7, 1834 his brother Thomas Leflore, was elected to that office.[21] Nitakechi and Mushulatubbe were reëlected chiefs in their respective districts that same year, but the latter was soon succeeded by Joseph Kincaid. Mushulatubbe's district, named for him lay on the Arkansas River and had a population then of about 2,000. About the same number comprised Nitakechi's district which was named Pushma-taha and lay on the west side of the Kiamichi River. East of the Kiami-chi, the dense settlements of Red River District contained more than 7,000 Indians until they began removing higher up the Red River.[22]

About three weeks after their arrival in the West the treaty captains of Nitakechi's district at Horse Prairie wrote the President that they were well pleased with their new homes; but they objected to having to cross the Kiamichi River and travel to Doaksville to receive their annuity. They particularly objected to the great number of white traders who were swarming into the country to the great disadvantage of Indian merchants who could supply the wants of the Indians if left to themselves, but who could not compete with their white rivals. With the coming of the Indians the little town of Doaksville had grown up near Fort Towson, consisting entirely of white traders, except two Indian merchants.

21 Armstrong to Choctaw Chiefs, *Talk*, March 25, 1834; Armstrong to Herring, April 25, 1834; Brown to Herring, October 11, 1834, OIA, "1834 Choctaws West." Colonel Nail was the opposing candidate. They were nominated by their respective parties in May (*Missionary Records*, Vol. LXXII, No. 146).

22 Byington to Bullard, December 30, 1834, *Religious Intelligencer*, XIX, 722.

Some of the more enterprising of the immigrant Indians not only conducted trading stores among their own people, but embraced the opportunity for profitable hunting and trading expeditions among the western Indians. Capt. David Folsom left with a party of twelve men in October, 1835, and returned in February. They went to Coffee's trading post on the Red River west of the Cross Timbers, which he made his base of operations. From here they traveled west and southwest sixty or seventy miles where they were in frequent contact with the Comanche Indians, whom they reported as friendly to them, the Cherokee, and Creeks, but bitter against the Delaware and Shawnee hunters.[23]

Armstrong had issued licenses to five white traders in the Choctaw country, and the war department held that the Indians had nothing to say on the subject; that the white traders would "prevent the prevalence of a monopolizing spirit among the native Choctaw traders, very injurious to the great body of people." The white traders were required to keep for sale stocks of goods suited to the use of the Indians, and they were forbidden to farm or keep more stock than that required for family use. They were also "forced to close their doors on the Sabbath."[24]

But the principal object of the communication of Nitakechi's captains was to request the annuity to which by the terms of the treaty they were entitled on their removal, including plows, iron, steel, anvil and blacksmith's tools, saws, knives, hoes, wedges and other implements needed by the pioneer. In addition to 600 blankets, strouds, domestics, plaids and calico for the individuals, the chief needed his "fine frock coat laced with gold" at $140, and one pair of fine pantaloons at forty. They wanted a blacksmith and thirty three small medals, three larger ones, and one still larger for the chief; they wished also "a drum, fife, and a flag for the use of our district."[25]

Pursuant to the terms of the treaty, the Government ordered for the immigrant Choctaw articles for their use in the West. For those

23 Stuart to Seawell, February 10, 1836, OIA, Choctaw file. Many of the emigrant Indians were going out on fall hunts and called on the agent for their annuities with which to equip themselves (Armstrong to Harris, August 16, 1836, OIA, ibid., A 25).

24 Document, III, 660; ibid., IV, 163.

25 Ibid., IV, 71.

who went in the winter of 1831-1832, the war department contracted for a number of agricultural implements on the supposition that they would be in the hands of the Indians for use in the following spring. Among these were 200 hilling hoes, five or six inches wide; 200 weeding hoes, eight or nine inches wide; 100 grubbing hoes, and 500 plows with wrought-iron plates. The buildings at Fort Smith had been repaired to house these farming tools so they would be ready for the Indians on their arrival in the West. They were shipped September 21, 1831, from the arsenal at Philadelphia and were received at Fort Smith March 29, 1832.[26] From here most of them were carried overland to Red River, where they arrived long after the Indians most needed them. 250 cotton cards and an equal number of wool cards were shipped to McClellan, the Choctaw agent at Fort Smith.

There were also 550 rifles contracted for; the Indians expressed a preference for those made by Mr. Derringer, and the contract was let to him. 350 were to be fitted with flintlocks, and the other 200 with percussion locks. However, after they were delivered the Indians asked the agent to take back the percussion rifles and let them have all flint-locks. The barrel was from three to four feet long with a half-inch bore; the rifle was furnished with ramrod, ball screw in lieu of wiper, nipple screw, bullet moulds and woolen cover to each. Another contract was made with Mr. Tryon of Philadelphia for 450 more rifles.[27] There were furnished also 20,000 pounds of lead for bullets, 10,000 pounds of powder[28] and 16,000 flints for the rifles; the latter cost three dollars a thousand. When the powder was delivered at Fort Smith and issued to the Indians they found it of such inferior quality that they could not use it.[29] The Indian agent notified the arsenal to take it away, and it was not replaced for a year. There were also promised to be delivered at Fort Smith for the Indians 1,000 spinning wheels;[30] a few hundred four-pound axes, which the Indians said were well-nigh worthless, were delivered, besides a few blankets.

26 *Ibid.*, I, 491.

27 *Ibid.*, II, 287, 297, 314, 345, 349, 373, 689.

28 *Ibid.*, I, 256.

29 *Ibid.*, III, 662.

30 The spinning wheels promised in the treaty were to be furnished with steel spindles and turned iron axle, the wood well seasoned. "The looms to be of the best seasoned materials, with hand shuttles, cast iron rag wheels, and wrought iron wrists. . . .

MURIEL H. WRIGHT

*Mushulatubbe in 1838, from the Catlin painting
in the Smithsonian Institution.*

First Choctaw Council House

The next year 500 more plows were sent to Fort Smith. They were shipped from the East May 2, 1832, reached Little Rock in July, and were stored in a warehouse and apparently forgotten; discovered again following the clamor of the disbursing agent at Fort Smith, who said his Indians were badly in need of them to engage in their spring plowing, these useful instruments were sent on their way up the Arkansas, where they arrived April 12, 1833, long after they could have been used to good purpose. There was some official jealousy and lack of coördination that occasioned the studied neglect of the plows. It happened that the 500 that were detained so long at Little Rock had been ordered by the Indian department; and the department of subsistence, which was in charge of the removal of the Indians, permitted them to remain in storage without any apparent effort to get them to the Indians in time to be of service.

The second winter there were engaged for the Indians other articles, including kettles, iron wedges, grindstones, drawing knives, hand-saws, four-quarter and three-quarter augurs, cross-cut saws, whip-saws, one bellows, anvil and set of blacksmith tools. Another lot of hoes and axes were ordered for the newcomers, but there was loud complaint when spring came that they had not received these useful tools, without which they could not clear the brush and timber and prepare the land for tillage; and as if to mock their efforts, these implements arrived at Fort Smith on July 11, too late to be of any service for the crops of that year.

Perhaps the most picturesque item provided by the Government for the Indians, under the requirements of the treaty, was that calculated to enhance the pulchritude of the many headmen of the tribe. Nothing was done for the women, of course, but witness the amazing contribution to male vanity! Ninety-nine chiefs and headmen of the tribe were

---

in fine both of these articles to be what would be called first rate country looms and wheels" (ibid, I, 241). They were not delivered for a long time, and in April, 1840, a large number of Choctaw Indians petitioned the Government to carry out that part of the treaty agreement. In forwarding the petition to Washington, Agent Armstrong said his predecessor had delivered 220 wheels and 88 looms out of 1,000 wheels and 499 looms due them. Armstrong reported that he had let a contract for making the remainder of the wheels, 570 for the large district on the Arkansas River and the balance for the small district on the Red River (Armstrong to Crawford, May 26, 1840, "Western Superintendency," File A 807, 1840).

each provided with the following gaudy articles of raiment; a beaver hat with silver band, cockade and three scarlet plumes; one pair of calfskin puttees, a superfine blue frock coat with collars trimmed with silver lace, a superfine silver lace-trimmed vest, a superfine pair of pantaloons, one Irish linen shirt, patent leather stock and a morocco swordbelt with plates; eighty-seven of these brilliantly accoutered captains bore infantry officers' swords with bright scabbards, basket hilts with two guards and square ends, and the other twelve wore artillery officers' swords with plain bright-yellow scabbards, yellow bands and mounting, basket hilts, and two guards.[31] They were shipped from Philadelphia to Fort Smith in July, 1832, and it well may be assumed Indian Territory never looked the same after these ninety-nine warriors blossomed out in their effulgent splendor.[32]

By the autumn of 1836 a building in each of the three districts, to be used as a church and schoolhouse, had been erected pursuant to the promises in the treaty of removal. The first was constructed by Robert Baker and the other two by William Lowry. The Government was obligated also to erect a house for each of the three chiefs and a council house for the tribe. The Indians had selected sites for these buildings and there was considerable complaint by them because of the delay on the part of the government officials. The site chosen for the council house was near the residence of Vaughn Brashears, a half-breed Choctaw, on the upper part of the Kiamichi River, about midway between the Arkansas and Red rivers. The Indians had been holding councils there for a year or two.

A contract was let to William Lowry who constructed a commodious council house in time for the October, 1838, meeting of the council. The Indians took much pride in planning this building, which was constructed to meet their wishes. It was forty-five by twenty-five feet in size, containing a council chamber 25 by thirty feet and the remainder was divided into two committee rooms, where the district

31   These swords were made at the United States arsenal at Watervliet and cost $1,162.56 (Bomford to Garland, June 13, 1832, OIA) and were delivered to the war department at Washington in June, 1832.

32   Document, I, 99, 116, 452, 717; Thomas L. McKenney and James Hall, History of the Indian Tribes of North America (Philadelphia, 1854); in these three volumes are to be seen pictures of a number of the immigrant Indians garbed in similar uniforms.

delegations could meet for conference. The building was well constructed of trimmed logs six inches thick with fifteen-inch facing, chinked with short timber and pointed with lime mortar; the logs inside were trimmed with dressed plank, and the ceilings, fourteen feet high, were made with tongued and grooved boards; sawed rafters, joists and dressed flooring; a girder running the length of the house with the joists framed in and supported by a round column fifteen inches in diameter, with a Grecian cap; plank cornices with large Grecian moulding and caps; two three-foot doors, a large double door at the end, six windows of eighteen lights each, each light ten by twelve inches, and Venetian shutters, morticed blinds.

The whole rested on three sills twelve by twelve inches, in turn supported by fifteen stone pillars. The council chamber was provided with a platform three feet high and twelve long, one table twelve feet long and twelve benches ten feet long of plank two inches thick. For the accommodation of the spectators a gallery with seats was provided. Two stone chimneys furnished as many fireplaces. The inside of the house was painted white and the doors green. The building was surrounded by a seven-foot fence inclosing an area 150 feet square. Everything about the council house was ample and adequate; and withal it was an imposing structure in that far-off wilderness and gave dignity to the functioning of the Indian government.[33]

Lowry constructed also a house for each of the three chiefs in their respective districts; each house was fifty feet by twenty, having two rooms twenty feet square with a twelve-foot passage between, the whole under one roof; porches ten feet wide extended the full length of the house, front and back. The house was constructed of trimmed logs six inches thick, showing a face of fifteen inches, and the whole rested on twelve-inch sills; there were two stone chimneys with four-foot fire-places to cheer the large rooms with their twelve foot ceilings. The inside of the rooms, columns and hand rails of the porches were painted white and the doors and windows green.

Superintendent Armstrong advertised for bids to furnish 312 looms and 780 spinning-wheels to conform to the specimens at the agency, then in common use in the country. The Government agreed to furnish

33   The specifications are from the advertisement of William Armstrong for bids for the construction of the buildings, dated June 3, 1836, inserted in the *Arkansas Gazette*, June 8, 1836.

the iron for the looms, consisting of cast-iron rag-wheels, wrought-iron catches, iron screws for cross timbers and two shuttles; and for the wheel a turned cast-steel spindle and axle. The Choctaw Indians were for a long time denied the use of the spinning wheels promised them in their treaty. Because of the cost of transportation the Government declined having them made in the East where they could have been turned out rapidly. So their manufacture was intrusted to the laborious process in the Choctaw Nation by Robert Baker, "an individual entirely competent to the task, but whose slowness in the performance must be attributed to the disadvantage of his situation."[34]

Baker set up his shop near the Choctaw agency and after long delay in receiving the irons from Cincinnati, due to low water in the rivers, succeeded in turning out 220 wheels and eighty-eight looms for the Indians in Pushmataha District. For those on Red River he got out the timber and had it cut at Nail's mill; here he equipped a carpenter shop and set up a turning lathe operated by horse power. But there was much complaint concerning the delay in furnishing the looms and wheels necessary to enable the Indians to convert the cotton they were raising, into the clothing so much needed by them. Baker's contract was cancelled by Agent Armstrong, and the wheels and looms were not furnished the Indians for several costly years.

The Choctaw Nation was governed by a written constitution and laws printed in English and Choctaw. Each of the three districts was represented by a chief and ten councillors elected by the qualified voters—males over twenty-one years of age. The councillors and chiefs met on the first Monday of each October in general council for the transaction of the business of the Nation. All measures passed by the council were subject to the veto power of the three chiefs, though when passed by two-thirds of the council they became law regardless of the chiefs.[35] Judges were appointed, juries and executive officers provided for to enforce the law, light-horsemen were employed to seize whisky and destroy it.

When the council met, a speaker and secretary were selected[36] and

34 United States House, *Executive Document* No. 2, p. 291, Twenty-fourth Congress, first session.

35 *Report* of commissioner of Indian affairs for 1838: *Report* of William Armstrong; *ibid* for 1836 in *Arkansas Gazette*, February 14, 1837, p. 1.

36 *Ibid.*, for 1841.

each chief in turn delivered a message to the council, recommending such laws as he thought needful. The council usually remained in session for ten to twenty days; the members received two dollars per diem and mileage, and the chiefs $250.00 annually. The strictest order prevailed and all proceedings were recorded. Observers said that few deliberative bodies could have been conducted with greater order and propriety. The Choctaw Academy in Kentucky had educated many of the most intelligent men in the Indian country, and they were to be seen in their councils taking the deepest interest in the welfare and prosperity of their people.[37]

One of the first measures enacted by the new Choctaw government was a law dealing with the subject of witches; for "the Indians were still addicted to heathen rites and superstitions, fear of witches, ghosts, &c."[38] In 1834 three Choctaw Indians killed a man and a woman of the tribe who were accused of being witches. Superintendent Armstrong demanded the surrender of the murderers who were delivered up on his threat to withhold the autumn annuities payable to the tribe. The Choctaw council then enacted a law imposing the penalty of death upon any one who killed another accused of being a witch and sixty lashes upon any one charging another with being a witch.[39] Soon afterwards they passed a law forbidding Negroes in the nation to own any property and forbidding their being taught to read or sing except with the consent of their masters.[40]

The first exercise of the judicial functions of their government of which records are available was the trial of a slave named Bob, the property of John Caffery, for the murder of a Negro woman belonging to John L. Price; the owners of both slaves being white men with Indian wives and families. The case was tried September 10 and 11, 1834, in Red River District, before the presiding judges, George W. Harkins, Israel Folsom, and Silas L. Fisher, and a jury of twenty-four Choctaw citizens. Joel H. Nail represented the district, William Le-

37 Ibid., for 1842.

38 Williams to Greene, July 17, 1833, *Missionary Records*, ibid., LXXII, No. 107.

39 Armstrong to Harris, September 24, 1834, "Choctaws West." In spite of the law, in 1838 Indians of the Six Towns executed a woman believed to be a witch and caused much excitement in the nation (Hotchkin to Armstrong, July 23, 1838, OIA "School" File A 402).

40 Williams to Greene, January 18, 1837, *Missionary Records*, ibid., No. 35.

flore appeared for Price, and Thomas Hays and Jack Hays represented Caffery, owner of the defendant. Bazil Leflore was secretary of the district. Two-thirds of the jury found the defendant guilty and sentenced him to death. As neither the defendant nor his owner was a citizen of the Choctaw Nation, Superintendent Armstrong perceived difficulties in the situation and directed that the defendant be surrendered to the military authorities to be held in irons until he could consult the Indian department at Washington on the subject.[41]

Acting Superintendent Armstrong in 1836 said that the Red River part of the Choctaw country was "destined soon to be a fine cotton-growing country; the native traders have erected cotton gins, and they purchase all the cotton that is raised by the common Indians and half breeds. It is estimated that about 500 bales will go down Red River from the Choctaws this year. There is one good grist and saw mill near Red River, and another is building on the Poteau, from which large quantities of lumber will go down the Arkansas. To a great extent the trade with these Indians is carried on by the natives. I can state from my own knowledge that two native Choctaws on Red River have this year brought into the country $20,000 worth of goods;[42] and there are others engaged in smaller trade of from 2,000 to 10,000 dollars. They make their purchases in New Orleans, and, I understand are in good credit. The assistants in the three public smith-shops are natives, who in a year or two, will be able to take charge of them. Besides these shops, they have five others of their own, that are used in the farming season. The chase, for a living, is now nearly abandoned; many take a fall hunt, but it is more an excursion of pleasure than a pursuit of gain."[43]

41 OIA, 1835, "Choctaw West (Agency) F. W. Armstrong."
42 One of these Choctaw merchants was Robert M. Jones.
43 *Report* of commissioner of Indian affairs for 1836, *Arkansas Gazette*, February 14, 1837.

CHAPTER TWO / *Schools and Missionaries*

THE Choctaw Indians now occupied an advanced position in education and culture resulting from influences operating long before their removal. In the early part of 1820 the chiefs of the Northwestern District of the Nation by resolution appropriated $2,000 annually for sixteen years towards the support of a school for their children. They sent the resolution to the secretary of war[1] and, with the assistance of David Folsom, a second school was established by the missionaries, who named it Mayhew. The two schools, Elliot and Mayhew, were in charge of the Rev. Cyrus Kingsbury and the Rev. Cyrus Byington, each with a corps of teachers, instructing the youths in books and manual labor.

The treaty of 1825 with the Choctaw Nation[2] provided for the payment to it of $6,000 annually for schools in the Nation. Authority was given for the tribe to expend part of that sum in the education of twenty of their boys at the home of Col. Richard M. Johnson, who in later years was to become vice-president of the United States. Colonel Johnson lived at Great Crossing in Scott County, Kentucky; on his plantation he had two houses which he fitted up for the accommodation of the Choctaw youths and a teacher he engaged for them. He proposed that if he were allowed sufficient compensation he would clothe and feed them and devote much of his time toward establishing them in habits that would govern them through life.[3] Twenty-one Choctaw boys from Mushulatubbe's District, mounted on their

1 Calhoun to McKee, April 14, 1820, OIA, "Choctaw, War Department."

2 Charles J. Kappler, *Laws and Treaties*, II, 149.

3 Johnson to McKenney, September 27, 1825, OIA, "1825 Schools (Choctaw Academy)."

ponies, departed October 15 under the guidance of Peter P. Pitchlynn[4] and arrived at Colonel Johnson's home in time to start the school on the first of November. This was the beginning of the Choctaw Academy, a school destined, through many years of usefulness, to become celebrated in the annals of Indian education.[5]

The desire for education continued to grow among the Choctaw Indians, and four mission schools were flourishing in the Nation at the time progress was interrupted and school work wrecked by the removal of the tribe.[6] They had no sooner arrived in the West however, than, in 1833, they planned, in coöperation with the Government, to expend their annuity of $6,000 in the construction of twelve log houses, the purchase of schoolbooks and the pay of teachers, and they were discussing the expenditure of their annuity of $12,500.00 granted by the treaty of 1830 for the establishment of three more advanced schools. The boys were to be instructed in "the usual arts of husbandry. . . . and the girls in spinning, weaving, and housewifery," in addition to ordinary book learning.[7]

The story of the Indians would not be complete without some account of their friends, the missionaries, who accompanied them to the West and shared their hardships in order that they might minister to them and help rebuild their schools and churches. History of that

4 Johnson to McKenney, October 22, 1835, *ibid;* Report of Thomas Henderson, December 1, 1835, *ibid; Public Advertiser,* November 9, 1825, p. 3, col. 3. Mushulatubbe was called a pagan who was opposed to the work of the missionaries; and Indians of the other districts resented his sending boys to Kentucky to be educated at the expense of the tribe (Folsom to McKenney, June 27, 1826, OIA, "1826 Schools (Choctaw Academy)." The other districts were soon represented however; the next autumn twenty-seven more Choctaw were entered in the school, and in November Opothleyohola brought thirteen Creek boys including his eight-year-old-son.

5 For an extended account of the Choctaw Academy by Carolyn T. Foreman, see *Chronicles of Oklahoma,* Vol. VI, p. 453, and Vol. IX, p. 382, and Vol. X, p. 77; *Col. Richard M. Johnson of Kentucky,* by Leland Winfield Meyer, p. 336.

6 On the removal west of the Choctaw Indians, the American Board of Commissioners for Foreign Missions filed the following claims for improvements at the missions abandoned in the old nation: At Elliott, $6,000; Mayhew, $7,200; Bethel, $1,300; Emmaus, $1,230; Goshen, $1,185; Hebron, $670, and Yakanckchaga, $900 (OIA "Special File" 260). Before their removal was completed Peter P. Pitchlynn was writing to the secretary of war for the approval of teachers selected by them (*Document* II, 890).

7 United States Senate *Document* No. 1, Twenty-third Congress, first session.

trying and interesting period is under great obligations to these same missionaries for the intelligently written accounts of the events and conditions that came under their observation.

Alexander Talley, a Methodist, was the first missionary to depart for the West; he left Mississippi in November, 1830, with some of Leflore's emigrants; though he seems to have been with the Indians in their new home until 1833, there is no record of his having established a mission. After the treaty was ratified and Choctaw removal seemed assured, the Presbyterian missionaries prepared to remove with their Indian charges. Alfred Wright[8] with the assistance of Israel Folsom[9] as translator, had completed the translation into Choctaw of part of the Gospel of St. Luke, and in October he and Mrs. Wright left for Utica New York with his manuscript to have it published. In the following October they sailed from New York and arrived at New Orleans, December 1, 1831. At Vicksburg the next month as they were about to board a boat for Little Rock, Mr. Wright was seized with a spasmodic affection of the heart to which he had been subject for six years.[10] Waiting until he had sufficiently recovered, they sailed February 11 and a week later reached Little Rock where Mr. Wright's condition became so alarming that he was obliged to remain until the fourteenth of the following September; he and Mrs. Wright then drove in a dearborn wagon 190 miles to join their Choctaw friends of the Six Towns in their new home.[11]

In the meantime, Loring S. Williams, another missionary, with his family left Utica, New York, on October 13 and traveled by canal to Buffalo, then by lake to Erie, and stage to Pittsburgh; a steamboat brought them to Memphis where they took a wagon for Mayhew Mission station. Mrs. Williams became ill, they encountered storms

8 "Mr. Alfred Wright, a licensed preacher, on a mission from the South Carolina Presbyterian and Congregational Missionary Society," called on the missionaries at Brainerd on August 6, 1819. Three days later he "took an affectionate leave of us this morning, to prosecute his mission in east Tennessee" (American Board of Commissioners for Foreign Missions, ibid., vol. XVI, No. 2).

9 Israel Folsom and McKee Folson were students at the Indian school at Cornwall, Connecticut, in 1820 and 1821 (Morse, ibid.).

10 Harriet B. Wright to D. Greene, April 6, 1832, Missionary Records, ibid., Vol. LXXII, No. 136.

11 Missionary Herald (January, 1832), Vol. XXVIII, 26; Williams to Greene Missionary Records, ibid., LXXII, No. 100.

and high water, and were obliged to abandon their wagon and continue by canoe. They arrived at Mayhew November 25, and remained until January 16, when they set out for their new station with the immigrant Choctaw Indians. They traveled in a wagon 200 miles to Vicksburg where they joined Mr. and Mrs. Wright whom they accompanied to the mouth of White River, where they ". . . .had to wait for a boat in the western trade. At length we sailed in the *Saratoga* first a few miles up White River, then through the 'cut-off' into the Arkansas," and up that stream to Little Rock.[12]

On the second of March Williams set out with his family for the Choctaw country. He attempted to travel over the roads recently cut up and rendered almost impassable by the thousands of emigrants with their wagons, oxen and horses. He traveled on foot, driving two ox teams hitched to his wagon, and his family rode horseback. But finding it almost impossible to make any progress with a wagon he abandoned it before reaching Washington, Arkansas, and continued with three horses, on one of which they packed their tent, ax, clothing, blankets, and provisions; and on the other two, five persons, including three children, rode, while the remainder walked. When they arrived at Washington, Mr. Williams left his family while he continued to the Choctaw Nation, and on March 24 he arrived at a white settlement on the line. Across the line he found the Indians, some of whom had taken possession of old houses and fields formerly occupied by white people who, by the Government had been removed from the Choctaw land; in some instances several families were industriously tending one field, for the food they so much needed; some of them had put up tents and other temporary quarters and were building houses. Companies of Indians were arriving daily.[13]

Mr. Williams, the first of the Presbyterian Missionaries to arrive in the Choctaw country, located on July 12, ten miles west of the Arkansas line, on Mountain Fork, the stream called by the Indians Nonih Hacha (or Mountain) River. Here he bought a house and other improvements and a fine spring formerly owned by a white man. This was at a crossing or ford on Mountain Fork River where all the emigrants passing to the west were obliged to cross. With a pretty senti-

12   *Religious Intelligencer*, Vol. XIV, 723.
13   Loring S. Williams *Report*, April 12, 1832, *Missionary Records*, Vol. LXXII, No. 100.

ment he named the place Bethabara. Bethabara of old, he said, was beyond Jordan and at or near the crossing place of the children of Israel where they entered the Promised Land. Here on the west side of the stream on August 19, 1832, they organized the first church, embracing fifty-six persons, which they called Nonih Hacha. It was to this home of Mr. Williams that Rev. Alfred Wright came September 14, 1832, when he was sufficiently recovered to leave Little Rock.

In December Mr. Wright was able to leave the Williams's and establish himself at a place ten miles from Fort Towson centrally located between the Mountain Fork and Kiamichi rivers, which he named Wheelock, and here, in December, 1832, he organized the church of Wheelock.[14] The next year, that of the devastating fever, when hardly one in twenty escaped, the little log house of the Wright's had to accommodate also the family of Rev. Ebenezer Hotchkin during the period of six months that they were helpless. They arrived in the West the early part of the preceding winter and were received in the home of Mr. Williams after Mr. and Mrs. Wright had left. Here they remained until March when Mr. Hotchkin, with a little native assistance, constructed a log house fifteen feet square on Clear Creek, in which he and Mrs. Hotchkin and their children established themselves. It was not long, however, before they were taken ill and Miss Eunice Clough, a teacher recently arrived, went to their house to care for them. Soon she also became desperately ill, and the whole household thereupon, was carried to the little cabin of the Wrights, which they shared for six months.

On their arrival in the West the Indians concentrated on the streams near[15] the stations where their rations were to be issued; many were

14 Wheelock was named in memory of the first president of Dartmouth College, who was a devoted friend of the Indians, and first opened his Indian school (afterwards transferred to Hanover, New Hampshire), in Lebanon, Connecticut, the native town of Mr. Wright. "That portion of the Choctaws among whom he labored before their removal, are settled compactly around his station, there being as many as 2,000 within the distance of 10 or 12 miles. . . . . The church there was organized on the 2nd Sabbath in December, including 87 members, 80 of whom belonged in the old nation." At Mr. Williams' station, about twenty-five miles north of Wheelock, ". . . .there is a dense settlement of Indians amounting to 1500 within a distance of 5 miles, and not less than 3,000 within 25 miles" (Account in *New York Observer,* copied in *Cherokee Phoenix,* April 19, 1834, p. 1).

15 "Mr. Nail's party (known as the Christian party of the Southeast District) are settled between these two rivers (Red and Little); the Six Town people on

influenced also by the prospect of being near their missionary friends, and the churches and schools they hoped would soon be established. As a result, within what are now McCurtain and Choctaw counties, there were nearly five thousand Choctaw Indians located in the early part of 1833. They erred in settling in dense communities along the streams[16] instead of scattering out on the more healthful prairies; when warm weather came in the summer of 1833, accompanied by excessive rains and flooded lowlands, they were stricken with an epidemic of what the missionaries called remittent fevers. In some families every individual was down, and in seventy families within a radius of three miles of Mr. Wright, seventy deaths occurred that year. Almost every individual in the Red River settlement was ill. Mr. Hotchkin reported that in his neighborhood embracing four to five hundred souls, not a single child under one year old was left.[17]

The nearest doctor was sixty miles away and his charge of $70 for coming to see Miss Clough appalled the little household. Indian doctors or medicine men were in great demand, but as their impotency was exposed by the fearful mortality of the stricken ones, the Christian Indians placed their reliance in the feeble Mr. Wright, and he was called upon from near and far. Mrs. Wright, a most competent helpmeet

Little River, from the bend where it turns from the east ten or twelve miles down the river. The Chickeashahoy people (Nail's people) on Red River from the mouth of Clear Creek about the same distance, in an easterly direction. East of Mr. Nail's people and between them and the line are Mr. Hotchkin's people. North of Little River are Col. Folsom's; east of Mr. Nail's people and between them and Kiamichi and extending 50 or 60 miles up that river are Col. Folsom's people—West of Kiamichi are Nitakechi's, called by the missionaries, the pagan party (Koonchas or Six Towns); Mr. Nail has from 1800 to 1900 in his party settled in nearly equal divisions on Little and Red River. These rivers are from 8 to 12 miles apart. The people are generally settled near the rivers. The intervening country is a high prairie 5 or 6 miles in width" (Alfred Wright to David Greene, January 14, 1833, *Missionary Records*, Vol. LXXII, No. 142).

16 An observer cataloguing the resources of Miller County where the Indians were locating, said: ". . . .cane is found in abundance on the lands from Cantonment Towson to the Louisiana Line. In many places on these bottoms, are to be found, in plenty, large, tall, straight cedar trees, which are very valuable timber. This tree seldom grows except among rocks, but here it is found of enormous size, growing in the richest bottom land, where a stone cannot be seen" (*Nashville (Tennessee) National Banner and Whig*, January 15, 1828, p. 3, col. 3).

17 *Cherokee Phoenix*, May 17, 1834, p. 2, col. 2.

and observer of events, writes on August 13, 1833, that she has found on Mr. Wright's desk part of a letter "which he commenced, to send by to-day's mail, but he was called up at midnight to attend to a sick patient"; his "whole time has been taken up with the sick—since the first week in June he has attended 322 individual cases; he is frequently called up in the middle of the night, though he is still very feeble, and can't sleep well on account of obstructed respiration and circulation." The convalescent Indians often suffered relapse from want of suitable food. Tea was very expensive and quinine twelve and a half cents a grain.[18] "The wretchedness of the people without suitable food or medicine or nursing, was heart rending and altogether beyond description."[19]

The missionaries labored long hours to cheer the despondent, homesick, and suffering immigrants and they were called on almost daily to minister to dying members of their churches. Rev. Mr. Williams was summoned to the home of a Choctaw captain named Walking Wolf, who was near the point of death. While twenty-five of his neighbors looked on, the missionary held a service over the dying man who lay on a bearskin in his dooryard between his friends and a fire. "The sick man as he lay lifted up his withered hands & in a low faltering voice prayed fervently to his heavenly father."[20]

The suffering of these poor people who came begging to the homes of the missionaries evoked their compassion, but they could do little for so many; Mr. Hotchkin wrote in April, 1834, that "many Choctaws are suffering for food. I know of families that have not an ear of corn nor the least bit of anything that is eatable. What will they do before corn is raised?" In June he said "The Choctaws are suffering extremely. More than ever they suffered before from hunger. It is not uncommon for persons to call who have not eat any bread or meat for 10, 12, and 15 days. It is enough to draw tears from a rock to hear some of them relate their trials and distress. One woman said the other day 'for myself I can bear all without a murmur but when my children cry for bread day after day it almost breaks my heart'."[21]

18   Harriett B. Wright to D. Greene, August 13, 1833, *Missionary Records*, Andover-Harvard Library, Vol. LXXII, No. 144.

19   Letter from Rev. Loring S. Williams to *Vermont Chronicle*, copied in *Cherokee Phoenix*, February 22, 1834, p. 3, col. 1.

20   Williams to Greene, April 24, 1834, *Missionary Records*, Vol. LXXII, No. 113.

21   Ebenezer Hotchkin to Henry Hill, June 9, 1834, *Missionary Records*, *ibid.*, No. 126.

Earlier in the year Choctaw Agent Armstrong reported to the Stokes Commission at Fort Gibson that there were 1,100 Indians on the point of starvation from the lack of corn which they could not secure by their own efforts until autumn. Armstrong had neither money nor authority to buy corn for them and the commission, though uncertain of their power, adopted a resolution directing the agent to purchase for the starving Indians, 2,750 bushels of corn which they sent to the commissioner of Indian affairs with a resolution requesting Congress to make an appropriation to pay for it.[22]

The Missionary Board in Boston sent devoted young teachers to the mission stations in the West, which they reached after laborious travel; some overland and some by long ocean voyage from New York to New Orleans. Among the Choctaw they labored for a stipend of twelve to fifteen dollars monthly. Invariably they succumbed to the unhealthful climate in which they labored, and suffered through long sieges of enervating illness, and often their emaciated bodies were interred in the malarial soil of that far-off wilderness. But in spite of difficulties, with the coöperation of the Indians a few schools were soon provided; but there was difficulty in securing teachers as soon as the more progressive Indians desired them. Of this class were the Indians who settled at Nonih Hacha, or Mountain Fork, in 1832. Prominent among them were the brothers Israel and David Folsom,[23] merchants who improved the opportunity for enterprise. Thanks to the terms of the treaty of 1830 by which they were signally favored, they arrived in the West in a considerable degree of affluence; to their credit it must be said, however, that they were public spirited and used their influence and means for the advancement of their people. Israel Folsom[24] loaned Mr. Williams $200 with which to purchase the improvements for his station at Bethabara. Early in 1833 the people of this settlement began the construction of a schoolhouse without waiting for outside assistance and engaged Miss Eunice Clough to teach their school in the fall. Some of them decided to call their settlement a village and fifty captains, headmen, and whites signed a petition to the post office

22   Stambaugh to Herring, February 24, 1834, OIA *Western Superintendency.*
23   Folsom had several hunters in his employ (OIA *Western Superintendency*).
24   In the summer of 1835 Israel Folsom got the missionaries to order for him *Scott's Family Bible, Vose's Astronomy, Blair's Rhetoric* in two volumes, *Watts's Logic of the Mind,* a history of the United States and an Indian biography.

department asking that a post office, to be named Eagletown, be established at that place. The petition was granted on July 1, 1834 and Rev. Loring S. Williams was named postmaster.[25]

However, in the autumn of 1834, Israel Folsom decided that the Mountain Fork settlement was too unhealthful for a home, and after an exploring tour of what was then called the "far West," selected a new home[26] on Blue River, to which he removed some years later. Rev. Loring S. Williams desired to leave the unhealthful surroundings of Bethabara for a location three miles away in the pine woods, where there was no water but a living spring. Peter P. Pitchlynn had built a cabin there and was taking his family to it in the hope of restoring his broken health.[27] Many other members of the tribe wished to remove in 1833 from the dense settlements to the Blue River, but were deterred by fear of the "whiskey traders who immediately settle on the south bank of Red River opposite any settlement of Indians."[28]

The Choctaw were essentially a temperate people, but the demoralization by which they had been overwhelmed in the recent few years brought much intoxication among them. "We came here sober," said their chief to the United States commissioners in 1801; "we wish to go away so; we therefore request that strong drink which we understand our [white] brothers have brought here may not be distributed."[29] And when they made the treaty[30] at Doak's Stand in 1820, it was provided in section 12 that "in order to promote industry and sobriety among all classes of red people in this nation, but particularly the poor," the agent should have full power to seize and confiscate all whisky brought into the nation without his permission, or that of three chiefs.

25 Post Office records.
26 In 1833 Colonel Vose at Fort Towson reported that ". . . .the Choctaw settlements extend as far up as the mouth of the Boggy—on the Kiamichi there is a dense population" (Vose to Macomb, Report, June 5, 1833, AGO, OFD, 23 V 33).
27 Williams to Greene, August 8, 1834, Missionary Records, LXXII, No. 114.
28 The Blue River country was a very remote and unexplored region for some years. Buffaloes were still very numerous on the Blue and Washita rivers. Colonel Vose reported that part of his command at Fort Towson went on a buffalo hunt in April, 1833, on Blue River and they "saw large herds of buffalo very near the opposite bank."
29 United States Senate Executive Document No. 1, p. 193, Twenty-third Congress, first session.
30 Kappler, op. cit., II, 135.

Dr. Alexander Talley, the Methodist missionary, planned to remove west with the Indians. They were alarmed by talk of abandoning Fort Towson, which was proposed with a view to constructing another post farther west, to give better protection to the emigrant Indians.[31] Nitakechi, who lived above the Kiamichi River, and about eighteen miles from the post, protested against the move. Colonel Vose said the fort was necessary to preserve peace between the Choctaw Indians and the inhabitants without the boundaries of the United States, and would be necessary any way as ". . . . long as Miller County contains a population of the present description."

Several Choctaw schools were in operation in 1835 and more the next year. The missionaries were occupying the field in Pushmataha and Oaklafaliah districts, but in Mushulatubbe District the Government constructed five log schoolhouses. One of these near the agency was occupied by Francis Audrain, who was termed a "Treaty Teacher." His school began in April, 1835, with eight pupils in a log building eighteen by twenty feet in size, with no benches or desk. The other teachers were called "United States teachers"; of these Dr. Alanson Allen occupied a schoolhouse near Cavinole Mountain. Another school was being prepared by Rev. Joseph Smedley near a fine spring at Pheasant Bluff on the Arkansas River; but in the midst of his labors Mrs. Smedley died of bilious fever July 6, 1835, survived by her husband and eight children. A school was constructed near the Sugar Loaf Mountain taught by Eben Tucker, and later by Thomson McKenney, a Choctaw. Another school was located on the Fourche Maline River.

Henry K. Copeland, a "United States school teacher" at Eagle Town on Mountain Fork River had forty pupils through 1836, though many of them thought more of their "ball plays" than they did of their studies.[32] Moses Perry had a prosperous school at Shawnee Town on the Red River. One hundred women in the neighborhood, he said,

31 Gaines to Macomb, July 6, 1833, AGO, ORD, Western Department, *Letter Book No. 6, p. 289.* This was attempted the next year by the temporary establishment of Camp Washita (Grant Foreman, *Pioneer Days in the Early Southwest*).

32 The farmers in the vicinity were raising corn, oats, cotton, potatoes, and some wheat. One Choctaw in the neighborhood made looms, spinning wheels, and tables. There were also a shoemaker, two blacksmiths, one merchant, and several carpenters among them.

could spin and weave, but only eighteen of them had wheels and looms promised by the Government in their treaty of 1830.[33]

H. G. Rind, a "Treaty Teacher," began a school at Rattle Snake Springs in Oaklafaliah District with twenty to thirty-five pupils, all boys but one. He said an apparatus had been purchased that year to manufacture salt from a spring near by, and two smith's shops were operated by Indians. "Numbers of them have fine stocks of horses, cattle, sheep and hogs; the men are getting to wear pantaloons, the women to dress like the whites, and in general the people of the Oakla-faliah district, a thickly settled section, are on the rapid advance to civilization." Another school was conducted at Fort Towson by J. B. Denton.

The Government did not establish a school in Pushmataha district for some years but there were two "common schoolhouses" constructed by the Indians. Rev. Ramsey D. Potts, in 1835, at his own expense erected a schoolhouse in this district, in a neighborhood populated principally by full-blood Indians who were indifferent about schools; he employed a woman teacher for the girls who attended, and boarded the teacher in his house. The next year Mr. Potts reported that his school was not adequately provided with books and stationery, and he said he had seen only one spinning wheel and no looms in the district. About forty miles above the mouth of the Kiamichi River was a salt spring which yielded a large quantity of water and had been worked for family use. Two years later a white man manufactured considerable salt from it. There were 200 slaves in the district. Another United States district school named Bennett was started in 1838 by Charles G. Hatch, four miles north of the Red River on a bluff forty feet above the bed of Standing Whiteoak Creek.

The missionaries had in operation twelve schools attended by 300 children in 1835 and 1836; the names of eleven of these schools with

33 Shawnee Town was about six miles southwest of where is now Idabel, on the Red River on the road to Clarksville (Authority of Peter Hudson). Pheasant Bluff is on the south bank of the Arkansas River, five miles below the mouth of the Canadian, and twelve below Webbers Falls. Swallow Rock, or Herrold's Bluff, the site of Fort Coffee, is between Pheasant Bluff and Fort Smith (*Document*, I, 839, 846). For the Choctaw Schools Armstrong requested "slates and pencils, Smilie's arithmetics, cyphering books, copy books, Webster spelling books, Parley's geography, and 12 dozen good quills" (OIA, Choctaw Agency, "Schools," Choctaw File A 98, A 191).

their teachers were: Ah Pah Kah (A pe ha) east of Mountain Fork, Elizabeth A. Merrill and John Q. Adams, a Choctaw; Eagle Town, Louisa M. Williams; Lukfata Creek (White Clay or Greenfield), Eunice Clough; Glover's Fork, Ellen Carney; Wheelock, George Reed; "Near Col. Garland's," Samuel Moulton; "Near Clear Creek," Mrs. Ebenezer Hotchkin; Pine Ridge (Chuahli), two miles northwest of Doaksville, Miss Anna Burnham; "West of Mountain Fork," J. Cogswell, a Choctaw; Boktuklo, seven miles northwest of Lukfata; Red River, James Brewer, a Choctaw.

The missionaries Rev. Cyrus Byington and Rev. Cyrus Kingsbury did not accompany the Choctaw people on their migration. It was not until the summer of 1834 that they crossed the Mississippi River at St. Louis and under orders of the American Board of Commissioners for Foreign Missions proceeded on an inspection tour of some of the western missions. In October they entered the Indian Territory from the present southeastern Kansas and on the twentieth of that month reached Union Mission, then scourged by an epidemic of cholera. A week later they arrived at the mission of John Fleming in the Creek Nation and on the thirty-first reached Dwight Mission. Some weeks later they made their way to Fort Towson. After planning their locations and future labors they returned to the East and brought out their families in 1835.

By the summer of 1836 Mr. Byington was able to report that they were quite comfortable in their log dwelling. "I have a slab floor in my study and a window of 6 lights. In our house we have a floor made of plank but they are not planed or 'laid' by a joiner. . . . We have two glass windows in our house which is more than many of our neighbors have." Where dirt floors were common even a slab floor was a sign of affluence.

Mr. Kingsbury stationed at Pine Ridge reported in September, 1836 that there had been no opportunity to establish boarding schools and that the attendance at the day schools had been irregular. However those who came studied in books and some of them learned spinning in which they could have been instructed by their mothers had they been furnished the spinning wheels promised them in the treaty. "Some of the men weave well. George Hudson who was educated and learnt his trade at Mayhew in the Old Nation, makes wheels on Mountain Fork, the best I have seen in the nation." Crops were good that year

Reverend Cyrus Byington

Mrs. Cyrus Byington

PHOTOGRAPHED BY GRANT FOREMAN AT THE HOME OF
MRS. TENNESSEE HUNTER, CHOCTAW NATION, IN 1900

A primitive cotton press used by the Choctaw Indians

and the Indians began putting up some good improvements, including a saw and gristmill by Colonel Nail, to be operated by water power. Two salt springs and two sulphur springs were known and preparations were being made to work one of the former. David Folsom was making salt at a spring near Eagle Town, reported Rev. Mr. Byington.

The Indian department reported in 1837 that there were 15,000 Choctaw Indians in their western home and that they were prospering and improving.[34] They were raising corn, potatoes, peas, beans, pumpkins, and melons and those located along the Red River were raising more cotton than they required for their own use. They had erected two cotton gins which were expected to stimulate the growing of cotton. They had a surplus of 50,000 bushels of corn, most of which was sold to the garrison at Fort Towson. There were six native traders in the Choctaw Nation doing considerable business; two gristmills and sawmills were operated by water power and three others were being erected. There were 217 boys and 46 girls taught in the ten public schools, and 98 boys and 82 girls taught in the twelve missionary schools in the Nation.[35]

But in the dense settlements on Little River and Mountain Fork there had been an appalling death rate that is not noticed in any official published reports and there was such a thinning out of settlers that several schools were broken up and abandoned. The Folsoms removed from here to the vicinity of Blue River[36] where they were

34   In 1835 the Choctaw government enacted laws instituting marriage and prescribing its form and responsibilities (*Laws of the Choctaw Nation*, Edition of 1869, p. 70; *Report* of the commissioner of Indian affairs for 1837. There were then eleven public schools in the Choctaw Nation conducted by the Government in addition to the missionary schools (*ibid*).

35   *Ibid*. Official reports, always optimistic concerning official achievements, need to be supplemented by others: Mr. Byington, writing August 2, 1837, says: "The Choctaws are not so industrious as they were. They drink more and spend more time at their plays. Since about the first of January, 1837, ten persons living within ten miles of me have died in consequence of drinking whiskey. Provisions are scarce and dear" (*The Missionary Herald*, XXXIV (November, 1838) 445). At Lukfata Miss Clough had taught a term of nine months and three weeks; at Bok Tuklo where Mrs. Wood taught and where the pupils gave monthly concerts, ". . . . one heathen woman followed her little boy to school with a whip" (Rev. Joel Wood to Rev. D. Greene, June 6, 1838, *Missionary Records, ibid*., Vol. 139, No. 93).

36   In 1838 there was a considerable settlement at Pheasant Bluff including "The Widow Folsom," "The Widow Coleman," Charlie Jones, John Riddle, Robert M.

joined by a large number of their friends; many others of the Mountain Fork settlement left there for a more healthful and desirable location on Red River, within what is now Bryan County, Oklahoma.

David Folsom developed and operated a salt works on Boggy Creek near Blue River and about fifteen miles from the Red River. Here he made twenty bushels of salt a day and had an accumulation of 1,000 bushels which he planned to market down the Red River as soon as the removal of the Great Raft from that stream would make navigation possible. He had a ready market also for his output in the Choctaw Nation and across the Red River in Texas.

The missionaries and other teachers regarded their field of labor with much optimism at first; they said the Indian pupils learned as readily as white children, but they found their labors involved in many difficulties. Many parents and children were only mildly interested in education; the equipment of the government schools was woefully inadequate; the parents who were engaged in farming needed the labor of their children during the warm season and in the winter many of them had not clothes to keep them warm enough to attend school. One teacher reported that some of his pupils wore nothing but a shirt. Neither did many have food to eat away from the taful-la kettles at home. Always in season the pupils were more interested in their "ball play" than in their lessons. The Rev. Cyrus Byington at Eagle Town found the Indians too fickle to keep their children in school regularly. His neighbors, he said, were poor farmers and much of what they raised was taken across the line into Arkansas and traded for whisky.

A great change for the worse took place in 1838. A serious drought had ruined their crops which, added to a great deal of sickness and many deaths, thoroughly discouraged the Indians. In this state they yielded to the lure of intoxicants, brought into the country by the white people, in large quantities, which they were everywhere drinking. A wave of intemperance swept the country. The Indians were neglecting their crops, their stock was dying from lack of attention, and their schools were sadly neglected. The Indians spent their time

---

Jones, a white man named John Walker, and Nathaniel Folsom, all with their Choctaw families. Robert M. Jones had a double log cabin of hewn logs which he occupied as a store. John Jones and Anderson Perry lived near the site of Fort Coffee (*American State Papers*, "Military Affairs," Vol. VII, 976).

attending "ball plays," drinking and carousing. To combat this situation the missionaries organized temperance societies that recruited large numbers of Indians; some of the prominent Indians themselves, even those who were not members of the churches, alarmed at the situation, took a leading part in the temperance movement. Rev. Cyrus Byington reported much drinking in the vicinity of Fort Towson where he performed most of his labor. He organized temperance societies in a number of places in that territory.

Besides other disastrous influences, when the Chickasaw Indians arrived in the Choctaw Nation in 1838 they brought with them the smallpox[37] which, spreading through the Nation, was particularly devastating on the Arkansas River where it caused the deaths of four or five hundred Choctaw people, the breaking up of schools and neglect of crops.[38] During this epidemic there occurred near the Choctaw agency the death of Mushulatubbe, the famous Choctaw chief. He died August 30, 1838, at the age of seventy-five or eighty years.[39] Ravages

37 "It was, however, in the Northwest where the greatest amount of human life was extinguished among the more savage and unsettled tribes. It is computed that among the Sioux, Mandans, Riccaaras, Minnetarees, Assinabornies, and Blackfeet Indians, 17,200 persons sunk under the smallpox" (*Report* of commissioner of Indian affairs for 1838). This epidemic took a heavy toll in the Southwest also (Foreman, *Pioneer Days*, 253).

38 *Report* of commissioner of Indian affairs, *ibid.*

39 Coleman Cole to Lyman C. Draper December 1, 1884, *Draper Manuscript Collection*, Vol. 4, YY; *National Intelligencer*, October 10, 1838, p. 1, col. 3. Mushulatubbe was the son of a chief of the same name who died prior to 1820, who, under General Jackson, had led his warriors against the Creeks in 1812. The second Mushulatubbe had signed the Treaty of Treaty Ground, Mississippi, October 18, 1820; of Washington, January 20, 1825, and of Dancing Rabbit Creek, Mississippi, September 27, 1830. He took a prominent part in the conference with the western tribes at Fort Gibson in September, 1834. One of the three districts in the western Choctaw Nation was named for him. During the discussion in Congress of Jackson's Indian Removal Bill, the people of Mississippi, to win the favor of the Choctaw, made a gesture conferring citizenship upon them; and induced the chief Mushulatubbe to announce himself in the April first issue of the Port Gibson *Correspondent* as a candidate for Congress. To flatter him and his tribesmen, the press pretended to regard his candidacy seriously (*Niles' Weekly Register*, XXXVI, 327, 362). That these blandishments were not wasted is seen in the fact that he was one of the signers of the treaty of removal. Mushulatubbe, Pushmataha, and Apuckshunnubbee were members of the delegation sent to Washington in 1824 to negotiate the new treaty. Apuckshunnubbee died on the way, and Pushmataha died in Washington before the treaty was signed. Pushmataha,

of this disease had "been truly appalling. Some large families have been entirely swept off. And in others perhaps one or two survive to mourn the loss of all that was near and dear to them." This summer also some of the benighted Six-towns Indians killed an old woman charged with being a witch. In addition to the visitation of smallpox, droughts and prairie and timber fires caused great destruction of crops, and hostile Indians continued to disturb the peace of the Choctaw people.

Disorder developed at this time along the Red River in Pushmataha District. It was caused in part by Mexican emissaries seeking recruits among the Choctaw for service against Texas. There had been much friction between citizens of that republic and their Indian neighbors north of the Red River, a number of whom departed for service under the Mexican flag. The reactionary old ex-chief Nitakechi had not forgiven the more progressive people of his district for choosing Thomas Leflore in his place; "since that election the old chief has been in constant and violent ferment. His malicious feelings have been mostly directed towards white men and half-breeds." Nor was he on good terms with his white neighbors, and he made his home a rendezvous for Mexican agents. Efforts were made by the military and Choctaw officials to arrest at the home of Nitakechi one of these agents for whom a large reward was offered by Texas. This greatly exasperated the former chief and his partisans, and a small civil war impended. "Powder and lead were procured & a day fixed upon for the parties to meet. But a timely letter from Col. Vose prevented. In the meantime the old chief has been using his utmost endeavors to break down all civil law and institute in its place the ancient customs & he has succeeded so far that two old women within the last year have been most unhumanly murdered on the supposition that they were witches."[40]

Mushulatubbee, Col. Robert Cole, and Maj. John Pitchlynn, Choctaw representatives, together with the chiefs of the Chickasaw tribe, were presented to General Lafayette in Washington November 24, 1824. Four sons of Mushulatubbe were named Peter, James King, Hiram and Charles (Mushulatubbe to Eaton, January 16, 1831, *Document* II, 393.)

40 Hotchkin to Green, May 22, 1839, *Missionary Records*, Vol. 139, No. 143. J. W. P. McKenzie a Methodist missionary who had been at Shawnee Town two years reported that "The quantity of ardent sold to the Choctaws is indeed astonishing and unless a stop is put to it certain ruin must ensue to the full blood Choctaws" (McKenzie to Armstrong July 21, 1838, OIA "School (Western Supt'y)" A490).

CHAPTER THREE / *Signs of Improvement*

ERMITTED by the terms of the agreement[1] between the two tribes, the Chickasaw Indians settled throughout the Choc-taw Nation rather than go to the more remote western district purchased of the Choctaw where they would be sub-jected to depredations by the wild prairie Indians. The treaty gave them equal privileges with the Choctaw except in the national funds. The latter changed their constitution to admit the Chickasaw to their council as one district, so that in the common government they were represented by one chief and ten councillors. It was believed by the United States officials that as their language was similar and they had somewhat intermarried, they could be amalgamated as one tribe; but in this folly, as in the fatuous hope of uniting the Creek and Seminole tribes, the Government was to be disillusioned after causing irreparable harm and delay to the progress of both tribes.

In 1841 the Chickasaw held their first election of councillors since their emigration and at the October session of that year participated for the first time in the joint council which then consisted of forty members from the four districts. November 10, 1842 a new constitu-tion was adopted which among other things defined the boundaries of the new Chickasaw as well as the other districts into which the Choctaw-Chickasaw country was divided.[2] Judges in the Choctaw Nation were nominated by the chief of the district and received a small compensation. Trial by jury was guaranteed in all capital cases. Singularly there was no law to enforce the payment of debts[3] but as

1   *Indian Removal, op. cit.,* 203.
2   *Report* of commissioner of Indian affairs for 1941, p. 334.
3   In October, 1846, William Armstrong, Acting Superintendent, reported from the Choctaw Agency: "Their national council, which is now in session, has before

credits were extended with knowledge of this situation debts were seldom incurred and those few usually paid. Their laws were generally respected and punishment followed a violation. Acts of violence were rare and every individual felt safe in his own property. Travelers passed through the Choctaw Nation with every feeling of security.

That year witnessed continued improvement and progress of these people. The Choctaw on Red River owned and operated eight or ten gins and shipped between seven and eight hundred bales of cotton; there were also a number of sawmills and gristmills in operation; many of the Indians had built comfortable houses and were preparing their farms with every indication of substantial farmers; many of the women spun, wove and contributed much to the clothing of their families. The industry of the Choctaw women was indicated by the report of Rev. Cyrus Byington for 1842; in his mission neighborhood, Stockbridge, near Eagletown, there were thirteen looms, and in nine families they had made 2,227 yards of cloth; two families had made 1,250 yards; "there were 35 yards of linsey. Mr. Calvin H. Howell a son-in-law of the late Major Pitchlyn, has a cotton gin. He ginned 64 bales of cotton last winter. The Messrs. Harris have a horse mill and at this time are erecting a water mill. There are two flocks of sheep owned by my neighbor."[4] Stocks of cattle, hogs, and horses were

---

it a proposition to pass laws for the collection of debts, which heretofore has not been done, though their courts frequently try the right of property in cases of some magnitude. At this time a suit is pending in one of them involving an estate valued at $20,000. These courts are regularly organized, with judges and juries, and the suits are conducted on both sides by professional advocates, of which there are a large number. . . . . The three districts of the Choctaw nation are sub-divided into sixty companies, each headed by a captain, living in the midst of, and personally acquainted with, his people and their condition" (House Executive *Document* No. 4, Twenty-ninth Congress, second session, 268).

4 *Report* of commissioner of Indian affairs for 1842, *Report* No. 69. *The Natchitoches Herald* in 1841 published an interesting account of the progress of these people. The Choctaw planters on Red River had seven cotton gins with a prospect for more, the paper said, and would produce and ship down the river 1,000 bales of cotton that year and twice as many the next. There were eight or ten blacksmith shops. On Boggy River Col. David Folsom "has an excellent salt works which supplies even Texas planters with a large quantity of salt." In the Choctaw Nation were to be seen "comfortable frame and log dwellings; the matrons sewing, spinning, and weaving, and around them large plantations, yielding corn, oats, pumpkins, potatoes, and a great

owned by them, and little feed was required, the range, both summer and winter, being abundant. However, the price of cotton fell so low in 1842 many of the Choctaw farmers around Fort Towson planted their land largely to corn to supply a contract for 20,000 bushels of that grain needed at the garrison where a portion of the First Dragoons were to be located.

The Indian Superintendent reported that trade was carried on in numerous suitable places in the Choctaw Nation but the most extensive trading was done at Doaksville, within a mile of Fort Towson. There were five stores at the place, three of which were owned in part by the Choctaw and the other two[5] by white men. The extent and assortment of goods carried was ample for the Indians, who required sugar, coffee, and other luxuries the same as the white people. Doaksville was an orderly and prosperous village, boasting, besides the stores mentioned, a resident physician and a good tavern, blacksmith shop, wagon maker and wheelwright. A church had been erected, in which there was preaching once or twice on Sunday, by the missionaries living in the neighborhood. A temperance society included a large portion of the most respectable Choctaw and Chickasaw, as well as white people.

The Rev. William H. Goode visited this place in November, 1844, and described it:[6] "Doaksville I found to be a flourishing town, the largest in all the Indian country. It is mainly surrounded by large cotton plantations, owned by Choctaws and Chickasaws, mostly half-breeds, and worked by slaves. It is a brisk, neat-looking place, with a good church, an excellent public house, kept by my host, Colonel Folsom, on temperance principles, quite a number of stores, mechanics' shops, etc., and all the marks of thrift and prosperity. It commands a

---

variety of vegetables. There have been lately erected several splendid mansions, entirely by native mechanics, and they are now filled and adorned with all fashionable furniture" (Copied in *New York Tribune*, February 26, 1842).

5   Doak and Tims was one firm; the other was Berthelet, Heald and Company, the "company" being the Choctaw Indian Robert M. Jones. Mr. Joseph R. Berthelet was appointed postmaster there in 1847. In 1849 the adjutant at Fort Towson reported that mills recently erected in the vicinity made excellent flour that was available to the post in any quantity required (Commissary to Gibson, November 27, 1848, QMG.).

6   William H. Goode, *Outposts of Zion*, 187.

fine view of the garrison buildings at Fort Towson, a mile distant, and is within a few miles of Red River and the Texas line." On the site of this once flourishing village, now entirely erased from the map, stands one log house said to have been the home of Colonel Folsom.

"Some of these tribes," said the commissioner of Indian affairs, "have received patents for the lands they possess, describing the limits and conditions under which they held their country. These things are well calculated to inspire confidence, giving hopes that their present homes are permanent, creating thereby a general incitement to industry and the adoption of such laws and regulations as are calculated to give protection to a people in the incipient stage of civilization. The Choctaws have long since justly acquired for themselves, not only from the Government of the United States but from the citizens with whom they have intercourse, a name of honesty and fidelity at least not surpassed by any of our Indian tribes. They have by a steady attention to their own business since they emigrated to their present homes, greatly increased in wealth. They have not been unmindful, at the same time, of educating their rising generations; and they have by these means added to the general intelligence and standing of the Nation. . . . The wealth and intelligence of the nation is confined mainly to the two districts on Red River. The Choctaws may be considered as an agricultural and stock raising people; farms on Red River will compare with many in the states."[7]

The missionaries were still laboring to regain the ground lost in the devastation of removal, but their efforts were embarrassed at this period by acrimonious discussion of slavery; some of the slave-owning members of the tribe were particularly bitter at the missionaries for their views on abolition. The years 1839 and 1840 had witnessed a recurrence of the fever epidemic of 1833 though in a milder form.[8] However, there were many deaths, a number of schools were closed, and the missionaries were constantly busy; Mr. Byington wrote that there were forty deaths in his neighborhood during the year 1839;

7 *Report* of commissioner of Indian affairs 1842, p. 438.

8 Armstrong reported that much of this sickness was attributable to the fact that there were few wells among the Indians, who procured their drinking water in the summer from stagnant pools where streams had ceased to flow (*Report* of commissioner of Indian affairs 1838, p. 73).

while he was preaching the funeral sermon for one of his flock he would hear the gun fired that announced the death of another.

When Rev. Cyrus Byington arrived in the new home of the Choctaw people early in the year 1835, he was placed in charge of the station at Stockbridge near Eagletown on the east side of Mountain Fork about four miles from Bethabara. Though his school was broken up by the migration of the people to the Blue River country, he was exceedingly busy ministering to the Indians in their illness; besides, he employed nearly two years in the translation of the Acts of the Apostles with the aid of an interpreter; he then started on the Book of Genesis,[9] but when he had reached the seventeenth chapter he was obliged to stop as his Choctaw interpreter quit to look after his farm. However, he finished it in April, 1839, and sent the manuscript to Boston for publication. Mr. Kingsbury's station was at Pine Ridge where a school was established and placed in his charge.

If one would know what privations these missionaries were willing to endure, consider the testimony of Mr. Hotchkin: "During the first nine years of Mrs. Hotchkin's missionary work she received only five dollars in cash. This was paid by Mr. Cushman for teaching his children two years at his station. This was the only money that passed through her hands for 9 years." When Miss Clough had been seven years with the Choctaw Indians the missionaries requested of their superiors at Boston permission for her to return to New England long enough to regain her wasted strength. After receiving $120.00 for a school year of toil her summer vacations had been spent in nursing the sick. Many teachers who had not died from the fatal miasma in that virgin country lifted their emaciated frames from sick beds to mount a horse or ox-cart or other conveyance that would carry them forever away from the fever-blighted home of the Choctaw; but some labored through every hardship as long as their lives were spared. The testimony of Mr. Hotchkin is pertinent again: "We have had some sickness this spring. Intermittent fever, pleuresy, scurvy, worms, bots, lice, vermin &c. But after we got through the old scurf and dirt, the little girls come out as bright as other children. To effect this change strong nerves are necessary."[10] Miss Anna Burnham, of advanced

9 Rev. Mr. Byington compiled a Choctaw-English dictionary and a Choctaw-English almanac (Transcript of Byington manuscripts Oklahoma Historical Society).

10 E.Hotchkin to David Green, May, 1840, *Missionary Records*, Vol. LXII, No. 370.

age, for several years taught a little school on Red River, more than seven miles from any white habitation and there she lived alone in a little log house constructed by the Indians.

In spite of the inconvenience under which Mr. Wright toiled by reason of having to share his little home with other people in 1833, and his tremendous labor while, in the frailest health,[11] ministering day and night to the hundreds of afflicted who looked to him for succor, and his preaching engagements at three places, he resolutely carried forward his translations. In August, 1835, he completed and forwarded to Boston to be published his manuscript of *Chahta Nolisso* or spelling book; in September, 1837, he completed the translation of the Gospels and Epistles of John, but he was obliged to stop the work as he had no more funds to pay his interpreter. In July, 1839, he reported that as he had the health and opportunity to do so, he was engaged in his translations and had completed the Gospel of Matthew. By July of the next year he translated the Epistles of John and sent his manuscript to Mr. Worcester at Park Hill to be published. One of the difficulties under which he labored was illustrated by the fact that a box of books sent by water from Park Hill,[12] was two years in reaching Wheelock and then it was transported by way of New Orleans. As Mr. Joel Wood, the missionary at Boktuklo, had been compelled by sickness to leave, Mr. Wright was preaching at Wheelock, Red River, seven miles distant, Boktuklo, ten miles away, and "at the home of Colonel Garland who for more than two years had been confined to his bed by the fall of a tree upon his back."

At the earnest solicitation of the Indians Mr. and Mrs. Wright took some Choctaw children in their household to teach them, but they had not the means nor room to care for many. In 1841 Mrs. Wright wrote to the Mission Board begging them to raise their meager annual allowance of $450.00 to the sum of $600.00, so that with the additional $150.00 annually they would be able to receive in their

11 Mr. Wright had been so feeble ever since he came west that he said he could perform no manual labor "or even do so much as to cut a stick of wood" (Harriett B. Wright to D. Green, *ibid.*). Mrs. Wright was also in feeble health.

12 Park Hill was in the Cherokee Nation about five miles south of Tahlequah. Of the twenty-five or thirty homes, stores and churches that made up this community, only two or three remain. See the map of the place in Grant Foreman, *Advancing the Frontier.*

home and educate for at least five years a number of Choctaw orphan girls. In May, 1842, at the urgent request of some of the influential half-breed members of the tribe, they had commenced a boarding school composed of several orphans and those children whose parents were able to pay the meager actual expense of board; they had begun on a small scale and with additions in May there were sixteen in attendance, but there was no room to care for others who desired to enter. However, they later managed to take a few more and by September they had twenty-five.

The Choctaw people became dissatisfied with the expenditure of their school funds in Kentucky; the students returning from there, disappointed their people as they had acquired no knowledge of agriculture or other practical subjects. In 1840 the chiefs notified Superintendent Armstrong that they would send no more boys to the Choctaw Academy in that state, and that they proposed to use funds expended there in the construction of an advanced school for boys in their own country. However, they were prevailed upon to send them again the succeeding year by the promise to appoint Peter P. Pitchlynn as superintendent of the school. In the winter Pitchlynn went to the Kentucky school armed with a commission from his tribe to investigate the condition of the students; after spending fifty days there, he received from the Indian department an appointment as superintendent of the school which he accepted with the condition that it was only temporary pending the opening of a school in the Choctaw Nation.[13]

In the summer, however, the Choctaw chiefs, James Fletcher, James Gardner, and Johnson McKenney, informed Armstrong that they had definitely determined not to send any more boys to Kentucky, as they intended soon to have a school in their own country where mechanical arts and agriculture would be taught. And at the October session of the General Council of the Choctaw Nation a resolution to that effect was adopted. They resolved at the same time that at the next meeting of the council a committee consisting of two from each district, with the agent, be appointed to select a site for a girl's school. This resolution, bearing the signatures of Johnson McKenney, James Fletcher and Isaac Folsom, Chiefs, and Sloan Love Speaker, was sent to the

13 Pitchlynn to commissioner of Indian affairs, March 2, 15, and 29, 1841, OIA, "School File" p. 850.

commissioner of Indian affairs.[14] The progressive members of the tribe were becoming keenly interested in the subject of their schools, and before the council adjourned, a committee was appointed to select immediately a site for the boys' school.

The movement of many of the members of the tribe from the dense settlements in which they first lived for some years, and the occupation of more remote parts of their domain was in part responsible for the necessity of setting up new schools and discarding others in sections abandoned in part by the settlers. In planning for the future it was decided to abandon the three district schools taught by Wilson, Potts, and Rind August 1, 1843, and send the pupils from those schools to the new school that was to be called Spencer Academy.

While the construction of their first boys' academy was under way, a general awakening by the leading men of the tribe to the importance of education was manifest. Their plans took larger form and it was proposed to appropriate for school purposes the annuity of $18,000 derived from the sale of their lands to the Chickasaw. A large portion of the tribe was opposed to this use of the per capita payments they had been spending upon themselves, but in spite of stout opposition, in November, 1842, the Choctaw council decided to carry this plan into effect, and enacted legislation[15] which became the basis of their excellent school system. With these funds and the further sum of $8,500 provided by treaty for school purposes, they made provision for a number of schools to be operated by the Presbyterian, Baptist and Methodist missionary societies. Spencer Academy, the boys' school, was then in course of construction. The next to be inaugurated under the new legislation was at Wheelock in Apuckshunnubbee District, where a school was already in operation on a small scale under the direction of Mr. Wright.[16]

14 Armstrong to Crawford, July 15 and October 14, 1841, *ibid.*, A 1048 and 1108.

15 *Laws of the Choctaw Nation* (New York, 1869), 78.

16 Pitchlynn to Armstrong, December 12, 1842 in *report* of commissioner of Indian affairs for 1843, *school report* 69. Pitchlynn said also he was directed to request that by virtue of the terms of the Treaty of Dancing Rabbit Creek, ten Choctaw youths be educated at Jefferson College, Cannonsburg, Pennsylvania; ten at Ohio University at Athens; ten at Asbury University, Greencastle, Indiana, and ten at some other school to be selected by the Indian department. In his letter Pitchlynn stated that the school that was later to be called Spencer Academy was at first named

Education of Indian youth in far distant states was not always a blessing; they were usually sent while quite young and kept away for five to ten years; by this time they had forgotten how their people lived at home and on their return found their own condition so changed in these strange surroundings that it became intolerable. In 1842 two of the Choctaw young men who had recently returned from the academy in Kentucky committed suicide—one because he found his relations in extreme poverty, and the other because the affections of his father were estranged from him, his mother having died during his absence.[17]

Mr. Wright's enlarged school at Wheelock, authorized by the Choctaw council, went into operation on Monday, the first day of May, 1843.[18] There were, at the beginning of the school, fifty-two pupils, forty-eight girls and four small boys. Thirty-four of the girls were boarded at the school and the others found quarters with some of the employes of the school. So great was the desire of members of the tribe for admission of their girls to the school, that, to avoid the appearance of favoritism, at first seven girls were selected from each of the three clans, Ahepotukla, Olilefeia, and Oklahoneli, and three from the Urihesahe. The list was made from twice the number of applications and only one was taken from a family.[19]

Noincoaiga; The secretary complied to the extent of sending ten to Asbury and ten to Lafayette College at Easton, Pennsylvania (Crawford to Armstrong, May 8, 1843, in *report* of commissioner of Indian affairs for 1843).

17   Wilson to Armstrong, August 30, 1842, *report* of commissioner of Indian affairs for 1842, *report* No. 72.

18   *Reports* of commissioner for 1849 and 1851.

19   *Ibid.*, for 1843.

CHAPTER FOUR / *Institutions Take Form*

T
HE vicinity of Fort Towson was selected for Spencer Academy because in that thickly settled region bordering on the Red River, the people were more concerned with education than in any other part of the Choctaw Nation. The committee met at Doaksville and selected a site about ten miles north of the Fort on the military road which ran from that post to Fort Smith. The place combined the advantages of an elevated situation with good soil and a fine spring of water. Plans were prepared, contracts were let, and construction of the buildings began in 1842. The school was opened February 1, 1844[1] and the Choc-

1 *Report* of commissioner of Indian affairs for 1844; McKinney to Armstrong, August 29, 1844, OIA, "School file" A 1718. Spencer Academy was named for John Spencer, secretary of war from 1841 to 1843, who donated to the school a valuable bell weighing 250 pounds. The buildings first erected were constructed of hewn pine logs with shingle roofs; there was a storehouse, a smokehouse with room for ten tons of bacon; farmer's and workmen's houses, springhouse twelve by fifteen feet paved with stones; a servants' house and a dormitory, the latter named Jones Hall. Superintendent McKinney was assisted by William Wilson, principal, and Reuben Wright and Jonathan E. Dwight, assistant teachers, the latter an educated Choctaw who acted as interpreter. George C. Farquehar was in charge of farming operations (*Report* of commissioner of Indians affairs for 1844). Oliver P. Stark, a graduate of Princeton, was the principal teacher in 1846.

The school was visited in 1847 by P. P. Brown who remained a week and gave an interesting account of it: "As you approach the Institution from the south," he said, "the first building met with is a good sized stable and shed, about 200 yards from the dwelling houses. Entering the large yard on the north side of the farm, before you stand two large two-story frame buildings painted white. Pitchlynn Hall is on the right, is occupied on the lower floor by Rev. Mr. Ramsey, the Superintendent, and one of the teachers; the upper story by part of the boys.

"Jones Hall is on the left, is occupied by the principal teacher, with another portion of the pupils. Passing into the square formed by the buildings, on the extreme left,

taw people were very proud of it. It was built to accommodate 100 boys who were to board at the school and receive instruction in manual training as well as in book learning.[2] The trustees arranged at first to admit sixty students, one from each company in the nation and by the end of February, fifty-seven of that number had been received. Later forty more were invited, to be selected from the districts according to their population and they had all presented themselves by May 1.

With increasing zeal in the pursuit of learning the Choctaw people continued to establish schools. For those living on Arkansas River two schools were established: the old garrison buildings at the abandoned Fort Coffee on that river were turned over to the Choctaw Nation and funds were provided for their repair, for the erection of other buildings suitable for school purposes, and the whole under the management of Methodist missionaries, was called Fort Coffee Academy.[3]

---

you see the school house; it is built of logs, one story high, divided into one large school room and two small recitation rooms. On the north side of the square fronting to the south, stands Armstrong Hall, of the same size and form as the other; occupied on the lower floor by the primary teacher, and the Institution carpenter; on the second floor by the remainder of the boys, principally the smaller ones.

"On the right or east side of the square, is a two story building, occupied by the steward and family, and some female helpers. In the rear of this, the dining room attached to which is the kitchen, bakery, and 'Ton Fuller' [ta-fu-la, food made of crushed corn], room. To the east of Pitchlynn Hall, and a little back, stand the store room, smoke house, and a lodging room for hired help. The three halls have large piazzas extending the whole length, which renders them very pleasant and agreable" (The Indian Advocate (Louisville, Ky.) September, 1847).

2   In 1846 the management of this school was entrusted to the Board of Foreign Missions of the Presbyterian Church. Mr. Reuben Wright, former acting superintendent, then resigned (Report of commissioner of Indian affairs for 1846).

3   "When we came to Fort Coffee which is on the Choctaw side of the river, it had begun to grow dark one evening. It was then occupied as the Mission premises and boarding school, under the care of the Methodist church. The buildings were old log houses on the top of a bold bluff, and the river bends itself around its foot. The boat was bringing stores for the mission and her shrill whistle brought out the teacher, and twenty or thirty Indian lads and they came running down the hill.

"It was a romantic spot, and a scene which a painter would love to sketch. The cone-shaped hill bearing stately trees on its sides, those weather beaten block houses on its summit; Indian boys scattered here and there, their dusky features revealed by the torch light, and the river laving its rocky foundation. That fort once grinning with cannon through its port holes; that hill once bristling with infantry, now serving a better purpose, and now a far better defense for the tribe than when armed men

It was opened February 9, 1844[4] as a boys' manual training school, and sixty acres of land adjoining was cleared and enclosed as a farm in connection with the school.[5] A girls' school called New Hope was established five or six miles southeast of Fort Coffee and one mile east of the Choctaw agency.

The pupils who attended Fort Coffee Academy presented certificates signed by the chiefs and trustees of the three districts. "In a few days we had received thirty pupils into the school to be clothed, fed, and taught. . . . The lads came dressed in the prevailing fashions, having generally shirts, pants, and calico hunting shirts; a few had shoes and moccasins, but the majority with bare feet. Not more than two or three wore hats; the balance were either entirely bareheaded or had a cotton handkerchief twisted around the head, making a sort of turban. According to Indian taste they all had long hair, and a few of them wore it braided.

"Our first work after their arrival was to wash and clothe them; we had entire suits prepared in advance for them. The coat and pants were of Kentucky jeans; good stout shoes, seal-skin caps, white shirts of stout cloth, and cotton handkerchiefs completed the outfit. We had a tub of water for ablutions; then Mr. P. armed with stout shears, soon reduced their hair to our notions of taste and comfort. . . . . One little fellow, about eight years old, had come a distance of 120 miles. When dressed warmly and neatly, in new clothing, he manifested great delight with his improved circumstances; but just in the dusk of the evening, he was seen standing behind the dining-room weeping most bitterly. When asked through an interpreter, the cause of his trouble, he replied that he 'had good pants, good jacket, good shoes and cap,

---

were quartered there; for now it is fostering an army of teachers, and men who will be friends of education and religion" (Augustus W. Loomis, *Scenes in the Indian Country*, 34). The Rev. William H. Goode was the first superintendent at Fort Coffee Academy, assisted by Rev. Henry C. Benson. On August 12, 1850, Rev. John Harrell was appointed superintendent of this school and New Hope. He afterwards served as superintendent of Asbury mission, where he and his wife died in 1867; their remains rest in neglected graves in a cotton field near the site of that old school about two miles northeast of Eufaula, Oklahoma.

4 William H. Goode, *Outposts of Zion*, 130; Henry C. Benson, *Life Among the Choctaw Indians*, 186.

5 *Ibid.*

and was much glad, but he had no blanket to wrap himself in, and thought that lying upon the ground without a blanket he would be cold.' We took him into the dormitories and explained to him the mysteries of a bedstead, with its mattress, pillows, sheets, and blankets; and, pointing to the particular one upon which he should sleep, we left him with his eyes sparkling and his face beaming with happiness."[6]

Other schools later established were Chuahla Female Seminary at Pine Ridge, one mile from Doaksville, opened in 1845, under the superintendence of Rev. Cyrus Kingsbury and attended by thirty-five pupils. Partly destroyed by a tornado[7] it was closed for eight months, but after reconstruction school work was resumed. Iyahnubbee, a female seminary in charge of Rev. Cyrus Byington, located near Eagle Town on the east side of the Mountain Fork River, not far from the Arkansas line, was commenced December 14, 1844, and accommodated fifty pupils. Norfolk School opened in February, 1846, five miles northwest of Wheelock Academy, with thirty-five pupils. In this school the pupils were reported as especially proficient in singing. Koonsha Female Academy located near Goodwater in Pushmataha District began operations May 1, 1844 in charge of Rev. Ebenezer Hotchkin with thirteen pupils, but later accommodated fifty. By 1846 they reported three academies, besides several small schools for boys and five seminaries

---

6 *Ibid.*

7 March 19, 1848 (*Report* of commissioner of Indian affairs for 1849). "The large two-story house occupied by Miss Bennett and Miss Slate & the girls under their charge, was entirely carried away, except the lower floor & the walls & sleepers to which it was nailed. . . . . Seventeen persons were in the house at the time of the disaster and yet, wonderful to relate, a hand unseen preserved the life of every individual; and the injuries sustained were few, & in most cases so slight as not to be regarded. . . . . Miss Bennett was attempting in vain to close the front door of her room, when she heard a crash, saw the house parting at the corners, & expected it was coming down on her head. The next thing she knew, she was lying on the ground near to where the house had stood. . . . My son & his hired man had just time to escape from the house in which they were, when it was levelled to the ground; and amid trees falling in every direction, and the fragments of broken buildings, which were hurled through the air with great violence, they were as by a miracle preserved from harm, except a few slight injuries. . . . ." Friends from Doaksville, Fort Towson, and Spencer Academy quickly responded with aid for the sufferers and assisted in repairing the buildings (Kingsbury to Rutherford, March 29, 1848, OIA, "School File" R 343, Choctaw Agency).

for the instruction of girls, all under the management of the Presbyterian, Baptist and Methodist churches.

While the school fund seemed considerable, it was insufficient to
care for more than 500 or one-tenth of the Choctaw children and the
applications always greatly exceeded the number that could be accommodated; the duties of selection became delicate and the trustees often
found it difficult to refuse urgent requests of persons beyond the proper
age. The tribal council appointed four trustees, one Choctaw from
each district, and one, the Choctaw agent, to supervise the schools
and select the pupils for admission. The missionary societies were
requested to report to the trustees annually concerning the conduct
of the schools and the expenditure of the tribal funds entrusted to them.

The miracle of recuperation and improvement of the Choctaw people
impressed observant members of the tribe and one of the most intelligent
of them, George W. Harkins, living at Fort Towson undertook in June,
1845 to describe it to his uncle Greenwood Leflore who had remained
in Mississippi: "Peace and harmony reigns among the Choctaw people.
Political strife that was existing between the different leading men of
the Nation while in Mississippi—I am happy to say all hostile feelings
are buried, and they are united as a band of brothers in trying to
promote the interest and happiness of their people.

"The Choctaws are progressing and are certainly making great strides
towards civilization. The Choctaw people if let alone by the United
States govt in the course of twenty years there will be found in this
Nation as intelligent men and women as can be found in your highly
refined state of Miss. The Choctaws are beginning to appreciate and
see the importance of having their children educated. . . . great numbers have embraced the Christian religion. There is places of worship
in nearly all the neighborhoods of this district. While I am now writing
I see from my window immense numbers traveling the road to the
meeting house 2 miles distant. If you were here you would take them
to be Mississippians from their manners and dress. . . . .

"The greatest evil we have to contend with is whiskey. Bordering
on the Arkansas and Texas line there are a host of grog shops and the
larger portion of them kept by your refined civilized brothers from
the State of Mississippi. They follow the Indians like buzzards. All
the murders and ravishments that are committed in the Nation generally
originates from drinking frolicks. . . . . Some 8 or 10 murderers running

at large in Mushulatubbe district. The civil officers of that district are afraid to execute the laws. Nat Folsom is chief of that district—he is not worth his weight in coon skins; the fact is the larger portion of the people of that district are the dregs or the last leavings of the Choctaw people. When such men as John McKinney gets to be chief you may know good men are scarce. Col. Thomas Leflore makes an excellent chief; he has energy and firmness about him; he keeps very good order and regulation in this district. . . . . The election for chief will take place in Pushmatahaw district the second Wednesday in next July. The candidates for chief are Nitter cachy, James McCoy, and Eyarcha-hopia. Old Nit is now chief and I think will be elected. He is the smartest full-blood I have ever seen; his feelings are changed entirely for the better; you know he was very hostile while in the old nation towards civilizing the Choctaws.

"Our election for chief will not come on in this district until in July, 1846—the same time in Mushulatubbe. We have a Senate and house of representatives and meet once a year. Our representatives are elected yearly and the senators every two years. One member is allowed for one thousand souls. I would send you a copy of our laws but we have no correct copy at this time. There is men selected to revise, correct, and put it into proper form, and so soon as that is done we intend to have them printed, then I will send you a copy by the first chance."

The Choctaw people demonstrated their pride and interest in their schools on occasions such as the final examinations of the pupils at Spencer in July, 1846, when many parents came to witness the achieve-ments of their children.

"Our examination came off the day before yesterday, Tuesday, much to the satisfaction of all parties. The evening before a great many people had arrived, besides the trustees, the chiefs and head men; and during the morning they kept coming in from all directions, almost every one leading another horse for one of the boys to ride home; so that at dinner we had above 150 guests. We had killed, the afternoon before, a beef, three hogs, and two sheep, which together with a moderate quantity of bacon, had nearly all disappeared the next evening. There were a number of gentlemen and some ladies from Doaksville and Fort Towson present; among others Col. Pitchlynn's two daughters, and sister-in-law. Capt. Jones also, who you may be aware is one of our trustees, a very intelligent man, and of polished manners, and a partner of Mr. Heald, brought his family along in a very handsome coach—the only thing of the kind I have yet seen in the nation. Our exercises commenced about $7\frac{1}{2}$ o'clock, and continued, with about an hour's recess for dinner, until about three. The schoolroom, which however is intolerably small, was crowded all the time, but not a fourth part of the people were in at once that would have been had our accommodations been better.[8]

"The classes first examined belonged to Mr. Dwight's[9] department, whose sole duty since I came has been to teach the English language to those who cannot speak it. As we have had no books suitable for this, it has required great labour on the part of the teachers; and the examination which was a sample of the daily teaching, was conducted simply by giving the names of various objects in Choctaw, and requiring from the scholars the English; repeating short sentences in Choctaw, and requiring a translation in English, and some conversation. . . ."

This was followed by the examination of classes in reading, writing, and arithmetic, geography, natural philosophy, United States history, algebra, Latin reader; "after which I examined one boy in Horace, who had been reciting to me since I came. Occasionally between classes we had a speech or two from some boys previously appointed to prepare, which tended somewhat to vary the exercises, and add to their interest. All at the close appeared pleased, and freely expressed their approbation." After the examinations were concluded the people assembled under the trees to hear Mr. Ramsey address them on the subject of education and the plans for the next session of the school. His talk was then interpreted by Mr. Dwight for the benefit of those who did not understand English. The exercises were then closed by a prayer delivered by Rev. John H. Carr, Methodist missionary.

"Col. Harkins, one of the trustees, then rose, and after making a few remarks in Choctaw, invited Col. Leflore, the chief of this district,

8 Letter from Rev. James B. Ramsey, July 16, 1846, in *The Foreign Missionary Chronicle*, XIV (October, 1846), 289.

9 Jonathan E. Dwight was the name given to a Choctaw youth who lived in the family of Amos Smith Jr., his teacher at Yale College in 1836. Smith and Professor Silliman of the same school wrote letters to Indian officials commending him highly for his moral character and studious habits, though he had much difficulty in mastering the English language (Ellsworth to commissioner of Indian affairs, October 13, 1837, OIA "School file—Ellsworth").

to address the people. He was followed by Col. Fisher, the chief of the upper or Arkansas district; and he by Mr. McKinney, one of our trustees, who is also Maj. Armstrong's interpreter. After which Capt. Hudson gave a speech, which I learned from Mr. Dwight was a very good one indeed; he is a very able, strong-minded Indian, was instructed in Mr. Kingsbury's school in the Old Nation, and though not a professor of religion, is one of the very warmest supporters of the school and of temperance. He spoke with real Indian energy and eloquence of gesture. Mr. McKinney appeared to be also a good speaker. All these speeches were in Choctaw, and of course unintelligible to me. Their general drift, as I learned from Mr. Dwight, was to show the advantages of education, and to enlist the feelings of all in behalf of the schools; and as addressed to the boys, recommending diligence and obedience, &c.

"Col. Harkins closed with a few remarks, and the company began to scatter, and such a scattering—the saddling of horses, and running hither and thither, and shaking of hands and packing of saddle-bags you never saw, or rather I never saw; and in less than two hours, though it was after four o'clock considerably when they finished speaking, there were scarcely twenty students and strangers together, and it appeared truly desolate. They seemed nearly all determined to start off, if they could only go five or six miles, and camp out, which by the way is the common custom."

The next day the writer, Mr. James B. Ramsey, superintendent of Spencer Academy, "went down to Mr. Kingsbury's, to the examination of his school; this you are aware is a girl's school, and close by Doaksville. The examination commenced between 8 and 9 o'clock; I, in company with Mr. Bissel and Dwight arrived a little while after they had commenced, and was much pleased with the promptness and correctness with which they answered the questions proposed to them. Indeed I believe that no company of white girls could have stood an examination better. It was a cheering sight, to see nearly fifty of these girls, thus trained up under religious influences, and growing in useful knowledge, and a large number of their fathers and mothers present, looking on and listening with countenances of deep and lively interest. . . . . Specimens were then shown of their work in plain and fancy needlework, some of which were very pretty.

"After the examination, which occupied some three hours or more, we had a series of speeches from the chiefs and trustees and other head men. . . . . Col. Folsom, one of their principal men, gave a very good speech in English, rather broken indeed, but not the less interesting. He urged the girls not to forget the things they had learned at school, as too many he was sorry to say, had gone back to the habits of their forefathers, and thrown all they had been taught behind their backs."

The efforts of these people justly inspired the following appreciation and prophecy: "The Choctaw, who have earned for themselves so much credit by the establishment of schools in their own country, and who have bestowed so liberally of the tribal means to the great cause of education, continue to press forward in their noble course. The ex-ample they set to other tribes is worth more than the expenditure; and the improvement socially, morally, and religiously among themselves is priceless; it cannot be estimated. Their policy in this particular will be an enduring monument to their forecast, and at some future time they will receive as they well deserve, the gratitude of those that will profit by their example. This people are sowing in other respects the seeds of prosperity. I have samples of cotton and woolen cloth (linsey) manufactured by them, that make very good ordinary clothing, and such as I have often seen worn in Pennsylvania. They have shown an improvement in their legislative body, a sagacity and sense of justice infinitely creditable."[10]

The commissioner's reference is to a change in their constitution by the Choctaw people in 1843 so that their legislature, instead of one, was composed of two bodies called collectively the General Council.[11] "The cause of this change" said Superintendent Armstrong, "is worthy of notice. The nation is divided into three districts, one of which con-tains more than half the entire population. Experience satisfied them that the interests of the two smaller districts were likely to suffer in the general council, from the prepondering influence of the larger one. To remedy therefore an actual practical inconvenience, a new body

10 *Report* of commissioner of Indian affairs for 1844. There were now 12,419 Choctaw people in the West (*ibid.*), thousands having died during the emigration and within the first two or three years after.

11 *Ibid.*, for 1843. While they had only one legislative body the smallest of the three districts complained that it was overshadowed by the largest one. "To silence this discontent the strong district had the good sense and good feeling to agree that the legislature or council should consist of two bodies, in which each of the districts should be represented in its corporate capacity "(*ibid.*, for 1844).

was organized, somewhat resembling the Congress of the United States in its structure. What is chiefly remarkable in this, is the fact that the most populous district, which could have prevented the change, had the wisdom to foresee the bad consequence that might result from resistance, by arousing local and hereditary prejudices."

Other indications of improvement were not less striking, said Armstrong. "At the annuity payments may be seen full-blooded Indians in the fanciful dress of their tribe, either as captains, calling to the pay-tables persons enrolled under them, from registers in their own hand-writing, or as traders, referring to their ledgers or memorandum-books in settlements with debtors or creditors. Different trading stands exhibit large quantities of cloths manufactured by Choctaw women; and more than half the Indians are clothed in fabrics made in their own families. Before any part of the annuities are paid, enough is taken from them to support, during the spring months, for farming purposes, eleven blacksmith-shops over and above those furnished by the government, besides moneys required for other purposes of a public character. The disposition of these sums is managed by the auditor and treasurer of each district, under the direction of the general council, to which they are obliged to render a strict account."[12]

Before the change, the laws of the Choctaw Nation were enacted by a legislative council of forty members; under the new form the joint concurrence of their two houses was necessary to the passage of all laws. They had four chiefs, one for each of the three Choctaw districts and one for the Chickasaw district; a majority of the chiefs could veto a measure enacted by the legislature, which in turn could be overcome by a two-thirds vote of the law-makers; judges were to be elected, and trial by jury was guaranteed to every citizen. In 1850, at the session of the general council, a change was made in their judicial system. Instead of a local judge for each district, one circuit judge was appointed for the entire nation, who traveled about and once every three months held court in each of the four districts. These districts were divided into counties, each of which had a judge for an inferior court, which had cognizance of minor offences, and all cases where the amount involved did not exceed fifty dollars. Cases tried in the county courts could be appealed to the circuit courts and from

12 Armstrong to Crawford, October 1844, *ibid.*

the circuit to the national court, which was composed of one supreme and three associate judges. The judges of the supreme and district courts were elected by the council, the former for four and the latter for two years; the judges of the county courts were elected by the people.[13] The supreme court sat once in six months at the council-house of the nation.[14]

The education of their children continued a paramount consideration with the Choctaw. In September, 1849, the school facilities not keeping pace with the demand, a largely attended meeting was held in Mushulatubbe district on Arkansas River, where speeches were made by the chiefs, captains and other principal men, urging the parents to establish neighborhood schools; holding up for their encouragement the accomplishments in other parts of the nation; urging them to work harder and raise more corn that they might be able to build schools and pay their teachers.

Armstrong Academy[15] was located near the center of Blue County, two miles south of the road leading from Fort Towson to Fort Washita, fifty-five miles west of the former and thirty east of the latter. It was near the dividing ridge between the waters of Blue and Boggy rivers. The buildings were not completed on time, and the school did not begin operations until December 2, 1845. A farm of fifty acres was connected with the school, on which the boys worked when not attending their classes.[16] Rev. Ramsey D. Potts was superintendent and Rev. P. P. Brown, teacher.[17]

The progress achieved by the Choctaw people in the first two decades of their residence in the West is indicated by the establishing of a newspaper in their nation. The *Choctaw Telegraph*, edited by Daniel Folsom, a Choctaw Indian, and published by D. G. Ball at Doaksville, made its appearance in the autumn of 1848. It had a brief career and was followed by the *Choctaw Intelligencer* in the summer of 1850. Like its predecessor it was published weekly at Doaksville and was printed in English and Choctaw. D. D. Alsobrook was publisher, and J. P. Kingsbury and J. R. Dwight were the editors.

13   Cooper to Drew, September 3, 1853, *ibid.*, for 1853.
14   *Ibid.*, for 1851.
15   Under the American Indian Mission Association of Louisville, Kentucky.
16   Capt. Robert M. Jones was trustee and Col. Silas D. Fisher chief of this district.
17   *Report* of commissioner of Indian affairs for 1846.

Armstrong Academy for Boys, Bokchito, Bryan County, 1843–1921

Peter P. Pitchlynn

By permission of the terms of the Treaty of Dancing Rabbit Creek, about 7,000 Choctaw Indians remained in Mississippi after the larger part of the tribe emigrated west; but the citizens of Alabama and Mississippi demanded their removal. The laws and treatment by the white people were bringing the Choctaw every year into a more deplorable state, and the Government made repeated efforts to get them away. On March 3, 1843, the secretary of war made a contract with Alexander Anderson to remove them by water from Vicksburg to Fort Coffee, but the Indians refused to go on boats and the contract was cancelled. Another was made September 4 of the next year, with Anderson, Cobb, Forrester, and Pickens. But the Indians still refused to remove until they could receive the script to which they were entitled from the Government for their land. The failure of the Government to provide this script on time entailed considerable delay and loss both to the Indians and the contractors. Others refused to leave without their oxen and horses and only 550 were removed that year.[18] In April, 1845, emigration was renewed when 1,280 of these people passed through Southern Arkansas to join their brothers in Indian Territory; and the next year a thousand more came;[19] this latter was a community of Choctaw people who were peculiarly fortunate in their condition and were not at all like the destitute members of the tribe. Many years before, one of their number named Toblee Chubbee

18 *Ibid.*, for 1844 and 1845. White speculators exercised their influence over the Indians and agents and secured their script at a fraction of its value (*ibid.*, for 1847).

19 Said to have been 1786 (*ibid.*, for 1846); see also *ibid* for 1851. Toblee Chubbee's band left Vicksburg on the afternoon of Friday, May 22, in the steamer *New Hampshire*. They encountered low water in the Arkansas River fifteen miles above Little Rock, immediately below "Free Nigger's Bend." Here they landed part of their cargo on May 28, and continued up the river but on June 3 the boat struck a snag and sank near the bank below Titsworth's Landing in McLean's Bottoms. The conductor of the party, J. B. Luce, then secured twelve ox-wagons and oxen to carry the Indians and their personal effects. It was with the greatest difficulty the party was removed to the south side of the river as a violent storm prevailed, and the white ferrymen abandoned the boat; but the Indians took their places and the crossing was effected. After several days of preparation the march was begun, but the ground was so soft from recent heavy rains that the wagons repeatedly mired down. One required eight yoke of oxen to extricate it. They finally reached and crossed the Poteau River at Phil's ferry on June 10 and camped at the western edge of Ring's Prairie (J. B. Luce to William Armstrong, June 3 and June 10, 1846, OIA, "Choctaw Emigration" File A 2058).

became converted to the Christian religion and exerted all the influence of a man of strong character to the uplift of his people. He converted them to Christianity, induced them to live sober, industrious lives, to abandon the habits of Indians and live like the better class of white people. Most of them had comfortable homes and it was with difficulty they were induced to emigrate; in fact, they would not consider moving until they had seen some of their western brothers and heard their accounts of schools and churches and other improvements in the West.[20] When they did go, they not only had more property, but were altogether superior in appearance to any other Indians in Mississippi. Unfortunately, the change was not at first a happy one, for they suffered many deaths and much from disease.[21]

In 1847 there were 1,623 more emigrants who came in eight parties. "Of these, 360 were of the Shuk-hu-nat-chee band; formerly settled on a stream of that name, flowing into the Tombigbee; 425 were Mogolushas, chiefly from Neshoba county, Mississippi; 650 were Sixtowns, from the southern section of Mississippi and Louisiana; and the rest were from the country watered by the Big Black and Pearl rivers. About half the entire number settled on the Arkansas, and the remainder on the waters of Red River. The different parties vary considerably in their habits and character. Some are sober, industrious,

20 When Superintendent Armstrong went to Mississippi to further emigration of the Choctaw remaining there, he took with him a delegation from that tribe living west of the Mississippi to present the inducements of life in their new home. Among them was the doughty old chief Nitakechi of Pushmataha District, who contracted pleurisy from which he died November 22, 1845, in Lauderdale County, Mississippi (Arkansas Intelligencer, December 27, 1845, p. 2, col. 1).

21 "Nothing is allowed them by government for medicines or medical attendance. . . . . They leave against their own inclination, at the solicitation of the government. On the route, when they seldom need it, medical aid is furnished; but after their arrival, when sickness is inevitable, they get none. By affording very little assistance, many lives might be saved. Besides health and strength are more essential during the first year after their removal than at any subsequent period, as they have their cabins to build, farms to open, and others labors to perform, incident to a change of residence" (William Armstrong in House Executive Document No. 4, Twenty-ninth Congress, second session, 268). "The United States could not confer a greater boon upon the Indians than by holding out encouragement in some way for the location of scientific physicians among them. Thousands die for want of proper medical advice and medicine" (Agent Douglas H. Cooper in Report of commissioner of Indian affairs for 1853).

thrifty, and anxious to improve their condition. Others, again, are indolent, improvident, and intemperate. To the first class the Shuk-hu-nat-chee, with but few exceptions, belong. They are, in general, decently and comfortably clothed; about one third of them are members of religious societies, and nearly all have provided themselves with cabins and fields, making this year, notwithstanding the usual acclimatory sickness, respectable crops of corn.

"The Mogollushas differ widely from the Shuk-hu-nat-ches. They have always been regarded as improvident, turbulent, and reckless. Many of them had, on their arrival, large sums of money, derived from the sale of land script. These spent most of their time in drinking and fighting, to the infinite annoyance of the more peacable and well disposed of their neighbors. Their means, however, soon gave out, and, I understand, about half of them have shown a disposition to labor.

"The Sixtowns are said to be, with the exception of one or two small bands, the most ignorant of the Choctaw race. They have, hitherto, been more strongly attached to the customs of their ancestors, and more obstinately opposed to innovation, than any other portion of the tribe. They are not so quarrelsome as the Mogolushas, and not so industrious as the Shuk-ha-nat-chees. Prior to their emigration, they led wandering lives, ranging over a considerable scope of country, and seldom remaining long in one place. It was, therefore, supposed that the greater part would return to their former haunts. It is said, however, that not a single family has gone back. On the contrary, they bid fair to make very good settlers. A portion of those included under the head of Six-towns are better known as Bay Indians. These came up the Washita [Ouachita of Arkansas] in April last, and settled in the southeastern corner of the Choctaw country. They have intermarried with the French, and adopted, in a great degree, their manners and peculiarities. I have not seen them, but understand that in dress and appearance they resemble the lower classes of the creole population of Louisiana. Considering their mode of life and peculiar condition, it is rather remarkable that, apart from the Bay Indians, who are a distinct body in many respects different from the others, there are no half-breeds among the Sixtown emigrants.

"The Bay Indians and other Sixtowns, who came about the same time, arrived too late to plant corn this year. Those who came in January last, and in the spring of 1846, are said to be doing tolerably well. The other emigrants that removed during the last year generally resemble the Mogollushas in their character and habits. They did not reach this country until long after the usual planting season."[22]

The party of Sixtowns Indians who arrived in April 1846 came through Southern Arkansas. A. M. M. Upshaw went to the state line and brought them to the home of Chief Thomas Leflore. The contractors, wrote Upshaw from Doaksville, had "got all the waggons except one and a good many of the Indians this side of the line, but Col. Jack Johnson" who had stopped three-fourth of a mile east of the line made the Indians take all their baggage back to where he was. They remained here for three days camped near a grocery, most of them drunk; "they sold there blankets, guns, and every thing they could to get whisky; the women got drunk; in fact they were the most awful set of Indians I ever saw, and Col. Johnson is certainly to blame for it all." Upshaw said the contractors were quarrelling and all was confusion. The sordid scheme of Johnson, said the agent, was to keep the Indians drunk in Arkansas until the contractors had exhausted their resources, when he would bring them into the Choctaw Nation and demand pay for rescuing them and completing their emigration.[23]

Several hundred Choctaw came yearly for the next few years. On their arrival they set about building homes and adjusting themselves to their new surroundings; but it was said that these people who had been living with the whites in Mississippi were greatly addicted to drunkenness and whisky shops multiplied along the Arkansas line. Many of their children died from whooping cough. However in 1847 the Choctaw settlements on Red River produced 1,000 bales of cotton for shipment besides a surplus of corn.[24] But this year the Choctaw in

22 *Report* of Samuel M. Rutherford, acting superintendent of Western Territory: with *Report* of commissioner of Indian affairs for 1847. In May, 1849 Rutherford was removed and John Drennan appointed in his place as Choctaw agent and acting superintendent of the Western Territory.

23 Upshaw to Armstrong, April 30, 1846, OIA "I. T. Misc. Upshaw." Two parties of Choctaw emigrants arrived at Fort Coffee in March 1847 on the steamers *Nathan Hale, Cotton Plant* and *Arkansas No. 5* (*Arkansas Intelligencer*, March 20, 1847, p. 2, col. 1). A few weeks later the engineer of the steamer *Alert* was swimming in company with his pet bear; becoming too frolicsome the pet drowned his master (*ibid.*, June 19, 1847, p. 2, col. 1).

24 *Ibid.* The Chickasaw Indians furnished most of the supplies used at Fort Washita (*Report* of commissioner of Indian affairs for 1847).

common with the Chickasaw and Creeks complained much of the wandering Kickapoo who stole their horses and killed their cattle.[25]

Two years later 547 more Choctaw removed from Mississippi to their new home in the West.[26] Most of them settled in Mushulatubbe District where they built cabins and planted corn. These emigrants brought the cholera into the nation, resulting in the closing of Fort Coffee Academy and New Hope Seminary April 19, 1849.

Jefferson Davis, then a United States senator, was among those still determined to expel the remnants of those aboriginal owners of the soil. From the senate chamber he addressed a letter to the commissioner of Indian affairs, forwarding with his approval a letter written by D. N. Haley, who had long been active in efforts to remove the Indians, and who had engaged in securing the Treaty of Dancing Rabbit Creek in 1830: "It is an object of great importance to us that the Choctaws should be removed and prevented from returning and I commend the proposition to your favorable consideration."[27]

George S. Gaines, a tried and trusted friend of the Choctaw Indians, was then in Washington vainly trying to secure compensation due him nearly twenty years for conducting an exploring party of Choctaw Indians to the West.[28] One hundred of his Choctaw friends residing in and about Jasper and Newton counties, Mississippi, appealed to Gaines, saying: "Our tribe has been woefully imposed upon of late. We have had our habitations torn down and burned; our fences destroyed, cattle turned into our fields & we ourselves have been scourged, manacled, fettered and otherwise personally abused, until by such treatment some of our best men have died. These are the acts of those persons who profess to be the agents of the Government to procure our removal to Arkansas & who cheat us out of all they can, by the use of fraud, duplicity, and even violence." They asked Gaines to aid them in securing removal agents whom they could trust.[29]

A few small parties, aggregating four or five hundred, were got under way from the southern part of Mississippi during the winter and spring of 1850. Ineffectual efforts were continued through the

25 Ibid., for 1847. This year on September 24 occurred the death of their leader David Folsom, who was born January 25, 1791.
26 U. S. Senate *Executive document* No. 1, Thirty-first Congress first session p. 948.
27 Davis to Brown, March 27, 1850, OIA, "Choctaw Emigration."
28 *Indian Removal, op. cit.*
29 "One hundred red men" December 6, 1849, OIA, Choctaw File G 156.

spring and summer, but the extreme heat and cholera made the work difficult and caused great suffering among the Indians. After much sickness and many deaths among the emigrants, survivors wandered back to their old homes in Mississippi. Their agent, Douglas Cooper, attributed their sickness to their manner of living and to the stupid policy of issuing to them beef to last them two, and sometimes as much as six weeks, when it was almost certain to spoil on their hands. "The Indians gormandize for a short time, aided by numerous friends and acquaintances and then have to subsist themselves. If they did not eat up the beef, no doubt it would spoil on their hands, although they have salt issued. You know the improvidence of these people. It is rare they take the trouble to save their meat by salting."[30]

Among the recent arrivals in the Choctaw Nation was a party of Catawba Indians who left South Carolina in December, 1851, and after six had died on the way, the surviving nineteen reached the Choctaw agency in February following. They were peaceable and inoffensive people and begged to be admitted into the Choctaw Nation.[31] They had recently made similar application to the Chickasaw Nation and had been refused. On November 9, 1853, the Choctaw council passed the necessary legislation admitting to the tribe as members the following Catawba Indians: William Morrison, Thomas Morrison, Sarah Jane Morrison, Molly Redhead, Betsey Heart, Rebecca Heart, Phillip Keggo, and the infant child of Phillip Keggo and Cynthia Keggo, Rosey Ayers, Betsey Ayers, Julianna Ayers, Mary Ayers, Sopronia Ayers, and Sally Ayers.[32]

In the spring of 1853, another party of Choctaw numbering 383 emigrated to the West, but becoming homesick and dissatisfied with the change, more than two-thirds of them wandered back to Mississippi. Emigrants who arrived in 1854 also returned to Mississippi because of the diastrous drought of the two preceding years.

30 Cooper to superintendent, June 10, 1853, OIA *ibid.*, C. 348.
31 Drew to commissioner of Indian affairs, September 23, 1853, *ibid.*, D 418.
32 Cooper to commissioner of Indian affairs, January 4, 1854, *ibid.*, D 504.

CHAPTER FIVE / *Threat of Civil Disorder*

B
Y 1850 there were five schools in the Choctaw Nation under the management of the American Board of Commissioners for Foreign Missions: Koonsha, Chu-ah-la, I-yan-nubbe and Wheelock Female Seminaries, and Norwalk Male Seminary, the two latter under Rev. Alfred Wright; Armstrong Academy, a Baptist Mission school was conducted by the American Indian Mission Board; the Presbyterian Board of Missions conducted Spencer Academy; Fort Coffee Male Academy and New Hope Female Academy were under the direction of the Methodist Episcopal Church, South. In these and three smaller schools there were 528 pupils.[1]

The facilities of these schools and those maintained by the Government and the tribe were taxed to the utmost to provide for all who wished to enter and the Choctaw people evolved the interesting and novel expedient of what were called "neighborhood" or "Saturday and Sunday" schools. Within the Nation there were dozens of these schools attended by pupils who lived at home; they were taught reading, writing and arithmetic in the Choctaw language. The teachers were usually Choctaw who had gone through the mission schools. "Two

1   Armstrong Academy was in successful operation until November 15, 1858, when it was closed by an epidemic of malignant measles, and it was not reopened until the first Monday of the next February. In addition to the four schools at this academy a new brick building was erected here at a cost of $10,000 in time for the opening of school the first Monday in October, 1859. One hundred and thirty-six boys were instructed in 1852 at Spencer Academy by four teachers. At the end of the school year the pupils were examined in the presence of two of the trustees, Col. P. P. Pitchlynn and Stephen Cochausur, for a period of twenty hours (*Report* of commissioner of Indian affairs for 1852).

of the teachers are young ladies of about eighteen years of age, native Choctaws. They conduct the schools and deserve great credit for their ability and exertions in behalf of their people. They speak the Choctaw language and have the entire confidence of the Nation." The pupils were not limited to children, for so eager was the desire to learn that many adults of both sexes attended to secure the elements of an education that had been denied them when they were children. Mr. Wright reported the desire for education so keen that within the sphere of his ministerial labors there were seven of these Saturday and Sabbath schools. Some of them were attended by as many as twenty-five to fifty pupils.[2] In Mr. Wright's school at Wheelock arithmetic, grammar, geography, natural philosophy, astronomy, botany, chemistry, geometry, and history of the Bible were taught. So avid were the Choctaw to get all they could out of their schools that Mr. Hotchkin was moved to protest that teachers and pupils were over-worked and insisted that the school should not be run more than nine months out of the twelve. It is only fair to consider also the heroism of the pupils. *Vide* Mr. Wright again: "In reading, the teacher has not only endeavored to have her pupils read correctly but has collected such books as will lead them to think and such also as will have a moral and religious influence— as Conversation on Common Things; Child's Book on Repentance; History of Jonah; Natural Theology, by Gallaudet."[3] Despite these formidable studies some of the children rode their ponies as far as ten miles to school. In 1848, both female teachers at Koonsha Female Academy died; and scarlet fever, whooping cough and mumps successively attacked the students.[4]

A temperance society in the neighborhood of Wheelock numbered 300 members. The Indians in that section in 1849 circulated a petition to the Texas legislature praying that body to stop the sale of whisky to the members of their tribe.[5] The Choctaw council, immediately after the tribe's migration, had enacted a law to prohibit the introduction of whisky which they claimed antedated the Maine law on the subject. "Indeed I think Neal Dow must have been a boy

2 Armstrong to Crawford, October 6, 1841, *ibid.*, for 1841; *ibid.*, for 1856.
3 *Ibid.*, for 1851.
4 In 1851 Spencer Academy was overwhelmed by measles and out of 100 boys present seventy were ill; of these four died (*ibid.*, 1851).
5 But it went unnoticed for several years.

when the first 'council fire' against whiskey was kindled in this nation. Their laws have been quite well executed. This people deserve
credit for not ever having had a distillery or a national debt, as well
as for doing so much in the cause of education."[6]

Maj. Thomas Wall and Thomson McKenney, interpreter, erected a
good grist-mill on James's Fork, one of the tributaries of the Poteau,
about ten miles from the Choctaw agency on the main road from Fort
Smith to Fort Towson, thus encouraging the Indians to raise wheat.
In this, Mushulatubbee District, they were experimenting with the
culture of cotton, which theretofore had been almost exclusively grown
on Red River. The largest planter in the Choctaw Nation was Capt.
Robert M. Jones, who had four plantations on Red River and in 1849
raised 700 bales of cotton.[7] Maj. Pitman Colbert and Jackson Kemp
were also extensive planters.[8] "Domestic manufacture is on the increase. Cards and looms are now more used. Last winter, at late hours
of night, I heard the hum and buzz of the spinning-wheel. . . . .
The subject of education may be termed the great subject among the
Choctaws. Schools! Schools! sound on the ear wherever I go. Inquiries
are often made—'When can you give us a school teacher?' "[9]

The Lennox neighborhood school opened in October, 1853, with
forty-eight pupils. "Our last examination was attended by almost every
parent and friend, and for nearly five hours they listened to recitations,
interspersed with singing, followed by speeches by the Choctaws for
two hours, expressing their great satisfaction in the result of the school,
and their continued confidence and interest.[10] Indians improving; better
treatment of the female sex. Formerly the wife, barefoot, followed the
husband on horseback, with hose and shoes; now in our settlement
if either is obliged to walk, it is the man."[11] "Our young brother Allen

6 Cyrus Byington: *Report* of commissioner of Indian affairs, 1858.

7 Even in those early days it was said, "the Choctaws. . . . who raise cotton,
it is true, have lost a great deal from the ravages of the worm" (*ibid.*, for 1846). The
adjutant at Fort Arbuckle reported to the commissary general in November 1848
that mills had been erected in the neighborhood during the year that made excellent
flour which could be furnished to the post cheaper than it could be purchased at
New Orleans (QMG, L to P, 1849, No. 1).

8 *Report* of commissioner of Indian affairs for 1852.

9 Ebenezer Hotchkin, *idem.*

10 Simon L. Hobbs, July 24, 1856: *Report* of commissioner of Indian affairs for
1856.

11 *Ibid.*

Wright completed his course of study and returned to labor for his people. He was ordained to the Gospel Ministry in April last.[12] I. P. Folsom, graduate of Dartmouth College taught a day-school at Bennington."[13]

Epidemics took a sad toll of lives in the autumn of 1852. At Fort Coffee Academy says Rev. John Harrell, the superintendent, ". . . .32 of the boys were prostrated with measles, in their worst form. They all, however, partially recovered, when whooping-cough, pneumonia, and the flux followed. The scene was truly appalling. Every room was a hospital, and the groans of the sick and dying were heard in every direction. In vain did we resort to physicians and medical aid, all was unavailing; and for four long weeks the angel of death, with his raven wings, hovered over us. . . . ." Fifteen of the pupils died; the school was suspended and did not resume until the next fall;[14] in the meantime the buildings were repaired and whitewashed and eight fireplaces added to rooms that formerly must have been cheerless and unhealthful habitations through the winter months. The epidemic involved the pupils at New Hope near by, and there were a number of deaths including that of one of their teachers.

On March 27, 1853, occurred the death of Rev. Alfred Wright[15] and the next report of Wheelock was made by his very capable widow, Harriet B. Wright, who submitted the following sketch of Mr. Wright's life: ". . . .Mr. Wright was a native of Columbia, Connecticut, and was born March 1, 1788. He received his collegiate education at Williams College, Mass., commenced the study of theology in Andover, Massachusetts, but was compelled by ill-health to go south, where he was licensed and ordained to the work of the gospel ministry. In December, 1820, he joined the mission of the Choctaws, and has been for thirty-two years devoted to this work. He found them without a written language, without the instruction and restraints of the gospel, without written laws, and with but few of the usages and habits of

12   *Ibid.*
13   *Ibid.*
14   Some years later these schools were again suspended; New Hope resumed on November 29, 1858, and Fort Coffee Academy on the first Monday of January, 1859.
15   Mrs. H. B. Wright to S. B. Treat, May 4, 1853, *Missionary records*, Vol. 243, No. 360.

civilized life. Amid many hindrances and difficulties he learned the language, assisted in reducing it to writing, and translated and published some sixty books and tracts in the Choctaw language for the use of those who can never learn English. He also translated and printed the New Testament and six books of the Old Testament. Besides, he was the only physician in this part of the country, his calls in sickly seasons amounting to fifteen or twenty patients daily. He was also superintendent of the schools at Wheelock and Norwalk, and had a large pastoral charge. From the time that Wheelock church was organized in this country, in December, 1832, till his decease, in March, 1853, he had been permitted to receive to the communion and fellowship of this church five hundred and seventy members.'"[16]

The 383 Choctaw immigrants who came in 1853 brought cholera with them and fourteen deaths occurred on Arkansas River; but ". . . .by camping the Indians in the woods in small detachments, and by proper remedial agents, the progress of the disease was arrested."[17] Buyers went among the Indians, purchasing all their cattle which they drove through to California to supply the great demand there;[18] Indian Territory was thus so nearly denuded of cattle as greatly to increase the price of meat, bringing prosperity to those who had it to sell and distress to others.[19] This situation was greatly aggravated by an unusual drought; during 1854 and 1855 little rain fell[20] for fourteen months and there was almost a complete crop failure in 1854. There was much suffering among the Indians as they had not been able to raise enough grain to sustain them; the water in Red and Arkansas rivers had been too low to permit boats to ascend with grain or other provisions, and many of the poorer Indians were forced to scour the woods for wild vegetables and other sources of food. This lack of water in the rivers, however, had been a blessing in disguise as it prevented the introduction of large quantities of whisky usually

16   *Report* of Commissioner of Indian Affairs for 1853, p. 170.
17   *Ibid.*, for 1854.
18   In the summer of 1850 Captain Forrest, heading a party of twelve Americans, four Mexicans and two Delaware Indians, left Indian Territory for California with a drove of 774 cows and 231 calves. They crossed Arkansas River on June first, and traveled west on the Fort Smith route. Some of this great drove was collected in southwest Missouri (*Arkansas Gazette and Democrat*, June 21, 1850).
19   *Report* of Commissioner of Indian Affairs for 1854, p. 131.
20   *Ibid.*, for 1855, p. 170.

brought up the streams by boat, and the cause of temperance was greatly promoted. The drought compelled the Indians to renewed industry and improved methods of farming, with the result that in spite of slight precipitation in 1854 some good crops of corn were made, though their oats failed entirely; the next year their crops were nearly destroyed by grasshoppers. In the spring of 1855 some of the Choctaw people were in a starving condition and were depredating on others who were more fortunate. And after these years of adversity the hopes of the Indians for a fruitful year in 1857 were blasted when on April 16 the thermometer registered a temperature of 18 that destroyed all their corn, fruit, and most of the wheat. At this time the Indians were much disturbed and excited by events in Kansas and Nebraska, and the bill introduced in Congress by Senator Johnson of Arkansas to "erect the Cherokee, Creek, and Choctaw countries into qualified Territories of the United States."[21] Nothing came of it however.

Indians who had immigrated during that period, homesick and discouraged with the prospects of life in the West, had wandered back to Mississippi. Their agent, Douglas H. Cooper, visited Mississippi, Alabama, and Louisiana, and reported there were more than 2,000 ignorant Choctaw Indians remaining there leading a vagrant life after their primitive customs.[22] But encouraging accounts continued to find their way into official reports. Rev. Cyrus Byington reported in 1855[23] "within fifteen miles of me [Stockbridge, Eagletown] there are five horse-mills and one water mill, and a sawmill. At some of these mills they have made, or are making, preparations to grind and bolt wheat. There are five cotton gins. . . . . I can count ten wells and as many chimneys built of rock. In some of these wells there is the old fashioned pump, and in others the chain pump. . . . . There is a good ferry boat on Little River and another on Mountain Fork at Eagletown. There is a store at Eagletown. There are three cotton gins within six miles of this place. Last winter and spring about 200 bales of cotton were ginned at these gins."[24] "The Arkansas synod will meet at Doaksville on September 21, 1854,"[25] and a little later, "a good saw and flouring

21   Ibid., 132.
22   Ibid., for 1856.
23   Ibid., for 1855.
24   Ibid., 1854.
25   Ibid.

mill has been erected at the bridge on the Blue. This will afford encouragement to the people in regard to raising wheat."[26] Farmers were already raising some wheat. From Goodwater, Rev. Ebenezer Hotchkin reported: "Within the bounds of this church we have eight places for preaching. At six of these places we have meeting houses; four are built of logs; two are frame buildings, forty-two by thirty-two feet; one has been built this year at an expense of $700.00; and no debt on that account." In the warm seasons their meetings were held under brush arbors.

Injection of the slavery question into local affairs resulted in the withdrawal of the American Board of Commissioners for Foreign Missions from the conduct of the schools in the Choctaw Nation. Armstrong Academy was transferred from the American Indian Mission Association to the Domestic Board of the Southern Baptist Convention located at Marion, Alabama.[27]

The National council in 1853 enacted a new school law creating a board of trustees and a general superintendent. It was provided that no slave nor child of slave should be taught to read or write in any Choctaw school. And the school authorities were required to remove "any and all persons connected with the public schools or academies known to be abolitionists or who disseminate or attempt to disseminate directly or indirectly, abolition doctrines."

There was always the handicap of the flood of whisky from Texas and Arkansas to demoralize the Indians, against which the Choctaw government waged a constant but ineffectual fight; the occasional drought, the cholera, smallpox, and epidemic of measles took their toll of strength but the resolution of the Indians continued to carry them forward in spite of these obstacles. By 1856 it was reported that the farms of the Indians were not only more numerous but were larger and better fenced than formerly, for the protection of both stock and crops. The farmers were raising cotton, wheat, oats, rye, corn, peas, potatoes, turnips, and pumpkins. Some of them had apple, peach, pear, and plum orchards. Other evidence of the increase of industry was seen in the number of wagons, carts, plows, hoes, axes, carpenter's tools and in the opening of new wagon roads. To a large extent the

26 Ibid., 1857.
27 Ibid., 1855.

people dressed in cloth of their own manufacture. Few attempted to support their families by hunting.

Their horses, cattle, cows, working oxen, hogs, sheep, geese, turkeys, guinea fowls and chickens testified in their favor. Many families kept track of the days by notching sticks which they laid away weekly and monthly; but good cabins with plank floors, stone chimneys, and glass windows; roofs put on with nails instead of "rib poles"; dug and walled wells; improvement in their household furniture and wearing apparel; the great number of horse mills, cotton gins, grist- and sawmills, blacksmith shops and ferry boats; all these things indicated a people who were not only industrious and provident, but who were heartened by their situation to a sense of permanency, and who were in fact a nation of good citizens, fit progenitors of the civilization they were so surely establishing.

Rev. Cyrus Byington was not only a zealous laborer for the spiritual welfare of the Choctaw Indians, but he learned to speak their language fluently and continued his translations; in this work he was assisted by the Rev. Alfred Wright. Mr. Byington assembled his manuscripts and left home in the autumn of 1850 for New England and New York to look after the printing of his translations, which included a Choctaw hymn book, the Books of Joshua, Judges, Ruth I and II, Samuel, and an abridgement of Gallaudet's *Sacred Biography* and the *Choctaw Definer*. He did not complete his work and return to his family until the spring of 1853.

While in New York he wrote an interesting account for the New York *Evangelist* descriptive of the improvements achieved by the Choctaw people. He said that now instead of the labor of the field being performed by the women with hoes, "the men plow the fields with cattle or horses, and plant them or else help the women to do it. Instead of a brush fence the laws require fences to be made ten rails high. Instead of seeing men without hats, shoes, and pantaloons, it is rare to meet them on public occasions without all these. The houses are now to a great extent furnished with floors, chairs, tables and beds. The meals are taken more regularly and the table is supplied with plates, knives, forks, metal spoons, with bread, meat, sugar, and coffee." He mentioned their constitution and trial by jury secured to all. "Marriage between one man and woman is regulated by law, and is to be solemnized by a judge, or minister of the Gospel. The legal fee is $2. Widows are entitled to dower, and children inherit their father's estate. Their laws forbidding the introduction of ardent spirits, first enacted nearly thirty years since, before there was a Christian Choctaw to be found, and before the chiefs could read or write should not be forgotten."[28]

Among the teachers in the Choctaw Nation were graduates of Mt. Holyoke, Dartmouth, Williams and other eastern colleges, as well as native Choctaw, who had been graduated from good schools. The course of study in the schools was practical, and calculated to make youths into useful citizens. Attached to each of the academies was a farm cultivated mainly by the boys who were instructed in agriculture. In the girls' schools after recitations from their books they were instructed in spinning, weaving, sewing, knitting and ornamental needle-work, and by turns performed the duties of the household and dairy. This work prepared them for usefulness in after life and fullblood graduates formerly indifferent and ignorant, cherished the knowledge so gained to bestow it on their daughters in after years. Girls returning home from these schools proudly carried with them bed quilts or clothing they had made for their parents. At Chuala Female Seminary they made a large quantity of clothing for the boys at Spencer Academy, and the boys at Fort Coffee Academy wore clothing made for them by the girls at New Hope Seminary six miles away. One year the girls of this school made 100 pairs of pants and shirts for these boys, besides making much of their own clothing.

Boys in Fort Coffee Academy were instructed in spelling, reading, arithmetic, geography, English grammar, chemistry, algebra, geometry and Latin grammar. The girls at the branch school, New Hope, had the same studies except chemistry, algebra, geometry, and Latin grammar. Some of the girls from this school were sent to more advanced schools in Mississippi and Tennessee. Among the Choctaw boys in the sopho-more class of Delaware College in 1849 were Pitchlynn, Hall, Wright, and Garland.

As about two thirds of the Choctaw people were living on the Red River, Choctaw Agent Douglas H. Cooper and Superintendent Thomas S. Drew in 1853 recommended the abandonment of Fort Towson as an army post so that it could be occupied by the Choctaw agency which

28 *New York Evangelist* copied in *Indian Advocate* October, 1852, p. 3, col. 4.

would then be more convenient to the great majority of the Nation. Drew suggested that if this were done it would draw to that part of the Nation most of the Choctaw Indians living on the Arkansas River, thus "opening up for a cession of the Arkansas and Canadian districts, one of the most eligible routes for a Pacific Railroad."[29]

Fort Towson was abandoned by the army the next July; and the quartermaster general directed that the buildings of the post be delivered to the agent for the Choctaw and Chickasaw Indians except those occupied by white people. Agent Cooper turned over the buildings of the old agency to Tandy Walker and went to Fort Towson to set up his office there.[30] He found at the abandoned post seven sets of officers' quarters and soldiers' barracks for two regiments together with a large hospital and blacksmith shop, not only in an advanced state of decay, but badly damaged by a hurricane that had swept through them in the preceding June. The buildings, he said, were too numerous and extensive to be kept up for the use of an agency unless disposed of for residences and stores.

The Choctaw council had requested that some of the buildings at the post be turned over to the Nation for council house, courthouses and other uses and Cooper recommended that their wishes be granted. After permission had been given for them to use the buildings at the post, the council passed a resolution reciting: "Be it enacted that hereafter the meeting of the General Council shall be held at Fort Towson on the first Wednesday of November, and the law directing it to be held at Doaksville is hereby repealed."

"It is a pity," said Cooper, "to allow so many valuable buildings as are here, to rot down, and I would respectfully ask authority to dispose of them in such manner as will be most beneficial to the public and in such way as to keep the place in good repair; otherwise the decaying timber will render the Post too sickly to be used for the residence of the Agent. It will cost more money to tear down & remove the buildings (which are of logs) than the department will be

29 The route for this proposed railroad through their country had been surveyed in 1853 (*Report of Explorations for a Railway Route near the Thirty-fifth Parallel of North Latitude, from the Mississippi River to the Pacific Ocean by Lieutenant A. W. Whipple, 1853-54*).

30 Cooper to commissioner of Indian affairs, September 14, 1854, OIA, "Choctaw" 1004.

willing to expend for the purpose. It is difficult even to determine how to arrange & repair buildings for Agent's residence, Offices, dwelling for Interpreter &c., without knowing what disposition will be made of the residue.

"I shall still delay extensive repairs, or the final appropriation of buildings for use of the Agency, until I know what conclusion the Department will come to. It is necessary I think, to authorize the Agent here to dispose of all buildings not needed for the Agency to the Nation and to Traders. As long as the present system is kept up, Trading Posts will be required. This place will make a delightful village where the Council & Courts of the Nation can be accom-modated and the Traders located under the jurisdiction of the Govern-ment Agent. And in the event of the adoption of the Territorial form of Government, suitable buildings can be had for the Governor and other public officers."[31]

Following the abandonment of Fort Towson the country was plagued by a great increase in the amount of whisky introduced from Arkansas and Texas. Peddlers from Fort Smith in violation of law undertook to ply their trade without giving bond and secur-ing a license. One firm that dealt in so-called patent medicines made by itself and composed mainly of intoxicants, constructed a peddler's wagon full of compartments and drawers stocked with these "medi-cines, liquors, and fancy articles without end," wrote the super-intendent Charles W. Dean. Much of the contraband went into the Indian country under the name of sarsaparilla.[32] Merchants and so-called doctors were introducing into the Choctaw country other nostrums called "John Bull," "John Brown," "Johnny Jump-up,"

31 Cooper to Drew, November 20, 1854, OIA "Choctaw Agency," D 742. Mrs. Esther Gooding, widow of the late sutler, George C. Gooding, occupied a house on the reservation 150 yards from the fort. Her husband had built there a "house and store with the necessary outbuildings, barn, and stables, store, and ware room with the approbation of the commandant. His widow wishes to have her title to the prop-erty recognized by the Choctaw Nation. Her husband was the son of Capt. Gooding of Tippecanoe memory, in which engagement he rendered good service and was severely wounded" (Babbitt to adjutant general October 6, 1854 (with Jefferson Davis to commissioner of Indian affairs, October 10, 1854) OIA "Choctaw" D 460). The buildings of the old fort were nearly all destroyed by fire a few years later.

32 Dean to Manypenny, October 24, 1855, OIA, Southern Superintendency, D 991.

"Bay Water," and "Schnapps."[33] The purchase of horses from the Choctaw and Chickasaw Indians that had acquired the name of "pony trade," had developed to such an extent that it required special regulations.[34]

The ill-advised situation under which the Choctaw and Chickasaw Indians occupied the same country and shared in the same government, with its endless contention leading to the verge of disorder and violence, was terminated by a treaty of separation in 1855[35] though the agencies for both were consolidated under Douglas H. Cooper[36] with headquarters at Fort Towson. The tribes, requested to indicate preferance for a new location, did so in their autumn councils. The Choctaw chiefs voted in favor of Boggy Depot and the Chickasaw divided, eleven voting for Boggy Depot and ten for Upshaw's old agency near Fort Washita as some of the buildings of that agency were standing and the location was near the Chickasaw council grounds. William R. Guy wished to sell the Government his house at Boggy Depot for the sum of $4,500 to be used as an agency.

Cooper retained his post at Fort Towson for some time and in the autumn of 1855 he was engaged as a sort of examining magistrate in connection with the killing at Doaksville a mile from the post of Noah Folsom in April, 1855, by W. E. Gildast a white man. Cooper reduced to writing voluminous depositions given by witnesses from which one learns the names of several residents of that once important trading village of which scarcely a trace remains. Folsom and Gildast were playing cards and drinking in the store of Henry Folsom when a quarrel arose between them and Gildast killed Folsom with a butcher knife. Dr. Francis Pugh, Dr. A. E. Greenwood, a Mr. Bourland, Henry Berthelet a merchant, and Simpson Folsom, brother of the deceased, all of Doaksville, gave testimony which Agent Cooper forwarded to the commissioner of Indian affairs.[37]

The Choctaw council held a special session at Fort Towson in the summer of 1856 with Daniel Folsom, president of the house of repre-

33 Pitchlynn to Manypenny, October 10, 1856, OIA "Choctaw" C 220.
34 Dean to Manypenny, September 4, 1856, OIA, "Choctaw" C 229.
35 June 22, 1855 ratified by the tribes in council, and finally approved by the President March 4, 1856 (Kappler, *op. cit.*, II, 531).
36 Cooper to Manypenny, May 3, and May 30, 1856, OIA, "Choctaw," C 229.
37 Drew to Manypenny, October 23, 1855, OIA, *ibid.*, D 994.

sentatives, Kennedy McCurtain, speaker of the house, George W. Harkins, N. Cochnaner, and Peter Folsom, chiefs respectively of Apuckshunnubbee, Pushmataha, and Mushulatubbe districts. At the regular session in the following October the Choctaw council adopted a resolution authorizing Peter P. Pitchlynn to enter into arrangements for establishing at Fort Towson an academy of a high order and in connection therewith an orphan school. The removal here of Spencer Academy and the establishment of an insane asylum at the old post were planned.[38]

Still at Fort Towson, Agent Cooper in November 1856 made a payment to the Choctaw orphans. But the next month he temporarily located at the old Chickasaw agency near Fort Washita, "bringing with me the archives of the Choctaw agency, those of the Chickasaw agency having never been removed from this place." However the chiefs of both tribes agreed that in the future the agency should be located at Boggy Depot. In 1857 the commissioner of Indian affairs directed that in view of the difficulties between these two immigrant tribes and the wild Indians of the prairies, the Chickasaw agency should be removed to Fort Arbuckle and a separate reserve was laid out for the agency south of the fort.[39]

After the separation of the two tribes it became necessary for the Choctaw people to adopt a new constitution appropriate to their new situation. A convention of delegates representing a faction of the tribe met at Skullyville[40] on January 5, 1857, and adopted a constitution for the Choctaw Nation vesting the supreme executive power in a governor. The terms of the constitution were devised with a view to its further

38 Cooper to Manypenny, March 6, 1857, *ibid.*, C 779.
39 Cooper to Mix, June 2, 1857, *ibid.*, C 923; Cooper to Denver November 1, 1857, *ibid.*, C 1222; *Advancing the Frontier, op. cit.*; until the Civil War Cooper transacted his business as agent at Fort Arbuckle, Fort Washita and Scullyville. In September 1859 he obtained lumber to repair the old agency buildings at Fort Washita (Cooper to Rector September 3, 1859, OIA, "I. T. Misc. Agent Cooper"). The agency buildings at Boggy Depot were destroyed in 1875.
40 The payments were made at the agency to the Choctaw Indians whose name for money is "iskuli-fehna," whence the place became known as Scullyville. In the report of the Choctaw agent for 1857 the name made its first appearance in these reports. The place now consisted of "about thirty houses, the greatest part of which are stores or entrepots of merchandise for the use of the Indians" (Abbe Em. Domenech, *Seven Years Residence in the Great Deserts of North America*, vol. I, 154).

adaptation to the forms of a territorial government[41] and it therefore met with the bitter hostility of the majority of the tribe. Soon after its adoption, persons opposed living on Red River assembled in Blue County and recorded their objections to it. The authorities holding under the new constitution called an extra session of the legislature, adopted amendments to meet these objections and provided for their submission to a popular vote in accordance with its provisions. The opponents then held a convention at Doaksville, framed a constitution, and elected a rival legislature and chiefs under it. The first legislature again offered to submit to the people any amendments to the constitution they desired, but their opponents insisted upon holding to their new constitution.

At an election held in August, 1857, called by the Skullyville government to fill the offices, some of the counties on Red River failed to vote, and in October the council provided for another election to be held the first Wednesday in December; again these counties refused to vote at the call of the opposition. Operation of law throughout the Choctaw Nation was about to be suspended, peace of the country was seriously threatened; and the efforts of the United States Government were engaged to restore peace destroyed by its schemes for forcing a territorial government on the Indians in violation of their treaty stipulations. As in the case of the Cherokee nearly twenty years before, the department of the interior espoused the cause of the minority; the majority were characterized as rebels and warned by the secretary of the interior that if they did not cease their opposition to the constitution of Skullyville, a military force would be sent into their country to compel obedience.[42] Great excitement and disorder prevented the peace and quiet that should have prevailed in the presence of bountiful crops.[43]

The opposition wanted to return to their old system of having a chief for each district, and charged that the more modern system of government adopted at Scullyville was but a subterfuge to promote

41 *Report* of commissioner of Indian affairs for 1857.
42 *Ibid.*, for 1858.
43 Forts Smith, Washita, and Arbuckle had been abandoned and in view of threatened disorder in the Choctaw Nation and other conditions on the frontier, it was urged that these posts be reoccupied (Pulliam to Mix, January 27, 1858, OIA, Southern Superintendency R 643).

territorial government. Gov. Alfred Wade, who had been elected governor of the nation under the Scullyville constitution, resigned on January 12, 1858, and the duties of his office were assumed by Tandy Walker, president of the senate of the general council, who, within a few days, called a special election of the legislature to meet on April fifth next, at Boggy Depot, the seat of government.[44]

In October, 1858, the Skullyville council adopted conciliatory measures which averted further disorder in the Choctaw country then at the brink of anarchy. A compromise was reached whereby it was provided that the Skullyville government should be regarded as controlling until another constitutional convention could be held.[45] The office of chief in each of the two districts, Apuckshunnubbee and Pushmataha, was recognized, to be filled by the two leaders of the opposition. This, of course, was but a makeshift, but it restored order; and October 24, 1859, at the general council, a new constitution was adopted, providing for a principal chief, and three subordinate chiefs representing the three districts, all to be selected at the general elections. The legislative functions were vested in a body composed of a senate and a house, and a judicial department was provided. Their new government, modeled on the laws of Mississippi, was installed in October, 1860, and with the return to the old system in accordance with the views of the majority, peace again rested on the country. The opponents to the Skullyville constitution prevailed, vindicated their opposition and forced the removal of the seat of government from Boggy Depot to Doaksville.[46]

An extensive commerce had "sprung up between the Choctaw and Chickasaw Indians and the adjoining, and even some of the remote states of the Union, in cattle, horses, and hogs, of which both the Choctaws and Chickasaws rear a large surplus over their home consumption and wants." But they were handicapped in this commerce by archaic intercourse laws which the Government, though often solicited, had not taken steps to liberalize.

"Their legislature and general councils consist of a senate and house of representatives, with the usual presiding officers; and their deliberations are characterized by a degree of order and decorum worthy of

44   Ibid.
45   Report of commissioner of Indian affairs for 1859.
46   Ibid., for 1860.

imitation by their white brethren of the United States. These tribes have each a governor, national secretary, auditor of public accounts, treasurer and attorney general. . . . . As yet they do not quite understand the working of the new system; their laws are defective, the machinery of their government and the practice in their courts do not work smoothly. But it is not to be expected that any people can suddenly throw off their dependence on chiefs, captains, and head-men, and become at once fitted to take part in the administration of a new, and to them, complex form of government."[47]

"The Chickasaws in proportion to numbers, appropriate a much larger sum to educational purposes than the Choctaws; while their school system lacks an important feature, which is obtaining prominence in that of the Choctaws; I mean the system of common or neighborhood schools. These among the Choctaws are mainly taught by natives and form an interesting and important adjunct to the academies."[48]

A route for a wagon road from Fort Smith to Texas was now being surveyed by Lieut. E. F. Beale along the Canadian River and the Indians were greatly concerned about it, as it involved the project also of constructing the railroad contemplated by Lieut. A. W. Whipple's survey six years before. Choctaw Agent Cooper reported that an abundance of cedar along the Canadian would furnish the necessary cross-ties.[49]

Upon the completion of the survey Beale in 1859 directed H. B. Edwards to contract for the erection of bridges where the road crossed the Poteau River, Sans Bois and Little Sans Bois, Longtown and Little rivers, according to plans made by "Mr. Crump the civil engineer ordered by the War Department to accompany me as my asistant." The Poteau bridge was to be at McLean's ferry about ten miles above the mouth of the stream; but the people of Fort Smith and officers of the Overland Mail Company protested the location vigorously as they desired the river crossed at the edge of the village and near the fort. The result was that work on the bridge was suspended and available information does not disclose whether it was renewed before the

47 *Ibid.*, for 1859.
48 *Ibid.*
49 *Ibid.*

breaking out of the Civil War.[50] Remains of three of the other iron bridges destroyed during that war are yet to be seen; in Little River at Edwards' Trading Settlement two or three miles above the mouth when the water is low one may see the bases of two of the piers. In Sans Bois Creek near a locality known as "Iron Bridge" fragments of the metal of the old bridge project above the water. On Red Bank Creek about seven miles northwest of Spiro are to be seen abutments of the bridge over that stream.

They were "at liberty to move from place to place as inclination or their interests lead them," said the missionary O. P. Stark of the Indians near Goodland. "I have known families to move four and five times in the course of a year. This state of things has the effect to perpetuate habits of vagrancy and idleness, and to counteract the benefits which, in other circumstances, they might derive from the establishment of churches and schools among them. Another serious difficulty arises from the low estimate in which the marriage relation is held. Separations of husband and wife are common occurrences, and the effect upon children is disastrous. They are left uncared for, with no homes, to wander about and grow up addicted to the worst of vices. We have been accused too of being abolitionists, and the emissaries of abolition societies," Mr. Stark added with great indignation.[51]

Elias Rector of Arkansas, recently appointed superintendent for the Southern Superintendency, could not see the Indians in the favorable light with which others viewed them. He reported that most of the five tribes cultivated the ". . . . soil to a small extent; but having no individual proprietorship therein, they are continually on the wing, moving from place to place; and one sees, in travelling through their country, more deserted than inhabited houses.[52] They are generally poor farmers and poorer livers, without gardens or orchards, with plenty of cattle, but no milk or butter, caring to surround themselves with few of the luxuries or even comforts of life." And with this back- ground for justification he urged his views in favor of authorizing the

50 Beale, Edwards, Montgomery, and Crocker to secretary of war, May 6 and June 30, 1859, AGO, ORD, WDF, M 162, C 124, and E 111; U. S. House *executive document* No. 42, thirty-sixth Congress, first session: "Letter from the Secretary of War transmitting the report of Mr. Beale relating to the construction of a wagon road from Fort Smith to the Colorado river."
51 *Report* of commissioner of Indian affairs for 1858.
52 *Ibid.*

sale by the Indians of their lands, to facilitate the population of the country by white people; for, he said ". . . .The country possessed by them, picturesque and fertile, must at some day become a State of the American Union. . . . ." The good faith of the United States toward the Indians must be maintained, ". . . .But necessity is the supreme law of nations. All along the Indian border the country is now populous, and the railroad will soon reach the frontier. Necessity will soon *compel* the incorporation of their country into the Union, and before its stern requisitions every other consideration will give way, and even wrong find, as it ever does, in necessity its apology." This highly immoral view candidly expressed those held by most of the white neighbors of the Indians and shows how, in spite of the treaties made with the Indians, in their execution the promises to keep whites out of their country were flouted and entrance made easier rather than harder; it shows what tremendous difficulties opposed the Indians, presaging the final surrender by the Government to the whites. Rector was very impatient with and intolerant of the Indians because ". . . .they will not now hear to any proposition for parting with any portion of their land, and cannot be made to see the advantages of retaining part and selling the residue to individuals. And their aversion to parting with their land, of which they do not need one acre in a hundred and their strong feeling of nationality, are played upon by the more intelligent, who find it well enough for them to use without price as much land as they want and pay no taxes. . . . ." Ever since these Indians had known the white man they had been wheedled and ravished of their lands on one specious pretext and another; and now that they were located on what was promised them to be their last home, within which white people were not to be allowed to intrude, and which would "never be made part of a state of the Union," where they could maintain their own government, an Indian official joins the white people in trying to justify and facilitate the breaking down of those promises.

A devastating drought brought destitution and suffering to all the Indians in the Southwest in 1860 and Rector warned that many of the Choctaw and Chickasaw would perish from want of food if the Government did not go to their relief. New Hope School was closed by whooping cough and measles from March 1 to May 1, and Fort Coffee Academy was closed by measles.

BOOK TWO / *Chickasaw*

CHAPTER SIX / *Chickasaw Description*

THE habitat of the Chickasaw Indians was the northern part of Mississippi adjoining the Choctaw, to whom they were related. The latter had become notable for their devotion to agricultural pursuits while the former were still a turbulent warlike people. The Chickasaw were noted from remote times for their bravery, independence and warlike disposition. But due to the influence of the missionaries and other associations with the whites, early in the nineteenth century they began to make rapid strides in civilization. An illuminating picture of their progress and condition at the time of the enactment of the famous Indian Removal Bill is furnished by their agent John L. Allen: "The buffalow and Bare are gone, and there are but few Deer, not sufficient to justify an Indian to depend upon for support, more particularly those that have familys. Consequently the Chickasaws are compelled to Subsist by different means than those of the chase. They have plenty of Horses of a superior quality. . . . large herds of Cattle, Swine, Sheep, and Goats, and poultry of every description." They raised cotton, corn, wheat, oats, peas, potatoes, and beans. In 1830 they exported 1,000 bales of cotton and a considerable amount of beef and pork.

"The proceeds from the sales of Cotton, Horses, Beef, Cattle, Hogs &c after retaining a sufficiency for their home consumption is Generally applied to the purchase of necessaries and Luxuries of life; to-wit, Slaves, Shugar, and Coffee, as well as dry goods of various descriptions, which are calculated to render them comfortable and ornament their persons. Every family cultivates the earth more or less, as his thirst for gain, or his imaginary or real wants increases. Much to the honor of the Chickasaws, for the past eight years the practice of the men of requiring the woman to perform all the labours of the field is much changed—the men now, with a few exceptions, cultivate the earth themselves, while the female part of the family is engaged in their household affairs. They spin, weave, make their own cloathing, milch Cows, make butter, Cheese &c. They keep themselves decent and clean and in many instances particular attention is paid to fashions that are in use by the whites. It is their constant practice to appear in their best apparel at their public meetings, also when they visit the Country Villages in the white settlements.

"Many of the Chickasaws profess Chrisitanity; I attended a camp meeting in Novr. last at the Missionarys. Devine worship was performed alternately by white, and red men, in the English and Indian Languages; and for the first time I saw the Sacrament taken by the Indians. Every thing was Conducted with the utmost good order, and decorum. As a Nation the men are brave and honest; the women (the half breeds in particular) are beautiful and virtuous; and I am of the opinion that there has been greater advancement in Civilization in the last eight years than there was in twenty previous."

The chiefs of the tribe desired to improve the facilities for education of their youth which then were enjoyed only by those Indians of part Indian blood. "There are at this time several white men that have identified themselves with the Indians by Marriage, and Several half breeds that have sufficient education to enable them to transact a considerable portion of the business for the Nation.

"The Municipal laws of the Chickasaws consist in written Laws or resolutions commanding that which is right and prohibiting that which they conceive to be wrong. Their laws are few, easily understood and rigidly enforced and are highly calculated to promote peace and good order among themselves.

"As I have already mentioned the state of agriculture, I have only now to say something on the Subject of the Mechanic arts, the knowledge of which is Generally confined to the white men that have identified themselves with the Indians. . . . towit—House Carpenter, wheelright, Mill rights, Blacksmiths &c. All the arts necessary for farming use, Stocking plows, helving axes, does making slides, Truck wheels, draw bars, &c, is Generally confined to the Common Indians and Slaves."[1]

1   John L. Allen to Indian Commissioner, February 7, 1830, OIA, "Chickasaw sub-agency;" Report of secretary of war for 1830; The Arkansas Advocate, June 23, 1830, p. 3, col. 3.

The Chickasaw people were sending some of their boys away to school. One named James Perry, after spending two years at Elliot Mission, at the age of nineteen was sent to Jefferson College; here he delivered a commencement address September 30, 1824, that was widely copied in the press of the North and East.[2] For a number of years they appropriated annually $3,000 for the education of their youth in schools in the North. A school was established at Monroe in the Chickasaw Nation in 1821 by the Missionary Society of the Synod of South Carolina and Georgia, which conducted it until 1829, when it was transferred to the American Board of Commissioners for Foreign Missions of Boston. Another school named Charity Hall was established in 1820 three miles from Cotton Gin Port by the Cumberland Missionary Board. Another school was begun January 15, 1827, on Caney Creek, nine miles west of Tuscumbia. Many Chickasaw who later became prominent and useful in the affairs of their tribe were educated at these schools. They were maintained in part by the funds of the tribe and by appropriations made by the Government. However, the Government assistance was withdrawn about 1830 as part of the program of aiding the southern states in driving the Indians from within their borders.

Just as this advanced state of civilization of the tribe had been achieved and with still greater progress within sight, Congress enacted Jackson's Indian Removal Bill and the State of Mississippi extended her laws over the Chickasaw Nation. This hastened and facilitated the oppression of the Indians as it was intended it should, and their country was overrun by the whites. The lives of the Indians were made intolerable and they at last were induced to sign a treaty in 1832 yielding up their lands in Mississippi in return for a promise by the Government to find them a home west of the Mississippi River where they hoped to live in peace.[3]

The major part of the Choctaw tribe had emigrated west by the end of 1833 and it was then planned to remove the Chickasaw Indians and cause them to be united on the same domain and under one tribal government. The efforts to effect a union of these tribes were responsible for much dissatisfaction on the part of the Chickasaw people and

2   *Pittsburg Recorder*, copied in *Western Citizen* (Paris, Kentucky), November 13, 1824, cols. 4 and 5; *Jackson (Tenn.) Gazette*, January 8, 1825, p. 3, col. 3.
3   Grant Foreman, *Indian Removal*, 193.

delay in their removal. Thus it was not until 1837 that their emigration began, but it was practically completed within a year.[4]

Most of the emigrants at first encamped in the vicinity of Fort Coffee
where they awaited the construction of a road to their future home.[5]
A depot for the issuance of their supplies was located in the western
part of the Choctaw Nation on Boggy River near a place that became
known as Boggy Depot, and a large part of the emigrants settled on
Boggy and Blue rivers convenient to this place of issue. Others settled
in other parts of the Choctaw country, in many cases purchasing the
homes and improvements of the earlier arrivals. Some of the Chickasaw
were prosperous and brought with them large numbers of slaves.

The Chickasaw Nation had purchased for a new home the western
part of the Choctaw domain, but as it was overrun by wild Indians
of the prairies and predatory Indians of other tribes, the newcomers
could not occupy it until the Government complied with its promise
to establish a military post in the country for their protection. Before
the completion of their emigration, in the winter of 1837-38 the chiefs
of this tribe addressed a communication to the officers of the Government asking that a fort be located near the mouth of the Washita
River. A large body of wild Indians, who assembled on the south side
of the Red River opposite the mouth of the Washita, planned an
attack on the white settlers of Texas. Volunteers were organizing
to proceed against them and Indian Superintendent Armstrong feared
these Indians would take refuge in the Chickasaw country to the
great annoyance and injury of the immigrants. And he added his
appeal to that of the Chickasaw for military protection. However the
Government did nothing about the matter for nearly four years, thereby
entailing costly delay to the immigrants in getting settled in their new
home.[6]

Emigration of the tribe had arrested all progress they were making
in the East and introduced in its place almost a state of demoralization.
After removal this condition was continued and little was done to
correct it. For want of adequate protection in their own country the

4 Ibid.
5 George Colbert and others to William Armstrong, December 13, 1837, OIA.
6 Armstrong to Harris September 4, 1838, OIA, Western Superintendency File
A 456; Report of commissioner of Indian affairs for 1838; Armstrong to Harris, December 26, 1837, OIA.

Chickasaw led a restless, unsettled life on the lands of the Choctaw Indians with no incentive nor opportunity to establish their government, schools, and other institutions, nor land upon which they could build their homes. To aggravate the demoralization resulting from their forced migration, the emigrants on the way through Arkansas, contracted smallpox from which between 500 and 600 of their tribe died before the disease was checked by vaccination. Because of the destitution following this epidemic and consequent inability to raise crops that year, Congress authorized an additional issue of rations to them for seven months.[7]

The largest Chickasaw settlement in the Choctaw country was on Boggy and Blue rivers, reached by them over a road they opened from Fort Coffee on the Arkansas River, from where a large part of their supplies were forwarded.[8] Steps were taken at once to ameliorate the condition of the new arrivals by the erection of a gristmill and a sawmill on the Boggy, where but a year or two before the wild Indians roamed. A number of wealthier half-breeds settled on the rich bottom lands near Fort Towson where they engaged on a large scale in raising cotton and other farm products. One of them, Col. George Colbert, the first year after his arrival prepared to plant from three to five hundred acres of cotton with the labor of his 150 slaves.

For many years George Colbert had been a conspicuous and valuable member of the Chickasaw tribe. He lived to see his people through their great crisis, and then died in their new home, honored by all who knew him. The following account is from an army officer:[9] "Fort Towson, November 7th, 1839. We this day buried with the honors of war, General George Colbert, the head chief of the Chickasaw Nation, a man of superior intelligence, the greatest of warriors, and the white

7 Ibid., for 1839, p. 14; Indian Removal, op. cit.
8 Corn for the immigrants was shipped by the contractors up Red River to Boggy and boated up that stream to where a depot was established, and then hauled thirty miles to the place of issue. The beef part of the ration was driven from Arkansas and delivered on the hoof (Report of commissioner of Indian affairs, 1838). Here at Boggy Depot were Saffarans & Lewis and Berthelet Heald & Co., merchants who kept large stocks of goods for sale to the Chickasaw, including "blankets, domestics, calicoes, with various other dry goods, sugar, coffee, axes, hoes, chains, augurs," and other commodities (William Armstrong to commissioner of Indian affairs, January 9, 1841, OIA).
9 The Army and Navy Chronicle, January 9, 1840, p. 26.

man's friend. He was a revolutionary veteran; he served under General Washington in our struggle for independence, from whom he received a commission of Major of Militia in the U. S. Service, and a sword.

"He served under General Wayne, and also under General Jackson in the Florida War against the Seminoles; for his bravery General Jackson presented him with a colonel's commission, and afterwards a sword, when President of the United States. He gained the entire confidence of the officers he served under for his integrity and valor; he was physically and mentally a great man; although 95 years if age, he walked as upright as a man of 25.

"The commanding officer, on having received and read the commissions, ordered an escort from the fort, of three officers, a captain and two subalternes; also all the men doing military duty, to escort his corpse to its last resting place with reversed arms and buried with the customary salute due his rank; he was interred with his saddle and bridle, the swords presented to him by Generals Washington and Jackson, and a United States flag. He was of great importance to the cause of civilization among his people by his examples of industry; he was a planter, his fields of cotton whitened the hills and dales near the fort. He educated his sons[10] and located them on plantations among his people, and worked moral influence among them; he was looked up to as a father, and exercised a father's influence over his people."

Further information is given by the press of Tennessee: [11] "He was born in the Chickasaw country, now north Mississippi, near Tennessee river, and was a half-breed. Early becoming attached to the whites, he united himself and nation to their interests and was regularly commissioned a Colonel by President Washington. At St. Clair's defeat he was taken prisoner and after his release, accompanied Gen. Wayne to the western frontier. He was with Jackson in all his campaigns; and in all situations on all occasions, proved himself the devoted friend, the sagacious counsellor, the gallant soldier, uniting in a happy combination, the ennobling qualities of the Indian and the white man. His unwavering firmness, unbending integrity, immaculate truth, noble generosity, and amiable frankness, were proverbial with all who knew him." He was survived by three daughters and an adopted son.

10 He sent his son Pitman to school in Washington in 1803.
11 *Memphis World*, January 1, 1840.

Soon after Colbert passed away another conspicuous member of this tribe, old Chief Tish-o-mingo, died in his western home. The high sense of appreciation of his tribesmen is indicated by the twelfth section of the treaty of Pontotoc:[12] "The Chickasaws feel grateful to their old chiefs, for their long and faithful services, in attending to the business of the nation. They believe it a duty, to keep them from want in their old and declining age—with these feelings, they have looked upon their old and beloved chief Tish-o-mingo, who is now grown old, and is poor and not able to live in that comfort which his valuable life and great merit deserve. It is therefore determined to give him out of the national funds, one hundred dollars a year during the balance of his life, and the nation request him to receive it, as a token of their feelings for him, on account of his long and valuable services."

Old Chief Tish-o-mingo lived for several years after the removal of the tribe and died May 5, 1841.[13] The following touching account of the beloved chief was contributed to the press[14] by a Choctaw: "Choctaw Nation May 6, 1841; Captain Tish-o-mingo, a veteran warrior of the Chickasaws departed this life on the 5th inst. Although but little known beyond the limits of his nation, yet he was a man that had seen wars and fought battles—stood high among his own people as a brave and good man. He served under General Wayne in the Revolutionary War, for which he received a pension from the Government of the United States; and in the late war with England, he served under General Jackson and did many deeds of valor. He had fought in 9 battles for the United States. As a friend, he has served the white man faithfully. His last words were: 'When I am gone, beat the drum and fire the guns.'

"I hear the sound of the drum—the report of 'Death guns'[15] is roaring in our valley—a warrior spirit is passing away. The brave Tish-o-mingo, the veteran warrior of our tribe, is gone. His clansmen

12 Kappler, op. cit., II, 263.
13 Draper Manuscript Collection, Shane Scrapbook, Vol. 1, 26 CC.
14 Arkansas Gazette, May 26, 1841.
15 There was a custom among the Choctaw and Chickasaw people to fire a gun to announce the death of a member of the tribe. Cyrus Byington's son the next day wrote from Eagletown of Tishomingo's death in that neighborhood. He said they painted the dead chief's face black and red. Referring to another death in the vicinity he says they "shot the gun, blew the horn" (Byington letters, Oklahoma Historical Society).

are gathering around his corpse. Long years have passed away since first his native hills re-echoed his war whoop—when gray headed warriors gathered around his war dance, and said, 'Go, young warrior, go. It is the beloved Washington who calls for help.' Our aged warriors and chieftains are all gone. Tish-o-mingo, the last of the braves is gone. They are all gone. (Signed) Pitchlynn."

The disposition of the Chickasaw to industry and progress was very similar to that of the Choctaw, but the former suffered from a demoralizing influence for some time after their arrival; many of the members of the tribe had large sums of money received from the sale of their land in the East and were but little disposed to work while the money lasted. However, many others used these funds for purchasing horses, cattle and hogs from the Choctaw and starting herds of live stock, which brought prosperity to individuals of both tribes. For years few of the Chickasaw dared locate on the land ceded them by the Choctaw. There they would have been much exposed by their frontier location, with Texas immediately opposite them. That state was engaged in constant warfare with the western prairie Indians who frequently took refuge in the Chickasaw country whence they were hunted out by Texan troops and between the two opposing forces the Chickasaw were the sufferers, losing lives of their citizens and much livestock.

The Chickasaw had been annoyed by roving bands of Delaware, Shawnee, Kickapoo, Cherokee, Caddo, Yuchi and Koasati, who claimed to be hunting but were also engaged in stealing the livestock of the Chickasaw and trafficking with the Comanche for the horses the latter had stolen from white people in Texas. They became so threatening and hostile towards the Chickasaw that the agent called on the commanding officer at Fort Gibson for assistance; three companies from that post were sent into the Chickasaw country during April and May, 1841,[16] and they drove the troublesome Indians out; after the troops departed, however, some of the Indians returned, and continued to steal horses and Negroes. In August an armed band of whites from Texas crossed to the north side of Red River and killed two Indians, a man and a woman; the other Indians made their escape, but their property was destoyed. Two or three weeks later a company of sixty

16 *Advancing the Frontier.*

or eighty armed Texans crossed Red River above the mouth of the Washita and scoured the country between the Washita and Red rivers, committing depredations on the property of the Chickasaw.[17] This situation hastened the establishment in 1842 by General Taylor of Fort Washita;[18] a portion of the Chickasaw tribe were then encouraged to settle in the limited extent of country under the protection of this post.

On these fertile lands the Chickasaw raised considerable corn and other produce, part of which they were able to dispose of to the garrison; they still had a surplus of corn, however, which was of little value to them, as Red River did not provide navigation and they had no other facilities for shipping it. They had need for this market for their produce, as the remote white settlements offered little; the merchants at Fort Smith and Van Buren advertised Choctaw stripes, red and blue stroudings, flour, coffee, sugar, and other supplies in exchange for hides, peltries, coon skins, beeswax, tallow, chickens, eggs, and such produce.[19] And while flour, sugar, and coffee sold for prices not much different from those obtaining in modern times, the merchant retailed the farmer's produce very cheaply indeed; beef, one and one-half to two cents a pound; tallow, four to six cents; beeswax, twenty-two to twenty-five cents; mutton and veal, four to five cents; butter, six to eight cents a pound; eggs, six to eight cents per dozen; chickens, seventy-five cents to a dollar a dozen;[20] and whisky of a kind, at thirty cents a gallon lured the Indians to market many miles from home and accounted for much unhappiness and disorder among them.

Berthelet, Heald & Co. were advertising that they had coming up the Arkansas 500 packages, casks, and bales of merchandise, which ". . . will be swapped on very accommodating terms for peltries, furs, skins, cotton or cash."[21] A lot of buffalo tongues was just received and offered for sale by Austin Clegg.[22] Another advertised "Buffalo and

17 *Report* of commissioner of Indian affairs, 1841, p. 340.

18 Fort Washita was located about twelve miles east of what was called the small Cross Timbers on the route followed by wild western tribes crossing the Chickasaw country on their way between Texas and the country to the north.

19 *Arkansas Intelligencer*, (Van Buren) May 10, 1845, p. 3, col. 5.

20 Ibid., July 19, 1845, p. 1, cols 3 and 4; *ibid.*, July 12, 1845, p. 2, col. 1.

21 Ibid., March 29, 1845, p. 3, col. 5.

22 Ibid., July 26, 1845, p. 4, col. 1.

horse dressing combs and horse tuck combs," and announced the highest market price for ginseng and snake root.[23]

In 1843 individual Chickasaw Indians had as much as 500 acres in corn, besides cotton, wheat, oats, and rye which they were able to cultivate with the labor of a large number of slaves. There were three fine cotton gins owned by Chickasaw, and a horse-mill for grinding corn owned and operated by a Chickasaw woman. Early in 1845 William R. Guy, a white man married to a Chickasaw, started a saw- and gristmill on Boggy Creek operated by water power.[24] "Several of the Chickasaws have spinning-machines, and are making cloth to clothe their negroes." The Chickasaw still clung to their old custom of permitting an old chief to select his successor.[25] They were annoyed by Indians between Washita and Red Rivers who harbored their runaway Negroes and sold them to the Comanche; Shawnee and Delaware Indians would then bring the Negroes into the Chickasaw country and compel the owners to pay large sums for their return. In the summer of 1843, a Negro belonging to Sloan Love, a Chickasaw commissioner living near the mouth of the Washita, was attacked and wounded with arrows by Kichai Indians, who carried off a number of Love's horses; the latter pursued them across Red River in vain. Maj. Benjamin L. Beall, with forty-one troops from Fort Washita, then took up the chase, but as the Indians were well mounted and the troops on foot, naturally the former escaped.[26] These Indians were included among remnants of several tribes that menaced the peace of the immigrant Indians and prevented their settlement farther west. There were 900 Wichita and 300 Kichai who were intermarried and living together in a village on Rush Creek, sixty miles west of Fort Arbuckle, near the site of the present town of Rush Springs, Oklahoma.

23   Ibid., January 31, 1846, p. 4, col. 5.

24   William R. Guy came west with the Chickasaw in 1837 as commissary and assistant conductor.

25   Their agent reported difficulty in taking the Chickasaw census: "The rule that the Chickasaw have adopted is to leave out a great number that lived with them in the old nation, and all those who have married amongst them, whose mother is not a Chickasaw. For instance, an Indian may be half Choctaw and half Chickasaw; but if his mother was not a Chickasaw, he is not to be taken in the census, nor is he to draw an annuity" (Report of commissioner of Indian affairs for 1845).

26   Taylor to adjutant general, July 22, 1845, AGO, OFD, 202 T 43.

Col. Joel H. Nail, an intelligent and enterprising Choctaw, was building a fine saw- and gristmill on Blue River and Col. Sloan Love was beginning a horse-mill and cotton gin on his farm.[27] The desire to improve their condition persisted with the leaders of the tribe. They ventured tentatively on the eastern part of their own land under the protection of Fort Washita, and began to build homes as the menace of wild Indians seemed to diminish, and they looked forward to setting up their schools and churches. They had elected a body of commissioners with some powers of government, composed of Isaac Alberson, Benjamin Love, Sloan Love, James Gamble, Joseph Colbert, James Wolf, Winchester Colbert, Capt. Chickasaw Nah nubby, Ish hit tata, E bah ma tubby, New berry, and William Barnett. The commissioners on December 15, 1844, passed an act providing for the establishment of a manual labor school in the Chickasaw district, to be conducted by the missionary society of the Method- ist Episcopal Church. An appropriation of $3,600 annually for the operation of the school was made.

There had been many distractions during the year. The great flood of 1844, the greatest perhaps in the history of the country next to that of 1833, had caused much loss to the Indians living on the streams where most of them had settled. Agent Upshaw accompanied a number of Dragoons from Fort Washita and some Chickasaw Indians to the Wichita town in an effort to recover some boys captured in Texas. The agent was having trouble with white men who were intruding in the Chickasaw country. Greasy Ballard had been killing the hogs of Captain Caudle, the public smith near Doaksville. The Chick- asaw commissioners took a census of their tribe and July 23, 1844 re- ported they had found the number to be 4,111, the most of whom were still living in the Choctaw Nation.[28] Upshaw warned his friend Major Armstrong that Pierce Butler planned to succeed him as Indian super- intendent as soon as Clay was elected president; so sure was Butler of this issue of the impending election that he had offered to wager four mules on the result. And when it was found that Polk was the winner Upshaw proposed to meet Armstrong and his brother Robert

27 *Arkansas Intelligencer*, March 15, 1845, p. 1, col. 1; *Report* of commissioner of Indian affairs for 1844.

28 Isaac Alberson and other commissioners to Upshaw, July 23, 1844, OIA, "I. T. Misc. Upshaw."

in Washington, where they would "eat oysters and drink a glass of wine." In January one of Mrs. McDonnel's Negroes and Pitman Colbert's nephew broke open Mr. Anderson's trunk and extracted $300. Upshaw thought the culprits should be handed over to the United States marshal, as the greatest punishment prescribed by the Choctaw laws for theft was only thirty-nine lashes on the bare back.

CHAPTER SEVEN / *Difficulties With Wild Indians*

A s GREAT a *rascal* and as deceitful a fellow as ever was raped up in so much hide" was Agent Upshaw's description of a white man named L. I. Alsoobroke, who was accused of inciting the Chickasaw people to turn from their progressive leaders and revert to old customs. In particular it was said that they proposed to abandon their modern style of government and restore that by hereditary chiefs and thus throw the whole power of the tribe into the hands of two or three of the most ignorant of its members, dominated by Pitman Colbert. The purpose of this movement, said Upshaw, was to secure to a few designing members through the agency of nominal rulers, the control of the large revenues derived from the Chickasaw annuities.

A great council called by Colbert was held at the Boiling Springs near Fort Washita on Monday, July 14, 1845. "All the officers of the Post were invited by Pitman & accordingly on Tuesday morning all hands went down; from the rumors in circulation 'twas supposed there would be some great works & that P. wished the officers present to see him triumph. . . . . The people were doing nothing but eating beef, a bountiful supply having been furnished by Sampson Folsom to the tune of 32 steers." Mercenary political methods employed there did not differ greatly from those by white people today.

There were bitter differences between Colbert's faction and the commissioners, who were charged with betraying their trust and making improper use of the public funds handled by them. Isaac Alberson and Benjamin Love denied it and much oratory and vituperation were expended in airing the views and relieving the feelings of the members of the council. Love gave Colbèrt "particular thunder & frequently after he had spoken some minutes in Indian, spoke the same in English so that the officers who had been invited by Pitman could understand what was going on."[1] King Ish to ho to pa made a speech in which he said he was their king, that he was born so and would remain king until his death, though he was willing to abdicate if they wished him to. But the Colbert following would not permit him to do so and he was confirmed as king to convene and preside over all councils of the Chickasaw people. Edmund Pickens was appointed "second controlling chief" to act as treasurer and to handle all tribal funds. Sampson Folsom, William P. Stuart, Dougherty Colbert,[2] and James Davis were appointed as assistants to Second Chief Pickens, to hold office during good behavior; in the event of vacancies the king was to make temporary appointments.

The Chickasaw Nation was divided into four companies—Tishomingo's Company, McGilvery's Company, Alberson's Company, and Thomas Seeley's Company; this arrangement was to be continued for the purpose of dividing their annuities. Pitman Colbert wrote Superintendent Armstrong of the proceedings at the council and said: "we have placed our friend Edmund Pickens in the same situation as my old uncle Levi Colbert was in the old Chickasaw Nation." He said that his uncle had been impoverished by the large number of people who came to see him and were fed at his table. And as Pickens would have similar calls upon him it was hoped that a salary would be provided that he might be able to carry this burden. Although Colbert had some education he had at the council asked the editor of a Clarksville, Texas, paper to assist him in drawing up the resolutions and outline of the new government, which are therefore expressed in lucid English.[3]

The success of the Colbert faction, said Upshaw, was due largely to the jealousy of the people, of their district officers and their preju-

1 Johnson to Armstrong, July 22, 1845, OIA "I. T. Misc. Agent."

2 Colbert to Armstrong, August 1, 1845, OIA "I. T. Misc. Agent;" Dougherty Colbert was educated in the East having lived two years in the home of Indian Commissioner Thomas C. McKenney at Washington (OIA, Letter Book IV, P. 3, 1827). William Armstrong, acting superintendent, corroborated the statement of Agent Upshaw regarding the determination by a majority of the tribe to "restore the old and long since abandoned system of governing by hereditary chiefs. . . . . to benefit a few designing persons" (*Report* of William Armstrong, September 30, 1845, *Arkansas Intelligencer*, February 7, 1846).

3 Colbert to Armstrong, August 1, 1845, OIA, "I. T. Misc. Agent." He had served as a captain of a company of Chickasaw warriors in the war against the Creeks in 1814.

dices in favor of the old Indian customs. The king selected to rule over them, he said, was an uneducated Indian of inferior capacity, and Pickens was no better. However, Armstrong refused to deliver the money to the officers they selected, but instead paid it to the individuals as formerly. This proved satisfactory to most of the tribe, though much ill feeling and excitement resulted and two of the rival leaders attacked each other during the payment. "It was with the utmost difficulty" said Armstrong, "that I succeeded in separating them, and preventing a general row, which, if it had occurred, must have led to fatal results." Pitman Colbert, the leader of the reactionary faction attempted to keep the Chickasaw Indians in the Choctaw Nation under his control, while Alberson pursued the more enlightened course of endeavoring to have them go to their own domain, establish themselves under their new system of laws and begin their schools.

But conditions were slowly improving. The Chickasaw were industrious and in favorable seasons they raised good crops of cotton, wheat, oats, rye, and corn. In 1843 they had a surplus of 40,000 bushels of corn. But they were handicapped by want of a market denied them by lack of transportation. Red River which sometimes served was wholly inadequate at the season it was most needed. However, they, as well as the Choctaw, found relief in the great movement of white emigrants to Texas in 1846 and subsequent years. Said Armstrong: "For nearly 200 miles on the main traveled road from Missouri and Northwestern Arkansas to the Northern and Northwestern sections of Texas, emigrants and travellers depend entirely for subsistance and forage upon Indians of this tribe, generally of the full blood. Their cabins, usually constructed by themselves, are generally sheltered by Shade trees, and in Situations chosen with a degree of taste, and a regard for comfort not always found among frontier settlers. At several of their homes I Saw looms and Spinning wheels of their own manufacture, some of them made by self taught mechanics. . . . . It has been remarked of them that they spend less of their money at the pay ground than is usual among Indians, reserving it for their future wants and requirements."[4]

The Texas emigrants established a well-marked trail from the north, called the Texas Road, which traversed both the Choctaw and Chick-

4 Armstrong to Crawford, September 30, 1845, OIA, "Western Supt'y," file A 1911.

asaw countries.[5] Travel on this road during the Texas migration was attended by perils that the Chickasaw Indians were unable to prevent. Said their agent, Upshaw: "Maj. George W. Anderson is now command-ing at Ft. Washita with two companies of Infantry, in all 47 men; if we had one or two companies of Dragoons here I think I would apply for them to go on Boggy and Washita and burn up the Cherokee settle-ments on those Rivers; they are in the habit of lurking along the road from Ft. Smith to Coffees on Red River, and stealing horses from emigrants on their way to Texas. About 8 days since they stole from some emigrants 3 fine horses. I got two of them yesterday morning; the other had been taken to the Canadian.[6] I gave two or three Chickasaws the description of the horses and sent them to the Cherokee settle-ment. . . . . They found them with the Cherokees and that night they got the horses and brought them to the depot on Boggy by day light the next morning. They are a pair of splendid match horses worth at least $300. Should you see Genl. Arbuckle I think you had better advise him to send one or two companies of Dragoons here as soon as con-venient."[7]

With the Gold Rush in 1849 another great thoroughfare was added, which crossed the Choctaw and Chickasaw country from east to west along the south side of Canadian River.[8] Some of the more enterprising

5   This road proceeded southwest past Fort Gibson and Honey Springs, crossing the Canadian River at North Fork Town, near where is now Eufaula, Oklahoma. Other stations built on the Texas Road were Perryville and Boggy Depot. At the lat-ter place after the road was joined by the one from Fort Smith, it divided and one branch went directly south to Warren's on Red River, and the other reached the river at Preston by way of Fort Washita. Lieut. J. W. Abert an army officer, traveled the Texas Road from Fort Gibson in October, 1846, by way of Maysville, Bentonville, Springfield, and Waynesville. He said in an official report: "The way from Fort Gibson was literally lined with wagons of emigrants to Texas, and from this time until we arrived at Saint Louis we continued daily to see hundreds of them" (U. S. Senate *Document*, Twenty-ninth Congress, first session, No. 438, p. 74).

6   The Starr gang of horse thieves whose rendezvous was at Younger's Bend on the Canadian River in the lower part of the Cherokee Nation, ran stolen horses to Texas and there stole horses they ran to the Cherokee country. One of the Starrs was killed near Fort Washita.

7   Upshaw to Armstrong, January 20, 1846, OIA, "I. T. Misc. Upshaw."

8   This route for a number of years had been employed by traders going to Santa Fé and Mexico; May 1, 1839, a caravan under Pickett and Gregg left Van Buren with an assortment of merchandise, principally dry goods; they traveled on the north

citizens of both tribes established themselves on these public roads where for the next ten years they catered to the needs of the emigrants on their way to new homes; these provided a market for some of the surplus crops and live stock of the Indians and thus contributed measurably to their prosperity.

Mr. Upshaw, the agent, reported in 1847, that the Chickasaw were "improving every year in their habits of industry. I know of but few in the nation who do not make more corn than will subsist them; they raise a good many fowls, and those that are situated within from 10 to 20 miles of Fort Washita furnish it with butter, potatoes, chickens, eggs etc. The merchants generally get contracts to furnish the fort with corn, but they are furnished by the Chickasaws. This year the contract is for only seven thousand bushels; the Indians could furnish forty thousand at the contract price, which is 43 cents, but their corn will be of little use to them, as they have no way of shipping to any foreign country. Had they navigation, their country would be much more valuable, but they can in this country live very independently."[9]

However, they were still without schools. A young man named Akin, of the Methodist Episcopal Church, had taught a school for a few months, but he gave it up for some reason. For nearly three years, said Mr. Upshaw, the Chickasaw had been trying to make arrangements to establish a manual labor school. "The Chickasaws have great anxiety to have their children educated, and what is most astonishing, the full-bloods show as great a desire as the half-breeds; but they are all very anxious on this all-important subject, and I am in hopes, in a few years, to see at least three large institutions of learning in the Chickasaw district." No preachers either had located in the Chickasaw country.[10]

Many Chickasaw were deterred by fear of the hostile Indians from moving to their own district where those who did go were still harrassed by Cherokee, Shawnee, and Kickapoo Indians living on Canadian River, who stole their horses and killed their cattle and hogs. Rev.

---

side of Canadian River and reached Santa Fé on June 25, and the twenty-second departed for Chihuahua (*Little Rock Gazette*, May 15, in *Army and Navy Chronicle*, June 13, 1839, p. 383; Josiah Gregg, *Commerce of the Prairies*, Thwaites, *Early Western Travels*, Vol XX, 104). Subsequent expeditions traveled sometimes on the north side of the Canadian and sometimes on the south side.

9 *Report* of commissioner of Indian affairs, 1847.

10 *Ibid.*

E. B. Duncan, a Methodist minister, and his wife conducted a small school for about two years. Mr. Duncan also preached to them and Rev. Cyrus Kingsbury came twice a month from Fort Towson to preach. A contract had just been made with the Missionary Board of the Methodist Episcopal Church for the erection of a manual labor school. A few more Chickasaw removed from the Choctaw country in 1847, and a body of forty emigrants came from the old nation east of the Mississippi. This year they raised fine crops of cotton, corn, and pota-toes. Their horses, cattle, and sheep were improving, but they were not so fortunate with their hogs. The unsettled condition of affairs and lack of police force made it possible for desperadoes to take refuge in their country and add to the difficulties of Chickasaw settlers.

The Alberson faction of Chickasaw met at Post Oak Grove in the Chickasaw district January 29, 1848, and addressed a memorial to their chief and captains requesting that two schools be established in their district, one of which should be for girls. And as some of their people were removing from the Choctaw Nation to their own district they requested that the appropriation for smith's shops on the Kiamichi River and Brushy Creek be reduced to provide for only six months shops instead of twelve months; to provide for a shop on Jacks Fork and that the one on Brushy Creek be removed to Perry's Court Ground (near McAlester, Oklahoma) and another be established at Fourche Maline, one at Boggy Depot and one on Red River. This was signed by Isaac Alberson as chairman of the committee, Benjamin Love, Winchester Colbert, Edmund Pickens, Jackson Frazier and eleven other members of the committee, Sampson Folsom secretary, and James McLaughlin chief of the district.[11]

Construction of the first Chickasaw school on their domain, the Chickasaw Academy, by the missionary society of the Methodist Church, was commenced in January, 1848. On the first of the month, Superintendent Wesley Browning says, they had opened a road to the site of the proposed school. "We immediately pitched our tent, which with one wagon afforded us shelter, while two men went to making boards and the balance of our force engaged in cutting logs and putting up a cabin. The weather continued unusually dry and pleasant, and we plied our axes with such success that by the 10th of February we were

11   OIA, School File U-30 Chickasaw Agency, 1848.

enabled to move over the whole of our family from near the council ground. About the middle of Feby. I was offered the hire of 5 or 6 laboring hands—negroes—and finding I could do no better for the present season, I determined to hire them tho' at high rates—ranging from about 13 to 18 dollars per month." By March 31 they had completed "one log cabin 14 by 20 feet with a clapboard shed at each end, which with our tent affords shelter to our whole family of 18 persons in all; a hewed log smokehouse 18 by 20 feet well covered and ready to point; and a corn house, 10 by 20 feet, shedded round for horse and wagon shelters and nearly covered." They had logs cut for a large carpenter shop which they planned to use as a residence while they were building the large boarding house for the mission family. Thirteen thousand rails were being cut for fencing their mission and farm.[12]

Work on the mission was delayed for some time while Mr. Browning went east to secure "some good steady and pious laboring hands, some more materials and supplies, and to consult with the board of the Missionary Society about the expediency of building a saw mill." Between fifty and sixty acres of woodland were cleared, enclosed with a fence eight rails high and eighteen acres planted to corn. A well and poultry house had been constructed, and logs cut and hewed for the construction of the large carpenter shop. Mr. Browning had brought back from the east the necessary irons and in the autumn a wheelwright was engaged to erect a water mill on a creek about three miles from the mission, to saw the lumber for the buildings and grind the wheat it was expected would be grown on the farm.[13]

The Chickasaw people wished the Rev. Thomas C. Stuart to have supervision of their girls' school, and the boys' school to be managed by the Episcopal Church. Rev. Mr. Stuart had recently been engaged in removing a party of Choctaw Indians from Mississippi. There were twelve Chickasaw boys attending school at the Choctaw Academy in Kentucky and in June a delegation of Chickasaw Indians in Washington requested that these boys be sent to other schools. They said they were determined not to send any more boys to Kentucky and they were

12 Browning to commissioner of Indian affairs, March 31, 1848, OIA, School File R. 285, 324-363, Choctaw Agency.

13 Browning to Medill, June 30, 1848, OIA, School File R 285.

hopeful that schools might soon be in operation in their own country where all their youth could be educated.[14]

The factions were now united and Pitman Colbert, Isaac Alberson, Edmund Pickens, James McLaughlin and others formed the delegation to Washington where they were engaged in securing an adjustment of their claims against the Government.[15] They had employed Col. Peter P. Pitchlynn to go to the Choctaw Academy and take the Chickasaw boys from there to other schools to be selected for them, and they asked that funds be given him to defray the necessary expenses. Pitchlynn conducted eleven of these boys to Plainfield Academy, Norwich, Connecticut, where they arrived August 22, 1848; they made good progress in their studies. In March, 1848, seven more Chickasaw boys, conducted by Robert Love, were sent east to school, including A. V. Brown, Holmes Colbert, Frederick McCala and Benjamin McLaughlin. The commissioner of Indian affairs was requested to select the schools for them and he designated Delaware College, at Newark, Delaware, for young Colbert, who proved an apt student. "His appearance," wrote the principal, "is very prepossessing. I find on examination, that he has not studied any Greek, and very little Mathematics, altho he has made more proficiency in Latin."[16]

The spring of 1849 found the Chickasaw Academy still incomplete; the work had been confined to the sawmill and now after a year of difficulties, discouragement and delays, it was hoped to have the mill in operation by May. At a meeting of the chief and captains of the Chickasaw Nation on July 16, 1849, an additional appropriation of $5,000 was made to complete the school, and $300 to send Zach Colbert and Colbert Carter to school for three years; and funds with which the sixteen boys at Norwich could purchase clothing to wear on Sundays and other occasions when they appeared in public.

The people of the Chickasaw Nation were shocked by the assassina-

14 In May, 1832, the Chickasaw complained that of twenty-one boys sent away to school five had died and several were in the last stages of consumption.

15 Pitman Colbert, Isaac Alberson, and others to Medill, June 9, 1848, "National Records, 1848, Chickasaw Nation," Superintendent for the Five Civilized Tribes, Muskogee, Oklahoma.

16 Wilson to Medill, May 8, 1848, OIA, "School File" W 333. At the same time four Choctaw youths, Pitchlynn, Hall, Wright, and Garland were members of the Sophomore class at Delaware College (*Report* of commissioner of Indian affairs, Senate *Executive Document* No. 1175, Thirty-first Congress, first session.)

tion on July 3, 1849 of Benjamin Love, the interpreter, five miles from his residence while returning from a Biloxi village where he had gone to recover a stolen horse. He was killed by a Shawnee Indian who was captured and confined at Fort Washita. He admitted his guilt, but implicated also two Chickasaw Indians, whom he charged with hiring him to commit the murder, though the Chickasaw authorities ascertained that there was no ground for his charges. Love "left a vacancy in the nation that cannot be filled," said Upshaw; "he was the most talented man in the Nation; he understood and knew how business ought to be done." Upshaw then appointed as interpreter Col. James McLaughlin; he was late chief and was one of the delegates to Washington the preceding summer.[17]

The year 1849 found the Chickasaw "situated much as they were last year; very few changes of residence having taken place among them. Some few have moved upon the Washita River, west of Fort Washita, and some from near Fort Towson have moved upon Blue River, and some few have moved upon Red River some distance above the mouth of the False Washita. But it is to be regretted that so large a number of the Chickasaws are yet scattered through the different Choctaw districts. There never will be that unity of feeling among them which is desirable, until they get together. I have but little doubt but what some few influential ones among them is the cause of a great many more not moving into their own district."[18]

The eccentricities of the weather of that year subjected the Chickasaw to considerable reverses. Early in the year there was such an excessive rainfall that the crops were planted with great difficulty; and after they had come up a sleet and snowstorm destroyed their corn, oats, wheat and all their fruits. The weather continued so cold that the people required winter clothes and fires in their homes through the month of August.[19] The extraordinary high waters washed away the fine grist- and sawmill of Col. William R. Guy on Boggy River, and the saw- and gristmill of G. L. Love the night after he had received it from the builders; the sawmill just completed for the Chickasaw Academy which was to cut lumber for that institution was seriously damaged. The commissioner of Indian affairs had made a contract with

17 Upshaw to commissioner of Indian affairs, July 5, 1849, OIA, Chickasaw file U 67.
18 *Report* of commissioner of Indian affairs, 1849.
19 *Ibid.*

the Presbyterian Board for the erection of an academy for girls, authorized by the tribe several years before, but nothing had yet been done
on it. Nor had any progress been made on the male academy planned
by the Episcopal church. So that there were as yet no schools in the
Chickasaw Nation.

By 1850 the carpenters at the Chickasaw Academy had hewed out
the long timbers for their first large building which was 125 feet long,
34 wide, two stories high with double porches on each side. The lower
story contained two living rooms, a large dining room, kitchen, pantry
and storeroom, with a cellar thirty-two by eighteen feet. The upper
story contained bed rooms. By June, 1850, the walls were up ready for
the roof. After a long painful effort the little sawmill had cut the
necessary lumber and it was hoped to open the school the first of the
next year, if some way could be found to construct the chimneys, said
Browning, who, in spite of his obvious inefficiency, was still in charge
of the work. He had secured a farmer from Arkansas to look after the
crops, but "by the last of April his wife became so dissatisfied and homesick that he left and went back again." They succeeded in planting
"35 or 40 acres in corn, but the birds and squirrels were so annoying
that a considerable portion of it had to be planted the third time."
They were delayed also by the failure to receive from the Government
the $6,000 appropriated by the Chickasaw Nation.[20]

Three months later Browning reported that the sickly season and
slow operation of the little sawmill had permitted the large building
to progress only to the extent that it was two-thirds weatherboarded;
the rafters and lathing for the roof had not been sawed. The carpenters
and laborers had all been ill and Browning still did not know how he
was going to get the chimneys built. However, he had cut twenty-five
tons of hay and had an undetermined amount of corn in the field to
feed his six yoke of oxen with which he had timber hauled for the
construction of the school. At the meeting of the Chickasaw council
near the end of 1849 it was discovered that the tribe was nearly
$20,000 in debt. In order to reduce their expenses to the extent of
$3,000 a year they decreased the number of their captains from twenty-
five to twelve. It was said to be an honest and economical government.[21]

20 Browning to Brown, June 29, 1850, OIA "School File" D 310.
21 Letter from Fort Washita, January 14, 1850 in *Fort Smith Herald*, January 26,
1850, p. 2, col. 6.

-{ 118 }-

After the induction into office of President Taylor, Chickasaw Agent A. M. M. Upshaw, who had served continuously since 1838, was removed and he was succeeded by Gabriel W. Long, who was married to a Chickasaw woman. There was much complaint concerning the payment of their annuity in January, 1850, when the Indians suffered from cold. At the payment at Perryville in December, 1850, there was much drinking, and Christmas night in the little village was characterized by that evil and disorder which included one murder as the result of a fight between two drunken men. Kenton Harper was appointed Chickasaw agent to take effect July 1, 1851, but because of illness did not assume the duties of his post for several weeks. Soon after, he was succeeded as agent by A. J. Smith.

The condition of the Chickasaw people showed little improvement. Their progress was much retarded by the unrestrained introduction and drinking of whisky. Many grocery stores were maintained along the border to cater to this appetite and two steamboats on Red River retailed whisky freely. The current rate was a quart of whisky for a bushel of corn. A company of Seminole Indians headed by one Bill Nannubbee were engaged in carrying whisky from Preston on the south side of the Red River, through the Chickasaw Nation to Tukpafka Town in the Creek Nation, where it was retailed by a man who stored it in a cellar under his house. The Chickasaw light-horse undertook to prevent this traffic through their country; one of these officers named Chin chi kee encountered this band and though he was armed only with a knife he killed three of the whisky runners before he was in turn killed by Nantubbee, who shot him in the head.[22]

The Chickasaw continued to be annoyed and harrassed by the wild Indians who prevented their peaceful occupation of the country owned by them. The Kichai tried to settle on the Washita River against their opposition. The Wichita, who lived on the western part of the Chickasaw domain, stole a number of horses from the Caddo Indians. When the demand of the latter for the return of the stolen horses was refused, the Caddo with Jim Ned, a Delaware, and a few Biloxi Indians made a descent upon the Wichita village and drove off some of the horses of the Wichita. The latter fired on them and precipitated a general fight in which two Caddo and a number of Wichita

22 *Ibid.*, January 10, 1852, p. 2, col. 1.

Indians were killed. "The Wichita who escaped the massacre, came into the Creek country, and implored them to save their tribe from extermination"; they said that thirty of their men, women, and children had been killed in the attack. "The Caddoes and their leader told the Wichitaws that Col. Upshaw the Chickasaw Sub-agent had given them liberty to kill the Wichitaws, as they were a very bad people. Col. Logan, the Creek agent at the request of Echo Harjo, Creek Chief, immediately upon this information addressed a letter to Col. Upshaw, upon the subject."[23] Naturally, where such disorders prevailed it was impossible for the unwarlike Chickasaw people to occupy their land and build homes.

Emigration to California through the Chickasaw country which was now in full tide, brought a measure of prosperity to the Indians. The Comanche Indians in the spring of 1850 had broken up their winter camp west of Fort Washita, leaving the road to California free from interruption except from a small band of Waco Indians. But the Chickasaw farmers were suffering from the devastation of immense flocks of rice birds that destroyed their wheat fields. A sixty-acre field of wheat, they said, "would not last their vorarious maws over three days."[24] A letter from "Skitty Hay's Town on Blue (Chickasaw Nation)" July 20, 1850 said: "We have not had a rain for a long time past; the drought is ruining us. . . . . Capt Ed Pickens was re-elected chief of the Chickasaws last week, after a closely contested election."[25]

23 *Ibid.*, June 6, 1849, p. 3, col. 2.
24 *Ibid.*, June 15, 1850, p. 2, col. 4.
25 *Ibid.*, August 3, 1850, p. 2, col. 4.

CHAPTER EIGHT / *Union With Choctaw Dissolved*

THE Chickasaw had no sooner arrived in the West than they repented their bargain which united them with the Choctaw Nation. Each tribe was jealous of the other, and as the Choctaw outnumbered the Chickasaw three to one, the latter were suspicious and fearful of the former lest they would find some way to appropriate or confuse with theirs, the large amount of tribal funds the recent arrivals possessed. They served notice on the Indian department that they would never consent to have their tribal funds combined with those of the Choctaw for the purpose of building schools, a plan suggested by the commissioner of Indian affairs.[1] The result was that while the Choctaw were building schools and making rapid strides in education, the Chickasaw had no schools of any consequence until they removed to their own country. They were constantly agitating the subject of schools with no effect. Every year from the time of their removal the report of the Indian agent contains accounts of the distrust and dissatisfaction growing out of the anomalous relation of the two tribes, and the futile discussion of establishing schools. The Chickasaw seriously considered removal to some other country, remote from the Choctaw.[2]

In 1846 the Chickasaw met at Boiling Spring near Fort Washita and adopted what they called a constitution, though there were not more than a third of the tribe living in their own district;[3] but on October 13, 1848, they again met in convention at the same place, and on November 4 subscribed to a more formal document also called a

1 *Report* of commissioner of Indian affairs for 1842.
2 *Ibid.*, for 1846.
3 *Ibid.*

constitution, which repealed the former; it was signed by Winchester Colbert, Edmund Pickens, Benjamin Love, William Kemp and fifteen others. It provided for an executive to be appointed by the Chickasaw council, with the title of Chickasaw District Chief; and a council of thirty members to meet the first Monday of each October; eight members were to be elected from Pushmataha District, two from Apuckshunubbee, seventeen from Chickasaw, and three from Mushulatubbee; thus indicating the distribution of the Chickasaw through the respective districts. The polling places were Boiling Springs, Good Spring and Perry's Court Ground in Chickasaw District; Blue Springs, Arch McGee's and Running Water in Pushmataha District; Candell's Old Shop near Doaksville for Apuckshunubbee District; and "Fooshna-line, where the road leading from Fort Smith to Fort Washita crosses it," for Mushulatubbe District.

Edmund Pickens was the first Chickasaw chief under this constitution and the first council was held immediately after the constitution was adopted, beside which little other business was transacted. The second session convened at Boiling Springs November 6, 1849, when it was determined to remove the deliberations of the council to Post Oak Grove. A called session was held September 4, 1850, where it was resolved that the Chickasaw tribe decline to receive the Catawba Indians living in North and South Carolina, whom the Government was trying to locate in their country. Five dollars was appropriated to pay William Kemp for the use of his house and an equal amount for beef he furnished at the council on November 10, 1849.

The most urgent business of that session, however, was a memorial to the President against the presence of the "Tonqueways, Caddoes, Keechies, Kickapoos, Quappaws, Boluxies, Cherokees, Shawnees, Ironeyes, & Witchitaws, who are intruders upon us." They represented that these wild Indians infested their country, and committed many depredations by stealing their horses, hogs, cattle, and other property; that these outrages were driving the Chickasaw to such exasperation as to endanger the peace of the frontier by threatening a general war among the Indians. And they invoked from the President the protection promised them in their treaties. They also prayed ". . . .that the force at Fort Washita may not be diminished as the safety of our people from the incursions of the prairie Indians, depends upon the United States forces stationed there. They respectfully suggest that mounted men or dragoons give them more perfect security than Infantry."[4]

The Chickasaw excepted from the proposed removal, however, certain Indians who had been exempted by the Choctaw from an order to remove enacted in October, 1844, by which the latter tribe called on the Government to exclude from their limits all the intruding tribes except ". . . .the Caddoes, who at a previous session of the General Council, having obtained permit to live in the Nation, shall be exempt from the operation of this act; and also the following named families of Indians be allowed to remain unmolested by the operation of this act, viz: Charley, Mike, McCoy, Cherokees; Little Boy, and Frank's family, and Strong Man, Delawares; Capt. Beaver, Panther, and Oats, Shawnees, and their families; and one family of Quapaws, living above the mouth of the Washita, on Red River."[5]

The Chickasaw constitution was framed primarily to control the use of their large tribal funds against the possibility of their being diverted by the Choctaw, of which they were in great fear; and the business of the succeeding sessions of their council was taken up largely with consideration of their schools, the securing of their tribal funds, and measures for securing a separation from the Choctaw Nation.

At the meeting of the Chickasaw council at Boiling Spring in November, 1849, Chief Edmund Pickens, Pitman Colbert, and Cyrus Harris were appointed delegates to go to Washington. At the annuity payment an extra session of the council was called and Jackson Frazier introduced a resolution appropriating $200 of their funds to be donated to the construction of the Washington Monument "in such a way as to have the name of the Chickasaws inscribed on the monument, to perpetuate their love and remembrance of their Great Father, who always gave his red Chickasaw children good advice."[6]

With the establishment of Fort Arbuckle[7] the Chickasaw moved

4 Laws of the Chickasaw Nation from 1848 in manuscript, in custody of superintendent for Five Civilized Tribes. These prairie Indians said they would fight before they would remove (*Fort Smith Herald*, June 15, 1850). The establishment of Fort Arbuckle the next year was expected to relieve this situation.

5 *Choctaw Laws*, edition of 1869, p. 88.

6 *Fort Smith Herald*, February 2, 1850, p. 2, col. 2.

7 The first location of this post, called Camp Arbuckle, was on the south side of the Canadian River, near where is now the line between McClain and Pontotoc counties, Oklahoma. See, *Advancing the Frontier* by Grant Foreman.

from the Choctaw country to their own domain in larger numbers until in 1851 approximately two-thirds of their total population were living in their own country. As Fort Washita supplanted Fort Towson in usefulness, so Fort Arbuckle, being still further west, rendered both of them of diminishing importance.[8]

Discontent on the part of the Chickasaw over their relations with the Choctaw people steadily increased. In 1851 the delegation in Washington presented their grievances to the commissioner of Indian affairs and urged a separation from the other tribe. They claimed that in their joint council they were ignored by the majority and "their voice is neither felt nor heard in that body; practically they have no participation in making the laws to which they are subjected. . . . . They are completely at the mercy of the Choctaws, and every Chickasaw feels that he is oppressed by them. . . . The Choctaws regard and treat the Chickasaws everywhere out of their own district as intruders, and it is frequently thrown up to them as a reproach that they have no rights in the country. This is the cause of many private difficulties, frequently ending in the death of one or the other of the parties, and the number of these are constantly increasing.

"The boundary between the Chickasaw district and the rest of the nation has never been designated. A margin about twenty miles wide from one extremity to the other is disputed—both parties claim and exercise jurisdiction over it. The Choctaws have repeatedly refused to enter into any fair arrangements to have it settled, but exert their own laws in violation of their constitution and the compact between the two peoples. This has recently created much excitement and irritation and came near producing an open rupture between the two tribes."[9]

Jealousy of their financial interests and disbursements of tribal funds provoked and kept alive animosities; their association tended to alienate rather than to unite them and amalgamation appeared more and more impossible. "There is I find a deep and abiding feeling on this subject." They believed themselves "oppressed and down-trodden by their more powerful co-partners in the government. The Chickasaws number about one-fourth as many as the Choctaws, and the depressing influences

8 Quartermaster general's *files*, Fort Myer, Book 33 No. 204.
9 Colbert, Folsom, and Frazier to commissioner, April 26, 1851, OIA, Chickasaw File.

MURIEL H. WRIGHT

Cyrus Harris, first governor of the Chickasaw Nation, 1857

Chickasaw Capitol, Tishomingo City

of such a conviction are plainly visible in their conduct. They act as a people who feel as if they had no country. Restless and dissatisfied, they are continually breaking up their homes and seeking new locations; and the same unsettled and distracted spirit pervades their councils and mars their enterprises. For evils so momentous there must be found a remedy, or the Chickasaws must perish."[10]

However, at this time 3,134 Chickasaw had already settled in their own country and on October 6, 1851, they met in convention to amend their constitution. By this document and the laws then enacted, they set up a government for themselves in which the executive power was vested in a district chief, theirs being one of the four districts in the Choctaw-Chickasaw union. They provided also a council of thirty members with a president and secretary, to meet once each year. They were thus armed to cope with a real or imaginary peril of aggressions by the Choctaw. The agent reported[11] that the Chickasaw council was composed of intelligent men; they disbursed the funds usually handled by the agent ". . . .and have taken on themselves the entire management of their own affairs." Many of the Chickasaw maintained trading houses in the Nation.[12]

While the Chickasaw people had not established a school system, they succeeded in 1851 in beginning the operation of the Chickasaw Academy, long in process of erection. Under the auspices of the Methodist Episcopal Church South, this school began with Rev. Mr. J. C. Robinson as superintendent; sixty pupils attended at first though in a short time the full quota of 120 for which the school was planned were in attendance. It was located twelve miles northwest of Fort Washita, two and one-half from the Washita River and fourteen west of the line dividing the two nations. The girls in the school made fancy work that was exhibited on examination days and sold to the visitors, the proceeds from which were used to purchase books for the library. Six "neighborhood schools" also were soon put in operation.[13]

10 Harper to Drennan, September 1, 1851, *Report* of commissioner of Indian affairs for 1851.

11 *Ibid.*, for 1853.

12 *Ibid.*

13 *Ibid.*, for 1851. An interesting account of the Chickasaw Academy and the superintendents who served there is to be seen in *Chronicles of Oklahoma*, Vol. IV,

The "Female Labor School" an imposing structure of stone was located "on the grounds of Wah-pa-nucka" in the eastern part of the Chickasaw Nation and forty miles north of the Red River. It was conducted under the auspices of the Presbyterian Board with James S. Allen as superintendent; the ten teachers received from $100 to $150 annually, besides their board and room and traveling expenses to their homes once in three years when they desired to go there to visit. The Chickasaw council having appropriated $6,000 to complete the buildings[14] the school under the name of Wapanucka Female Institute was opened in October, 1852, with a capacity for 100 girls.[15]

The Chickasaw Manual Labor Academy as it was later called, soon passed through a serious epidemic of typhoid fever. Many of the students left to attend the local schools now being started in their several neighborhoods. They had just burned 170,000 brick to erect an additional building three stories high, 52 feet long and twenty-two wide, having six rooms nineteen feet square with a fireplace in each end. A disastrous flood had done much damage to the school property, including the water-mill. The school had also a horse-power mill.[16] Colbert Institute, also a Methodist school, was opened November 8, 1854, in the settlement called Perryville, and continued there until 1856, when it was removed west on the headwaters of Clear Boggy, eighteen miles north of Wapanucka, where it was resumed in November. It was on the military road constructed between Fort Smith and Fort Arbuckle. This school contained sixty boys and girls.[17]

---

p. 116. After 1880 the school was badly damaged by fire and by authority of an act passed by the Chickasaw legislature October 20, 1885 a new school was constructed here that became known as Harley Institute from Joshua Harley, the principal. It was located about a mile north of the present town of Tishomingo on the bank of Pennington Creek. It was a large two-story brick building with a two-story addition making it a T shaped structure.

14 *Laws of the Chickasaw Nation.* In October, 1852, $1,600 was appropriated to complete the buildings at Bloomfield Academy, and $2,500 for those at Wapanucka Institute.

15 *Report* of commissioner of Indian affairs for 1856.

16 Bloomfield Academy, a Methodist school for girls, was established in 1852 with J. H. Carr in charge (*ibid.*, for 1856).

17 *Ibid* for 1856 and 1857. In 1859 there were applications for the admission of forty more pupils in Colbert Institute who could not be accommodated (*ibid.*, for 1859). Bloomfield Academy had 45 pupils; "it was suspended for seven weeks last

The early fifties brought the handicap of a great increase in the traffic in whisky, which was introduced from trading houses on the Texas side of Red River. It was impossible to induce state authorities in Arkansas[18] or Texas to promote any effective measures to prevent the introduction of liquor into the Indian country. The Chickasaw agency was then conducted in a one-story log building[19] constructed with four rooms and a passage through the center located in a clump of trees on the edge of the prairie 600 yards west of Fort Washita, and near a fine spring of soft limestone water. Here the annuities[20] were paid to the Indians and much criticism was directed at the authorities in Washington for causing these payments to be made in the winter when the Indians, including infirm and aged people, were compelled to travel long distances and camp out through the most inclement weather, a measure of administration that was attended with much suffering and loss of life by the Indians.[21]

The year 1851 saw the Chickasaw settlers around Fort Washita

---

fall by measles and whooping cough;" then when an effort was made to resume the school measles again broke out from which three pupils died. Chickasaw Manual Labor Academy twelve miles northwest of Fort Washita has 100 boys. All three were conducted by the Methodist Episcopal Chuch, South (ibid.). Wapanucka with 100 girls has a department of domestic "or family training" (ibid.). "I have not seen an Indian drinking or drunk for four years" (ibid.).

The Chickasaw laws were not well enforced from the fact that the nation "is composed of two or three very numerous and influential families. In almost every case brought before the Chickasaw Courts, judges and jury are related by consanguinity or affinity to one or other of the parties litigant" (ibid. for 1860). At their boarding schools 305 boys and girls were being taught in 1860 (ibid.). There were "four academies among the Chickasaws and another will go into operation this fall" (ibid.).

18 Governor Drew of Arkansas in 1844 submitted a special message on the subject to the legislature which paid no attention to it. The governor reported that public sentiment did not support the effort to give this protection to the Indians (ibid., 1847). However, about ten years later Texas passed laws prohibiting the sale of liquor to members of the tribes of the Indian Territory, but they were not enforced.

19 Ibid., 1856. The Chickasaw agency buildings were constructed here in February 1842 after the site for Fort Washita had been selected but a few months before its establishment (Foreman, A Traveler in Indian Territory, 165).

20 The Chickasaw tribe had realized the sum of $2,000,000 from the sale of their land that was held in trust by the Government and yielded them an annuity of $70,000.

21 Report of commissioner of Indian affairs for 1851.

entering upon the cultivation of corn and oats to a considerable extent, "and bid fair in a few years to be able to supply fully all the requirements of forage for this post. . . . . The Chickasaw district commences a few miles to my east and runs west to the 100° of west Longitude about 120 miles from here; their settlements however, are principally confined to the Washita River on either bank from its mouth, to about 20 miles northwest of this. Within this district is located the Caddoes, about 300 in all, near the oil spring and not over 15 miles from where Capt. Marcy is ordered to locate a post on Wild Horse Creek [Fort Arbuckle]. They are disposed to cultivate the soil and live peaceably and friendly.

"On the headwaters of Cache and Beaver creeks near the Witchita Mountains live the Witchita and Wacoe's; in number the former have about 300 warriors; the latter fortunately not over 80, as they are much the most warlike and will hold no intercourse with the whites. These tribes are really the wild people of the Prairies; although I think the Witchitas an amiable people and could be easily turned to cultivation of the soil, if encouraged by the Government. The Wacoes are like the wolves, untameable and at war with every tribe they can war with. The northern band of Keiches, about 90 warriors strong, live on the Washita near the Caddoes; they never raise anything but roasting ears and pumpkins, are regarded friendly. There is a tribe recently come into this district from Texas—driven from their former country by all the tribes, and they are kicked and cuffed about by all here, that would seem as if the curse of God was on them. I mean the Ton-ka-ways, numbering about 150 warriors. They roam from the Canadian to Red River and dodge about, east to west, too glad if let alone for any brief space of time in any location. They are cannibals; they not only eat their enemies when taken dead or alive, *but eat their own people when they die.*

"The Northern Comanches under the chieftainship of Pa-ya-ho-kee roam with his numerous bands through this district, like lords of the soil—all pay homage to him; all court his protection. Whatever he orders is obeyed, if even to cease war among the small bands and make peace. It is only late in the Fall and during the winter that the Comanches approach near here. The chief has been once to visit me but brought no one with him but his servants. As he was encamped then not over 100 miles west from here, with, as was estimated about 5,000 warriors, I considered his visit then as a reconnoissance and held myself in readiness to give him a proper reception should he come nearer. Since then no Comanches have visited the settlements. All the Tribes I have named except the Caddoes, live upon Buffaloes, horses, and mules, and all steal; the Wacoes kill."[22]

The next year it was reported that the Chickasaw were improving in spite of difficulties. They had large numbers of cattle, horses, and hogs; several mills and gins operated along Red River beside others scattered through the country.[23] They said they could be happy if they were only separated from the Choctaw; they had made an appointment to meet delegates from that tribe at Doaksville to discuss the subject of a separation, but they charged that most of the Choctaw treated them with contempt and refused to keep the engagement. There was continued complaint of the Kickapoo, Caddo, Creeks and Seminole, who were engaged in trafficking in whisky they introduced from Texas into the Chickasaw country and beyond.

Oil Springs in the Chickasaw country were attracting attention ". . . .as they are said to be a remedy for all chronic diseases. Rheumatism stands no chance at all, and the worst cases of dropsy yield to its effects. The fact is, that it cures anything that has been tried. A great many Texans visit these springs, and some from Arkansas. They are situated at the foot of the Wichita mountains [now called Arbuckle mountains] on Washita River, and also on Red River."[24]

Contention between the tribes was reaching a critical stage in 1854 and commissioners were appointed to confer on the subject of permitting the Chickasaw to exercise exclusive jurisdiction over their country. There was bitter controversy also over the location of the boundary line between the tribes. The dispute was submitted to the

22 Col. Dixon S. Miles to Jesup, February 23, 1851, QMG, Fort Myer, Book No. 32, M 430.

23 In 1854 their oats brought eighty-five cents and corn $1.50 to $2.00 a bushel, due to the increased demand by the garrison at Fort Washita and emigrant trains going to California and to the draught (Report of commissioner of Indian affairs for 1854).

24 Ibid., for 1853. A. C. Love of Texas wrote a letter dated at "Oil Springs, Chickasaw Nation July 20, 1858" to the Dallas Herald in which he said "I have been here nearly three months watering." He had recently broken the tedium of his stay by accompanying Douglas H. Cooper and the Chickasaw Indians in their pursuit of a band of Comanche Indians who had stolen a number of their horses (Clipping enclosed in a letter of H. R. Runnells to secretary of war August 12, 1858, AGO, OFD, 144 T 58).

agent, Douglas H. Cooper, with right of appeal from his decision to the President. Hostilities seemed to be within the range of possibilities which Agent Cooper hoped he would be able to avert; but he expressed the opinion that there could be no peace between the tribes until they had dissolved their union. He employed Capt. R. L. Hunter to run and mark the line described in their Treaty of 1837; part of this line followed the old military road run and traveled in 1834 by General Leavenworth[25] from Fort Gibson to the Washita River; but it was so nearly obliterated in places as to be impossible to locate. Some claimed that where the treaty located the lower part of the line by "Island Bayou," "Allen Bayou" was meant. Cooper arranged a conference at Doaksville and November 4, 1854 commissioners from the two tribes agreed upon a new boundary line that disregarded the military road.[26] It was emphasized that the new line[27] should be run so as to include within the Chickasaw domain their new Wapanucka Female Institute, which was in peril of being left on the Choctaw side of the line by the old survey. As if the Indians did not have enough to plague them, in 1854 they were aroused by Senator Johnson's bill to incorporate their country in a territory.

The inevitable separation of the tribes was achieved in a new treaty[28] executed June 22, 1855, at Washington, which dissolved the union, though retaining the mutual right of living in either country and the boundary lines established in the Treaty of 1854 were preserved. In this treaty these tribes leased to the United States all their lands west of the ninety-eighth degree of longitude for the permanent settlement

25 Grant Foreman, *Pioneer Days in the Early Southwest*, 127 ff.

26 Kappler, *op. cit.*, II, 487.

27 By the provisions of this treaty the eastern boundary of the Chickasaw Nation was fixed: "Beginning on the north bank of Red River, at the mouth of Island Bayou, where it empties into the Red River, about twenty-six miles on a straight line, below the mouth of False Wachitta, thence running a northwesterly course, along the main channel of said bayou nearest the dividing ridge between Wachitta and Low Blue (de l'eau bleu) rivers as laid down upon Capt. R. L. Hunter's map; thence, northerly along the eastern prong of Island Bayou to its source; thence, due north to the Canadian River. . . . . Provided, however, if the line running due north from the eastern source of Island Bayou to the main Canadian shall not include Allen's or Wa-pa-nacka academy within the Chickasaw district, then an offset shall be made from said line so as to leave said academy two miles within the Chickasaw district, north, west, and south from the lines of the boundary."

28 Kappler, *op. cit.*, II, 532.

of the Wichita and such other tribes or bands of Indians as the Government might desire to locate therein.[29] But the Choctaw and Chickasaw retained the right to settle upon the leased territory. For this lease[30] the Choctaw received $600,000.00 and the Chickasaw $200,000.00.

August 11, 1856 the Chickasaw assembled in mass convention[31] to initiate the independent government secured to them by the new treaty. They adopted as their organic law a written constitution and provided for the election of a governor[32] and other officers assimilated in name and scope of their several duties to those of the state governments.[33] But their troubles were not yet at an end; the treaty gave to each Choctaw who should settle in the Chickasaw Nation all the rights, privileges and immunities of citizens thereof, except the right to participate in their tribal funds; and the Chickasaw feared enough Choctaw people might settle within their country to control their elections, and thus their tribal revenues and finances.[34] So there arose a new controversy as to whether an unlimited right to vote in their elections was meant by the treaty.

In the meantime the Chickasaw people, uncertain as to precisely what had been accomplished by their new constitution, and what advantages had been given over to the Choctaw people, sent this document into Texas to be printed, and the messenger who carried the

29 "The Indians from Texas and the Wichitas and other bands affiliated with them" removed in 1859 to this country on the Washita (*Report* of commissioner 1860); but they were in constant fear of citizens of Texas, who wrongfully charged them with depredations (*ibid.*, 242).

30 This lease, being in perpetuity, was treated by the Government as a cession, which was far from the intention of the Indians (*ibid.*, 1858).

31 This meeting was held at a place on Pennington Creek called Good Spring, to which the Chickasaw seat of government had been removed in 1853. In preparation for the important first meeting under their independent government the place was improved by the erection of a brush arbor fifty feet square, with log seats and benches and a platform, and the place was called Tishomingo after the illustrious old Chickasaw chief. Five thousand pounds of beef were contracted for to be consumed at the meeting. The first election under their new government was held there on August 17 and contracts were let for the erection of a council house, a chief's residence and other adjuncts of the new capital.

32 Cyrus Harris was elected governor, and H. Colbert was elected national secretary.

33 *Report* of commissioner of Indian affairs for 1856.

34 *Ibid.*, p. 147.

original, and only, manuscript of it disappeared,[35] and all trace was lost of their precious document.[36] The Treaty of 1855 provided that until other laws should be enacted the Choctaw laws would control in the Chickasaw Nation, but with the loss of their newly adopted constitution, no one knew what law was in force. Great disorder prevailed; murders and other crimes were committed, but in time their difficulties were adjusted. An abundant harvest in 1857 placed the people beyond want.

Daniel G. Major completed his survey of the ninety-eighth meridian, the western boundary of the Chickasaw Nation in August, 1858. He was under contract to proceed with the survey of the one hundredth meridian, the west boundary of the "Leased District," but on account of the numerous bands of hostile Comanche, Kiowa, and Cheyenne Indians collected about the Antelope Hills it was considered too hazardous to proceed without an escort able to resist encroachments of a thousand savage warriors, and the work was necessarily postponed. H. M. C. Brown and A. H. Jones surveyed the west boundary of the Creek and Seminole domain with a company of twelve people protected by an escort of fifty Creeks and fifty Seminole warriors against a large force of Comanche Indians assembled between the North Fork and the Main Canadian River.

Because of the hostile attitude of these plains Indians, Douglas H. Cooper recommended that a military post be established in the Wichita Mountains.[37] The secretary of the interior also urged upon the secretary of war this military protection, a plan that was later realized in the creation of Forts Cobb and Sill. In June, 1859 two companies commanded by Capt. D. B. Sackett from Forts Smith and Washita departed with a train of ninety wagons containing baggage and supplies bound for Antelope Hills. This expedition resulted in the establishment of Fort Cobb near the site of the present Anadarko, Oklahoma.

35 The messenger was afterwards seen in Shreveport.
36 *Report* of commissioner of Indian affairs, 1857.
37 Cooper to Mix, August 19, 1858, OIA Southern Superintendency, C 1618. For extended accounts of the hostilities of these prairie Indians at this time see Grant Foreman, *Advancing the Frontier*.

CHAPTER NINE / *Relations With the Military*

THE lives of the Chickasaw Indians were influenced in their new home by the military arm of the Government more than those of the other tribes. Protection from the aggressions of the prairie Indians was promised them in their treaty of removal. More than three years before the necessary military establishment was built, General Arbuckle recommended the location of the post "at or near the mouth of the False Washita on the Red River, where two companies of Infantry ought to be stationed. The necessity for troops at that position results from the Chickasaws and Choctaws being about to extend their settlements that high up Red River, which is about as far west as their country is valuable or the necessary supply of timber can be had; and it is about that point on Red River that the Comanches, Wichitaws and other prairie Indians (now at peace with the United States and the emigrant Tribes on this border) frequently visit, and from the former habits of these Indians it is believed that they will require to be frequently counselled to remain at peace and that it will be necessary occasionally to call them together at the new post proposed, for the purpose" of settling difficulties between them and their neighbors.[1]

Pursuant to the recommendation of General Arbuckle and General Zackary Taylor, Fort Washita was located on a trail long used by the Indians and traders on their expeditions to and from Texas. With the evacuation of the positions held by our troops in Mexico after the war with that country, weary and travel-worn detachments of the army

1 Arbuckle to Jesup, January 14, 1838, AGO, ORD, Headquarters Second Military Department, Western Division, *Letter book No. 111.*

labored homeward over those early trails through the Choctaw and Chickasaw country. On November 13, 1848 a part of the Fifth Infantry arrived at Fort Washita from Mexico; it consisted of a train of thirty-five wagons and teams and a number of extra horses. In spite of the long journey the wagons were in fair condition, but the harness was much worn and the horses were broken down until they were mere skeletons; one died on arrival at the post and thirty-five were condemned. Ten days earlier another detachment from Mexico on the way to Fort Leavenworth reached Fort Smith; it contained eighty-one men, one ambulance, fourteen wagons, one traveling forge, and seventy-five horses; 1,212 mules traveling in four divisions were herded along the route by fifty herdsmen. Large numbers of mules from Texas and Mexico were constantly passing through the country for the Fort Leavenworth market and the quartermaster at Fort Smith asked permission to purchase some of them to use in place of oxen.

From the beginning of Fort Washita in 1842 it furnished a measure of protection for the Chickasaw Indians from the wild Indians of the prairies; with changing conditions and the emigration of white people through the country it became necessary to enlarge the fort. Col. Dixon S. Miles who was in command, reported late in 1849 that new quarters were so far completed that the infantry moved in the day he wrote; and during the week he would complete the basement as a kitchen; he was planning to erect a hospital, and requested permission to board up the western piazza so as to make a two-room shed for bachelor quarters and a place to entertain visitors to the post.[2]

The movement of California emigrants through their country exercised a notable influence on the lives of the Chickasaw Indians. Beginning in 1849 large and frequent trains of emigrants bound for the "gold diggings" of California passed through the Chickasaw country, some of them along the Canadian River to Santa Fé and others bending their course southwest past Fort Washita into Texas and westward to El Paso. These parties of emigrants left considerable sums of money in their wake through the Indian settlements expended for food, grain, and live stock. One large party of about 500 that traveled along the Canadian River was escorted by a detachment of the Fifth Infantry from Fort Smith commanded by Capt. R. B. Marcy, who was ordered

2 Miles to Jesup, November 29, 1849, QMG *Book 31*, No. 363.

to explore and recommend a permanent route through the country for future emigration.

The next year, 1850, General Arbuckle commanding at Fort Smith recommended that troops be taken from Fort Smith and Fort Towson to establish a new post beyond Fort Washita for the protection of the California emigrants and the immigrant Chickasaw Indians from the annoyance and depredation of the Comanche Indians.[3] In May General Arbuckle relinquished his command of the Seventh Military Department and departed on leave because of his health for the hot springs in Arkansas. He was succeeded by Gen. W. G. Belknap. Before the end of the month, pursuant to Arbuckle's recommendations, the war department issued orders for Capt. R. B. Marcy to establish a new post on the Canadian River near the "Western Boundary of the Reserves."[4]

Company B of the Fifth Infantry left Fort Smith for Fort Towson and soon afterwards on August 22, 1850, Captain Marcy proceeded to his new station on the south bank of the Canadian River. Before he had completed the barracks for his troops he received instructions to suspend work as it was contemplated ordering him to change his location. However large quantities of supplies were sent to his command from Fort Smith by slow-moving ox-teams. One contingent started the round trip of a month in August and another a few weeks later.

Captain Marcy, having been ordered to remove his post to a point near Washita River, selected the site of a Kickapoo Indian village on Wild Horse Creek where his command arrived April 19, 1851. In order to convey supplies to this distant post far beyond the Chickasaw settlements, at the direction of General Arbuckle, Captain Marcy sent two men in canoes down the Washita River to Fort Washita to report on the navigability of the stream, and the commanding officer at Fort Smith directed Col. Dixon S. Miles commanding at Fort Washita, to have a keel boat constructed for the purpose of conveying supplies from his post to the new one about to be established by Captain Marcy. The specifications for the construction of this boat are interesting; the use of a barrel of whisky as a standard of measure illuminates the customs of the country.

3   Arbuckle to Jones, March 13, 1850, AGO, ORD, WDF, A 46.
4   Jones to Belknap, General Orders, No. 19, May 31, 1850, AGO, ORD, WDF, A 93.

The boat to be built at Fort Washita was to be seventy or seventy-five feet long, fifteen feet wide in the clear; "two feet between the floor and the thwarts or cross piece which hold the sides of the boat together, this being supposed to be sufficient to stow a whisky barrel under the thwarts." It was to have a cargo box extending from near the stern to the bow, leaving sufficient room in the bow for one or two oars on each side, and doors on each side about the middle to receive the cargo and for the purpose of bailing the boat. The bottom of the boat must be flat and the ribs let into the bottom of the keel, the keel being inside. The straight part of the sill to be from eight to nine feet and curve up three or four inches above the thwart; and on the top of these will be placed the running board on which the men will walk to pole the boat. The cargo box will rise from the running board, the sides inclining inwards and about four or five feet above the running board which will make the cargo box from top to bottom of the boat about six or seven feet and the sides inclining inwards so that the top of the cargo box will be about ten feet wide. This box to be planked up with light plank about 5-8 inches wide. The bottom boards of the boat ought, it is supposed, to be of oak an inch and a half thick. For the convenience of Cordelling a light mast should be placed about 1-3 back from the bow and about 15 or 20 feet in height above the Cargo box and a ring in the bow through which to pass a rope for a bridle which is attached to the Cordell by an open noose and used by a man in the bow to prevent the boat shearing round in a rapid current. The curved sides if possible should be sawed out of crooked timber and the flooring inside should be of light inch plank. The boat will have a small deck in the curve of the bow and stern outside of the Cargo box."[5]

From the Chickasaw settlers around Fort Washita, large quantities of corn were purchased for the remote Fort Arbuckle in the west where the Chickasaw people had not yet ventured to locate. Three thousand bushels of corn was shelled and sacked to be transported to the new fort, besides seventy-nine barrels of flour, forty-six barrels of pork, 1,744 pounds of sugar, and 545 pounds of coffee from the well-provisioned larders of Fort Washita. These activities caused the distribution of funds in the Indian country where they were much needed.

The next month the quartermaster at Fort Smith sent to the new

5 General commanding Fort Smith to Miles, March 25, 1851, AGO, ORD, Headq. Seventh Military Department, *Letter Book No.* 87, p. 35.

post a quantity of supplies that were conveyed by a train of nineteen wagons propelled by 152 oxen, four yoke to each wagon. But he thought mules should be substituted for oxen as they stood the hardship better. The oxen, he said, were subject to a disease known as the murrain, (now known as anthrax or Texas fever) which was more prevalent in that region than any other he had ever known. The assistant surgeon said that when cattle were removed from the range where they were raised to another even if only a few miles distant, almost invariably they were attacked by murrain during the succeeding summer and fall. One-third of the oxen used in hauling to Camp Arbuckle had died from this disease, and he had been obliged to send to the Choctaw settlements in Sugar Loaf valley for more. Some of the losses of the immigrant Indians on arrival in their new home are better understood in the light of this explanation. As to the comparative pulling qualities the quartermaster said, one would often find carcasses of oxen in boggy places, but never a mule.[6]

Marcy's new post was named Fort Arbuckle for General Matthew Arbuckle who died at Fort Smith of cholera at 11.45 A. M., on June 11, 1851. "A few hours before his death he knew he was going to die and expressed much anxiety concerning the forward movement of the Fifth Infantry into Texas, and the supply train. On being assured that measures had been taken to carry out his instructions he appeared well satisfied and happy that he had performed the last duty assigned him by his government."[7] Captain Marcy laid out a road from Fort Smith to Fort Arbuckle which continued to Red River and beyond. It attracted settlers of immigrant Indians who found there opportunities for sale of their produce and a measure of security from wild Indians. "This road," says Marcy, "for the first 150 miles traversed the Santa Fé route. . . . . The Choctaws have settled along the road for 120 miles out from Fort Smith; after which with the exception of a small settlement around Fort Washita, the road passes over a perfectly wild

6 Montgomery to quartermaster general, April 22, 1851, QMG, Book No. 32, M 506.

7 Page to adjutant general, Fort Smith, June 12, 1851, AGO, OFD, 132 A 51. Page's letter is endorsed by the adjutant general of the army: "No officer of the army was more devoted to the public interest or discharged his duty more faithfully, and this devotion to the good of the service is exemplified, even in his dying hours. Respectfully laid before the General in Chief, July 5th., R. Jones, A. G." Twenty-five men at the post had died of the dread disease.

and uncultivated country. . . . . On leaving Fort Arbuckle the road for the first six miles follows up the valley of Wild Horse Creek south 50 degrees west, then four degrees south and passes through a gap in a chain of low mountains running parallel with the creek. It then enters the Cross Timbers, here twenty miles wide. . . . . At 30 miles from Fort Arbuckle the road emerges from the Cross Timbers."

The roads through the Choctaw and Chickasaw country were now teeming with activity that exerted a decided influence on the lives and fortunes of the immigrant Indians: California emigrants in parties ranging from a single wagon load to great caravans winding over the hills and through the forests and prairies were familiar sights to the Indians for several years. The military too, entered upon an era of great activity in the country. General Belknap then stationed at Fort Gibson was directed to lay out a route to Dona Ana in Texas and his regiment, the Fifth Infantry, was ordered to Texas to occupy a post to be established on the Brazos River in the performance of a newly announced policy intended to protect the settlers of Texas from the Comanche and other wild Indians. The Seventh Infantry was to return to the Indian country to relieve the Fifth. Five companies of the Fifth Infantry marched from Fort Smith, one from Fort Towson and one from Fort Gibson to Fort Washita where they were organized for the march to the Brazos.

Equipment was assembled at Fort Washita for Belknap's organization that preceded the remainder of the regiment and laid out the new road. This equipment included ten range horses selected for their ability to live on the prairie grass, fourteen wagons, eight mule teams and ox teams. Beef cattle and arms were taken from Fort Gibson, one piece of artillery from the same place and one from Fort Washita. The explorers carried thirty rounds of canister, thirty of grapeshot, cartridges, and round shot. They proceeded along the road and crossed the Red River at Preston then a vicious little settlement built up on the California trail. In the meantime a year's supply for the Fifth Infantry was coming up the Arkansas River by boat to be hauled over the road through the Indian country into Texas. Col. John J. Abercrombie in command of two companies of the Fifth Infantry arrived at Fort Smith from Fort Towson May 31 and the next day the cholera broke out in his command, twenty-seven men dying by the middle of June. The survivors were then moved six miles from the post to an isolated camp where they recovered their health. [8]

The headquarters band and "C" company of the Fifth Infantry departed from Fort Gibson June 14, 1851 en route to the Brazos River by way of Fort Washita. All military movements converged on this post making it a busy place and bringing prosperity to the Indians roundabout.

New quarters were being constructed at Fort Smith when the order came for abandoning the post as part of the plans for extending the military establishment farther west. Enough men were to be retained to finish the lathing and plastering; and herdsmen to care for the oxen and other animals to be used in transporting supplies to Fort Arbuckle. [9] Before the end of the year another commander of this military department was removed by death when on November 10, 1851 General Belknap died in an army ambulance bearing him from Preston to Fort Washita on his way to join his family at Fort Gibson. His body was interred at Fort Washita.

The activities of these army establishments were not in all respects such as the Indians could approve. The officials of the tribes in endeavoring to prevent the introduction of whisky in their country ran counter to the habits and wishes of the officers and men at these posts. Five Indian officers, George Perkins, Imihl-hla-tubbe, Chafa, Wilson Beams, and Ka-li-tish-ka intercepted and destroyed a shipment of 100 gallons of whisky being taken from Preston, Texas to Bergwin and Eastman, traders at Boiling Springs near Fort Washita. The officers at

8 AGO, ORD, Seventh Military Department, Fort Smith *Letter Book No. 87*; Page to adjutant general, June 17, 1851, AGO, OFD, 117 B 51.

9 AGO, ORD, Seventh Military Department, Fort Smith *Letter Book No. 87*, p. 38. Maj. T. J. Holmes was now in command of Fort Washita and Col. Henry Bainbridge of Fort Gibson. Headquarters of the Seventh Military Department was removed in December, 1851 from Fort Smith to Fort Gibson. Col. Henry Wilson in command at Fort Smith thought the change a great mistake. The mail routes to all the different posts in the Seventh Department diverged from Fort Smith he said; "All communications coming by mail to Fort Gibson pass through Fort Smith and the road from Fort Smith to Fort Gibson crosses the rivers Salisor and the Illinois which are without ferries and frequently impassable from high water causing a detention of the mail for two weeks at a time." The citizens of Fort Smith protested long and bitterly at the abandonment of their fort (*Fort Smith Herald*, December 12, 1851). Colonel Wilson removed his troops to Fort Gibson overland, but the regimental band and the heavy baggage were carried by water.

Fort Washita took the loss of the whisky much to heart; Colonel Miles sent a detachment of men who took the Indian officers in custody and incarcerated them in the dungeon at the fort. The captives addressed a memorial to their chief and council in session at Nunih Waiya asking them to solicit General Arbuckle and the commissioner of Indian affairs to order their release from imprisonment which they said was a violation of their own laws and the intercourse laws enacted by Congress.[10]

As plans developed for protecting the frontier of the Chickasaw country and Texas, other changes were inaugurated: The road between Fort Smith and Fort Arbuckle became so badly cut up by the heavy supply trains that it was necessary in 1853 to select a new route. The headquarters of the Seventh Military Department was now transferred to Fort Washita which thus became the headquarters of the commander of the Seventh Infantry. The regimental band of this organization was ordered to remove with Company F to Fort Washita from Fort Smith and the public buildings at the latter place were ordered turned over to the superintendent of the southern Indian superintendency.[11]

Captain Marcy was ordered out on another expedition in 1854 and many interesting features along his route through the Choctaw and Chickasaw country were described in a series of notes made by a member of his party.[12] Soon after their departure from Fort Smith they witnessed a "ball play" near Skullyville. Here they saw the old council house "a long rambling building built of logs, and not different except in size from their ordinary houses. . . . . The place of assem-

10 *Cherokee Advocate*, October 8, 1850, p. 2, col. 1. The year before, the commandant at Fort Washita made a requisition for whisky for extra duty men and reported that the supply on hand at the post was contained in old, rotten, and leaky barrels and that it was necessary to secure new barrels in order to prevent further waste (quartermaster to Gibson May 1, 1849, QMG, A to C, 1849, No. 45). The fort was then commanded by Maj. Daniel Ruggles of the Fifth Infantry recently returned from service in the Mexican War; Ruggles was a popular officer and the settlement on the post reservation was called Rugglesville.

11 AGO, ORD, Seventh Military Department, *Order Book No. 86*, p. 45, order No. 14, October 29, 1853.

12 *Notes Taken during the Expedition Conducted by Capt. R. B. Marcy, U. S. A., through Unexplored Texas in the Summer and Fall of 1854*, by W. B. Parker, attached to the Expedition.

bling in Council having been changed to Doaksville." At some of the homes along the way they saw vessels used by the Choctaw Indians made of clay mixed with ground muscle shells; they would hold water, Parker said, and would withstand the heat of a fire sufficiently to be used for cooking food.

At times they passed parties of emigrants—and at Boggy Creek where the water was very high, they met a drove of over 1,000 cattle being driven from Texas to Missouri and Illinois: "They are very beautiful to look at, symmetrical in figure, with sinewy limbs, and very long sharp pointed horns." The drivers were a rough set of men, skillful riders who rode a small horse bred in Mexico, thick set and of great power of endurance. It was an exciting sight to see the herd of cattle driven off the high bank, plunge fifteen feet into the water and swim across, with nothing showing above the water but their taper heads and long thin horns.

Mr. Parker enjoyed the beginning of the day's march: "At dawn of day we were again enroute. It was a beautiful sight in the dim light and bracing air of morning, to see the long line of white covered wagons rolling quietly over the slopes of the prairie; the lowing of the oxen, the snorting of the horses, the shouts and cracking of whips by the drivers, with all the bustle of breaking up camp made up an enlivening scene, which must be experienced to be enjoyed. One thing however marred the enjoyment to me, and that was the awful profanity of the drivers. . . . it struck me as ill-timed and unnatural when endulged in, in the midst of natural beauties which might fire a dying hermit."

About two weeks from their departure from Fort Smith they arrived June 15 at Fort Washita "sore, sunburnt, and fatigued, to experience all the comforts and pleasures which unaffected and disinterested hospitality could offer and accomplish." The fort was then garrisoned by part of the Seventh Infantry commanded by Maj. T. H. Holmes. "Plain but comfortable quarters stand upon the brow of a hill, commanding a fine view of the place. . . . a little babbling brook meanders through the green sward at the foot of the hill, the whole forming a scene of picturesque beauty, compensating in some measure for the isolation from society and the daily peril concomitant to a frontier life. . . . We enjoyed the hospitalities of our friend, S. Humes,[13]

13 Samuel Humes was sutler or post trader at Fort Washita for a number of years.

whose heart is as open as the prairies around him. . . . our friends got up many little social soirees for us and we were also enlivened by a wedding. One of the garrison belles, leaving parents and friends, cast in her lot with a young subaltern of infantry." "During our stay here," says Parker, "many Indians came in to trade at the sutler's store. They were Caddos, Chickasaws and Wichitas, a dirty squalid and uninteresting set."

"Whilst in camp one evening during our march, I observed two Indians ride up and dismount. One of them stooped down, pulled up something from under his horse's feet, and walking to the camp fire, held it over the flames. Prompted by curiosity, I went over and found him preparing *sumach for his evening's smoke*. He had pulled a bunch of the green branches of the plant and now held them in the flame just far enough and long enough to singe and curl them; he then rubbed them in his hands, filled his pipe, lit it, and mounting, was gone, the whole process not detaining him five minutes."

Parker was not a sympathetic observer of the Indians, though he performed a distinct service by the notes he made of the things seen by him. He continues: "The style of building among this people is peculiar; two square pens are put up with logs, and roofed or thatched. The space between the pens is covered in and serves for eating place and depository of harness, saddles, and briddles, &c. A door is cut in each pen, facing the passage. They have no windows the doors admitting all the light used. This style is *called two pens and a passage* and is, in fact only a shelter for the family from bad weather, for of furniture they have but little, and that of the rudest and most uncomfortable kind. These buildings are stuck almost invariably upon the road; no neat door yard, with a substantial fence and neat gate encloses them; no flower or vegetable garden is seen, but the ornamental figure of a half-starved dog, grunts lazily on one side and a pack of miserable curs lounge on the other, the whole presenting an untidy picture of squalid discomfort, which even its temporary appearance cannot deceive." He evidently did not see some of the more attractive pictures of Chickasaw homes described by other travelers.

"At different points on our road we were witnesses to the absurd pow-wow and ridiculous incantations of the swindlers [medicine men]. Near the hut where lies the patient, they erect a pole, from the top of which flaunts gay ribbons and pieces of gay cloth. At the foot of the pole stands a frame, to which is attached a bale of muslin or woolen cloth, ribbons &c, and the door of the hut is festooned with ribbons and colored cloth. The mighty medicine man goes through with his mummeries, and leaves, taking the precaution to take with him as perquisites, all the cloth, ribbons, &c, which have been used and according to his wants, of muslin, woolen or ribbon, so will be the quantity required, and the quality of those infallible antidotes to the disease to be cured. What a commentary upon a people having all the advantages of the civilization and enlightenment of the nineteenth century."

After remaining two weeks at Fort Washita to collect, organize and provision his expedition Marcy departed with a company of forty noncommissioned men and officers and soon arrived at Red River. There the journalist notes a party of Seminole Indians who had come 150 miles to purchase Texas whisky which they intended to transport and sell to other immigrant Indians. They brought it across the river from Preston, Texas, in five-gallon kegs which they slung on their pack horses in netting of rawhide. However, they had not proceeded far on their route when a Chickasaw officer captured and destroyed the whole lot. The ferryman was also engaged in flouting the law by bringing whisky across the river and retailing it at two dollars a gallon, a vile concoction that cost him about fifteen cents a gallon, says Parker. He also saw a herd of 1,200 cattle crossing the river and 150 mustang mares on the way to Missouri—puny looking stock, he said.

Several hundred Wichita, Waco, Tawakoni, Caddo, Anadarko, Kickapoo, Shawnee, Delaware Hainai, and other Indians were still living on the diminished domain of the Chickasaw Indians whose legislature in 1857 ordered them to leave. The Wichita agent, A. H. McKisick, then addressed a letter to Cyrus Harris, governor of the Chickasaw Nation, requesting permission for them to remain until reserves could be designated for them on the "leased district." Nothing was done by the Government to locate these Indians and the next year witnessed a season of warfare and bloody depredation in the Chickasaw country.[14]

Later the necessary orders issued from Washington and Elias Rector superintendent of Indian affairs at Fort Smith departed from his station for the purpose of exploring the "leased district" with a view to determining on locations for the Indians who were to be removed there and for their agency. He traveled with several white men, and

14 Grant Foreman, *Advancing the Frontier.*

Indian chiefs and scouts to Fort Arbuckle where the post commander Maj. W. H. Emory furnished him a cavalry escort under Lieut. D. S. Stanley. On June 22, 1859, he reached the site of the old Wichita village on Cache Creek selected by Major Emory for a fort about to be established. He then made an exhaustive exploration of the country and designated as a location for the Wichita agency the site of the old Kichai village on the south side of the Washita River. He returned to Fort Arbuckle on the thirtieth where he met Robert S. Neighbors, superintendent for Indian affairs in Texas, and they planned the settlement of the Indians from that state.

Neighbors returned 170 miles to his agency on the Brazos River and under an escort of one company of infantry and two of cavalry all commanded by Maj. George H. Thomas to protect his Indians from the whites and wild Indians brought them, 1,000 Waco, Tawakoni, Tonkawa, Caddo, and 300 Comanche to the Wichita agency where on September first he delivered them to the agent Samuel A. Blain. Neighbors then started on his return to San Antonio and at Fort Belknap he was killed by a white man who resented Neighbors's defense of his Indians charged with atrocities on the whites, who refused to discriminate between the reserve Indians and the Comanche and other wild Indians of the prairies. Some of them were provided oxen and farming implements, and thus began the experiment of making settlers and farmers of these people on the "leased district." The Wichita were already known as agriculturists, and the reserve Indians from Texas had begun to farm there.

The Chickasaw Nation was now steadily improving in the elements making for an orderly and prosperous community. It was also rapidly approaching a crisis, the outbreak of the Civil War, that was to wreck all that had been gained through years of trial and stress. An evidence of progress that had been achieved was the launching of the newspaper, the *Chickasaw and Choctaw Herald* at Tishomingo City in January, 1858. This paper was published in English but it announced its purpose to provide material of particular interest to the members of the Chickasaw Indians, many of them having learned to read and speak the English language. It published a large amount of advertising of business and professional men located at Fort Washita and Tishomingo City that had become important little hamlets.

BOOK THREE / *Creek*

CHAPTER TEN / *Victims of Contractors*

PURSUANT to the terms of the Treaty[1] of 1826 about 1,200 Creek followers of McIntosh and as many more of the opposing faction emigrated and located in 1829 on the Arkansas River near the mouth of the Verdigris.[2] Much friction and discontent arose from the fact that the Cherokee Indians recently emigrated from Arkansas claimed the land on which the Creeks were located.[3] But their measure of unhappiness was filled to overflowing by the failure of the Government to comply with the terms of the treaties under which they had removed from the East. The traps, guns, and other things essential to their welfare promised them in 1826 were not furnished them for several years after their removal; in the meantime their hunters were obliged to travel far from home in quest of game in the country infested by savage western Indians. They were compelled to follow the chase to feed their families and to secure skins to make clothing for them. At home they were in constant alarm from the warlike demonstrations of the roving prairie Indians.

The new country of the immigrant Indians abounded in natural wealth according to white men who were acquainted with it. While the Choctaw treaty of 1830 was under consideration in the senate, inquiries concerning this western country and the Indians who had removed there were made by Senator Thomas H. Benton, chairman of the senate committee on Indian affairs, of Col. A. P. Chouteau, trader

1 Kappler, *op. cit.*, II, 188.
2 Grant Foreman, *Indians and Pioneers*, 297; *Pioneer Days in the Early South-west*, 210.
3 In 1842 Roley McIntosh wrote: "The rifles were delivered and some few small kettles and traps, but no money at all. The headright money due that party had never been paid."

at the Three Forks, Gen. William Clark, and John Campbell agent for the Western Creeks. Colonel Chouteau's long reply[4] is particularly illuminating. He said he had raised there forty-five to fifty bushels of corn to the acre and from eighteen to twenty bushels of wheat, thus fixing the growth of wheat in the country at a very early date. "The prairies are covered with fine grass; stock do well on it winter and summer; in the winter the grass of the prairies dies and cures, and the cattle and horses prefer it and keep fat upon it; but in cold, windy, wet weather they resort to the timber land to get cane, wild rye, and a winter grass." He stressed the ample water supply, both fresh and salt water. The deposits of salt on the salt plains were important. He had never seen them but had heard them described by the Indians and hunters. The Indians for hundreds of miles around came to gather salt and the Osage brought and sold bushels of it to Colonel Chouteau.

"The timber of the country is the oak, black walnut, hickory, ash, hackberry, locust, mulberry, pine, cedar, pecan, cherry, bois d'arc, and other kinds. . . . . Numerous fruits are found in the greatest abundance; they consist in a variety of fine grapes, plumbs, black haws, straw and black berries, pawpaws, persimmons, may apples, and a species of pome-granite, which is much esteemed for its flavor. Roots used as food are also abundant; and the rivers furnish an ample supply of good fish.

"The country abounds in wild game, such as the buffalo, elk, deer, antelope, bears, and furred animals; wild horses are found to the north-west in numerous herds. I have seen the face of the country covered with them as far as the eye could reach, and often I have been obliged to keep out guards to fire at and keep them from breaking in upon my camp or traveling line. The same remark is still more applicable to the buffalo."

Chouteau's trading house on the bank of the Verdigris River was

4 *Knoxville* (Tenn.) *Register*, April 13, 1831, p. 2, col. 5; p. 3 cols. 1 and 2. Rev. John Fleming located among the Creek Indians on the Verdigris River in January 1833. He thought these Indians were "idle, lounging about the greater part of the time. They have little houses and live and dress pretty much like ourselves; only they have no regular eating times through the day. A pot of hominy stands in the chimney corner and when any are hungry they go and eat. The women are learning to sew and spin on large wheels and some of them make out remarkably well."

within the Cherokee country and adjacent to that of the Creeks; he was a frequent visitor in the homes of his neighbors Roley McIntosh and other rich Creeks. "They have good log houses, many of which are double; and fields according to the means of the individual. I know some who have under fence and culture about 150 acres of land. They raise all the kinds of grains and vegetables common to that latitude; patches of cotton and tobacco and of upland rice, are common to them. Spinning wheels and looms are in use. Stocks of cattle, horses, hogs, sheep, and goats, are owned by these people. They have poultry, to-wit: chickens, turkeys, ducks, and geese. Their women ride on side saddles, and dress according to their respective means to do so in the manner and fashion of the whites; the same remark will apply to the dress of the men.

"The furniture of their houses comprises chairs, tables, beds, bed-steads, and in some instances bureaus. The table in many houses is neatly set; and a good comfortable dinner, supper or breakfast is served. Tea or coffee are in general use. They supply the garrison [Fort Gibson], their agents, and traders with poultry, butter, eggs, wild geese, and other articles that are usually brought into market at our towns. In the last year, (1830) the Creeks have raised a surplus above their needs of 50,000 bushels of corn."

But the great mass of Creek people had no money, nor, to them, much more than its equivalent—traps, guns, ammunition, clothing and food, and while they waited for that promised them by the Government, the traders A. P. Chouteau and Hugh Love on the Verdigris River provided them with the necessities they could not otherwise obtain; for these they were obliged to pledge a large part of their annuities payable to them under their treaty, and past due for several years while they waited and suffered. On March 1, 1832, Roley McIntosh, Chilly McIntosh, and fifteen other Creek chiefs and warriors of the Verdigris River settlements executed a power of attorney appointing Colonel Chouteau their attorney to secure and receipt for "guns, traps, kettles, blankets, etc., which is justly coming to us agreeable to our treaty."[5]

Finally, in December, 1834, a shipment of supplies promised them was ascending the Arkansas River when below Fort Smith the boat

5   Roley McIntosh and other Creeks to Augustus P. Chouteau, March 1, 1832, OIA.

sank. It contained articles intended for the Creeks and Quapaw Indians, including 1,000 rifles, 520 pairs of blankets, 5,652 pounds of lead, 2,230 pounds of iron, and 55 kegs of powder.[6] Some of these were recovered from the river in a damaged condition and brought up to the Creek Agency on the Verdigris River about three miles above the mouth. Among them were 305 rifles with percussion locks and 187 with flint locks; 486 bullet moulds, 445 wipers, and 443 beaver traps. Some of these were delivered to the Creeks along with a crosscut saw for each of the twelve towns, and a set of blacksmith tools including a bellows, anvil, vise, sledge, hammers, tongs, and numerous other tools.

For several years the immigrant Creeks had a wretched existence;[7] denied the necessities promised them in consideration of their removal and so vital to their existence in this wild western country, they were in addition afflicted with devastating fevers. By 1830 their numbers had grown to three thousand, but in the next three years over five hundred died from the fevers, an epidemic of influenza, and other prevailing diseases. Cholera and smallpox were epidemic at Fort Gibson and in the surrounding Indian settlements and in the winter of 1833-34 Dr. George L. Weed of the post vaccinated 790 Creek and Cherokee Indians for which the Government paid him six cents each.[8] Only one child in every four born in the new country had lived.[9]

As if this were not enough, their troubles were aggravated by contention with the Cherokee over the land they occupied, and the

6 Van Horne to Gibson, March 5, 1835, OIA "Creek Emigration."

7 When the Chickasaw explorers visited the Creeks in 1829 (Foreman, *Indians and Pioneers*, 310), they reported that "the Creeks are in a poor condition. They are continually mourning for the land of their birth. The women are in continual sorrow" (*Cherokee Phoenix*, June 10, 1829, p. 2, col. 4).

8 *Vaccination Accounts*, OIA "Creeks West" 1834.

9 *Document*, IV, 721, 722; a census of the western Creeks taken September 30, 1833, showed a total of 2,459, belonging to the following towns: "Coweta, 423; Broken Arrow, 326; Talledega, 251; Ufala, 131; Chow-woc-kolee, 95; New York, 50; Wockokoy, 117; Sandtown, 77; Koasati, 100; Hitchita, 166; Coiga, 120; Big Springs, 300; Oakela Ockney, 206; Sowocolo, 70; Hatchee Chubbee, 27." The total included twenty-six white men and two white women intermarried in the tribe, and 498 slaves belonging to the Indians (*ibid.*). And yet, while the Creeks were dying in such numbers, Secretary Eaton blandly told the delegation of Eastern Creeks then in Washington: "The country your nation possesses west of the Mississippi River you say is not healthy. This surely is not correct; all the accounts we have are opposed to your statement" (*Document*, II, 290).

fear that made them nearly desperate, that they were going to be driven from the homes and little farms they had wrested out of the forest on the Arkansas and Verdigris rivers. Many of the Creeks, sick of their treatment, ill, or nostalgic, wandered back to their old homes in Alabama.[10]

For some years the immigrant Creeks were clustered under the protection of Fort Gibson, from fear of the wild Indians. In the Creek settlement on the Verdigris and Arkansas rivers, the most populous community of immigrant Indians, they were settled so compactly for twelve or fifteen miles up those streams that their improvements adjoined;[11] and they continued so until 1834 when General Leavenworth directed the establishment of a military post at the mouth of the Cimarron River; then they felt safe in seeking out locations higher up the Arkansas River[12] where they would have more room to raise cattle and hogs.

These pioneer Creeks stood in fear of the wild Indians of the prairies and their appeal to the Government for protection was in a measure responsible for the Indian council held at Fort Gibson in September,

10 Ibid., III, 434.
11 ". . . .on the point of land formed by the junction of the Arkansas and Verdigris, extending twenty miles up the Arkansas and six up the Verdigris. . . . live 2,135. . . ." Creeks. ". . . .On the adjacent south bank of the Arkansas are 175, and on the north bank of the Verdigris, 50. The remainder (one hundred) live on the Canadian. The point between the Arkansas and Verdigris is compactly settled for twenty miles, and is a fertile and beautiful valley. . . . From 50 to 55,000 bushels of corn has been produced this season. The surplus quantity which can be spared for market is about 20,000 bushels. . . . The present current price of corn among the more extensive farmers, is seventy-five cents per bushel. The poorer class are every day selling considerable quantities of corn which they carry on their backs and sell to the traders for fifty cents in goods" (Van Horne to Gibson, October 7, 1834, Report of commissioner of Indian affairs for 1834, p. 256). Mr. Vaill wrote: ". . . .the country is one extended village, as thickly settled as some of the smaller parishes in New England" (Andover-Harvard Theological Library, Missionary Records, Vol. 73, No. 80).
12 In the fork of the Verdigris and Arkansas rivers the Talisi (or Tulsa) Creeks had cleared the ground of ". . . the peccan trees, the cottonwood, oaks, and hickory and a great many others, with their trailing vines; and some of these vines had trunks from four to six inches through" and established a considerable village (Augustus W. Loomis, Scenes in the Indian Country). Another village of "Talasee" is shown higher up the Arkansas River, where is now located the city of Tulsa (Map of Creek Country, Bureau of Topographical Engineers, 1850).

1834, where was laid the groundwork for treaties later made by the Government with the prairie Indians, of great importance to these and succeeding immigrants. But this did not end the troubles of the Creeks, who "made frequent and grevious complaints against the Osages for depredations committed by them, in killing their stock, stealing their horses &c, and have even threatened (as the Government does not afford them that protection which they have promised) to take satisfaction in their own way. . . . . They have also similar complaints against the Delawares who are constantly hovering round their borders, and destroying the game."[13]

Charges were renewed four months later by Chief Roley McIntosh "and several other Chiefs in a very grave manner, against the Delawares. Large hordes of them are said to be within and on the borders of the Creek country, killing and destroying the game; and destroying the cane and pastures; and at this time there are large encampments of them on the Seminole land. They have immense droves of horses pasturing on the cane, killing up all the deer, bear and turkeys; and destroying the Buffaloe that came in or near the Creek country, killing hundreds of them for their skins and tongues, stealing horses from the neighboring tribes and bringing them to the Creek country, by which means the Creeks apprehend being brought into collision with their neighbors; and they therefore claim the protection of Government from these troublesome people.

"They also have many grievous complaints against the Osages, who are continually depredating upon them by killing their Stock and hogs; and stealing horses and their property. There is now claims in this office of between nine and ten thousand dollars against the Osage for depredations of this kind. Unless protection is offered them in some way, it will hardly be possible to restrain them much longer from taking redress in their own way against these troublesome intruders."[14]

The tragic migration of the Creek Indians[15] brought more than ten thousand cold, suffering and destitute members of that tribe to Fort Gibson in December, 1836. "They had been hutted on the Military Reservation at that post when they were met in a friendly manner by the McIntosh's and on the 28th, 29th, and 30th December crossed over

13   McCabe to Armstrong, December 31, 1834, OIA "Creeks West."
14   *Ibid.*, April 5, 1835, OIA "Creeks West."
15   *Indian Removal*, *op. cit.*

the Arkansas River into their new country, near the mouth of Grand River."[16] Here they remained in camp for a time until they could organize for their next move. A few of them united with the McIntosh Creeks on the Arkansas River, but the great majority followed their trusted leader Opothleyaholo and located in the vicinity of the present Eufaula. Here they settled on the rich bottom land of the Canadian River where some of them who engaged in planting in the spring were rewarded by good crops.

On their arrival at Fort Gibson, in spite of efforts to reconcile their differences, they renewed the old bitterness over the killing of Chief William McIntosh and the selling of their lands in Alabama; and the tribe was torn by dissension, which at first threatened hostilities and for years prevented the united effort and coöperation essential to their best interest. The tribe was composed of nearly fifty towns, which were more political than geographical, divisions. The faction of Lower Creeks which had followed Chief Roley McIntosh, brother of the former chief William McIntosh, were located on the Arkansas River. The larger faction, the Upper Creeks, were combined under Opothleya-holo, though he was not the nominal chief. Upon the arrival of the emigrants in the Indian Territory in 1836 the two factions numbered nearly the same, making an aggregate of eighteen or twenty thousand. The members of the Upper Towns who located on the Canadian River soon began extending their settlements up that river as far as Little River. A few had even ventured farther west towards Camp Mason, where they would have more open grazing land and would be nearer the buffalo, though exposed to the incursions of the wild prairie Indians.

In 1837 the superintendent for the western Indians reported that the Lower Creeks living on the Verdigris and Arkansas dwelt in comfortable houses, had fine gardens and orchards, and raised forty to fifty thousand bushels of corn more than they needed for their own consumption. They furnished large quantities to the commissariat at Fort Gibson annually, and contributed greatly in supplying the late immigrants. They raised also more stock than was necessary for their own use, he said, and carried on a considerable trade with the garrison in grain, stock, vegetables, poultry, eggs, fruit, pigs, lambs, venison,

16 Batman to Harris, January 8, 1837, OIA, "Creek emigration," B 160.

ham, bear-meat and butter.[17] The numerous traders among them included two Creeks who did a flourishing business, selling eighteen or twenty thousand dollars worth of goods annually; they were also engaged in trade with the wild prairie Indians in the West. The Creeks were known as corn-growing people, and some of the principal farmers cribbed as much as five to ten thousand bushels of corn in a season.

The glowing published reports of the government agents are to be accepted with reservations, for they are often at variance with other accounts that for obvious reasons never found their way into print. However, the Lower Creeks, those on the Arkansas River, were, in fact, adjusting themselves to their new environment with measurable success. The next year reports were circulated that the Creeks had done no planting and that there was much discontent among them. This situation did exist among the Upper Creeks on the Canadian for the best of reasons. Driven from their homes without any preparation, and obliged to abandon their personal property, they found themselves in a strange country suffering from poverty and a want of provisions; they had no tools with which to till the soil and they could raise no crops the year after their arrival. Though they were without funds to purchase ammunition they were forced to go on hunting trips to procure deer skins and furs to clothe themselves and their families and food to keep from starving. These Creeks particularly bitter at the whites who had robbed them in Alabama, were the most destitute in their new homes; helpless to engage in farming, they were entertaining proposals to join the Texans in their warfare against the Mexicans.[18]

Governor Stokes, whose candor was always reliable, wrote in June, 1838 of these unhappy Creek people: "The circumstances under which a great portion of this Nation was lately removed to this country, has soured the minds of a great majority of the late emigrants. Very few of Opothleyohola's band are making crops for their subsistence. . . . the scenes exhibited on the Canadian River at this time, of drunkenness and riot among the Creeks are such as have rarely been exhibited in any country. There are no less than six dram shops at this time within two hundred yards of each other, where whiskey is openly and pub-

17 United States Senate *Executive Document* No. 3, Twenty-fifth Congress, second session, p. 579.

18 Stuart to Jones, June 9, 1838, OIA, "Fort Coffee."

licly sold."[19] The white vultures who had preyed on the Creeks during their removal fastened on them in their new home to add to their misery. There was much sickness among these recent emigrants and many died.[20] The homesick survivors wished to go to Texas whither they had planned to remove when confronted with the necessity of leaving their homes in the East. A drought in 1838 that destroyed their meager crops, added to the misery of all the immigrant Indians.

There was so much destitution among them that Congress appropriated an additional $150,000 to feed the Creeks, Osage, Chickasaw, Cherokee, and others. On February 1, 1839 an issue was made to 2,000 half-starved Creeks gathered at the depot on North Fork of the Canadian River, and later another to a large number nearer to Fort Gibson.[21] Issues were made later in the year to large parties of hungry Osage, Quapaw, and Seminole. Vaccination carelessly done had but little checked the smallpox then raging among the Creeks, Seminole, and Cherokee.[22]

The Lower Creeks, who were much more fortunately situated, feeling that an injustice had been done them by reports of neglect of crops, through Roley McIntosh, Fushhatche Micco and twenty-two other chiefs, caused a letter of denial to be published in the *Arkansas Gazette*. They said in early June that they had as good a prospect for a bountiful crop of corn, considering the late spring and the meager supply of farming tools, as they ever had.[23]

These Indians early began laying the foundation for herds of cattle and hogs. It was reported by the officials that the resources of the Creeks were equal to all their wants and comforts and it was thought that the superior fertility of their lands, aided by their evident tendency to industry, would in a few years place them in a condition equal to the Cherokee and Choctaw.

The emigration of the eastern Indians not only afforded opportunities for profitable employment by the emigration companies, but very materially increased the number of steamboats and the amount of

19 Stokes to Poinsett, June 5, 1838, OIA.

20 Foreman, A *Traveler in Indian Territory*, 120; letter from St. Louis, OIA, "Western Superintendency," file E 171.

21 Pew to Crawford, February 12, 1839, OIA, "Western Superintendency," file F 494.

22 McCoy to Poinsett, February 13, 1839, OIA, "Miscellaneous" file M 615.

23 *New York Observer*, July 7, 1838, p. 3, col. 5.

commerce on Arkansas River as far as the Verdigris. In the year 1836, seven of these boats were engaged in regular service to Fort Gibson and the Creek Agency on the Verdigris; and the next year there were twelve boats carrying Indians, rations, supplies and merchandise to Fort Coffee, Fort Gibson, and the Verdigris River.

The Government was under contract with the Indians to subsist them for a year after their arrival in the West until they could support themselves from their first crop in their new homes. The earlier arrivals, especially the Creeks on the Verdigris and Arkansas rivers, and the Cherokee near Fort Gibson, were raising an abundance of corn on the rich bottom land and each year had a surplus which they had been selling to the garrison at Fort Gibson, and which would have contributed measurably to the maintenance of the newcomers through 1836 and 1837. But for some reason, or lack of reason, the administration failed to consult the Indian officials of the West about the subject, and proceeded to let contracts for an enormous quantity of rations as if there were nothing whatever raised in the West; these rations were purchased at New Orleans and removed at great expense to Fort Gibson and Fort Coffee.

The nature of these shipments is shown by the ladings of three steamboats that left New Orleans for Fort Gibson in the month of May, 1837, loaded as follows: The steamboat *Privateer* with 473 barrels of pork, 596 barrels of flour, 25 sacks (or 100 bushels) of salt, and 35 casks (37,111 pounds) of bacon. The steamboat *Caspian* with 700 barrels of pork, and 450 barrels of flour; the steamboat *Cocchuma* with 25 casks (13,750 pounds) of bacon, 341 barrels of flour, and 392 barrels of pork.[24] One boatload followed another, and they had not all reached their destination when it was discovered that somebody had made a monumental blunder; that the supply purchased by the Government greatly exceeded the possible demand, and in addition there was promise of bountiful crops on the farms of the resident Indians.

The provisions were being piled up on the banks of the river at Fort Coffee and Fort Gibson, and hasty efforts were made to care for them—no adequate consideration, apparently, having been given to the matter before their arrival. Lieut. Jefferson Van Horne was sent to Fort Coffee to erect sheds to contain 1,000,000 rations, and Capt.

24   Lieut. John B. Grayson to commissioner of Indian affairs, May 25, 1837, OIA.

James R. Stephenson went to Fort Gibson to construct as quickly as possible a number of sheds to house twice that amount. On the bank of the river at Fort Gibson, four of these sheds each more than 200 feet long, were erected; labor and lumber were difficult to obtain, and it required weeks to complete them. The casks stood in the hot sun, and what with the heat and rough handling the hoops dropped off, the brine ran out and the meat began to spoil.[25] On June 16 there were piled up at this post on the bank of the Grand River in the hot sun 881 barrels of pork, 2136 barrels of flour, 207 hogshead of bacon of 700 pounds each, and 200 sacks of salt, with large quantities yet to arrive.[26] They turned desperately to the chance of reshipping these supplies to New Orleans to salvage those that were not spoiled; but the water in the Arkansas River had fallen so low that no steamboats were available to carry any of the stores down the river; and the government officials were forced to turn for relief to traders, contractors and others who were prepared to supply the immigrant Indians.

Much of this immense quantity of damaged provisions was sold to the firm of Harrison, Glasgow and Company, contractors for rationing the Indians and it thereby entered into the scandal that involved the care of these helpless people along with the prodigal and defenseless purchase of supplies at New Orleans and Cincinnati out of their money.

A ration for the Indians—food for one person for one day—consisted of three articles: meat, bread, and salt. The meat was either three-quarters of a pound of salt pork, or a pound of fresh beef; the bread ration was a pound of wheat flour or three-quarters of a quart of corn; salt was furnished at the rate of four quarts to every 100 rations. There was much complaint on the part of the Indians of the quantity and quality of the rations issued to them. A. J. Raines who had been employed by the contractors Harrison and Glasgow and afterwards discharged, wrote to the war department and members of Congress as early as 1837 making specific charges of the grossest frauds and impositions on the Indians. The authorities in Washington were disinclined to credit these charges and little attention was paid

25 Capt. R. D. C. Collins to Commissioner Harris May 31, and July 27, 1837, OIA; Stephenson to Collins, August 9, 1837, ibid.
26 Joel Crittenden to Harris June 16, 1837, OIA.

to Raines's letters nor was anything done to remedy the conditions exposed by them. Raines was finally silenced by the payment to him of the sum of $13,500 and he left Fort Smith with a large trading expedition bound for Mexico. Similar charges and complaints in connections with the rationing of the Chickasaw, Seminole, and Cherokee immigrants were lodged in Washington, and finally the matter became so notorious that in September, 1841 Maj. Ethan Allen Hitchcock was commissioned to proceed to the Indian Territory and make an investigation of the whole field covered by the charges since the arrival of the Creeks in the West.

Major Hitchcock interviewed many of the most intelligent Creek citizens who related incidents disclosing the truth of all the charges that had been made.[27] Capt. James R. Stephenson of the Seventh Infantry supervised the issuing of rations until April, 1837 and there was little complaint. At that time however the contractors Harrison and Glasgow took over this function and the complaints began. A few examples illustrate the whole field of villainy practiced by the heartless contractors on helpless Indians.

The fraud consisted mainly in the use of a false measure in the issue of corn so that the Indians received only about three pecks for a bushel; and in the issue of cattle on the hoof the usually ignorant and helpless Indians were obliged to take an animal at forty to fifty per cent more than its true weight. Benjamin Marshall, an intelligent Creek Indian whom Hitchcock regarded highly, said that he was asked by some of the ignorant Indians to go to Sodom a place of issue near his home and protect them in their rights. Samuel Mackey, a white man living on the Illinois River with his Cherokee family, represented the contractors locally. The issuing agent at the place was a man named Kirk and later Eli Jacobs, both white men. Marshall who had dealt extensively in cattle and was a judge of their weight said that Kirk was gambling in a house about 200 yards from the cattle pen; at least he was playing cards and Marshall saw money on the table. When the Indians came for cattle he would interrupt his game long enough to write an order to the contractor to issue a certain number of rations to them. The Indians would then go to the pen and present the order to the contractor who would turn out as many and such cattle as he chose to comply with the

27 Hitchcock *Report*, U. S. House *Executive Document* No. 219, Twenty-seventh Congress, third session.

order. Their weight, Marshall said, was greatly overestimated; an animal which would not weigh more than 350 pounds was issued to the Indians and credited to the contractors as from 500 to 550 pounds. When he saw this done repeatedly Marshall reported it to Captain Stephenson at Fort Gibson who resented Marshall's interference and they had some hot words. Chief Roley McIntosh, Alexander Berryhill and other reputable and intelligent Indians killed cattle that had been issued to the immigrants at 600 pounds and found that they weighed only a trifle over 400. And when informed of the fact the contractor refused to make good the difference. This form of fraud was many times related to Major Hitchcock.

The other most common method was the issuing of corn in the husk measured in a barrel for two bushels when it was contended that it would not shell out more than a bushel and a half. Another measure used was a square box for a half bushel which when tested lacked several pints of holding a half bushel of shelled corn. Seaborn Hill told of seeing a wagonload of corn in the shuck thrown on the ground for the Indians and delivered to them at forty bushels. He said the bed could not have held more than twenty-five bushels of shucked corn and with the shucks on it was much less. Hill said this was part of 5,000 bushels of corn he had sold to Gov. James Conway of Arkansas who was a partner of the contractors Harrison and Glasgow.

Samuel Smith related that in February 1838 an issue of corn was made at Sodom to a company of Seminole Indians under Nocose Yohola. It had been in a keel boat stranded on a sand bar where for two months through the winter it had been rained and snowed upon so that it was fit only for hogs. The agent wished to issue it at the rate of a bushel and three pecks a barrel, but Smith told him the Indians were doing him a favor to take it at all. Some of it was so rotten the husks were falling off.

J. L. Alexander, a white man, came west with Opothleyaholo's company of Creeks of whom 2,321 survivors of the 2,700 who left Alabama arrived at Fort Gibson December 7, 1836. He was employed by Captain Stephenson as issuing agent, but he was discharged on the complaint of the contractors that he was issuing excessive amounts to the Indians. The contractors had given him half a dozen square boxes in which to measure the corn; but when tested Alexander found that they did not hold half a bushel and by authority of Stephenson he substituted a regular half bushel measure. Raines, who was then in the employ of the contractors, made the charge and Alexander went to see him. Raines too was playing cards. It seemed that everybody played cards and gambled where there were so many rations being issued and so much money about. Raines left the card table and went to the door to speak to Alexander whom he accused of issuing 1,200 bushels too much corn to the Creeks. After his discharge the contractors held out that amount to make up for what they claimed to have lost. Alexander was then employed by the Creeks as clerk to protect their interests. At a certain issue of cattle he had them killed and weighed and found them 7,000 pounds under the weight for which the Indians were charged. By order of the chiefs he wrote to Captain Stephenson informing him of the facts but the Captain never replied. On one occasion when Alexander was working for the contractors, Harrison told him that he had some corn for the Indians at Webbers Falls about thirty-five miles from the place of issue on the Canadian River; and he said that if the Indians would transport it from the boat landing he would pay them "three bits" (37 1-2 cents) a bushel. The Indians having been without corn for a long time, many of them accepted the offer; some went on ponies, and some even went on foot and packed the corn on their backs the full thirty-five miles. For they were desperately poor, their families were hungry, and most of their ponies had died on the long march from Alabama.

Artus Fixico, a Creek chief at the head of a company of seventy-eight persons, said that his party was given an issue of five barrels, four of which contained sour flour and one was filled with lime. The provisions issued to them were so scant and so bad that as soon as the roasting ears came in the Indians lived on them until autumn when the new corn was available for crushing. The contractors then paid them seventy-five cents in satisfaction of their claim for food for the remainder of the year. At times there was complaint of complete failure to issue the rations to which the Indians were entitled and many of them were on the point of starvation. On other occasions the Indians were compelled to return home empty handed and visit the place of issue more than once before they could secure their rations. Cowed and discouraged they were then induced for a grossly inadequate consideration to sell to the contractor their claim for food.

There were several reports of barrels of lime being included with barrels of flour issued to the Indians. Instances were related where Indians complained to the issuing agents of the quantity or quality of the rations, only to be cursed and told that if they did not like what they were given they could do without. One Creek who represented his and other families requested to have the cattle to which they were entitled delivered as early as possible as he had to travel a long distance and cross a river. He was rewarded by being told that he should be the last one served; it was late in the day and night overtook him before he crossed the stream, the wild cattle he was attempting to drive home escaped in the timber and underbrush, he lost every one of them and the hungry families he represented were destitute of meat for a long time.

One witness told of seeing an Indian woman picking up grains of corn where the contractor's horses had been eating. At times, on the verge of starvation, some of the Creeks "were obliged to dig for the wild potato in the prairies; a good many have died, and but for the wild potato, a great many more would have died. The want of provisions occasioned a great deal of suffering, and, in my opinion, many deaths. Very few had guns, and there was very little game about." The investigation showed that no one representing the Government or the Indians took any steps to protect their interests or witness the issue of rations to them and these ignorant people were helpless victims of the rapacious contractors.[28] Raines said that in 1837 the contractors bought up the claims of the Creek Indians for corn rations for $20,000 cash which the latter expended for whisky; that at the issuing depot

28 Glasgow and Harrison, James S. Conway and Thomas T. Turnstall of Little Rock advertised that by the name of Glasgow & Harrison they had formed a partnership to trade and furnish rations to the Creek and Seminole emigrants for twelve months from April 1, 1837, and any contracts made by any of the members would be attended to by James S. Conway of Little Rock (*Constitutional Journal* (Helena, Arkansas) February 9, 1839, p. 2, col. 5).

Confidential papers in the Hitchcock collection of manuscripts charge that a disbursing officer at Little Rock connected with the rationing of the Indians was a defaulter in the sum of $200,000; but that he was the victim of a gang of rogues who surrounded him and taking advantage of his easy-going nature induced him to loan them large sums of Government funds for speculation in schemes that would yield them enormous profits. Names of some of the men supposed to have secured this money are given; men prominently identified with the country and times. The defaulting army officer was abandoned to his fate by his associates and he died just before Hitchcock made his investigation.

at the North Fork (later North Fork Town) 400 barrels of whisky was sold to the Creeks and that in one day he had seen 2,000 drunken Creek Indians; that in many homes entire families were prostrate with sickness so that not one was able to help another; and the next June when he wrote, one half of the 16,000 Creeks were without a mouthful of provisions.[29]

29 Raines to Harris, June 4, 1838, OIA, "Western Supt'y (Emigr.)" File R 269, 289.

CHAPTER ELEVEN / *Efforts to Unite the Tribe*

ANY of the Creek Indians were thoroughly demoralized for sometime after removal. "The nation was divided into two parties, each rivaling the other in animosity and bitter hatred, excited with jealousy and discord, and requiring great exertions on the part of the government officers to prevent bloodshed and bring about an amicable understanding." Drunkenness, carousals and gambling by both sexes were common in public places; prostitution and poverty abounded and the former was so general as to cause several portions of the nation to acquire a notorious fame;[1] religion was scoffed at and efforts to introduce schools and promote education were vain. Against this background there stands out the figure of their leader, Opothleyaholo, who, immediately on their arrival in the West in 1837, urged General Arbuckle to secure a good teacher for them.

Governor Stokes, who sympathized with the Indians in their troubles, voiced their complaints in interesting letters to Washington. He said the McIntosh Creeks on the Arkansas were doing better than those on the Canadian. ". . . .Most of those who are wealthy are making good crops; but many of them have or think they have cause for dissatisfaction by some of the regulations of Government.—In a Report which I made in 1834, I stated what was a fact, that the Garrison of Fort Gibson was considered by the Creeks and Cherokees and the Osages and Delawares as their inland market, where they could readily sell their pigs, their lambs, their poultry, their eggs, their venison hams, their Bear meat, their butter, their melons and fruit.—

1 Logan to Madill, November 9, 1847, *Report* of commissioner of Indian affairs for 1837.

They were pleased with the market; and it encouraged them to raise the articles purchased by the wives of the officers and soldiers of the Garrison. Thousands of dollars worth of these articles were annually sold, and the proceeds laid out in necessaries. By a late Military order, this traffic is totally supressed. The stores at the Garrison are forbidden to buy or sell to an Indian to the amount of one cent.—If these Indians could be made sensible of the policy or necessity of these restrictions, they might be better satisfied.—They apply to me for an explanation, but I can give none. Both the Creeks and Cherokees think it hard and unfriendly that here in their own Country they are denied the benefit of a convenient market, when at the same time the people of Arkansas are coming daily with their waggon loads of all sort of marketing, and purchasing in return whatever they think proper.—If there is any good cause for these restrictions, I confess it has escaped my notice. . . . . There are many Wealthy Cherokees settled in this country; The Ridges, the Vanns, Judge Martin, the Adairs, the McDaniels, McKeys, the Coodies, the Rogers's and many others who live as the Whites do. They buy their sugar and coffee by the bag; and when they come to the Garrison to buy their groceries and table ware, and kitchen utensils, they bring their Jersey Waggons and Carry-alls, to take home their purchases. These people are displeased at not being allowed to buy what they consider necessary.—The county traders do not deal in the heavy groceries of Sugar, Coffee, Tobacco, &c and therefore by the late regulation, the most wealthy and reputable portion of Indians are cut off from necessary supplies."[2]

The Creeks were trying to increase their meager herds of stock, but they were harrassed by their neighbors, the Osage, who would raise no stock of their own; to keep from starving they even killed and ate that given them by the Government to propagate herds, besides killing large numbers of animals belonging to the Creeks and Cherokee. The condition of the Osage had become pitiable in the extreme; they knew not how to change from the life of the hunter to that of the agriculturist such as the immigrant Indians led; their annuities were exhausted, their crops had failed, their game was destroyed by the inroads of immigrant hunters, and they were in a state of starvation.[3] The condition of this tribe is well described by Governor Stokes

2 Stokes to Poinsett, June 5, 1838, OIA.
3 *New York Observer*, February 24, 1838, p. 3, col. 4.

in a communication to the secretary of war: "Osages—When you cast your eye over the map of the immensely extensive and valuable country obtained from this nation, for the accomodation of the Emigrants from East of the Mississippi and without which cession the Emigrants could not have been provided with a country, you will readily perceive that every principle of Justice and Equity demands from the Government of the United States, that this people should not be abandoned and driven to the condition of robbers and perhaps shortly annihilated. Their annuities of $8500 dolls. was never sufficient to buy a blanket for each family, after paying their outfit for hunting on the great Western Prairies, where they are compelled to go three times a year in order to procure subsistence for their families. Upwards of three fourths of their annuity will cease this year by limitation. The greater part of their nation are now actually in a starving condition,—The recent death of their Principal Chief, Clermont, will cause their turbulent warriors to go to War before winter with the Pawnees, Kioways, and other tribes of the great Prairie, with whom they have been at peace ever since our late Treaties.—In the year 1833, Maj. F. W. Armstrong who was a good man, with the aid of Genl. Arbuckle, Genl. Dodge, Col. Chouteau and myself made a good Treaty with the Osages, which would have preserved that nation from the ruin that now threatens them.—President Jackson rejected this Treaty; But in the very sentence of rejection, he says that something shall shortly be done for 'them.'—Nothing has been done."[4]

The Government since 1831 had been promising to remove the Osage and thus put a stop to their depredations, and to compensate the emigrants for their losses; but as nothing was done to redeem that promise, the Creeks, now driven almost to desperation by the starving Osage, notified General Arbuckle that they would make no more appeals to the Government, but would themselves take up arms against the Indians who had been running through their settlements, stealing and killing their stock, and Arbuckle warned the war department that the Creeks were on the point of making their threat good.[5]

At last in October, 1838, Capt. William Armstrong and Gen. Matthew Arbuckle were commissioned to hold a treaty with the Creeks

4 Stokes to Poinsett, June 5, 1838, OIA.
5 Arbuckle to Jones, April 16, 1838, AGO, OFD; idem, OIA, Western Superintendency, A 378.

to adjust claims for the great losses sustained by them in their enforced removal. The conference began in October at Fort Gibson, but adjourned from time to time until November 23, when the treaty was agreed to and signed.[6] An adjournment was then taken to January 1, 1839, to "enable the secretary to make out a copy of the accounts presented, and at which time it was expected from information received, the Osages would be in from their fall hunt."

As all the Osage chiefs did not appear at the post on the day appointed, runners were sent to notify those who were absent and the meeting was adjourned. On Sunday, January 6, a sufficient number of chiefs having arrived, the next day was appointed to hold the council. After several meetings and adjournments, the Osage treaty was agreed to and signed on January 11.[7] The principal features of the treaty were those by which they agreed to remove from the Creek and Cherokee land to their own in the present Kansas, and the agreement of the Government to pay $30,000.00 for depredations committed by them on their neighbor tribes and white people.

In the spring of 1839 General Arbuckle ordered Lieut. G. N. Bowman with his company of dragoons to Clermont's town, to demand the surrender of horses stolen from the Creeks and Cherokee and to notify the Osage that they would not be permitted to raise another crop of corn on the Verdigris River; and that they would be required to leave the country at once, except those who were down with small-pox, who were to be allowed to remain with their attendants until their recovery.[8]

Directly after the arrival of the emigrant Creeks Eneah Micco died in 1837 near Fort Gibson, but his place as chief of the Lower Creeks was filled by the competent Roley McIntosh, who had been serving

6 Kappler, op. cit., II, 388; M. Arbuckle, January 12, 1839, Journal and accounts, OIA, Western Superintendency.

7 Ibid.; Kappler, op. cit., 389. The Osage chief Belle Oiseau (Beautiful Bird) came to Fort Gibson with twenty-one of his people in December and agreed to bring in sixty chiefs and braves on January 1.

8 AGO, ORD. Western Division, Fort Gibson Letter Book, 6, p. 9. White intruders were making trouble also and on January 2, 1839 General Arbuckle ordered Lieut. L. B. Northrup with his command to a settlement on the north side of the Arkansas River called Sodom; he was to camp there and send out parties to search for white men living on the Arkansas River whom the Creeks wished removed and bring them in to the Fort (AGO, ORD. Fort Gibson Letter Book III).

as chief of his faction removed under the Treaty of 1826. Creek Agent Logan made repeated efforts to induce the chiefs of the Upper and Lower towns to meet in council, compose their differences and unite the tribe. Twice they agreed to do so and twice failed to keep their promise. But on February 17, 1839 the much desired meeting was held.[9] It was attended by 1,500 warriors, nearly 1,000 of whom represented the Upper towns and the remainder were from the Lower towns. The meeting was described as a very interesting one. After certain rites and ceremonies, the several chiefs delivered their speeches with great oratorical effect and good feeling seemed to rest on the gathering. Colonel Logan addressed the meeting and his remarks were interpreted by Gen. Chilly McIntosh. The next year the united tribe began the erection of a tribal council house where representatives of the whole tribe met annually to transact business for all the people.

"And now," reported the somewhat too optimistic Agent Logan, "the ill feelings and jealousy which existed between the two parties, the Upper and Lower towns, and which at one time threatened to terminate in bloodshed, are entirely removed, and the most sincere friendship exists among them; their old established rule and custom of each party holding their own general council, and in all cases acting independent of each other, has been done away; the whole nation at present being represented in one general council by the chiefs of the different towns, Roley McIntosh, the chief of the Lower towns or the McIntosh party, presiding as the acknowledged chief of the united towns, and the whole Creek Nation. This council meets annually, and revises and passes such laws as affect the interests of the nation at large. Before it, individuals present their claims and receive redress for grievances; its general character is that of a court of justice; its decisions are however imperative, and from it there is no appeal; the laws passed by it remain in force for a year, at which time, if they are discovered to be inefficacious, they are repealed or abolished altogether."

A drought had cut their crops by half, but the happiness and general welfare of the Nation had been greatly promoted by a law of the last general council, suppressing the sale and use of all ardent spirits in the Creek country. In spite of all the precaution and vigilance of the

9   *Arkansas Gazette*, March 27, 1839, p. 31.

military at forts Gibson and Smith whisky in large quantities was at all times introduced into the Indian country and there was not an assemblage of the Indians met for the transaction of business, but large numbers of them could be seen beastly intoxicated. So much so, that it was a difficult matter to do any business in consequence of the chiefs indulging in the use of whisky equally as much as the common Indians. "The benefits of it have already become visible; heretofore scarcely a night passed but what was heard the yells and whoops of drunken Indians—now all is quiet, and there is every probability of that bane of the Indian, whisky, being fully abolished from the use of the inhabitants of the Creek Nation."[10]

The Government had promised to furnish the Creeks four mills to grind their grain but Logan reported that only one, a horse-power mill, had been provided, and he asked that the promise to the Indians be kept. The Indians complained, too, that the government had paid them paper money that was not good, and that some of the goods issued to them was rotten. When Maj. Ethan Allen Hitchcock visited them in February, 1842, on his official tour of inspection, Opothleyaholo and other chiefs met him in council. They detailed to him many grievances growing out of their enforced removal from Alabama, and the failure of the Government to adjust their claims as promised them at the time of removal and afterward.[11]

On his return to Washington the then Colonel Hitchcock gave the following frank advice to the secretary of war, who probably added it to his store of resentment against the fearless investigator: "I have only to repeat what I have already stated in former reports, that it is extremely unfortunate that any circumstances should leave the Indians under a sense of wrong from a non-compliance on our part with promises to them. They have but little else of importance to think of than the circumstances growing out of their intercourse with us, and promises either should not be made or strictly fulfilled, for the Indians dwell upon them and cling to them with great tenacity."[12]

During the next few years after the partial reunion of the tribe, it

10 Logan to Armstrong, September 30, 1841, *Report* of commissioner of Indian affairs, 1841.
11 Maj. E. A. Hitchcock, *report*, February 3, 1842, OIA, Creek file H. 1046.
12 Hitchcock to secretary of war, May 28, 1842, May 28, 1842, *Hitchcock manuscripts*, Library of Congress. See also *A Traveler in Indian Territory*.

was reported that in spite of the bitter feeling between the Upper and Lower towns, the Creeks were adjusting themselves to their new surroundings and improving in the character of their farming, homes and ordinary comforts. Some of them owned a considerable number of slaves they had brought with them, who aided in the cultivation of extensive corn fields. They tried to kill a missionary who had been preaching abolition. The Indians were suspicious of the motives of all white people and resentful of the efforts of the missionaries to turn them from their cherished tribal customs; their busk, dancing, ball-plays, racing—these things they were told, should be abandoned, and they were afraid the missionaries would try to rob them of what was an essential part of their life. They could not understand why they should quit drinking whisky at the behest of the white people when other white people drank and got drunk and brought whisky to the Indians so that they, too, might get drunk, and the missionaries and government did not stop them. "Go teach your white men," they said, "who cheat and lie and get drunk before you come to us." Many of them felt that the presence of missionaries was a violation of the promise made them that upon their removal to the west there would be no further interference with them by white people.

However, some of them observed the benefit of schools in the Cherokee and Choctaw nations, and asked for similar opportunities. They had no constitution or code of laws as had the Cherokee and Choctaw, though their chiefs met in council and passed laws and regulations from time to time. They were regarded as far behind those tribes in education, but, on the other hand, they were the most industrious of the emigrant tribes, as well as the most warlike. Their land was fertile and the most of the corn used at Fort Gibson was furnished by them. They had 40,000 bushels of corn to sell in 1838, the only tribe that had a surplus that year. Under treaty stipulations with the Government they had been furnished blacksmiths, wheelwrights, and wagon wrights. During this period they were afflicted with an epidemic of smallpox, which swept through the Indian tribes with much loss of life, but their progress was not seriously interrupted.

By 1841 a few schools had been established and fourteen boys were being educated at the Choctaw Academy in Kentucky. There were as yet no missionaries in the tribe, though two or three natives preached occasionally. The Creeks were slowly improving the form and substance of their laws, which were well observed by the people. When Agent Logan filed his final report in June, 1842, he gave an encouraging picture of his charges. Largely through his influence the two somewhat united factions entered in a more or less tentative way upon this new era in their history with promise of improvement: "The late emigrants or what is termed the upper Creeks, although much dissatisfied for a length of time after their removal to their new homes, owing mainly to their sufferings from sickness and the great mortality that prevailed among them, are now a happy and contented people, and are much in advance of the lower Creeks (or early emigrants) in the variety, quality, and quantity of their agricultural products, as well as in the management of their farms. They have larger and better stocks of domestic animals; they are likewise much in advance of the lower Creeks in domestic or household manufactures. They make quantities of cotton cloth from the raw material, planted and cultivated upon their own farms. They have also several useful mechanics among them— such as carpenters, wheelwrights, loom makers, smiths, &c.; In short I know of no people on this continent who are more happy and contented, or who enjoy a greater plenty than these people do of all the necessaries of life; and I do not hesitate to say that the present growing crop, if it meets with no disaster until it arrives at maturity, will equal three times the amount that may be required for home consumption."[13]

The Creeks held their preëminence as growers of corn with a substantial surplus nearly every year. A number of them on the Canadian River engaged to a considerable extent in the raising of rice, a branch of agriculture they had learned in their former homes in the southern states. Of this grain they produced a surplus that for a number of years they carried to Arkansas and the Choctaw Nation, where it found a ready market.[14] They were accumulating better stocks of horses, cattle and hogs, and erecting comfortable log cabins. Owning their country in common, some of them adhered to the old custom of cultivating large tracts of land by the combined efforts of the towns, under the direction of their chiefs; though many others worked their fields separately. In 1843 Agent Dawson reported that on Canadian

13   Logan to Armstrong, June 30, 1842, *Report* of commissioner of Indian affairs for 1842.
14   *Reports* of commissioner of Indian affairs, 1843 and 1846. Well cleaned rice could be bought on the Canadian River at a low price (*ibid.*, for 1846).

River the Creeks had a field three miles wide by eight long, which was a solid mass of growing corn and was worked by a number of towns in common.[15] They raised also quantities of sweet potatoes, beans, peas, melons, and peaches, besides their cotton and rice.

The New England and New York Meetings of Friends sent John D. Lang and Samuel Taylor, Jr., on a tour of the Indian tribes in 1842. In the autumn they visited the Creeks and Benjamin Marshall told them that every family in the Nation would raise produce enough that season to supply their wants throughout the year. "They are fast improving in agriculture and domestic manufactures and in their manner of living. They expect soon to manufacture all the material for their own clothing. Many of them live in comfortable houses, and dress like white people; but others still wear the blanket, and are much given to dissipation. . . . . They have lately passed severe laws to prohibit the vending of ardent spirits among them, and those who have been opposed to the laws have seen the good effects of them and become satisfied. Many of the slaves and Indians appear sober and religious. Some of the slaves are approved preachers and hold meetings regular on first-days. We attended one of these meetings, which was conducted in a moderate and becoming manner. It was composed of Indians and slaves and their masters; their minister was an uneducated slave. All seemed interested in the meeting, and several much affected, even to tears. A slave-holder told us that he was willing his slaves should go to these meetings for it made them better men and women. The Creeks have long been slave holders, and appear insensible on the subject of this great evil. . . . . A few days previous to our arriving there, about 200 slaves ran away from their masters. They belonged in the Creek and Cherokee nations. This caused great excitement, and a posse was sent after them from both nations.[16]

Logan found that part of the Creek Nation located on the Arkansas River flooded with whisky, and the people retrograding instead of improving. Their crops, he said, consisted of corn, sweet and Irish potatoes, yams, melons, pumpkins, and squashes. And some wheat, rice, and cotton were raised. "But little spinning and weaving is done by the Lower Creeks, or those living in the vicinity of the Arkansas. This

15 Ibid , 1843.
16 Report of a Visit to some of the Tribes of Indians Located west of the Mississippi River, by John D. Lang and Samuel Taylor, Jr. (Providence, 1843).

indolent feeling is to be greatly attributed to the quantity of whisky consumed by them, and also to their dependence upon the annuity; though this is bound to exist, in a greater or less degree, among any people who have anything else to depend upon besides their own resources."

CHAPTER TWELVE / *Hostility to the Missionaries*

C APT. JAMES L. DAWSON, formerly of the United States army, displaced Logan as Creek Indian agent in June, 1842, and served until July 8, 1844, when he became involved in a difficulty with his bondsman, Seaborne Hill, a trader on the Verdigris, whom he killed with a bowie knife sup' ported by his accomplice, his brother-in-law, Dr. John R. Baylor.[1] Dawson then became a fugitive and James Logan was again appointed agent. Logan was an intelligent observer of the Indians and in his report of 1844 makes interesting comparison of his charges. The Upper Creeks, the recent immigrants of 1836-37, were in a better condition than the remainder of the tribe; for located at a distance from the settlements of the whites, and also being further removed from the neighborhood "of their speculative and more civilized neighbors, the Cherokees, makes the importation of whiskey into their country a matter of more difficulty; there is consequently less of that pernicious article to be found. They generally live in good hewn log houses; are excellent farmers; are generally more reflective and economical than their brethren of the lower towns; and their females are generally occu' pied in the domestic occupations of spinning and weaving cotton, of which article a great proportion of what they manufacture is of their own country produce, of which they make nearly sufficient to cloth them. The lands they cultivate are fresh, rich, and, from every account

1 Logan offered a reward for the apprehension of Dawson, whom he described as "about five feet ten inches high, fine looking, dark complexion, Roman nose, and in all respects a man of genteel appearance" (*The Northern Standard* (Clarksville, Texas), September 4, 1844, p. 3, col. 4).

I can obtain, will this year produce them an immense crop of every-thing they cultivate."[2]

"The Creeks differ materially from the other large tribes in many respects," said Superintendent Armstrong. "They have not mixed so much with the whites; adhere more rigorously to the customs of their ancestors; have no written laws; and are governed entirely by their chiefs—the people having nothing to do with the making or the execution of the laws."[3]

A visitor to their country the next year observed that "the Upper Creeks care not for the world, and have no idea of what is going on in it; on the contrary the Lower Creeks have a smattering of general intel-ligence, and occasionally a news paper or an old book may be found among them. . . . . The Lower Creeks are agriculturists. They raise corn and sweet potatoes. I have been told that three of their Negroes can perform as much work as one of ours. Their negroes have to sup-port themselves with clothing and food. To do this they are allowed the Saturday of every week, and after their master's crop is laid by in July, from that time to September, or harvest time. Soon as the fall comes, all the fences fall and everybody rides wherever he may please, though there are thousands of roads running in every direction. Happy people! —no taxes to pay—no law to make them pay their debts. They are not harrassed like the whites with the eternal thought of money. . . . . We think the Upper Creeks their superiors; they have not degen-erated."[4]

A few more Creek emigrants were brought west at intervals. One hundred and four came in 1846 and in February, 1847, Paddy Carr arrived with his family and eight slaves. The former included his two daughters, Ariadon and Areanne. Their father was a reader of the classics and adapted the name of Ariadne to his daughters. He did not remain in the West but returned to Alabama. Refugees who had eluded capture or were detained when the tribe was removed in 1836-37 were brought from time to time. A contractor named Moses K. Wheat was

2 Logan to Armstrong, August 20, 1844, *Report* of commissioner of Indian affairs, 1844. Detailed descriptions of the Creek people in their new home in 1841 are to be found in *A Traveler in Indian Territory; the Journal of Ethan Allen Hitch-cock*, edited by Grant Foreman.

3 *Report* of commissioner of Indian affairs, *ibid.*

4 William Quesenbury in *Arkansas Intelligencer*, August 2, 1845, p. 1, col. 3.

engaged in collecting these remnants in the winter of 1845-46 and a company sent off by him in charge of Capt. A. Scale and Leroy Driver arrived at Fort Smith in February, numbering then 150. Wheat wrote the commissioner of Indian affairs that "in Coosa and Talledega counties I collected some 57 in number and put them in charge of the wagoner to carry them to camp, and when on the journey were persuaded to abscond by persons telling them that they were to be chained and carried off and sold as slaves. Genl. Blake writes me that in a scout in Barbour, Henry, Dale, Covington and Pike counties he found considerable but mostly females" held as slaves.[5]

The condition of these Creeks held in bondage by the whites of Alabama excited the compassion of their tribesmen who were able to do but little for them. The Federal Government seemed indifferent to their condition, but an enterprising Creek named Ward Co-cha-my went to their relief. Co-cha-my collected sixty-five Creeks whom he embarked on a steamboat at Sizemore's woodyard on the Alabama River and brought by water to Fort Smith, where they arrived June 24, 1848. From there they departed in wagons to join the Creeks in their new home. The next June, forty-four more Creeks were brought west.[6] Unfortunately they had traveled through a cholera infested region and brought the disease with them. However, it was confined to Chiaha Town, thirteen of whose members died.[7]

So badly had the wholesale emigration of the Creeks and Seminole been managed that a band of Apalachicola Indians were brought west and located upon the Creek domain. The Creek chiefs reported their

5   Wheat to commissioner, January 20, 1846, OIA, Creek emigration, W 2811. In 1840 information was furnished the secretary of war on this subject. The names of a number of citizens of Irwington including a circuit judge charged with holding Creek Indians as slaves, were given (Davis to Poinsett, June 20, 1840, OIA, Creek File D 522).

6   *Report* of commissioner of Indian affairs, 1849; *Cherokee Advocate*, July 10, 1848, Ward Co-cha-my who was later to be known as Ward Coachman, was a grandson of Sophia, sister of the great Alexander McGillivray and her husband Ben Durant, a Frenchman of North Carolina. He was well educated and after the forcible emigration of his tribe, until he was 22 years of age, he remained in Alabama at the home of his uncle Lachlan Durant, when he removed to the Indian Territory. It was three years later that he returned to Alabama to rescue his people and take them west. He was an intelligent and popular man and served two years as chief of his tribe.

7   *Report* of commissioner of Indian affairs, 1849.

presence on their land and begged the Government to furnish them with food, as they were "in a deplorable situation; a good many of them are naked and have no means by which they can obtain subsistence."[8] A band of Spaniards who lived by themselves on an island off the coast of Florida were enticed to Tampa Bay by whites who wished to be rid of them. There they were mingled with the Seminole prisoners with whom they were forced aboard the boats and shipped to the western home of the Seminole Indians. On their arrival in the West the mistake was discovered and as the Indian agents had authority to feed none but Indians they were destitute and hungry and Logan called on the Government to do something for their relief.[9]

The so-called union of the tribe in 1839 was by no means an amalgamation of the factions. Throughout their history there was always a line of cleavage between them, though in time their differences yielded slowly to their common necessities. It cannot be said, however, that they actually united under one government and one set of national officers until after the adoption of their constitutional government in 1867; this was forced upon the full-blood element that predominated among the Upper Creeks, by the more enlightened Indians, in many of whom was a considerable strain of white blood.

In 1842 soon after Logan had effected between the factions the beginning of the movement that he fondly hoped was to be a union of the tribe, they were visited by Maj. Ethan Allen Hitchcock who kept a series of diaries that provide an interesting picture of the Creek

---

8 Opothleyaholo and others to Armstrong, March 13, 1840, OIA, Creek file, "Main Canadian." Opothleyaholo sympathized with other Indians in distress. In March, 1840, he reported that "the Head Chief of the Shawnees is now at my house where he has been residing ever since last winter; he starts tomorrow in the Chickasaw Nation in search of his people, where they have been since the War Broke out in Texas; he expects some time this year to bring his people to this nation for the purpose of becoming one of our people, in consequence his people having been so much scattered they have become very poor. The treaty which they made [in 1817] secured to them forever $2,000 a year which amount he says that himself and people have never received the first dollar; therefore you will please represent the case to the government and ask the favor of them to send their annuity to this country with the Creek annuity, for we will by fall become one people" (Opothleyaholo to Armstrong, March 30, 1840, OIA, *Creek File* "Tuckabatchee").

9 Logan to Armstrong, May 19, 1840, OIA.

Indians.[10] The principal chief of the Lower Creeks, he said, was Roley McIntosh, and of the Upper Creeks, Tuckabatche Micco. "In general Council the two principal chiefs preside seated by the side of each other, but Roley McIntosh takes the right and is considered the senior or head chief of the Nation. For local purposes in the Upper Creeks there are four chiefs called Counselling Chiefs one of whom is called the King, who transact the current business of the party subject to the control of the principal Chief whenever the latter thinks proper to interfere, as on important occasions.

"After these are the Chiefs of the different towns. The whole nation is divided into towns having separate names. There may be forty-five towns, each of which has a principal chief or king and a subchief. In each town there are persons called *lawyers*, from four up to forty and even forty-five, acccrding to the population, whose duty it is to execute the laws; they are subject to the views of the Head Chiefs of the Nation who send them on important missions when necessary. The Lower Creeks have two persons in authority called Light Horse, who are a sort of Sheriffs for the collection of debts with other similar duties and are paid each a salary of $150 a year.

"There is a general council of the nation once a year in the Spring. All of the Chiefs of every grade are permanently in power unless they resign or from misconduct are deposed. The mode of filling a vacancy is assimilated to an election by the people but upon recommendations made by those already in power, to which the popular vote presents scarcely an obstacle.

"The general council for business is composed of the two principal chiefs and the Kings including those of the Towns. These constitute the Aristocratic portion of the government. There is another branch composed of one or two persons elected by each town from among the lawyers with one judge from the upper and one from the lower Creeks which constitute what is called a committee. This has the appearance of a popular branch. Sometimes the number of the committee is increased on important occasions.

"A law generally originates in the Committee; if approved there, it is sent to the principal chiefs for their approval. If approved by the principal chiefs it is a law. But practically the Chiefs made the laws

10   A *Traveler in Indian Territory, op. cit.,* 109.

and unmake them. Besides the written laws there are many usages in force which are not written. Their peculiar ceremonies and customs are not written.

"The Lower Creeks have to some extent abandoned their old customs, but the Upper Creeks who are less advanced in civilization, have retained most of their ancient ceremonies and customs."[11] Colonel Hitchcock learned that during the first twelve months after the arrival of the emigrant Creeks in 1836 more than 3,500 of them died, exceeding one-fourth of the entire population. One will look in vain through the published official records to find any estimate or mention even of that appalling catastrophe to these helpless people.

The Creeks were regarded as the most powerful tribe on the frontier. Many of them having been engaged in war with the United States and thousands of them forcibly removed from their homes east of the Mississippi, it was natural to expect a spirit of hostility against the Government, but these feelings were subsiding under the influence of Roley McIntosh, a man of undoubted attachment to the Government. The Creeks were becoming interested in the subject of education, but they decided that it was a waste of money to send ten or twelve of their youths to the Choctaw Academy in Kentucky; these young men returning after an absence of several years found themselves in a strange environment, isolated without companions or associates possessing the same advantages they had. Unable to adapt themselves to their surroundings, finding that their education was of no advantage in securing employment, they relaxed into "idle and dissolute habits and too often became a nuisance and curse to the nation."[12] The Creeks said that not one of their young men, educated at the Choctaw Academy had ever done any good after returning to the nation. It required an effort to convince many of the Creeks that education was not to blame for this condition. But to overcome the prejudice, the sending of their youths to the Choctaw Academy was discontinued; efforts were made to set up local schools instead.

After their expulsion from the Creek Nation in the autumn of 1836, there were no missionaries of any denomination for about five years except two or three illiterate preachers. "The darkness of heathenism brooded over the whole land. The wild whoop of the ball players and

11 *Ibid.*
12 *Report* of commissioner of Indian affairs, 1842.

the savage yells of the stomp dance were heard in all parts of the Nation. A fierce prosecution also was waged in some parts of the Nation against the few praying Indians who still clung to the Gospel, some of whom were whipped most unmercifully for attending religious meetings."[13]

Upon his appointment for the purpose by the Presbyterian Board of Foreign Missions, Rev. Robert M. Loughridge departed from Eutaw, Alabama, November 2, 1842, and traveled horseback 600 miles to the Creek Nation. After some delay the Creek council met to consider his application for leave to establish among them a mission school and to preach to them. Chief Roley McIntosh "as spokesman for all said: 'We want a school, but we don't want any preaching; for we find that preaching breaks up all our old customs—our feasts, ball plays and dances—which we want to keep up'." To which course Mr. Loughridge would not lend himself. Finally a compromise was reached by which it was agreed that if Mr. Loughridge would conduct a school for Creek children he might preach in his school but no where else. Encouraged by Benjamin Marshall that these restrictions might be relaxed as the people became better acquainted with his work, Mr. Loughridge signed a contract, mounted his horse and returned to Alabama to make his final preparations. On December 6, 1842, he was married to Miss Olivia D. Hills of New York, who was teaching school near Selma, Alabama, and soon afterward they set out by steamboat down the Alabama River to Mobile; thence to New Orleans and up the Mississippi and Arkansas rivers they proceeded and arrived at the Verdigris landing February 5, 1843.

"Although the old chief at first had manifested some fears of our religious influence interfearing with their old customs, yet he gave us a cordial welcome, and requested me to locate the mission in his town. This I did and called the station Kowetah, after the name of his town. It was situated about 25 miles northwest of Fort Gibson, and one and one-half miles east of the Arkansas River. There was on the place selected a vacant Indian cabin, 12 x 24 feet, with a dirt floor and covered with clap-boards; connected with it was a small unfenced field and a few fruit trees. For the whole premises I paid the owner ten dollars.

13 *History of Mission Work among the Creek Indians* from 1832 to 1888 under the direction of the Board of Foreign Missions of the Presbyterian Church in the U. S. A. by Rev. Robert M. Loughridge (unpublished manuscript).

As plank could not be had only by hauling a great distance, I had some hired men split out 'puncheons' and floor the house. In this little cabin we lived happily for more than a year, and in this our first child was born.

"As by agreement I could only preach at the Mission Station, my first object was to build a log house to answer the double purpose of a school and a church. As soon therefore as it was ready for use, my wife, June 23, 1843, commenced teaching a school of fifteen or twenty children, and the neighbors were invited to attend preaching there every Sabbath. A few persons only would attend. The outlook was altogether discouraging. The Indians around were friendly, but very shy and irregular in their attendance at the mission; while the most of them were devotedly attached to their old customs and superstitions." Mrs. Loughridge taught the school three months when the sickly season and inadequacy of the building caused it to be closed.[14]

Rev. Edmund McKinney and family arrived July 4 to assist in the mission work, and a cabin was built for them; but after a few months he departed for Spencer Academy in the Choctaw Nation. During the next autumn and winter Loughbridge erected a large log house one-story-and-a-half high, with seven rooms, hewed inside and out. Being thus prepared, May 13, 1844, they received eight boys and ten girls and inaugurated the boarding school. The school continued for four months, when the prevailing sickness closed it for a month. It was then reopened and continued until the next July.[15] Mr. Loughridge gradually overcame the prejudice of the Indians, who came in larger numbers to hear him preach. Their second child was born September 5, 1845, but they were unable to secure the attendance of the nearest physician who lived at Fort Gibson. Twelve days later at the age of twenty-nine, Mrs. Loughridge died of puerperal fever. "On the hillside, near the Mission, under a large bending oak, we deposited the precious remains of my dear Olivia; there with many others." To relieve the condition of the bereaved family Miss Nancy Thompson, "an aged missionary lady among the Cherokees," came and took charge of the motherless children and the household.[16]

14 Loughridge to Logan, September 8, 1845, OIA A 1911. December 4, 1846.
15 Loughridge to Logan, ibid.
16 Miss Thompson is celebrated in the annals of all the Creek and Cherokee Indians who had any contact with the Presbyterian schools prior to the Civil War.

In 1846 Rev. Mr. Loughridge reported that the people were anxious to have their children educated and that they could not accommodate all who applied for admittance to their mission school. Rev. W. D. Collins and Rev. Thomas Bertholf, Methodist missionaries, came to the Creek Nation in the fall of 1842 and organized a church in December. After holding several camp meetings they called a quarterly conference, where the Creeks, Peter Harrison, Cornelius Perryman, and Samuel Checote, were licensed as local preachers. In 1845 they had in the Methodist organization three local preachers, 16 exhorters, and 375 church members. However, they were obliged to contend with the opposition of some of the chiefs, who feared the Christian religion would destroy their influence. Some of the Indians were "driven from home! tied up and whipt, like slaves!! for no other reason than that they worship God."[17]

A small neighborhood school was started at Little River Tallassee Town September 6, 1845 by a Methodist missionary named James Essex. A small school had previously been conducted there by a Swiss who did not speak good English and therefore taught the Indian children an incorrect pronunciation which Mr. Essex had some difficulty in correcting. He had some opposition: "The persecuting Creeks have opposed their people in attending the preaching of the gospel; and from good authority I have been informed they have threatened that if they attended my meetings they should have 50 lashes upon their bare backs; and for the second offense, especially if they became religious, they should have 50 lashes and one ear cut off; and in fact some of them have talked about cutting my ears off."[18]

She was known far and wide for her acts of charity and devotion to those in need. She died in 1881 at the age of ninety-one at Tullahassee Mission, and was buried in the mission cemetery at Park Hill (authority of Mrs. N. B. Moore). Mr. Loughridge later married Mary Avery of Conway, Massachusetts, who came in 1840 to Park Hill where she taught four years, after which she was obliged by ill health to return to her eastern home. On her marriage she came to the Creek Nation; died at Tullahassee Mission in January, 1850. In 1843 the Creek council passed a law prohibiting Indians and Negroes from attending services where there was preaching (Judge to Crawford, October 22, 1843, OIA, Seminole File J 1173).

17 Collins to Logan, September 18, 1845 (with Logan's report) OIA, A 1911, "Creek Agency."

18 Essex to Logan, September 26, 1845, ibid.

CHAPTER THIRTEEN / *Progress Notes*

OST of the Creek emigrants settled on the rich bottom lands of the rivers and creeks, as there was a general belief that the prairies would not sustain human life. They cleared the timber, built homes and fenced their little fields with the walnut rails split out by them. A few years later they realized the hazards of their locations when they were overwhelmed with disaster. "The extraordinary floods of June last," said their agent, James Logan, in 1845, "in the different water courses of the Nation, particularly the Verdigris River, were marked with effects extremely and peculiarly destructive; many had the misfortune to lose their entire crops, with their fences, houses, and furniture, and large portions of their stock. So rapid was the rise of the water, that many who lived on the banks of the streams, had barely time to escape with their lives, from the devouring elements, leaving their *all* to be washed away, by the overpowering and rapidly accumulating flood, never again to see a vestige of it. An idea can be formed of the wonderfully rapid accumulation of the waters, from the fact that a portion of the Agency farm, distance 200 yards from the bank of the Arkansas[1] and equal to an altitude of 60 perpendicular feet, from the low water mark, was submerged after a duration of 12

1 The Creek agency at this time was on the north bank of the Arkansas River nearly due north of where is now Muskogee. The location and improvements were rented of Chilly McIntosh in 1833 and the next year were purchased by the Government, including about eighty acres of cleared land. The buildings were erected in 1827, a log cabin by Chilly McIntosh and one by the troops from Fort Gibson under orders of General Arbuckle. When Dawson became agent the buildings consisted of a double log cabin with two small rooms in the rear and kitchen, outhouse and crib. One of the rooms he used for his office; but he complained that the buildings were in

hours *only*, from the commencement of the rise, and even this was not equal to that of the Verdigris."[2]

There had been another extraordinary flood the year before which was long remembered by the Creek people, but it came early enough in the year that those who exerted themselves to the utmost were able to replant and raise crops of corn and the destitution that was anticipated did not result. "But this year the flood came at so late a period as to preclude the possibility of anything being expected from replanting; which added to the excessive drought of the summer throughout the Nation, will I am afraid in many instances create much want and suffering. . . . . From the low grounds that were overflowed, arises a noxious effluvia from the deposit left by the waters which greatly affects the health of the people living in their vicinity. The usual complaint of Billious and Intermittent Fevers greatly prevail, and more generally abound. This year they are remarked as being more fatal in their attacks. Much sickness still exists in every part of the Nation, although the season has arrived when it generally subsides, and many deaths are still occurring."

Logan continues his interesting description: "The governmental system of the Nation as it at present exists is one far from being calcu-lated to encourage the people in their desire for improvement or to bring about those results which it is the aim of the Govt to accomplish.

---

a bad state of repair (J. L. Dawson to Armstrong, July 5, 1843, OIA "I. T. Misc.") The first Creek agency was located on the east bank of the Verdigris River, about four miles above the mouth, in buildings purchased in 1827 from Col. A. P. Chouteau. In 1845 Logan strongly urged the removal of the agency to a more healthful location. The matter was agitated constantly by the Indians living on the Canadian River who objected to the long journey and dangerous crossing of the Arkansas River to reach the agency. They proposed that it be located at their new capitol "Ohiahulway" where they hoped to establish an important place as the Cherokee had made of Tahlequah. March 30, 1851 the "Chief and Head Men of the Creek Nation in Council assembled, in behalf of said Nation for and in consideration of the relinquishment by the United States of the Old Agency reservation" relinquished to the United States "two sections of land beginning at a certain post or stake, upon the southern bank of the Arkansas River, near what is known as the Hitchetee Ford, from thence running south two miles, from there west one mile, from there north two miles, from there east to the place of beginning" (OIA "Creek" R 58). On this tract of land was located the Indian agency near Fern Mountain until it was moved to Muskogee about 1876 and united with what was then called the Union Agency.

2   Logan to Armstrong, September 20, 1845, OIA 1911 "Creek Agency."

The nation is divided into two parties designated as the Upper Towns and the Lower Towns or McIntosh party. This division according to their traditions, has always existed; indeed it is stated that they have only been known to each other but little upwards of a century, and their first meeting upon the banks of the Chattahooche was in an hostile attitude, each deeming the other to be a belligerant and a separate and distinct Nation, and only upon the eve of battle did they discover their affinity of language, which tho' essentially the same has some peculiarities possessed by the one, different from the other. Scattered promiscuously among both parties are the remnants of the different Tribes subjugated by them, which consist of the following, towit, viz: Hitchatees, Uchees, Alabamas, Cawawsawdas, and Natchees. Of the last mentioned interesting Tribe but few remain; they still however as well as the rest retain their original tongue. There are many others, but they are now entirely extinct, and even their names are forgotten. The members of these tribes possess all the privileges and immunities of Creek citizens.

"Each party has its own Head Chief &c. &c. Roly McIntosh the Chief of the Lower Towns, is also vested with the dignity of Head Chief of the Nation which generally convenes once a year, but at no particular period. The deliberations are confined to subjects exclusively national and which affect both parties in common. Those subjects having reference to their own party concerns meet the action of their own councils which are held separate and distinct and in which neither interferes with the other. They are conducted precisely similarly and are composed of the Chiefs and Law Makers of the different Towns (or more appropriately clans) adhering to each party.

"These Chiefs are generally Selected from the oldest Citizens; in point of intelligence they cannot compare with private individuals, who generally do not desire such dignities; generally speaking they are extremely ignorant, are noted for their superstitious bigotry, for their old customs and ceremonies, and most bitter prejudices against all measures calculated to reform the condition or enlighten the minds of their people. There are however a few honorable exceptions but they are far in the minority and their councils have but little weight. They are opposed to religion, and to Education, more particularly the former, conceiving very justly that it has a tendency to lessen their authority and to abolish their old rites & Ceremonies, of which they are particularly tenacious. They have gone so far this year as to exact a fine of from two Dollars to three and a half Dollars per head upon all non-attendants at the 'Busk," green corn dances, &c, or who do not drink the Physic, a most nauseous compound of poisonous weeds. Their authority is often exerted arbitrarily, and their laws are unjust and unnecessarily severe. It is a standing law of the Nation 'if any person preach or hold religious meetings, whether white or red, he shall for the first offense receive Fifty lashes on his bare back, and for the second offense, one hundred lashes.' To maintain their authority they support out of the annuity an enormous number of subordinates, known as Law Makers, light horse, &c. &c. The people stand in much awe of them, and blindly pay them the obedience they exact. They have no voice in their appointment nor in their acts; when a vancancy occurs the place is filled, not by an election but by the nomination made by some noted chief.

"The two parties are about equally divided; the annuity amounting to $34,500 is paid to the principal chiefs of both and equally divided between them and by them distributed. . . . . The Chiefs appropriate the whole of this large amount to the pay of themselves and their subordinates. This mode of distributing it is much complained of by the intelligent portion of the Community who are now far from being inconsiderable, and the right thus arrogated by the Chiefs of doing what they please with the Annuities much questioned; but they are vested with so much power and have inspired so much awe and fear in the minds of the people generally that they are restrained from making a public expression upon the subject. Indeed I question very much whether there could be found many who would before them say that they object to their acts in any particuler. This I have sought for in regard to the Annuity and have failed to accomplish owing to the preponderance of the Chiefs, Law Makers &c, and to the cause above stated.

"The Lower Towns from their close proximity and greater intercourse with the Whites exhibit a much greater advance in civilization and manners than their Brethren of the Upper Towns.[3] The old custom of settling together compactly and cultivating the Town fields in common had been altogether abandoned and they are no longer visible in

3 When the Creeks lived in Alabama and Georgia those who resided in the southern part of their nation nearest the Gulf and the white settlements were known as the Lower Creeks and the remainder of the tribe farther inland as the Upper Creeks.

this portion of the Nation. The people are settled promiscuously throughout the country. Many of their farms and residences would do credit to the States. Ornaments, silver plates, ear rings, beads, and paint are grown into disuse and seldom or never seen except at their festivals or Ball plays. The dress of the Whites is becoming common with the exception of the Hunting shirt, which is generally of gay printed calico and may be conceived quite picturesque; it is tenaciously adhered to and is common to all Indians. Hats, Vests, Pantaloons, and shoes may almost be said to be the common habiliments of the Males; and dresses of the richest materials, of silks, Muslins, made too in accordance with the latest fashion, are often to be seen upon the persons of the female classes. Gold and silver watches, rich and costly articles of Jewelry, viz., Chains, rings, brooches, &c, &c, are also used by the rich.

"The English language tho' not generally spoken is understood by many, and a strong desire is manifested by the community at large to throw off all their old superstitious ways and customs and to adopt the ways of the whites; on the other hand however it can be said that the number of the indigent and needy is much greater here in this part of the Nation. The use of Whiskey too is more general and the effects more visible. . . . . . There is no Town, not even a village to be met with, yet the people are every year summoned to their great dissatis-faction to assist in building or repairing the Town council houses & in many instances to leave their crops and go a distance of 20 or 30 miles; this service is enforced too under a penalty of a pecuniary fine. The settlements of the Lower Towns extend from the Verdigris River on it and between it and the Arkansas on both banks of it to the Red Fork, a distance of about 80 miles and an average breadth of Fifty. They are separated from the settlements of the Upper Towns by an uninterrupted Prairie extending from the bottoms of the Arkansas south to those of the North Fork of the Canadian, a distance of about Forty miles."

The Upper Towns extended westward "between and on the Deep Fork, North Fork, and Main Canadian, to Little River, a distance of about 80 miles and an average breadth of about sixty. From their pecu-liar location they have less intercourse with the whites and conse-quently do not exhibit so much improvement. Their dress too is more of the aboriginal form; they are forbidden to adopt that of the Whites under penalty of lashes.[4] They are however generally more enterprising and industrious. They grow cotton and practice the domestic arts of Spinning and weaving to a greater extent than the others. Cases of extreme poverty are more rarely to be met with. The chiefs are more generous and their policy more liberal than those of the Lower Towns. In addition to the two Blacksmith Shops furnished them by Treaty stipulations they have a public shop which is supported out of their portion of the annuity; they have also devoted a portion of it to the erection of a Water Mill and the support of a Millwright; they have also a Wheelwright but he is supported by the Govt. They have not so much wealth as the Lower Town Chiefs, generally speaking. The McIntosh family are supposed to be worth $150,000 and B. Marshall some $50,000; yet they contribute nothing towards alleviating the distress of the poor, or to effecting any improvement in their country. However it is reported that Opothleyahola is by far the richest man in the whole Nation."

Repeated incursions were made on the lands of the Creeks, said Superintendent Armstrong, "Chiefly by Pawnees from the Platte—it is supposed for horse stealing purposes. These parties were in every instance driven back, generally with loss; several of their number were killed by the Creeks and the neighboring bands of Kickapoos and Quapaws. Although the settlers incurred but little real danger, great alarm was felt even as far down as the mouth of the Verdigris. Application was made to the officers commanding at Fort Gibson and Washita for asssistance, and parties were detached for their relief. The establishment of a garrison at Chouteau's trading house, an abandoned post 50 or 60 miles beyond the mouth of Little River was talked of; a measure clearly unnecessary, as sufficient protection will always be afforded to the frontier settlements by the various hunting parties of Shawnees, Delawares, Kickapoos, Miamies, Quapaws, and Caddoes.

"It is estimated that these various bands together muster among them a thousand fighting men, who form at once the barrier and the only channel of communication between the border tribes and the Coman-

4 The Upper Creeks held on to their ancestral homes in Alabama with greater tenacity than the other faction of the tribe; consequently they suffered more from the rapacity and cruelty of whites. They arrived in their western home with such bitterness in their hearts and hatred for the whites that for years they refused to conform to their ways and dress, especially in the matter of wearing trousers.

ches and other wild Indians south of the Arkansas. Through them the Creeks have made efforts to induce these tribes to meet them in council, hitherto without success. It was expected that an invitation sent during the summer to hold a general council at the Salt Plains would be accepted. There can be no doubt that the extension of the settlements and consequent destruction and scarcity of game have created a hostile feeling which it is desirable to remove. The Creeks have at considerable expense, taken great pains to conciliate the prairie tribes, and in my opinion their efforts should be encouraged and assisted by the government."[5]

Logan gives a long account of the difficulties of the Creeks with the roving prairie Indians and of the council held by them in 1845 in an effort to compose these differences.[6] Of the character of the Creeks, Logan says they "are grave and serious in their deportment and are dignified and imposing in their Councils; they are slow in the expression of their feelings, but are sure in the resentment of insult and affront. Tho' friendly to the White Man, yet they are easily influenced and prejudiced against him and are rather credulous than otherwise; when once an enemy, they are seldom afterwards a friend.

"Very little game now remains within the limits of the Nation or within 100 miles of it; their means of support therefore are drawn from the cultivation of the Soil. The Creeks have however been long noted as an agricultural people. The productions were principally Corn, oats, Wheat, Rice, Cotton & Tobacco, with every variety of esculent roots and vegetables. Orchards of Peach trees abound; apples, Pears, Plums & Cherries are also cultivated. The country is admirably adapted to the raising of Stock; it consists generally of Horses, Hogs, Cattle, & Sheep; domestic Fowls, Turkeys, Geese & Ducks abound in profusion. Weaving, Spinning, Sewing & Knitting too are practiced by the females who display both ingenuity and Industry."

Colonel Logan found that religion and education were beginning to arouse interest in some quarters where the Creeks solicited teachers and preachers. The expulsion of missionaries from their country some

5 *Report* of William Armstrong, September 30, 1845: *Arkansas Intelligencer*, February 7, 1846, p. 1. For an account of these border tribes see Grant Foreman, *Advancing the Frontier*.

6 Logan to Armstrong, October 1, 1846, OIA, "Creek Agency": *report* of commissioner of Indian affairs, 1846.

Opothleyohola, the great Creek leader. From McKenney and Hall,
History of the Indian Tribes of North America, 1838.

Tullahassee Mission

years before was due in part to some of the chiefs who were becoming jealous of their influence; they feared "that their own authority would be lessened, their old rites & ceremonies neglected and abandoned, and that veneration and obedience to which they had long been accustomed would no more be paid them." The cause of temperance too, he said, was gaining ground. He hoped that more of the funds of the tribe could be used for educational purposes and a school erected on the plan and extent of "that pride of the Indian country, The Spencer Academy," in the Choctaw Nation. In the Creek Nation was a school at Spring Hill and the Presbyterian Mission at Coweta, besides the little Essex school. Four other school houses had just been completed in the Indian settlements.

From a stupid misconception of the condition of these Indians the issue to the Creeks included large quantities of strouding, small blankets, squaw axes, pipes, beads, and such articles used by the wild Indians. The Creeks objected to these and requested that articles adapted to the use of civilized Indians be furnished them, such as large sized white and colored blankets, bleached and unbleached domestic, blue and assorted calicoes of gay and fancy colors, colored domestics, striped and plaid domestics, checks, bed ticking, a small quantity of which should be ready-made clothing, consisting of pants and vests for winter wear, men's and women's shoes, tin ware, brass kettles, pins, needles, coarse pant stuff of woolen and cotton and a small quantity of strouding.

Logan found twenty-seven white men in the tribe married to Creek women. The principal trading establishment was located near the agency in the Creek settlement on the north side of the Arkansas River and was owned by Napoleon B. Hawkins, an intelligent, educated and wealthy native, who kept an ample stock of goods similar to the stocks found in white settlements. Later the store was conducted in the name of his mother, Jane, the daughter of Chief William McIntosh, who was executed by his tribesmen in 1825 for signing the Creek treaty; she was the widow of Sam Hawkins, who was killed at the same time. "The Indians generally speaking have each sufficient stock for the support of themselves and families. I think the proportion of those who have not a cow, poney, and a little bunch of hogs is very small. Very little money ever comes into the hands of the common Indian. What little they do obtain is generally earned by labor done for the richer classes, and by the sale of Fruit and garden vegetables

&c, &c, to the Traders and Whites. The sale of Pecan nuts, the trees bearing which abound in the rich bottom of the water courses, is of considerable importance to this class. It is estimated that the quantity sold to the different Traders during the last fall and winter amounted to between 9 and 10,000 Bushels, the price paid for which, was from 50c to $1. per bushel, and was generally bartered for necessary articles of Clothing, Sugar, Coffee, Salt, &c, besides a large quantity was no doubt used for food. The Black Walnut and Hickory also abound in the Nation. These nuts, and the Pecan are used in the preparation of an article of food common to the Indian. The Acorn of the Black Jack, affords a rich oil which is also used by them as a substitute for lard and answers the purpose very well; in the construction of their houses, which tho' generally small, are tight and warm, they display much neatness and ingenuity. When we reflect that but little more than half a century has elapsed since these people were in what may be termed a savage state refusing to perform any offices of labor, but following the chase entirely for subsistence, having no occupation but War and Hunting, and compare them with their present condition, we most certainly cannot sufficiently applaud the fostering care of the Genl. Govt. which has effected so great a reformation." Logan recommended that an effort be made to induce the Creeks to abandon their present form of government and adopt a constitution and simple code of laws couched in language easily understood, which he thought could be accomplished by showing them the great benefits that had accrued to the Choctaw Nation by similar reforms.

The general council of the Creek Nation for 1846 convened September 22. One of the principal subjects to engage the attention of this session was the appointment of a second chief of the Lower Towns to fill the vacancy caused by the recent death of Ufaula Harjo. "The office has developed upon Mr. Benjamin Marshall, formerly national interpreter, an educated half-breed of wealth and standing. He is of course favorably inclined to religion and education, and much good may be anticipated to arise from his appointment. I am happy to state that the council is at present engaged in a revision of the laws of the nation, many of which, though not sanguinary, are unnecessarily severe and arbitrary. No change in the system of the government of the nation can be yet expected. . . . . The crops of the present year are abundant; so much so that a large surplus of almost every thing cultivated by them will be left for sale. Stocks of horses, cattle, and hogs are becoming abundant; and large numbers of the latter will be offered for sale during the approaching winter."[7]

Logan's prediction was well founded for the Creeks exported 100,000 bushels of corn, a large portion of which was purchased for shipment to Ireland and other foreign countries. Their reputation as raisers of stock had gone abroad and they sold 1,000 hogs to drovers from Illinois, Missouri, and Indiana, who traveled through their country buying their surplus.

Gradually, as the game disappeared, the Creeks had been taught the advantage of placing dependence upon their skill and labor. "Blessed with a country of abundant extent, well timbered and watered, of fertile soil and of comparative healthfulness, offering every facility for the rearing of stock and of following agricultural pursuits, they were ultimately persuaded to seize that which they so bountifully possessed, and which so alluringly tempted them to change their condition, and to become a sober, steady, and industrious community seating themselves at their homes, rendered permanent to them by the assurances of the government of the United States, and appreciating and enjoying all the comforts and endearments of the social circle. . . . . as their moral character and condition has improved, their mental capacities have increased as a consequence. They have become conscious of the advantages accruing to them from receiving and encouraging religion and education upon which subjects they feel a great interest."[8]

Logan's glowing account is somewhat qualified by his further description of the efforts to prevent the introduction of whisky in the Nation. He had labored to convince the chiefs of the evil of the traffic and had induced the general council on three occasions to decree the

7   Logan to Medill, November 9, 1847, ibid., for 1847. The education of Creek children had now become a subject of deep and general interest, said Rev. Mr. Loughridge at Koweta Mission. "Our greatest annoyance now is the constant & urgent applications by parents for their children to be received into our school. All feeling the importance of the subject & this being the only school in the nation, solicitations for admissions are received from every quarter. Today two men came a distance of 70 miles, bringing six boys with them to the school. Although we had already engaged as many as we thought we could possibly accommodate, yet their anxiety was so great and they could hear no denial, that we consented to take in two of them" (Loughridge to Logan October 22, 1847, OIA, "Schools.")

8   Logan to Medill, November 9, 1847, OIA.

destruction of all liquors found in their country, subjecting the punishment of a hundred lashes upon all who might thereafter introduce it.
"The consequences was, for a short time, none of it was to be seen;
but the high price of it, in consequence of its scarcity, was too great
a temptation to the cupidity of some of the chiefs themselves, and
others possessing great influence, who immediately entered into the
trade, and maintained the monopoly of it until it became known to
those in the habit of pursuing it as an avocation, who again engaged
in it. It is brought in by the Indians exclusively, who send or take
canoes or boats into the state; obtaining their lading about nightfall
they immediately depart, keeping under the high banks of the river
to evade notice; when they arrive home it is safely secreted and sold
out by jugfulls to others who attend the gatherings, and who retail
it out by the dram."

The next year the optimistic Creek agent was "surprised in travelling through the nation lately, to observe the many fine orchards, the
neatness and regularity of the fences around the farms and the improvements in their houses, and to see in many instances the furniture
in them neat, cleanly, and appropriate; the spinning wheel and the loom
are in common use; but that which struck me most was the introduction of Yankee clocks, an article not in general use among the Indians."[9]
But he despaired of persuading the Indians to have their annuities paid
to the individuals per capita. They were so completely under the domination of the large number of chiefs that no argument could break
down the customs of placing all tribal funds in their hands to be disbursed as they saw fit.[10]

The occasions of payments of the annuities to the Indians were picturesque. An observer of one wrote: "For some days I have been in a busy
crowd. This is the annual payment time of the Creek Indians, and the
tribe gathers here from every corner of the land, and with them every
white to whom they are owing five dollars. The Indians are waiting
for the money and the traders waiting to receive their long standing

9 *Report* of commissioner of Indian affairs, 1848.
10 March 31, 1848 James Logan, Creek agent, reported that the united Creek
tribe had established its capitol near a spring on a hill, four miles from Deep Fork and
about equally distant from the Creeks on the Arkansas and those on the Canadian.
They named the place O-hi-a-hul-way, meaning "high spring." The place afterwards
became known as Council Hill, which is the name of the town built nearby
on the K. O. & G. railroad.

dues. . . . . The Indians have received their money, and around them may be seen the white men they are owing. Perhaps the Indian owes a dozen, and hasn't more than that number of dollars. Every one is picking at him. He is not disposed to pay any of them, for his present wants crowd upon him, and he thinks that he must attend to urgent claims of his own for better clothing. At the close of the payment the Indian will not have a dollar.

"In this Nation there are about 400 chiefs, law-makers, light-horse-men, &c. At such meetings as the present one, most of the 400 are in attendance. They are a formidable force of themselves. They have been together a few days, and are a fine-looking assembly. Some of the number are speech-makers. I listened to several speeches; not a word could I understand, but the manner, the ease with which they spoke, the applause they received, enabled me to find out their best speakers. . . . . Murder is always punished with death; but the criminal has a fair trial, and often there is pleading in his behalf. Theft is punished here in a manner attended with more disgrace than in the States. For stealing small sums one ear is cut off; for larger sums both ears; and for the largest sums both ears and the nose is clipped.

"During this gathering of the people, I have noticed a few with these marks; it is a living disgrace; every child scouts the thief, and there is no power of concealing his punishment. The Creeks are honest and orderly. I have traveled through many parts of the nation, and have not been interrupted. Life and property are perfectly safe here.[11]

11 *Louisville Weekly Journal*, February 11, 1848. The specie disbursed to the Indians was principally gold. When Superintendent Rector drew $245,188.90 from the sub-treasury at St. Louis for the Indians, $200,000 of it was paid him in double eagles, $35,000 in eagles, $5,000 in half eagles, $500 in one-fourth eagles and $188.90 in silver (Sturgeon to Mix, October 16, 1858, "Southern Superintendency," S. 685).

The payments of annuities to the Indians were celebrated occasions, not only to the Indians, but the white people who had business there. One payment was concluded at the Creek agency on January 10, 1852, "and a joyous troop of merchants and clerks have departed from among us. . . . cold lunches of partridges, cheese, Boston crackers, and Bologna sausages, roast turkeys, etc." (*Fort Smith Herald*, January 17, 1852, p. 2, col. 2).

CHAPTER FOURTEEN / *Accounts by Observers*

Observing the progress of neighboring tribes who enjoyed the blessings of education, some of the Creek chiefs expressed the opinion that theirs was not advancing at the same rate and they exerted themselves to stimulate the interest of the people and the authorities in the establishment and maintenance of more schools. In April, 1847, Mr. Walter Lowrie, secretary of the Presbyterian Board of Foreign Missions, visited Kowetah Mission and learned the wishes of the Indians. A contract was then entered into at the "Old Agency," between Mr. Lowrie as the representative of the Board of Foreign Missions and the principal chiefs then in council, for the erection of a manual labor school. It was estimated that the mission would cost $10,000, of which the Creek Nation would pay one-fifth and the mission board the remainder. The Creek Presbytery was created, composed of Rev. Hamilton Ballentine, Rev. David W. Eaken, Rev. Robert M. Loughridge, and Elder John Lilly, and the first meeting was held at Kowetah Mission November 9, 1848. Mr. Ballentine was appointed to superintend the new Presbyterian manual labor school to be known as Tullahassee.

For a school site Mr. Loughridge purchased 70 acres of cleared and fenced land from Thomas Marshall. The building was constructed of brick, ninety-four feet long and thirty-four feet wide; it was three stories high, with a kitchen eighteen by thirty feet and two stories high. It was the most pretentious building yet erected in this western wilderness and was a formidable undertaking. Forty thousand feet of lumber was delivered by water at Fort Gibson; most of the supplies came from Cincinnati and New Orleans by boat, and 240,000 brick were burned near by;[1] 1,350 running feet of sleepers, 1,670 feet of

1 Lowrie to Medill, February 19, 1848, OIA, "School File" L 198.

joists, and 1,376 feet of rafters were hewed out of the forests and used in the structure. Work on the building commenced in the spring of 1848, the corner stone being laid the next September 26,[2] and it was completed in time to open the boarding school accommodating eighty pupils on March 1, 1850, a day school in a smaller building having begun two months earlier.[3]

The Baptists had been somewhat active among the Creeks for several years and Rev. Joseph Islands, a devout member of the tribe who lived and preached at North Fork Town, was highly esteemed by the missionaries of that church for his piety and industry. He died March 8, 1848, after the decease of his brother William, December 18, 1847, both of whose lives were given extended accounts in the columns of *The Indian Advocate*, a Baptist organ published at Louisville. William Islands was baptized March 23, 1845 at the time of a "religious awakening after a long curse of wickedness, drinking, and ball-playing." There were six Baptist churches in the Creek Nation in 1848. Besides the churches at and near North Fork Town[4] there was the Fountain or First Baptist Church on the Arkansas River near the Creek Agency; the Second Baptist Church on the opposite side of the Arkansas River; the Post Oak Baptist Church twelve miles from the agency; and the Elk Creek Baptist Church eighteen miles from the agency just off the road to North Fork; they had been much neglected, having to depend on the brothers Islands and a Negro preacher named Jacobs, until the missionary Americus L. Hay came in January, 1848 to organize the church and mission work.

Mr. Hay wrote from Fountain Church that the membership, 170, was so large that sometimes in the winter he was obliged to preach under an arbor. "There are many white people here, it being the principal trading place in the Nation. The improvements are larger and better than in other parts of the Nation." With the help of the Indians he built a schoolhouse. "My pupils" he said, "began in their alphabet.

2 *Cherokee Advocate*, September 18, 1848, p. 2, col. 1.
3 *Report* of commissioner of Indian affairs for 1851.
4 A protracted meeting by the Baptist Church at North Fork Town began on July 7, 1848. There were sixty camps on the ground. The meeting lasted four days and was attended by 1,500 people. The twenty-three who united with the church on that occasion included Gen. Chilly McIntosh (*Fort Smith Herald*, July 26, 1848, p. 2, col. 1).

I have the letters arranged into 'the musical alphabet.' The scholars commenced singing the letters; in one day eight learned their letters. In a few days all were spelling."[5] Hay, who was an intelligent, observing man, said that the Cherokee, Choctaw, Creek, Delaware, and Shawnee Indians produced great quantities of produce. "These tribes are well supplied with farming implements, and many wagons among them. On Sabbath day, at many of the churches, a number of families have their carriages. At many of the trading houses, Indians are employed as salesmen, and the simple trades are followed by some of the various tribes. . . . . At present there are 600 white men among the Choctaws" and not twenty Christians among them, aside from the missionaries.[6]

North Fork Town was a dense settlement between the Canadian and North Fork rivers, and the Methodists decided to locate their mission school there on the farm acquired from Mrs. Phips. It was on the south side of the North Fork of the Canadian River five miles above its mouth and included thirty acres of cultivated land, a good dwelling, outhouses and stables. In February, 1848 a contract was made with Webster and Reed of Fort Smith for the stone and brick work and in April a contract was entered into with J. J. Denny of Louisville, Kentucky to furnish material and do the carpenter work. The foundation was completed and the corner stone laid July 19. "The occasion was one of much interest to the Indians, many of whom attended, with several of the principal chiefs. Notwithstanding the day was very hot, the addresses and all elicited the closest attention from them. When they were told by a native speaker that this was what they had been trying to get for several years they responded most heartily."[7]

More than a year was required to construct the main building, which was 110 feet long by 34 wide and included a basement of stone and three stories of brick. A ten-foot porch extended across the front of the building which contained twenty-one rooms. The structure cost more than $9,000, of which the Government furnished $5,00᠃ and the Missionary Board of the Methodist Episcopal Church of Louisville the balance. The furnishings for the school came from Louisville by water and were much delayed by the low stage of the river. School

5 *The Indian Advocate*, May, 1848.
6 *Ibid.*, for August, 1848, copied from *The New York Recorder*.
7 T. B. Ruble to Logan, September 8, 1848, OIA.

had been taught in a log house while the mission structure was in course of erection. It was called Asbury Mission School and was opened in 1850 with a capacity of nearly one hundred pupils. The school was soon interrupted by the prevailing epidemic of measles and by a wind storm that cracked the walls of the building, from which teachers and pupils fled in panic. On "28th May our school broke up in great confusion, never, as I judge, to commence again."[8]

But Asbury Mission school did reopen and for years served the tribe well. It flourished under the superintendency of Thomas B. Ruble and soon had 112 pupils, thirty-two more than it was equipped to accommodate. In October, 1855, the school entertained a visitor in the person of Bishop George F. Pierce, who had just arrived after a journey over the drought stricken country of the Cherokee and Creeks, "a wild vacant country, dreary but for its beauty with here and there at long intervals, a hut or wigwam; and now, here is a large three-story brick building—a school-house—with superintendent, teachers, male and female, and an Annual Conference assembled within its walls! The bell rings, and we all descend to the dining-hall; the boys sit at one table, a teacher at the head; the girls at another, the guests at a third. All in order; no rushing and jamming; and now every one at his place awaits in silence the invocation of blessing upon the bounteous board. . . . . Nothing special occurred during the session [of the Indian Mission Conference] save the admission into the travelling connection of James McHenry—better known in Georgia as 'Jim Henry,' the hero of the Creek war in 1836. The lion had become a lamb—the *brave* a preacher. The War-whoop is hushed; the midnight foray is with the past; the Bible and the Hymn book fill the hands that once grasped the torch and tomahawk. The bold valiant savage, who spread consternation among the peaceful settlements on either side of the Chattahoochee, now travels a circuit, preaching peace on earth, good-will to men. . . . . He does not like to allude to his past.

"One day a brother informed me that the Indian preachers wished to hold a 'council' with me, and requested me to designate an hour for the interview. I did so, not knowing what they wished. They came to my room at the appointed time, and seated themselves in grave silence. I waited in vain for them to open their minds. *That* is not Indian eti-

8 Jarner to Lea, July 1, 1851: *Report* of commissioner of Indian affairs for 1851.

quette on such occasions. They were waiting for me, and so I inquired about what matter they wished to consult, and learned that they only desired to talk with me in their own way about the Church and the schools and the wants of the nation.

"In the midst of our talk, Chili McIntosh—well-known in Georgia in the days of 'Troup and the Treaty'—came in. The son of an old chief, himself a chief, the Indians all rose, in respect to the man and his title. They called him *General*. I had seen him at my native town (Greensboro), in my early boyhood, when, in the native costume of an American Major-General, and accompanied by some fifteen or twenty of his warriors, he visited several places in Georgia. The boys and the ladies were all greatly impressed, during that tour, with his manly beauty. He was caressed, and dined, and toasted everywhere. He made a triumphal march through the country. In conversation I found that he remembered every incident, private, and public in his visit to Greensboro. Among the rest, I reminded him of a question proposed to him by my father, and told him how as a boy I was impressed by his answer. The question was: 'Is there any word in the Creek language for blaspheming the name of God?' The answer was: 'There is not.' He remembered the conversation and reaffirmed his answer, appealing to his countrymen for its correctness. They all agreed he was right, and with one voice declared that 'If an Indian wanted to say bad words he must talk English.'

"McIntosh had not the height or majesty of person with which my boyish fancy invested him in other days. Though not an old man, he is now very gray; has a mild, gentle face, more expressive of humor than of boldness, and looks as if he would like a joke better than a fight. In conversation he is entertaining, quick-witted, and ready at any time for a little fun. Wishing to hear him talk, I asked him various questions about his people, the country, the soil, and the prospects of the Nation. He says it is a much better country than the one they left, though, for years, the people were dissatisfied. On their removal, sickness prevailed, many died, and they decreased fearfully in numbers; but trial and experience reconciled them. They could not be induced to return. He says every man coming to that region must pass through a process of acclimation."[9]

9 George G. Smith, *The Life and Times of George F. Pierce* (Nashville, 1888), p. 225.

McIntosh was rich and his family did not suffer from the privations and sickness that oppressed the great majority of the tribe. It is interesting to compare this impression Bishop Pierce received from McIntosh with that of Augustus W. Loomis, who came to Kowetah Mission in 1852 and taught for a year, "visiting the people in their homes and presenting the claims of the gospel through an interpreter." Said Mr Loomis in his quaint little book: "This tribe was removed to their present country, from Georgia, within the memory of those who are now not far past the meridian of life. They were very reluctant to remove; sorry to leave their old fields and orchards, their homes and hunting grounds, their council houses, and the graves of their kinsmen and their braves. To this day, they talk much of the happy country from which they were *driven*, as they express it; they discourse about its springs, and brooks, and rivers; its rich soil and abundant timber; its hills and valleys, and genial climate; and with it they are wont to contrast, depreciatingly, (like any homesick person,) the woodless and waterless country in which they are now settled; nothing is equal to what they had in Georgia; the summers here are hotter, the winters are colder, the rain is wetter, the crops lighter, the game scarcer, and their people are dieing off faster than ever before was known in the 'old nation.' "[10] In sentimental remembrance of the loved spots they left in their former home, they brought the old names with them and bestowed familiar appellations on the new places in the western country, that robbed them of some of their strangeness; and the nomenclature of their ancestral country became that of their new home in the West.

Surrounded by an abundance of the necessities of life, wrested from the soil by their prodigious industry, many of the Creeks were living a contented and fairly orderly existence. As a rule they lived in rude log cabins, having paid but little attention to more pretentious building; but there were a few wealthy men in the tribe whose houses were more imposing. Such a house was of a well established type, built of two log cabins under one roof, connected by a covered passageway and having a long gallery across the full length of the front.

The early Creek's establishment was primitive. If he had advanced to agricultural opulence, there was a little field of corn surrounded

10   Augustus W. Loomis, *Scenes in the Indian Country*, 7.

by a worm rail-fence; at a remote part of his possessions near a stream or spring, often out of sight from the road or trail, his domestic establishment; a little garden and a melon patch; some peach trees; a cow pen, and a log pen covered with thatch for a stable. A small square log house with one room, covered with long narrow pieces of oak split thin for shingles, and these not nailed, but held in place by heavy poles laid along the roof. There was not a sawed board about the premises. The floor, if not of dirt, was of what was called puncheon—segments of logs split, hewed and smoothed on one side; seats were of the same material with sprawling legs driven into holes in the bottom. The table was made with a hatchet, of such boards as cover the roof, and they were fastened together with wooden pegs. The door had wooden hinges and a wooden latch. At one side of the room were holes bored into the logs, into which were driven wooden pins; with supports at the other end, these sustained the bed; on other pins higher up were placed split boards; articles of dress hung on the pins, and a few dishes were set on the shelves. Over the door, a well kept rifle rested on its wooden hooks. Perhaps there were two cabins in the enclosure or near together; if so, the chances were the owner had two wives—an arrangement permitted by tribal custom, in the event he was able to care for both.

Frequently the logs of the house were not closely laid nor chinked so that the wind freely circulated through the room; the more pretentious dwelling was chinked and daubed; mud prepared in a pit near by was thrown into the chinks between the logs and smoothed with the hands in place of a trowel. A fireplace built against the outside of the house was sometimes constructed as high as the mantel with stone, but more often with logs thickly plastered inside with mud; above that it was carried as high as the roof with sticks similarly plastered.

In the more pretentious double log cabin, the ten-foot passageway through the middle, usually floored, served many purposes. It was cool and airy in the summer; a place in which to sit during the day, or to sleep at night. Frequently through the warm weather the beds were arranged out of doors on a staging to keep the sleeper above the reach of vermin, and of the pigs rooting around the house; here they napped at noon and slept at night; while the trees defended them from the sun by day and the dew by night.

A few standard domestic utensils sufficed; there was invariably the mortar made by hollowing out the end of a small log in which corn was crushed with the heavy wooden pestle, and with the corn they made their sofka or hominy. Shallow woven baskets for sifting and winnowing the grain; bowls and heavy spoons fashioned from wood. While they could cook over the fireplace in the house, that was usually done over an open fire out of doors.

When the members of the towns tilled their fields in common, each family was expected to do its share of fencing, plowing, planting and tending; it had its own crib, and these cribs were scattered about over the field. Crude vehicles were used by the poorer members of the tribe; sometimes cross sections of a log two feet in diameter with the heart chiseled out for the axle made the wheels for the primitive cart or wagon, to be drawn by oxen. Even the crotch of a tree, in the shape of the letter V, with the sharp end forward, and upright stakes set in to hold the load on made a vehicle to be dragged over the ground.

The prairie flowers and the moon were the almanac of the Indians. When such a flower showed itself it was time to plant this seed; when such another appeared another seed must be planted.[11] The days of important intervals were marked with sticks. Notice of an approaching busk or other public meeting was given by heralds dispatched by the town chief, with little bundles of sticks, one of which was left in each house, with the direction to throw one stick away every morning, and that morning on which but one stick remained they were to repair to the busk grounds; giving notice of an impending meeting was called "issuing broken days." The war of 1812, in which part of the Creeks fought against the United States, and a part of them for it under General Jackson, was called by the Creeks the Red Stick War; this from the fact that the warriors were assembled by means of bundles of red sticks which the runners left in each house, and which were employed to mark the days until time to go to the rendezvous.

Their amusements were simple; the ball game was a test of skill between rival towns, which frequently developed into riots in which heavy hickory ball sticks were sometimes used as clubs upon the

11 On the prairies of Oklahoma grows a luxuriant purple flower known as the Osage Almanac; this from the fact that when the Osage bands were far from home on their buffalo hunts, and they saw this flower blooming they knew the toothsome green corn was nearly ready to harvest and it was time to return home.

heads and naked bodies of adversaries until they were covered with blood. Dances and races contributed to their simple gaiety. The Indian at play or in feats of valor dissembled his pride of achievement with nonchalance; a traveler observed some of them in Van Buren: Some were racing their ponies through the streets for the mere excitement of the thing. Here you might see half a dozen swarthy faced young men, with long black hair floating over their bare shoulders, issue from a grocery, unhitch their apparently sleeping nags, spring upon their backs, and with a wild screech fly up the road, whooping and yelling till their noise dies away in the distance. "We have forgotten them and are occupied with other scenes, when suddenly in an opposite direction we hear the same frightful screeching and clattering of hoofs, then we see the foaming horses plunging furiously towards us, and on even to the hitching rail, where they halt in full career, and the riders slide down their sides, turn the bridle rein over the pony's head, hang it on the hitching peg, and lean themselves against a post or the side of the house, and, with eyes dropped upon the ground and one leg twisted around the other, they at once appear as listless and unconcerned as if they were alone by their own cabin in the woods."[12]

The Creeks were gregarious and enjoyed their barbecues and camp meetings. The most important gathering was the busk, an annual feast at the town busk ground to which all repaired. On this occasion they renewed their fires by rubbing pieces of wood together and from this they lighted all the fires used during the feast, and each family was expected to carry home some of it in order to keep disease and bad influence from the house. Water was drawn from the spring into which the medicine man blew a blessing through his reed, and the people all drank of it, supposing they were imbibing health-insuring draughts.

They were in session several days and nights, and one of the days was devoted to drinking a decoction passed around in a large vessel and known as the black-drink[13] made of roots and herbs boiled together and designed to operate as an emetic. A large feather accompanied the vessel, which was used by those who preferred to have their sickness

12 *Scenes in the Indian Country, op. cit.*
13 Black drink ("Carolina tea," Catawba *Youpon;* Creek *assi-luputski;* small leaves, commonly abbreviated *assi*), a decoction, so named by British traders from the color, made by boiling leaves of Ilex-Cassine in water (*Handbook of American Indians,* I, 150).

soon over. This day of cleansing was followed by the days of feasting and dancing. Houses were arranged around the sides of the square and facing inwards, and in the center a fire was built, around which dancing took place. The old Indians claimed that the Great Spirit gave them the dances and therefore they were bound with religious care to observe them and to teach them to their children. Some of the dances they said were learned from the bears; others were communicated to them from heaven, for it would be impossible, they said, for man ever to invent anything so intricate and so ingenious. The dances were mostly by night and by the lurid light of the great fire in the center.

The Creeks were a peace-loving people and had a shrewd appreciation of the blessings of quiet and tranquillity and both by precept and example they came to exercise a wholesome influence on their indigenous neighbors—more than did any of the other immigrants.[14] Capt. R. B. Marcy related that he had "learned from a Creek chief (Echo Hadjo) that his nation in a council with the Comanches, represented to them the fact of the rapid decrease of the buffaloes and that in a few years they would be almost entirely exterminated; when their present means of subsistence would be gone; and they and their children would be compelled to resort to some other modes of living; at the same time urging upon them the importance of abandoning their wandering habits, and learning to cultivate the soil. Thus the Creek Indians who are feared and respected by the prairie Indians, appear to have their interest and welfare at heart, and exercise a very salutary influence over them."[15]

The Creeks met the prairie Indians in a number of important peace councils and they and the Seminole were frequently called on for advice by the Comanche. In the spring of 1853 the Comanche Indians with 200 lodges were encamped in the Wichita Mountains. They sent messengers to the Creeks soliciting them to join in a council. But the Creeks a day or two before had sent Jesse Chisholm to the Comanche camp to make an appointment for the Grand Council fifty-five days from that time to be held at the Salt Plains which was intended to be

14 For an account of the efforts of the Creek Indians to establish peace among the prairie Indians, see *Advancing the Frontier, op. cit.*

15 Marcy to Jones, November 25, 1851, AGO, OFD, 489 M 51.

an extraordinary occasion.[16] In June 1500 Creeks departed for the Salt Plains to attend this Grand Council where large numbers of Comanche and other prairie Indians assembled.[17]

16   *Fort Smith Herald*, April 30, 1853, copied in *St. Louis Republican*, May 14, 1853, p. 2, col. 1.

17   *Indian Advocate*, June 1853, p. 3. This "grand council" held in July was attended by Comanche, Kiowa, Kichai, Creeks, Delaware, Shawnee, Chickasaw, and Choctaw Indians. Jesse Chisholm was selected as interpreter for all of them (Whipple's Journal: *Report of Explorations for a Railway Route from the Mississippi River to the Pacific Ocean, by Lieut. A. W. Whipple*, p. 19).

CHAPTER FIFTEEN / *Laws and Customs*

P HILIP H. RAIFORD became Creek agent in 1849 and after a survey of his field he concluded that the Creeks had "entirely abandoned the chase as a means of subsistence, as the men have become accustomed to the labor of the field, and convinced of its sure profits. The women, who but a few years since were the tillers of the soil, are becoming skilled in the art of housewifery; indeed their 'home-spuns' are fully equal in point both of texture and color to those manufactured by the ladies of the States. The neatness and comfort displayed in many of their homes is an indisputable evidence of their improving condition. I find the people of this tribe much less addicted to drunkenness than I had expected, from a limited knowledge of their habits some years ago. As a community they are as sober as that of any white people of the Union. . . . among themselves there are no factionists to disturb the settled and peaceful habits of the tribe. Their law-makers are abolishing by degrees many of their old and barbarous customs, and enacting in their stead sound and salutary laws."[1]

A disastrous drought in 1850 destroyed most of the corn crops of the immigrant Indians, the Creeks alone, by their superior industry, producing enough for their own use. However the next year the drought continued and even the Creeks were without this most essential article of food. "Crops are literally burned," wrote the missionary H. F. Buckner at North Fork Town. "This has caused many of the superstitious Indians to resort to their old customs of conjuring for rain, and should no other benefit result, I trust they will be taught

1 Raiford to Drennan, September 30, 1849, *Report* of commissioner of Indian affairs for 1849.

to look to the mediation of a higher grade than one of their own device. They have various methods of conjuring for rain, all of which are ridiculous enough. Some lacerate frogs and toss them up in the air. Others fast, three, four, or five days during which time they dive frequently, boil different kinds of vegetables, dip the tail of a buffalo in water and sprinkle the water towards heaven &c. Some have resorted to the method of burning the prairies; and woe betide the man who has a fence contiguous to them. My wife and I have twice exhausted our strength this week by fighting fires which caught our fence from the prairies. I had twelve acres of corn in cultivation, and the drought had ruined my crop, yet I was unwilling that the fire should consume my fence. I raised a shout for help, but nearly all the Indians in town had gone to a ball-play. One came however and rendered efficient aid."[2]

The Creeks had not advanced so far in the elements of civilization and the science of government as some of their red brethren by whom they were surrounded, said their agent. "Their rude and irresponsible form of government by chiefs still prevails among them. The chiefs all receive salaries in proportion to their grade and rank, or, in other words, a larger share of the common fund of the tribe than the great mass of the Indians. The result of this system has been a great increase in the number of chiefs, until they now amount to about 800; and, as the moneys due from the Government to the tribe are now paid to the chiefs, and they have it in their power to fix their own salaries, a large proportion of the funds of the nation is divided out among themselves, and but little left for the great mass. Great wrong and injustice are thus done to the common Indians," said Raiford; but he saw no remedy for it except under a different form of government, which he believed would result in a more rapid advance in their civilization.[3]

Boarding schools were believed to provide the only effective method of educating the Creek youth. Day schools had proved a failure, said Mr. Loughridge. As soon as the novelty of going to school was over, and the children became tired of their studies, as all children will, they deserted the schoolroom and returned to their sports. The teachers could not bring them back and the parents who exercised no discipline whatever over their children, would not, and hence they

2 *The Indian Advocate*, October, 1850, p. 3.

3 Raiford to Drennan, September 30, 1849, *Report* of commissioner of Indian affairs for 1851; *ibid* for 1853.

absented themselves at pleasure, returning only now and then, as curiosity might prompt them. This was the testimony also of the teachers and missionaries who had been laboring among the Cherokee and Choctaw for more than thirty years. Only in the boarding schools said Mr. Loughridge, where they could teach the children the English language, by precept and example were they able to show them the absurdity of their barbarous superstitions, and impart to them much important instruction which could not be taught in the day school-room.[4]

W. H. Garrett became Creek agent July 2, 1853, and he immediately recognized as the outstanding problem of his charges the form of government that subjected the great majority of the tribe to the un-restrained rule of a privileged class of so-called chiefs, a form of government that had been handed down to them from one generation to another for ages. While he believed it was essential for them to change their government if they were to develop and progress in company with the other immigrant tribes, he did not believe they were prepared to adapt themselves to a constitutional form of government modeled on those of the states.[5]

There were some fundamental peculiarities in the social organization of the Creek tribe that must be considered if one would understand their condition and belated progress. Prior to their removal to the West, as they were in the process of emerging from the hunter to the agricul-tural state, the institution of slavery, by which they were surrounded, and in which they participated gave a peculiar development to their industry. Chiefs, who were averse to work themselves, employed slaves, and thus the relation of planter and slave was established long before

4   Ibid. Mr. Loughridge wrote to the Creek agent August 23, 1853: "The cause of temperance too, is advancing. The 'Maine law,' which was in operation here before it was adopted by the State of Maine, is more faithfully enforced than formerly; and the people from principle are becoming more temperate. At the last annual meeting of the National Temperance Society we were much rejoiced to see the principal chief take a decided stand in favor of the temperance society. The old gentleman, whose head is silvered over with seventy winters, arose and warmly addressed the audience in behalf of the cause. He told us that he had *come to sign the pledge* not on his own account, for he drank nothing, but for the sake of the cause of temperance. He greatly deplored the evils of intemperance as the greatest curse to his people. He then put his name to the pledge and called upon others to do likewise."
5   Garrett to Drew, August 30, 1853, ibid., for 1853.

the question of their removal occurred. The effect of this was to exalt a portion of the nation above, and to depress others below, the average standing. The disparity which took place in habits of labor and in wealth also impressed itself on education, dress, manners, and information. This development together with the admixture of white blood enabled this and a few other southern tribes to send intelligent chiefs to Washington to transact their business, who astonished officials there with their sagacity and self confidence.[6] These intelligent and affluent individuals did most of the thinking for the other class that came to bear the name of "common Indians."

The Baptist missionaries provide further interesting sketches of the Creeks at this period. Rev. H. F. Buckner writes from Fort Gibson May 23, 1853 that he has preached the week preceding "at Tuckabatcheetown at night and had a good meeting. I was much delighted in a conversation with an old sister who was once scourged for praying to God, and who is now too infirm to attend church." In July he attended a "church-meeting at North Fork where I counted sixteen tents occupied by brethren from a distance with their families." At the Muskogee church on the Arkansas River he preached the funeral of "Sister Lizzie McIntosh." The preaching lasted three days and "an entertainment was given the whole time by Gen. Roly McIntosh, father of the deceased, and principal chief of the Creek Nation. A more sumptuous entertainment I never saw in my life. I think it much have cost the Gen. $500. There were from 800 to 1,000 people [to be fed] all the time. I could not avoid contrasting the difference in the general appearance of the congregation with what it was four years ago. Then there were not more than four sun-bonnets to be seen in a congregation of that size; now there is not a congregation in any country town in Kentucky that can excel this one in neatness of dress and good order." In the autumn he observed : "Three years ago we were not allowed to preach in Broken Arrow; now we have a flourishing church of about fifty members, and a house of worship."

In the winter they had preaching at Tuckabatchee and the crowd was too large to enter their little church; "so we prepared as many seats as we could outside. Such a congregation in the woods in the midst of winter, would have made a beautiful sketch for an amateur

6 "Our Indian Policy," *The United States Magazine and Democratic Review,* Vol. XIV (February, 1844), 178.

painter—a crowd of Indians dressed in their old-fashioned native costumes—many having been attracted to meeting for the first time, in all their native wildness and simplicity; some standing, some sitting on the grass or reclining against trees, some in the tops of saplings; and one youth in front and near to me, stood leaning upon the top of his bow, with spear-headed arrows in his hands; all giving earnest heed while I preached from 1st Timothy, i, 11, 'The Glorious Gospel of the Blessed God'."[7]

The gradual development of education in the Creek Nation in 1853 found the two manual training schools with eighty pupils, in addition to twelve neighborhood schools located by the chiefs,[8] and attended by about 500 pupils; their school work, however, was retarded by want of comfortable schoolhouses, a deficiency they were attempting to correct. The teacher at Cusehta, Thomas C. Carr, a Creek Indian who had been educated by the whites, wrote: "I was once like my pupils—could not speak a word in the English language; but the school and my kind teachers made a wonderful change in me and taught me to speak and write in the English language. I feel quite confident that I shall be able to make the change in them (in a few years) as was made in myself."[9] The cause of temperance was advancing: ". . . . 'the Maine law,' which was in operation here before it was adopted by the state of Maine is more faithfully enforced than formerly."

Five Creek boys were sent away to school in 1854, one of whom went to Center College at Danville, Kentucky. Four other boys, Richard Carr, Eli Danley, Lyman Moore and David Yargee, were sent to Arkansas College at Fayetteville. The Methodists maintained one school and three missions with between seven and eight hundred members; they were served by three white men and three native men. Thomas B. Ruble, who was then superintendent of Asbury Manual Labor School, reported that his school closed earlier than usual on July 8 because the parents wanted their children to come home before

7 *The Indian Advocate*, May 1852 to February 1854.

8 These schools were located in Creek District, Concharty, Chehaw, Creek Agency, Thlob-Thlocco, Choska, Old Creek Agency, Tuckabatchee, Little River, Tallasa, Hillabee, Cusehta, North Fork (*Report*, commissioner of Indian affairs, 1850). Thlob-Thlocco school was said to be ". . . .on the extreme frontier, in the neighborhood of the range of the trail of the Comanche" (*ibid.*).

9 *Ibid.* for 1853.

the weather became too warm to save them from sickness and so that they might attend the regular busks.[10] The excessive drought of the year before which destroyed their crops singularly enough contributed to the cause of temperance among the immigrant Indians by preventing navigation in the streams so that whisky boats were unable to ascend the rivers. A number of Creeks were now engaged in merchandising in their own country and others were carrying goods out on the prairies to traffic with the western Indians.

The oppressive government of the large number of so-called chiefs had caused such bitterness in the tribe as to force a reduction in that number from 800 to 500 in 1855; treasurers were appointed for the nation under some new enactments that indicated a desire of the Indians to improve their body of laws; though the agent, W. H. Garrett, gave it as his opinion that the tribe had not yet sufficiently advanced in civilization to comprehend a more intricate government.[11]

The Creeks, in common with the other immigrant tribes, experienced a crop failure in 1853 and 1854, and the next year would have suffered excessively but for the tardy payment to them of an appropriation to compensate them in a measure for their losses incident to their enforced hasty removal from their homes in the East in 1836, nineteen years before.[12] But they were resentful at their failure to secure from the Government any satisfaction on account of their claim for the loss of 9,000,000 acres of land taken from them by General Jackson at the Treaty of Fort Jackson, for which they never received a dollar. The Creeks were apprehensive at the impending abandonment of Fort Gibson considered by the Indian officials as the key to the whole of the Indian country west of Arkansas, and necessary for the protection

10   *Ibid.* for 1855.
11   *Ibid.*
12   But a more striking instance of deferred restitution is seen in the payment of what was known as the Creek Orphan Fund. In the Treaty of 1832 it was provided that twenty sections of land should be sold and the proceeds set apart for 598 orphans of the tribe who had no other lands allotted to them, and no one to represent them. This money was to be paid to these orphans on their arrival in Indian Territory. It was not paid for fifty years after the obligation was assumed by the Government; and in 1883, when the payment was finally consummated, 573 of those for whose benefit the provision was made had passed out of this world, and only twenty-five survived; and the necessities which justified the undertaking had been suffered to continue without redress. The payment, therefore, went to the heirs of those who were entitled to it.

of the immigrant Indians against the encroachments of those of the prairies.

The fearful toll of life visited upon the Creeks in the process of removal and adjustment to their new home is reflected in the census of 1857, showing a total of 14,888 members of the tribe. The number of Creeks enrolled for emigration under and after the Treaty of 1832 was about 22,000. These were to be added to 3,000 already living in the West, making in all some 25,000 Creeks before removal. This loss of 10,000 lives within twenty years time was caused by the casualties of emigration and the hardships and exposure incident to settlement in a new and wilderness country without the means of conserving their lives and health. Thousands of them died on the route and during the first two or three years after their arrival. "Another cause of their decrease has been the general prevalence among them of winter fever, (or, as it is called, pneumonia,) with which they are annually scourged; and this has been greatly increased by the delay in their annual payments until very late in the fall or commencement of winter when they have frequently to assemble to receive their money without any shelter or protection against the most inclement weather. This has been a frightful source of this most fatal disease, which evil should be remedied by an earlier remittance and payment of their annual dues."[13]

Some of the more enlightened members of the Creek tribe, said their optimistic agent Garrett in 1858, looked forward to a form of government similar to that of the states, but there was no immediate prospect of such an advance in the minds of the majority of the tribe. However backward they were in the matter of laws and government they were good farmers. "A large number of them have numerous herds of cattle and ponies, the reputation for which has attracted the attention of dealers in the neighboring States, who annually visit the nation to make purchases of the Indians, paying them just and remunerative prices." There were seven schools with 172 pupils in attendance

13 *Report* of commissioner of Indian affairs for 1857, p. 512. The Indians were sacrificed to the comfort and indifference of government officials. Their funds were made available at New Orleans in the warm weather when the annual visitation of yellow fever was raging, and the Indian superintendents refused to risk their lives by descending to that city before cold weather to secure the specie belonging to their wards (Drew to Manypenny, February 24, 1855, OIA, RFC, Southern Superintendency, 1855 D 804).

in Arkansas District and seven in Canadian District with 216 pupils, 33 females and 183 males.

The subject of religion was exciting a lively interest among the Creeks in 1858, said Mr. Garrett. "There is scarcely a settlement of the nation in which there is not a church under the visitation of white missionary preachers of the various denominations and under the direct ministry of native preachers. The Baptists appear to be the most numerous and successful, numbering among their converts some of the leading and most influential men of the nation. The Methodists have also made numerous converts, and they too regard their labors as successful and speak hopefully of the future. . . . . The cause of temperance too, has its defenders. The authorities of the nation have exerted themselves to the fullest extent in suppressing the trade in whiskey. The light horse are instructed to destroy all spiritous liquors, and a law has been enacted inflicting the penalty of four dollars a gallon upon all liquors introduced by natives into the nation, which is strictly enforced, and is effectual to a great extent in suppression the traffic."[14]

In Asbury Manual Labor School there were about seventy-five boys and girls from eight to sixteen years of age. The usual elemental studies were taught and vocal and instrumental music, the latter on the melodeon. Seventy acres of land were planted to corn, oats, millet, potatoes, and turnips. "Chinese sugar cane" was planted experimentally, with some success. "During the fall and winter the boys help to gather in the crop, chop wood, make fires, etc.; in the spring they assist in repairing the fences, cleaning up the grounds for cultivation, and do most of the hoeing in the fields and garden. Besides this they grind nearly all the meal we use on steel mills. . . . . The girls assist in the care and cleaning up of their own rooms, also in their own washing and ironing, sew, and work in the dining room. The girls as a general thing are more industrious than the boys; but, in a moral point of view, not more reliable."

The progress and plan of Tullahassee Manual Labor School were much the same, though it had a larger attendance, including ninety-six Creeks, four Cherokee and two whites. The management seems to have been somewhat more progressive, and Mr. Loughridge, with the aid of the interpreters, prepared several books in the Creek language.

14 *Report* of commissioner of Indian affairs, 1858.

On the staff of teachers now at this school were Mr. and Mrs. W. S. Robertson; on January 2, 1854 there was born to them Mary Alice, who was later to become identified with the education of the Creek people, and still later to represent the state of Oklahoma in the Congress of the United States.

The first paragraph of an undated manuscript volume of laws of the Creek Nation provides for dividing the Creek Nation into two districts to be known as the Arkansas and the Canadian districts, each with a principal and a second chief to serve no more than four years "unless reëlected by the popular voice of the office holders that may be present." The next thing in importance seemed to be a criminal code. It provided for the punishment of murder by death after a trial and conviction by a jury of twelve disinterested men. If a Negro killed an Indian the former should suffer death, but if an Indian killed a Negro the Indian "shall pay the owner his value otherwise suffer death." If a slave killed another the killer should receive 100 lashes on the bare back and the owner of the culprit should pay the owner of the victim one-half the value of the deceased. But no one should be punished for the killing of another in a "ball play." If one were found guilty of stealing a horse, mule, jack, jinny or a cow, for the first offense he should receive fifty lashes, for the second offense 100 lashes and suffer one ear cut off, and for the third, he should suffer death.

New laws were added from time to time and at some period, the date of which is not given, it appears that some of the slaves of the Creeks were freed. The law provided that Negroes so freed over twelve years of age should pay a tax of three dollars annually to the Creek Nation, except those who were recognized as members of the Nation. The freed Negroes should pay also a tax on their live stock and their wagons. Officials were appointed to take a census of all free Negroes in the Nation and collect the tax from them. And it was made unlawful for an Indian man to take a Negro woman for a wife. A fifty dollar fine or 100 lashes was the penalty for harboring runaway slaves.

No man could collect damages done his crops by the stock of another unless his field were enclosed by a fence nine rails high, "staked and ridered." But if the stock broke through such an enclosure the injured party could collect damages to be assessed by two disinterested persons. If a person refused to pay his debts the lighthorse was authorized to make up the amount out of his property. But no debt contracted by a citizen of the Creek Nation with an individual of another nation could be collected.

The making and proving of wills were provided for; and if one died without a will, provision was made for the distribution of the property of the decedent. Traders in the Nation were to be licensed. A citizen of the Nation could employ a white mechanic who might reside in the Nation only while engaged in the performance of his contract. No slaveholder should be held responsible for the debts of his slave. If two persons should swap horses and within five days one should prove that he was drunk when the trade was made it might be rescinded. Provision was made for requiring citizens to work on the public works of his town, after due notice.   There being as yet no courts, suits were brought before the general council, of which twenty days notice to the defendants was required. In case of default against one failing to appear he might show to one of the principal chiefs good reason for setting aside the default and a new trial should be had before the council. Incest was outlawed and punishment of fifty lashes provided for. The "ball play" was a serious business with the Creeks, so it was "enacted that if two Towns agree to play ball and it is afterwards found out that either had taken in the playmen from other Towns they shall forfeit a fine of fifty dollars."

With the passing of time they provided for a "committee" of twelve men, six from each district, separate from the Kings and Warriors, who should act as a court of first instance. Its duty was "to decide upon all difficult and complicated lawsuits and in all cases where this body shall decide according to law and the evidence there shall be no appeal from their decision." Stringent laws for the suppression of the introduction and sale of liquor were enacted. Some of the practices of the times are reflected in the law making it "Unlawful for any woman to use medicine calculated to cause infanticide" and a violation subjected the guilty woman to fifty lashes on the bare back.

Colonel Hitchcock related in 1841 how after the death of a man his widow could be sentenced to a period of widowhood from one year to four years, depending on the caprice of the relatives of the deceased.[15] A law was now passed providing that "no town or towns person or persons shall have power to keep any woman in widowhood

15   A Traveler in Indian Territory, op. cit., 128.

exceeding twelve months from the death of her husband" nor any man in widowhood more than two months.

Later the subject of succession received the attention of the council when it was provided that "the property shall be divided between the nearest relations of the deceased." No slave was "permitted to own or possess horses, cattle, or guns" and it was made the duty of the light-horse to dispossess slaves of such property which was to be sold and the proceeds turned into the national treasury. A treasurer was now provided for in each of the two districts to receive and receipt for all moneys due the Creek Nation. Benjamin Marshall was appointed treasurer of the Arkansas District and David Barnett of the Canadian District. No funds could be paid out except after appropriation by the general council and upon a warrant signed by the principal chief and clerk of the district in which the treasurer served.

Several sections were now devoted to the subject of stray horses taken up by the citizens who were required to deliver them to the captain of the lighthorse. It was made the duty of the finder to tell every one whom he might meet for the next two years of any stray cattle taken up by him, and if they were not claimed they were to be taken to the district council and sold, one half the proceeds to go to the Nation and the other to the finder.

Finally, the subject of education engaged the attention of the general council and in order to extend to their people the "means of a common education there shall be established throughout the Nation Fourteen schools" divided equally between the two districts; a super-intendent of schools for each district was authorized, whose duty required him to appoint a board of trustees for each school in his district. He was also directed to see to the erection of comfortable schoolhouses, visit them at least four times each year and report the progress of the school work to the general council. He was authorized to hire the necessary teachers; and determine the books to be used in the schools; but under no circumstance was a teacher to be employed who advocated abolition of slaves. It was provided that the expense of these schools should not exceed the sum of $6,000 annually.

Passing along to 1859 the council enacted that all free born persons, except those of Negro origin, "heretofore received and acknowledged by us as citizens of the Creek Nation are hereby declared bonafide mem-bers and citizens." Children of a Creek woman by a Negro man when not more than half Negro were to be counted as Creek citizens. No slave without a written pass was permitted to be found over two miles from the premises of his owner, at any time, nor any distance from his home at night. No slave after 1861 was permitted to carry weapons or to engage in mercantile business with property owned by him. No Negro was permitted to preach to an Indian congregation. Negroes were allowed to have religious worship within two miles of their owner's premises when there was some free person not of Negro origin to watch over them. On March 1, 1861, a law was enacted requiring all free Negroes in the Creek Nation during the next ten days to choose masters among the Creeks, or be put up and sold to the highest Creek bidder.[16]

Tuckabachee Micco of Canadian District and Roley McIntosh of Arkansas District were chiefs during the period when most of these laws were enacted and recorded. In June, 1859, an election for principal and second chiefs was held, which the agent reported[17] "was for the first time in the history of the Creeks, conducted after a civilized and democratic fashion, and passed off quietly." Roley McIntosh, a man of great force of character, who had been chief of the Lower Creeks for many years, made way for his successor, Motey Canard, as chief of the Lower Creeks or Arkansas District, and Jacob Derrisaw was elected second chief. Tuckabachee Micco, who had rendered valuable service to the government in the removal of the Seminole Indians, was succeeded as chief of the Upper Creeks, or Canadian District, by Echo Harjo, who had been second chief, and he, in turn, was succeeded by Oaktahasars Harjo. The retiring chiefs were "remarkable men, possessed of vast influence with their people, particularly McIntosh, whose power among his people was almost absolute. He has long been the ruling man of the Creeks, and his word has been law. Tuckabachee Micco was also a man of great influence, a staunch friend of his people, a maker of treaties, and a good man. Both were captains and soldiers in the Creek wars, and did effectual service to the United States."[18]

A census of the Creek tribe was completed in June, 1859, for the purpose of making a payment August 3 to 9 of the $200,000 fund, from which it appeared that there were 13,550 individuals in the tribe, an

16   Manuscript copy of Creek laws in library of Grant Foreman.
17   *Report* of commissioner of Indian affairs, 1859.
18   *Ibid.*

·{ 216 }·

apparent further loss in population in two years of 1,338. "All that can statistically be said of the Creek people is, that they are not increasing, in population, and that in property and improvements of schools and farms, they are only slowly advancing, but, perhaps, quite as much as could be expected of a people in their circumstances and condition."[19] "More Creeks were present at one time during the payment in August than ever assembled before in this country." There was, unfortunately, a great increase in the amount of whisky introduced in the country, and vice in proportion. "This lamentable change is not to be ascribed to any lack of enforcement of stringent Creek laws against the introduction of liquor, but to the fact that ever since the unwise abandonment of the military post at Fort Gibson, near this, in the Cherokee Nation, restraints have slackened in strength, laws have lost their moral force, while the bold, reckless, and criminal have daily more and more emerged into light, defying law and disregarding the rights and property of others, have exercised much influence for evil and produced melancholy results. The chiefs of this nation desire the reestablishment of a military post in this region on the south side of the Arkansas river."[20] "The abandonment of the military post at Fort Gibson, and the growing up of a vicious little town there, have given unusual activity to the whisky trade in that region of the Cherokee country, and in the Creek country adjoining," said Superintendent Elias Rector. "During the last Creek payment several hundred gallons were vended in small quantities, and at enormous prices, just within the Cherokee line, and disorder and violence were the natural consequences."

A military post on the south side of Arkansas River ". . . .is necessary . . . .to uphold the law, to restrain the vicious, and to prevent serious private and public disturbances which have already broken out between the Creeks and Cherokees. . . . and may avert the turmoil, anarchy, and crime now foreshadowed by late events. If it is considered at all important that the authority of the United States should be maintained, and peace and order enforced in the Cherokee country, a military post should at once be established at Frozen Rock. If that is not done, the agent should be withdrawn, and disorder left to take its

19 *Ibid.*
20 *Ibid.*

Oaktahasars Harjo

course."[21] "The congregating of desperate and reckless characters is an ordinary occurrence rendering traveling throughout the country somewhat dangerous."

In September, 1860, the superintendent reported the "Creeks peaceable and quiet. They adhere to their old system of government, by national and town chiefs, and their laws are respected and obeyed by the people. I imagine no great advance is to be looked for among them; there is an aggregate of several different tribes and portions of tribes, and most of the Yuchis and Upper Creeks speak no English, and have intermixed very little with the whites. They are an agricultural people, and live in houses, but have not the remotest idea of a constitutional government, and, I should think will not have in many years."[22] However, the next month some of the more enlightened men in the general council proposed a form of government to be headed by one principal chief and a second chief, and the division of the Creek country into four districts with a judge for each and five supreme judges for the Nation.

The Creek agent was so much impressed by this proposed departure, that he somewhat prematurely reported: "Some important changes have recently been effected in the government under the old system. The nation was composed of two districts, each governed by a first and second chief, and in a great measure independent of the other. During the last session of the general council a constitution was adopted which provided for the election by the people of one principal and one second chief, and the division of the country into four districts; also for the appointment of as many judges for the same, together with five supreme judges for the entire nation, who will take cognizance of all offenses committed within their jurisdiction. This instrument makes many other minor and unimportant changes, which nevertheless, are evidences of progress. It is certainly more satisfactory than the old form of government. More amply authority is also conferred upon their police, termed 'Light Horse,' whose duty it is made to destroy all spirituous liquors brought into the nation, and levy a fine or inflict a penalty upon all persons found guilty of introducing it, or of the commission of other offenses."[23]

21 Elias Rector to Greenwood, *ibid.*, 1860.
22 *Ibid.*
23 Garrett to Rector, October 15, 1860, *ibid.*, 1860.

However nothing came of the proposed change at the time, as the Civil War soon burst upon the country and not only arrested all normal activities in Indian government, but again divided the Creek tribe into two bitterly warring factions.

BOOK FOUR / *Seminole*

CHAPTER SIXTEEN / *Contemporary Descriptions*

THE Seminole Indians defended their liberty and homes in Florida at an appalling cost of life. They defied the efforts of the white people to drive them from their country to which they clung with a tenacity and desperation that have no parallel in our humiliating annals of Indian spoliation. By their courage, strategy, and resourcefulness they exposed to ridicule an invading army of more than ten times their number. Their homes and settlements destroyed, driven into wellnigh inaccessible swamps and hunted like wild animals out of their hiding places during a sixyear reign of terror, they were carried from time to time as prisoners to the Indian Territory.[1]

They were at last conquered by a long and expensive war of attrition, and except for a few hundred who escaped the soldiers, the removal was completed in the year 1842. By resistance to removal from their homeland these indomitable people had incurred the wrath of our Government that imposed punitive and humiliating measures upon them. One of the most harmful of these was the stupid policy of requiring them to be merged with the Creeks in their western home. Socalled treaties had been entered into in 1832 and 1833 wherein the Indians were made to say that they agreed to the terms.[2] All the available evidence shows that they were not favorable to this plan, but on the contrary were bitterly opposed to it for reasons fundamental in their history and conflicting interests.

The Creek domain assigned to the Seminole for their occupancy by the Stokes commission under authority of Congress[3] was the

1 For an account of this migration see Grant Foreman, *Indian Removal*.
2 Charles J. Kappler, *op. cit.*, II, 249, 290. For a further account of these treaties, see *Indian Removal op. cit.*
3 *Ibid.*; *United States Statutes at Large*, V, 316, act of February 13, 1839.

area lying between the Canadian River and the North Fork of the Canadian and extending west to the Little River. Black Dirt and his band, the first arrivals in the West in 1837, settled on Little River within the limits assigned his tribe. But the Creeks indiscriminately occupied the best part of these lands, the Tuckabatchee Town in the winter of 1836-37, headed by Opothle Yahola, locating on the choice area near the junction of the Canadian and the North Fork including the site of the future town of Eufaula. So, subsequently when the Seminole emigrants arrived they found their country already occupied. They were brought by water from time to time, and nearly all disembarked at Fort Gibson where they were mustered by the agents whose duty it was to count the survivors of those tragic journeys and provide for the issue of their rations.

They had been dragged from their homes, compelled to abandon their meager possessions and arrived at Fort Gibson destitute, cold, and hungry and were dependent on the rations issued there for their existence. The difference in climate, soil, resources and living conditions between their former home and the strange country into which they were thrust was so great and forbidding that these bewildered, embittered, and broken-spirited people preferred to remain in camp around the fort and receive rations, rather than to venture upon the uncertain hazards of extracting a living from the soil of a new country. Subsistence was furnished one party of Seminole near Fort Gibson in 1842 at a cost to the Government of three and one-half cents each per diem, which must have provided meager fare for these wretched people.

Chief Mikanopy was somewhat more tractable than many of the subchiefs and he was induced to remove with some of his followers to the Deep Fork; in 1841 this band had nearly eight hundred acres of land fenced and planted in corn. They also were raising beans, pumpkins, and melons and small quantities of rice.[4]

By March 1842 the Seminole immigrants numbered 2,833 and were distributed as follows: 1,098 of Alligator's and Halahtochee's bands from nine to fifteen miles north, 70 of Coachoochee's band three miles south on the Arkansas River, and 827 of Mikanopy's band scattered in settlements from ten to forty miles southwest of Fort Gibson, and

4 *Report* of commissioner of Indian affairs for 1841.

Concharte Micco's band of 479 twenty miles south of the fort. Black Dirt's band of 360 was living on the Little River at the western extremity of the Seminole domain.[5] Other bands were located on the Illinois River near Park Hill.

In February, 1842 a party of 220 Seminole under their head men in charge of Capt. T. L. Alexander of the Sixth U. S. Infantry were placed on a ship at Tampa Bay and brought to New Orleans; here they were confined in the barracks for nine weeks awaiting other parties of emigrants. When all had arrived Captain Alexander set out from New Orleans on the steamer *President*. In May progress of the boat was arrested by low water about sixty miles above Little Rock and the Indians camped on the river bank several weeks awaiting a higher stage of water. When it came, they renewed the journey, but were again obliged to stop June 1 at Webbers Falls where Alexander debarked his company of 302 Indians who were taken overland to their new home.[6] They included the young chief Waxie Hadjo who had surrendered the previous November with seventeen warriors and thirty women and children.

Another company of 102 Seminole captives brought from Tampa Bay to New Orleans in April were placed in charge of Lieut. E. R. S. Canby who embarked them on the steamboat *Swan* July 22, 1842, and on August 5, because of low water in the Arkansas River landed them at La Fourch Bar six miles below Little Rock. After a delay of a week wagons and teams were secured and the party set out by land. Incessant rains and the hardship of the journey resulted in much sickness and their progress was very slow so that they did not reach Fort Smith until the twenty-fifth. From here, at the suggestion of General Taylor, they proceeded by way of the Choctaw agency to the falls of the Canadian River. Here it was necessary to open a road for twenty miles to where it intersected the route[7] from Webbers Falls to the North

5 Clark to Armstrong, March 21, 1842, OIA, "Seminole emigrant file." A map in the war department made in 1845 shows "Alligator's Town" on the east side of Grand or Neosho River about ten miles above Fort Gibson; and "Wild Cat's Settlement" on the east side of Bayou Menard southeast of the Fort.

6 Alexander to Crawford, May 18, 1842; Alexander to Seminole agent June 1, 1842, OIA, "Seminole emigration file" A 1238.

7 This was an important thoroughfare later used by the emigrant trains to California during the Gold Rush.

Fork; over this route they proceeded to the Creek council grounds where, September 6, Canby delivered the Indians to their agent John McKee. This party included John Coheia or Gopher John, a Negro interpreter of some distinction and talents, whose shrewdness enabled him to possess $1,500.00 which he was able to loan to the conductor for the expenses of the party, Canby not having been able to negotiate a draft for the purpose.

Nearly fifteen hundred Seminole Indians under Alligator and Wild Cat, and other chiefs, were now encamped around Fort Gibson in a distracted condition, homesick and discouraged, inflamed by their forcible removal from their homes in Florida; destitute and bewildered; for want of tools, helpless to cultivate the land or build homes; without means of transportation to the land provided for them even if they wished to go there; but above all else resolved not to locate in the country of the Creeks, become subject to their control, and risk the loss of their slaves and free-born Negroes who accompanied them.

These helpless and wretched people were living on the lands of the Cherokee who took pity on them and permitted them to cultivate the soil;[8] but some of them rewarded their friends by killing stock to keep their families from starving. In 1842 Alligator and a large number of his followers at Fort Gibson waited on George W. Clark, their issuing agent; they desired to know when the Government would give them the axes, hoes, and rifles promised by the officers to whom they surrendered in Florida. They said that before they were marched to the boats, General Jesup, in order to lighten the burden of removal told them to throw away their old rifles, kettles, tools, and other cherished possessions, which would be replaced by the Government when they arrived in their new home. This promise had not been redeemed in the more than four years since the arrival of most of them in the West.[9]

Gen. Zachary Taylor, who was stationed at Fort Smith in command of the Southwestern Frontier, was directed in 1842 to visit Fort Gibson and investigate the situation of the Seminole Indians living near there with a view to removing them from the Cherokee Nation. Alligator and several hundred of his followers had surrendered to Taylor on the west side of Lake Okeechobee in the spring of 1838 and were brought west. He had now returned to Florida with a number of other Seminole

8 Taylor to adjutant general, May 15, 1842, AGO, OFD, 158 T 42.
9 Canby to Crawford, November 12, 1842, OIA, Seminole emigration file C, 1802.

chiefs in company with a detachment of the Fourth Infantry to use his influence with the remainder of the tribe in an effort to secure their removal. General Taylor was a just man who entertained much respect for these Indians and sympathized with them in their unhappy situation.

Alligator being absent, Taylor did not propose to take summary action against his people and told them that they would be allowed to remain where they were until their crops were gathered and their agent had returned from Washington. "His absence however, was so long protracted that it became an obvious dictate of humanity to postpone the removal altogether until spring, rather than drive women and children from comfortable huts, and expose them to the rigors of an inclement season," said Taylor. On the return of Agent Butler in the early winter Chief Ross was consulted about the matter and he said the Cherokee council had refused to demand the removal of the Seminole Indians then and had decided to postpone decision of the question until a general council of several tribes in the spring. "I learned moreover," said Taylor, "from a highly respectable member of the council at Fort Gibson that they were averse to any forcible removal of Alligator's party." In view of this attitude, said Taylor, he decided not to employ force to break up Alligator's settlement and enforce their removal until it was demanded by the Cherokee authorities.[10]

As claims by the Cherokee and Creek farmers, against these unfortunate people for stock killed by them continued to pile up, chiefs of these tribes met some of the leading Seminole Indians in council on the Verdigris River in the spring to devise some means of removing the trespassers with the result that a number of small bands, including part of Wild Cat's company and Alligator agreed during the year to remove if the Government would provide the means as the Indians were destitute.[11] But the inflammable subject of their slaves prevented the fulfilment of this engagement.

The year 1843 was a particularly distracting one for these unfortunate, homeless people. Spring, the season for planting was passing, and it was nearly June when some of the Seminole immigrants indignantly and vigorously protested to their agent and condemned the faithlessness of the Government that had promised them axes and hoes and

10 Taylor to Jones, December 23, 1842, AGO, OFD, 470 T 42.
11 Judge to Hartley Crawford, March 14, 1843, ibid., file J 1173-1350, "Subagency."

had failed to provide these most necessary tools so they could cut the timber, clear the land, build their humble log cabins and plant crops for their sustenance. It was imperative, said their agent Thomas L. Judge, that 350 hoes and 159 axes be provided at once.

Another party of 350 captives was embarked on February 5, 1843, at Tampa Bay, for New Orleans. In charge of Lieut. Henry McKavett, they left New Orleans on March 4 and on the eleventh reached Little Rock where they were detained by low water. McKavett landed his charges on the south bank of the Arkansas opposite the mouth of the Illinois River April 26.[12] They remained at Webbers Falls near by while awaiting transportation to their country. The spirit in which they came was evidenced by the retribution visited on their Negro interpreter. While in their Webbers Falls camp the interpreter "was lying down saying he was sleepy. Several Seminoles were also lying on the ground near him; one observed to him that it was now a year since he had decoyed them into Gen. Worth and as he was sleepy they would give him a long sleep, and immediately plunged several knives into him. They then buried him and told Mr. Judge that they had buried their interpreter. I have not received the account of Mr. Judge who is very much disturbed at the murder; when I do I will forward it to you. No other violence was offered, and as I have no doubt none intended. The object being to kill the Negro, which had been agreed upon doubtless before leaving Florida."[13] Agent Judge said that on becoming acquainted with the circumstances he was surprised that the Indians had not killed their interpreter sooner.[14] Wagons were then procured and the Indians were transferred to their new home, where they arrived destitute. The next year the Seminole near Fort Smith shot at the guide and interpreter, Gopher John.[15]

Agent Judge visited the various depots where during the summer of 1843 he issued corn and salt to some of the Seminole who had located in the Creek Nation. On this occasion he had an opportunity of observing some of the earlier settlers in their new homes and "noticing their

12   McKavett to Jones, March 31, 1843, AGO, OFD, 121 M 43; ibid., May 1, 1843, 45 M 43.
13   Armstrong to Crawford, May 22, 1843, OIA, Seminole file A 1457, "Choctaw agency."
14   Mason to commissioner of Indian affairs, July 10, 1844, OIA.
15   Judge to Armstrong, May 20, 1843, OIA "I. T. Misc. Seminole affairs."

domestic arrangements; and in every instance their Cabbins were Clean and Comfortable, and content seemed to be manifest in all their Countenances and a large vessel of sofka to which all who called were welcome, which for the first time I tasted, and it was very good; they dress corn in a great variety of ways, some of which would be considered a luxury in any Civilized society."[16] He was surprised at the progress they had made: "I found them in possession of as good land as any in the country, and generally satisfied; and things comfortable around them; they had raised a considerable surplus of rice which they sell at $3.00 per bushel and good demand for it. . . . . They are very desirous of having a school established; they have frequently named this subject. . . . . Wild Cat and Alligator both have agreed to move next fall."[17] However, a drought that summer reduced by one-half the corn crop of the immigrants, but to offset that loss some of them had good crops of rice and potatoes.[18] For these people living on their land on Deep Fork, the government blacksmith was making plows, wedges, troughs and other farming utensils. But when the axes were all distributed, they were two dozen short of a full supply.

Judge took the trouble to study and appreciate the Seminole Indians: "I am inclined to believe that the character of the subjects of this sub-agency had been little understood or appreciated. I find them a high-minded, open, candid and a brave people; they pay more attention to the wants and comforts of their women than any other tribe I am acquainted with; they keep them well clothed, and the men pay particular attention to appear in clean and appropriate costume. They appropriate most of their annuity to clothe their women and children; in this respect they set a good example to other tribes. If these people received a tithe of the aid and assistance that other tribes are the subject of, their advances toward civilized life would be second to no tribe. It is true thay have cost the Government much blood and treasure; notwithstanding which, I hope the Government will extend towards them an equal ratio of that fatherly care and protection of which other tribes have been such large recipients."[19]

16 Ibid., June 17, 1843.
17 Ibid., March 14, 1843.
18 Report of commissioner of Indian affairs for 1843.
19 Judge to Armstrong, September 15, 1843, Report of commissioner of Indian affairs for 1843.

The agent held a full council in July with the Seminole immigrants. Some of them proposed to disown Wild Cat and Alligator and their followers living at Fort Gibson. When this information was communicated to these chiefs, they declared that they were Seminole and acknowledged as their chief the old chief, Mikanopy, who had removed on the land set apart for the tribe. That they would go and look at the land and if they found some that suited them they would remove.[20]

At council, said their agent, there were 3,400 Seminole present, exclusive of their Negroes. "Notwithstanding the immense crowd and the country around in every direction full of whiskey, there was not an Indian on the ground the least disguised with liquor; I never saw a more orderly assembly in any country. Their object in getting their whole people together was for the purpose of hearing what was done at Washington for their relief in a pecuniary point of view, and the prospect of their obtaining a distinct section of country."[21] The Seminole, Judge says, had a much larger number of children in proportion to their population than the Creeks.

There were more than 1,000 Seminole Indians living in the Cherokee Nation[22] and John Howard Payne visiting them, noted their desire to be admitted into the Cherokee tribe. This sentiment is not hard to understand when one recalls the sympathy exhibited by the Cherokee for the friendless and harried Indians defending their homes and families in Florida against the invading white forces. In the autumn of 1837 a deputation of influential Cherokee Indians volunteered to visit the warring Seminole people and carry a message from Chief John Ross calculated to end the strife and bloodshed in their country. While the enterprise was carried out at the request of the war department, it was not given the necessary support by those in authority in Florida to insure its success. The delegation left their homes and endured great hardship and personal inconvenience and loss and were not even compensated for the expenses they incurred. The Seminole Indians had not forgotten that the Cherokee people were their friends in the hour of trouble, and their talk of being admitted to that tribe is quite comprehensible.[23]

20 Judge to Armstrong, July 14, 1843, OIA, "I. T. Misc. Seminole Affairs" 1843.
21 Ibid., August 11, 1843.
22 Butler to commissioner of Indian affairs, commissioner's report for 1844.
23 Indian Removal, op. cit.

But the stay of the Seminole people in the Cherokee Nation was an unhappy and profitless experience. A traveler who saw them there gives a drab picture of their destitution and aimless existence: "April 7 [1844]. Reached Fort Gibson on the Neosho. . . . . Four companies of infantry and two of dragoons are stationed here under the command of Lieut. Col. Loomis, a devoted Christian. April 8—had a talk with Micanopy, the principal chief of the Seminoles through the interpreter, Gopher John. Told him what I wanted. He said there had been a man talking something about a school, but he did not know much about it—could not tell whether his people would send their children or not. The 'governor', as Gopher John called him, seemed rather sleepy, and to care more about the contents of the bottle he carried with him, than whether his people were educated or not.

"Rode to the Seminole camp, half a mile from Fort Gibson; found 200 of the most miserable looking men, women, and children I had seen anywhere; the men had been on a drunken frolic, from the effects of which they had not yet recovered; the women usually select some day when their lords are sober, and do not require their care to enjoy *their* frolic. The night previous there had been a thunder shower, which failed however to break up their dance. One who recollects how they have been hunted and driven about in Florida for some years, can readily conceive the appearance their camp presented.

"The country assigned to them is between the forks of the Canadian: too cold in winter and too hot in summer for those who have been accustomed to the equable climate of Florida. . . . . The Seminoles who have been settled in the Canadian Fork raise corn and rice; have 1,000 blacks among them, slaves for the most part, who pay a small tribute to their master, say two or three bushels of corn, or when they raise stock, a beef or two.

"April 9—Rode out with Adjutant Belger of the 6th to pay our respects to Judge Fields[24] of the Cherokee bench. He had just finished a very fine and commodious house on a commanding eminence, but received us in his cabin. His lady, a Philadelphian of Quaker parentage; his daughter, educated in the East, very attractive. While there Micanopy, Alligator, and Wild Cat, followed by a troop of braves and *canaille*, some on foot and two on a horse, squaws at a respectable distance, came up to hold a council in regard to their matters.

24 Richard Fields lived east of Fort Gibson near Bayou Manard.

"Micanopy (the 'governor') brought an empty bottle, which with some significant gestures, he handed to the Judge. The interpreter (Gopher John) signified that the Governor was growing sleepy, whereupon something was produced to quicken the old gentleman's faculties. This after partaking himself, he handed to his brother chiefs, but not a drop to the parched throats of his followers, who, from the nodding in the course of the council, did not seem to have recovered from their late frolic. The governor began his speech by complaining that for sometime past councils had been held by the band near the fort without consulting him, and then alluded to a power of attorney given by some, not all, of the chiefs, to their agent, to negotiate for them with the government in reference to sundry matters of interest. Among these was entire discretion as to the point of their submitting to the Creek laws. Old Micanopy was alarmed lest his people would not submit to that rule, and had some apprehensions, no doubt, as to the two or three hundred blacks called 'Micanopy's slaves.' The Judge suggested their sending a delegation to Washington, which has since visited that city, with what effect we have not learned. . . . . Left the Seminoles debating among themselves what course they would take, and returned to the fort."[25]

By the spring of 1845 the Seminole Indians had all left the Cherokee Nation for their own home, except a band numbering 417 who expressed a wish to remain and live with their hosts. The Cherokee agent and the principal officers of the Cherokee tribe visited and held a council with them on March 17. They explained to the Seminole the terms of their treaty, the desire of the Cherokee for them to remove, and asked for their views on the subject. Addresses were made to them "in which their actual condition was kindly shown them and the advantage pointed out that will result to them by locating among their own people, having their own firesides, cultivating their own fields, living under their own regulations and maintaining a high spirit of self respect and independence. These and kindred arguments had very evidently no very little influence in reconciling them to the country, and to continue further westward their pilgrimage. Although strongly attached to the Cherokees, and disposed, as they expressed

25 *Journal of a Tour in the Indian Territory* by N. Sayer Harris in the Spring of 1844, edited and annotated by Carolyn Thomas Foreman, *Chronicles of Oklahoma*, X, 219.

themselves, to share the destiny of the Cherokees, to live where they live and to go where the mysterious hand that leads the Indian may guide them—we expect to see them speedily and voluntarily joining their own people. They will unquestionably remove at an early day.

"There is—perhaps, scarcely any subject upon which the Cherokee people, and most particularly the Principal Chief, has been more abused and misrepresented by one or two government agents on this frontier, than that connected with the residence of the Seminoles among the Cherokees. It has been represented that it was entirely owing to *his* influence and wishes, that they have not since quietly and voluntarily joined their own people, and settled down in the Creek country; and that they were kept here for selfish purposes, somewhat in the capacity of brave but mercenary Switzers. For a proper appreciation however, of the subject and of the feelings and circumstances that have suffered them so long to remain here, it is only necessary to state a few facts.

"The Seminoles were brought here by the U. S. officers, after the termination of a protracted war, and to suit the convenience of contractors, were tumbled in among the Cherokees and subsisted for one year at Fort Gibson. Having no country of their own, and not wishing to subject themselves and property to the laws of the Creeks, they were resolutely averse to settling down in their country and sacrificing their nationality and ancient customs. Under these circumstances, and heartily sympathising in their destitute condition, in their homeless state, and in the trials, wrongs, and keen sufferings they had borne for years with a manly and heroic fortitude, the Cherokees became their brothers, extended to them the hand of charity, bore with great generosity their depredations on property and were unwilling to raise their voice against them, and invoke the arm of the United States in forcing them away until some permanent and satisfactory provisions should be made for them.

"Such are briefly the considerations that have caused them to remain with us so long, but now that homes have been obtained for them, it is the wish of the Cherokees and the interest of both that they should go, as they will, and occupy them."[26]

In the autumn of 1845 a band of Seminole Indians were still living on Vian Creek and their Cherokee neighbors endeavored to have them

26 *Cherokee Advocate*, March 20, 1845, p. 3, col. 2.

removed. A resolution was adopted by the National Council on October 14 requesting the principal chief to invoke the assistance of the United States agent for the Cherokee Nation, in effecting that removal. Maj. George Lowrey, acting principal chief, returned the resolution with his disapproval for the reason that a compliance with it would necessarily enlist the service of the military arm of the Federal Government. The authorities of the Cherokee Nation had consistently and bitterly opposed any measure that would permit or encourage the intrusion of the United States forces in the internal affairs of the Nation; and the acting chief recommended that the Cherokee rely on their powers of persuasion on the unwelcome guests.[27]

Another unbiased observer of these much oppressed people visited them in their country near Little River where he wrote from Tustenuggee Town to the *Cherokee Advocate*. He described a Seminole as comfortable when he had a blanket "as old Abraham would say 'he full of sofky'; enough fire to light his pipe (at this time of year) his gun and 'tricks' thereto belonging—a hunting shirt, a girdle, handkerchief or shawl on his head, string of beads around his neck, a leather string around his leg, and last, tho' not the least in his estimation, a feather stuck in his hair and then if he has a piece of Tobac one inch square, he is, to use an Arkansas phrase, 'in town with a pocket full of rocks'..... Yesterday and day before, this place was crowded with Indians, several hundred being present. They had met to counsel on various subjects; one, the complaints made by Cherokees about certain Seminoles now in your country, whom they desire will immediately remove, and for that purpose have sent messengers to express the wishes of the chiefs. They say, however, that they expect a great deal is done on the credit of the Seminoles, as there are a heap of bad men among the Cherokees, who are just as willing to steal as anybody; but they do not wish their people to stay among their neighbors if they are tired of them. Another subject before them was the scarcity of corn, for want of which many are suffering, and to relieve whom they have drafted in advance on their annuity sufficient to purchase several hundred bushels to be distributed to the needy." The agent was to leave the next day for North Fork Town to negotiate for the corn.

"The chiefs deserve great credit for the promptness with which they called their people together and acted, when informed of the

27 *Ibid.*, October 23, 1845, p. 3, col. 4.

complaints of the Cherokees. While at the agency they also drew public hoes due them by the United States, for which they now have use; having fenced in considerable fields and nearly finished planting; some corn is now up; and if it is a good season, I have no doubt from experience, they will make a sufficiency of corn to do them the next year.

"Although several hundred were about the agency for two days, I did not see one that was intoxicated; they camped around within three hundred yards, in little parties, giving the place an animated and picturesque appearance, huddled around their camp fires in groups after nightfall. Being in open woods, they could be seen in all directions."[28]

28 Ibid., May 14, 1846, p. 3, col. 4.

HALLECK TUSTENUGGEE and his band of seventy warriors on April 16, 1843 fought with the United States forces the last battle of the Florida War. The Federal troops found the Seminole making a last stand upon an island in the Great Wahoo Swamp, and after an irregular fight of two hours, routed them. The loss was slight on both sides. Halleck Tustenuggee was a skillful warrior; bold and daring in his policy, yet capable of dissimulation and treachery. He had been the object of pursuit for two years, but his unceasing vigilance had enabled him to bid defiance to government troops. Now however, destitute of powder and provisions he was forced to sue for peace. He came into the American camp boldly, shook hands with Gen. William J. Worth, and proclaimed his pacific purpose. His professions were treated with great apparent respect. He wanted provisions for his people. They were encamped three miles from General Worth's quarters, and were fed at public expense. And when the whole band had come within the lines for the purpose of attending a feast, they were secured as prisoners, and immediately sent to Tampa Bay for emigration; and, on July 14, this entire band, consisting of 120 persons embarked for Fort Gibson by way of New Orleans.[1]

A large part of the Seminole emigrants could obtain no adjustment of their problems in the West. The failure of the Government to provide their needy people with implements with which to prepare their land for cultivation and shelters in which to live; the unalterable opposition of many of them to amalgamation with the Creeks and the contention over the Negro slaves kept them in a ferment, prevented their settling

1 Joshua R. Giddings, *The Exiles of Florida*, 313.

down and adjusting themselves to their new surroundings. So Wild Cat and Alligator, two of the shrewdest men in the tribe, organized a delegation to Washington to see what could be accomplished by interviewing the responsible heads of Indian administration. Wild Cat financed the journey and the Cherokee merchant Richard Fields, living at Bayou Menard seven miles east of Fort Gibson, went along to care for the party.

Through some influence, Black Dirt, Halleck Tustenuggee, Pascofa, and other Seminole chiefs remaining at home were induced to sign a statement condemning the members of the delegation and ascribing to them unworthy motives in making the journey.[2] When Wild Cat heard the charges against him he wrote a letter to General Worth denying that he was going to mix in politics: "It is true I am going to Washington on business of my people. We have been conquered. Look at us! A distracted people, alone without a home, without annuities, destitute of provisions, and without a shelter for our women and children, strangers in a foreign land, dependent upon the mercy and tolerance of our red brethren the Cherokees; transported to a cold climate, naked, without game to hunt, or fields to plant, or huts to cover our poor little children; they are crying like wolves, hungry, cold, and destitute."[3]

When the delegation returned home they found their people encamped on the prairies in the neighborhood of Fort Gibson, destitute of food. The great flood of 1844 in the Grand and Arkansas rivers had driven them from their homes, with the loss of practically all their possessions; not only destroying the crops in the ground, but sweeping off the old corn in the cribs. Two hundred and thirty-five sufferers by this calamity were left entirely destitute, subsisting themselves on berries and what they could obtain by begging. To relieve their suffering Col. R. B. Mason, commandant at Fort Gibson, issued rations to them.

The Seminole living on Deep Fork, Elk Creek, and Little River, in the Creek Nation, said their agent Thomas L. Judge, had a large amount of corn, potatoes, and rice on hand; and appearances promised a fair average crop in the autumn, in which event they would have a surplus.

2 Micco Nupper and others to Crawford, April 20, 1844, OIA, Seminole File M 1941.
3 *Arkansas Intelligencer*, March 30, copied in *United States Gazette* (Philadelphia) May 18, 1844.

They were also raising melons, pumpkins, and beans, and had increased their stock of horses, cattle and hogs. "And all about them evinces that they see the necessity of throwing themselves on their resources to procure the necessities of life.

"The great cause of dissatisfaction to the Seminoles is, that they have no country they can call their own; this has a tendency to depress their feelings, and is a continual source of uneasiness; and, until removed, it need not be expected that they will become content. They utterly repudiate the idea of becoming a constituent part of the Creek Nation, or submitting to the Creek laws in the remotest degree. . . . . And I am fully convinced it would be highly impolitic and improper that it should take place or that the government should make any attempt to make them a constituent part of the Creek nation. . . . . I have no hesitation in saying the farther apart these two people are the better for both."

"Among the poor, neglected and despised Seminoles, there is as much honor and integrity as among any other tribe, though they may be far advance of them in the habits of civilized life; and to their credit it can be said, that the intercourse of the sexes is confined to the connubial state—no cases of infidelity in this respect occur among them. They have great affection for their children; pay much deference to their wives; and when at home in their familes, appear to appreciate the enjoyments of the domestic circle. I admit, however, with all their good qualities, they have many bad ones; but if left to themselves, and not instigated by bad white men, they would have much fewer of these. They are extremely indolent; though, in view of their recent removal from a congenial climate, where the spontaneous production of the soil supplied them with nearly all their wants, so that little exertion was required on their part, this is not a matter of suprise. Under similar circumstances, the same result would have attended the whites. Most of them however, have become sensible of the change of circumstances, and that exertion is necessary on their part to obtain the necessaries of life; and they are applying themselves accordingly, and no doubt this eventually will be the case with most of them; and it would tend to produce this result if they had a country they could call their own."[4]

4 Judge to Armstrong, August 26, 1844: *Report* of commissioner of Indian affairs, 1844.

The Seminole tribe met in council July 31, 1844 and the agent availed himself of the opportunity to take their census. The total reported by all the towns or bands was 3,136 exclusive of Negroes. Of these, 400 belonged to the Apalachicola band, with Econchatti Micco as chief. "Blunter's Band" headed by their chief Co-ah-thlocco, numbered 114; and the remainder were Seminole proper.

John Douglas Bemo was a Seminole Indian with an interesting history, who distinguished himself in the service of his people. The son of a chief he was also the nephew of the militant and colorful Osceola. In 1834 while a small boy he was carried away from his home in Florida. One of his abductors was a man named Jean Bemeau from whom the boy received his name. He was taken to sea and for eight years sailed before the mast. In 1842 his ship made the port of Philadelphia and while there he visited the Mariner's Church and met the pastor, Rev. Orson Douglas. The minister said that Bemo was one of the most extraordinary characters he had ever met; he was greatly concerned about the persecution of the Seminole tribe at the hands of the Government, and expressed a strong desire to return to and serve his unhappy people.

Bemo was received into the church and plans were made to fit him to teach and preach to the Seminole people in their western home. Mr. Douglas in September 1842 "put him into the best schools our city affords, so that all the instruction needful to prepare him to be a blessing to his people had been furnished. He is so desirous to do them good that his mind is bent on returning" to them in the fall of 1843, "to live or die with them & for them. It seems to us a singular providence, that, while they are so prejudiced against the whites, one of their number should be raised up of God for their welfare. When Osceola died at the fort near Charleston, John was present and sent word by the warriors that so soon as they ceased fighting he would return & be their chief." It is the Rev. Orson Douglas who is writing the commissioner of Indian affairs for assistance in sending John Bemo to the Seminole Nation in the West; he offers to take the Indian to Washington for the commissioner to interview him.[5]

The next month Mr. Douglas wrote the secretary of war that he

5 Douglas to Crawford, August 15, 1843, OIA, Seminole File D 816. As Osceola died about January, 1838, Bemo must have returned from his wanderings to visit his uncle during his confinement in Fort Moultrie.

had done everything possible to prepare John for the field of usefulness among his people. "His whole heart is filled," he said, "with
the desire to return to his people to promote their temporal and spiritual welfare. For prudence, foresight, honesty, & real piety, he is
surpassed by few persons I have even known."[6] Bemo reached the
Seminole agency about November 1 and after reporting to the agent,
Thomas L. Judge, visited among his people and talked to them about
starting a school; his unselfish interest in and desire to serve his countrymen made a decidedly favorable impression on them.[7]

The agent said that Bemo was a very promising young Seminole.
His school was opened about March 15, 1844. "On the first opening,
there were forty children in attendance; they came under the impression that they would be found their meals; but finding that this was
not the fact, the numbers were soon reduced to fifteen; at which it
has remained stationary. . . . . Those are making good progress; all
of them have got through the alphabet and some of them commenced
spelling; they are much pleased and are very attentive, and no doubt
the school will increase. John Bemo's course has fully sustained the
good opinion his friends have formed of him; and, no doubt, if he continues faithful, he will be instrumental in dispensing much good to his
people. He preaches regularly once, and frequently twice a week, to
full houses; his congregations are principally blacks though several
Seminoles have joined the Church since he came among them; and a
marked change has taken place in the manners and habits of the Indians
immediately in the neighborhood of the school, which evinces that he
has exercised a salutary influence over them."[8]

"Many wealthy, influential friends of the Indians, believe that
John was raised up by Providence as an instrument in forwarding their
benevolent views towards them," wrote Rev. Mr. Douglas to the commissioner of Indian affairs. Among them a recent letter from the commissioner had "produced no little consternation, suprise, & sorrow"
because he opposed the plans of the church people to have Bemo return
to Philadelphia where they desired to lionize him and further prepare

6 Douglas to Porter, September 7, 1843, ibid.
7 Judge to Armstrong, November 7, 1843, OIA "I. T. Misc., Seminole Affairs."
8 Judge to Armstrong, January 29, 1844; ibid., August 26, 1844: Report of commissioner of Indian affairs, 1844.

him for church work in the Indian Territory. They had raised $100 for John's expenses home and supposing he was to be allowed to come, Mr. Douglas expressed their appreciation to an audience of more than 2,000 people. John had written that he would be ready to start as soon as the necessary funds should reach him. Mr. Douglas was at a loss what to say to his congregation to account for John's failure to return.

The delegation of Seminole Indian had recently been in Washington and Mr. Douglas raised "hundreds of dollars in money, cloaths, trinkets, & tools for Wild Cat & his party & paid all their extra expenses while here." Here then was the seat of the hostility of the commissioner who had no sympathy for Wild Cat or his grievances and because of the interest of the church people in their welfare, imagined that through John Bemo they might give aid and comfort to the dauntless Coacoochee and his partisans. Mr. Douglas said further that he had just heard from Wild Cat on his arrival home "that the high water had swept away their little property, & they must suffer unless rations are given them from Fort Gibson. Will you let us feed them? The poor creatures, many of them will be naked this winter. Shall we cloath them? They are ignorant. Shall we teach them? Then hasten John here to his friends, and we will furnish the means.⁹"

Bemo did come to Philadelphia, however, early in the spring of 1845 and through the aid of Rev. Mr. Douglas and his friends he was entered in the school at Easton where he applied himself to his studies until October when he returned to his people and resumed his labors.¹⁰

The Seminole agent was convinced that it was impossible to effect any marked change in the habits and character of the adult Indians; that the only way to make any permanent improvement in the tribe was through the children to be educated in the schools he hoped would be established in their country; and conducted by competent teachers who had dedicated their lives to the improvement of the Indians; teachers whose example and precept copied by the children would

9 Douglas to Crawford, September 10, 1844, OIA, Seminole File, D 970.

10 Bemo lived a life of usefulness as school teacher and preacher. He married a Creek woman named Harriet Lewis and located near the Creek agency northwest of Muskogee where he lived until his death. He had three sons and one daughter whom he named Iona in remembrance of the beautiful Ionian Islands among which he had sailed. His sons, were Alex Orson, Douglas, and John. Bemo's descendants lived until recent years on the old homestead which was taken as his Creek allotment by one of his sons.

unconsciously mould their character. He pointed to the example of Fort Coffee Academy and said that "the Choctaws (much to their credit, and to the honor of those who have aided them in the good work) are the pioneers in establishing a permanent system of education for their people in their own country"; and he thought that within the limitations of their means the Seminole might copy them.

Dissatisfaction and unrest were now becoming importunate. The Cherokee Indians thought they had tolerated the Seminole on their lands long enough. The Seminole refused to conform to governmental policies and submit to the Creek dominion over them. The Creeks were disappointed at not having the Seminole Negroes in their power, and the latter were in great alarm for their safety. All had been deceived; all had been wronged. And this feeling was growing daily until it seemed that hostilities were imminent. In vain had the officials endeavored to suppress this feeling.

The Government then decided upon another effort to bend the Seminole Indians to its policy. What was called a treaty between the Creeks and Seminole and the United States was entered into on January 4, 1845. The preamble of the treaty recited: "Whereas it was stipulated in the fourth article of the Creek Treaty of 1833, that the Seminoles should thenceforward be considered a constituent part of the Creek Nation, and that a permanent and comfortable home should be secured for them on the lands set apart in said treaty as the country of the Creeks; and whereas many of the Seminoles have settled and are now living in the Creek country, while others, constituting a large portion of the tribe, have refused to make their homes in any part thereof, assigning as a reason that they are unwilling to submit to Creek laws and government, and that they are apprehensive of being deprived by the Creek authorities of their property; and whereas repeated complaints have been made to the United States government, that those of the Seminoles, who refused to go into the Creek country, have, without authority or right, settled upon lands secured to other tribes, and that they have committed depredations upon the property of those upon whose lands they have intruded."

By the terms of the treaty the Creeks agreed that the Seminole Indians might settle in a body or separately in any part of the Creek Nation; that they could make their own town regulations, subject however to the general control of the Creek council, in which they should have representation. "The Seminoles having expressed a desire to settle in a body on Little River, some distance westward of the present residence of the greater portion of them," it was agreed that rations should be issued to them while removing and for six months thereafter. And the Government agreed to pay them the beggarly sum of $15,400 promised them in the Treaty of 1832 in exchange for their vast holdings in Florida. This meager consideration was payable to them on their arrival in the West and was therefore several years overdue. Annuities amounting to $17,000 promised them in the Treaty of 1832 and withheld for fifteen years were now again promised the Indians. And "in full satisfaction and discharge of all claims for property left or abandoned in Florida at the request of the officers of the United States, under promise of remuneration" they were belatedly to have the miserly sum of $1,000.[11]

The real bone of contention, the source of nearly all the bitter hostility, the controversy revolving round the Seminole Negroes, was disposed of in a few evasive words incorporated in section three: "It is mutually agreed by the Creeks and Seminoles, that all contested cases between the two tribes, concerning the right of property, growing out of sales or transactions that may have occurred previous to the ratification of this treaty, shall be subject to the decision of the President of the United States." This document drawn by officials of the Government made no allusion to the Seminole Negroes, but the Seminole delegates being persuaded that it had the effect of protecting them in their legal rights, agreed to it.

Pursuant to the terms of the treaty, in the following autumn and winter a number of Seminole and their slaves removed to the Creek country in the vicinity of Little River[12] where prairie land predominated. The Seminole Negroes established themselves in villages separate from the Indians, whereupon the Creeks proceeded to assert ownership over them. The Negroes then appealed to General Arbuckle for the protection promised them by General Jesup in Florida.

The Government had agreed in the treaty to subsist them for six months from June of that year and as they arrived in their new location too late to make a crop or adequately to house themselves against the

11   Charles J. Kappler, op. cit., Vol. II, 407.
12   Report of William Armstrong, September 30, 1845; Arkansas Gazette, February 7, 1846, p. 1.

weather, and as the succeeding winter was unusually severe, there was much suffering among these people so recently from Florida where they had never seen snow. The subsistence furnished by the Government terminated in the middle of the winter and most of them would have starved but for the fact that a kind hearted agent took the authority to provide them with food.

In the treaty the Seminole were guaranteed the right of self government so far as related to their "town laws" but were required to acknowledge the supremacy of the Creek general council. The Seminole tribe was divided into twenty-five towns or bands. There had been twenty-seven but upon the death of their headmen two attached themselves to other bands. Each town had its own governor or head man and town laws; the general council of the Seminole tribe having a supervisory control over all the towns.[13] In the council a majority of the head men with the approbation of the king or governor passed laws for the government of their people, provided they did not conflict with the laws of the Creek general council.

Many of the Seminole were accommodating themselves to their new environment in a better spirit, induced by the opportunity to govern themselves and relieved from the oppression of white people about them. Tending their fields in common they were raising some stock, corn, sweet potatoes, rice, beans, and ground nuts or goober peas. Their cabins were an improvement on their former habitations; simply furnished with a few necessities, a stool or two, pestle and mortar for crushing corn, sofka spoons, hominy baskets, two or three pots or kettles, with a buffalo or deer hide in the corner serving as a bed. The Seminole espoused no form of worship, said their agent DuVal; their views on that subject were expressed in the words: "to live as you please but die brave." In the presence of death and an opportunity to speak, the dying Seminole would say: "I am a man and a warrior, and not afraid to die."[14]

After Wild Cat returned from his visit to Washington in the winter of 1845-46 he accompanied Gov. Pierce M. Butler and M. G. Lewis to Texas to aid them in their successful effort to conclude a treaty with the Comanche of that state. Noting the opportunity revealed to him on

13 DuVal to commissioner, October 15, 1846: *Report* of commissioner of Indian affairs, 1846.
14 *Ibid.*

this western expedition, with Halleck Tustenuggee, Oktiarche and other Seminole, he went out on the western prairies on an "exploring hunt." "They were gone about six weeks and on their return Wild Cat held a meeting with his people on Little River when he told them of the scenes through which he had passed and the sights he had seen; of the Indians he had met and smoked with, and the word they had sent to their red brothers, the Seminole; of how pleasing it would be to the Great spirit when he saw the white smoke ascending to the heavens which arose from the pipe of peace smoked by the Seminole and their brothers of the prairies. He had met four different bands or tribes, and had a kind of council or friendly talk, and it was agreed among them to meet again about the first of September, and have a fuller understanding, so that they might always be friends. The agent informed Wild Cat and the other Seminole at the council of the recent triumphs of Gen. Zachary Taylor in Mexico. They were somewhat incredulous at first, but when satisfied of the truth of the report Wild Cat said "Mexicans, maybe so, they cant fight; maybe they better quit and make friends; might get whipped some more; Mexicans not as good as Seminoles to fight; General Taylor big man now, but I chase him back once myself; Seminoles make him run in Florida."[15]

Wild Cat soon headed another party of about 250 men to keep the appointment he had made with the Comanche Indians and engage in a protracted trading and hunting expedition. They took with them a large quantity of merchandise to trade to the prairie Indians, for peltries and mules, which they expected to dispose of for a handsome profit nearer home, and pay for the merchandise they took with them; and it was anticipated that if the venture were successful it would be followed by others. However the hunt was a failure and the price of peltries at home did not realize the profit they expected.[16]

At this period most of the Seminole Indians were living between the North Fork of the Canadian and the Little River on the north side of the main Canadian River. Their territory was mostly prairie land well adapted to farming and raising stock. The preceding winter had been one of the coldest ever known in the country and caused much suffering among these immigrants unused to such cold and unprepared

15 *Cherokee Advocate*, July 30, 1846, p. 3, col. 2.
16 *Arkansas Intelligencer*, October 3, 1846, p. 2, col. 1; *Report* of commissioner of Indian affairs, 1846.

to resist it. Mikanopy was the principal chief, and Wild Cat, his "Coun-sellor and organ, who has to assist him in determining what the king *ought to do;* there were also five sub-chiefs: Tussekiah, Oktiarchee, Pascofar, Echo-mathla, and Passuckee Yohola, who may be called the executive council."[17]

In 1847 the Seminole raised a bountiful crop of corn, rice, potatoes, pumpkins, goober peas and beans, and Mr. DuVal, their agent said they would bear comparison as agriculturalists with any other tribe on the border. Mutual jealousy between them and the Creeks continued but no serious difficulties had occurred. The subject of education, the agent observed, was little thought of; "As it was only intended for white people they feel themselves and desire to be considered, as perfectly satisfied to walk in the foot-steps of their predecessors, show-ing, as far as mental improvement is concerned, a philosophy in being satisfied with their present state."

By 1849 the condition of these Indians had changed but little. They paid scant attention to any kind of stock; if it prospered, all very well; but if not, they said that they had bad luck, or that if they had been in Florida their stock would not have required attention.[18] A good many of them went out to hunt, not so much for profit as from habit. They were on good terms with all tribes but the Creeks. The Seminole annuities were merged with those of that tribe and some of the former claiming they were discriminated against, believed they fared better by enrolling as Creeks.

There had been no school in the Seminole Nation but that of John Bemo;[19] and preparations were made by the Presbyterian Board to open one under Rev. John Lilley who arrived at the station on October 20, 1848. He erected a log structure for a mission school called Oak Ridge in which he and his wife, J. D. Bemo and his wife, and a few others instructed Seminole children. This school, the only one then in the Seminole Nation, was begun in October 1849 and continued for ten years. By 1854 it was reported that the Seminole were beginning to lay aside their Indian dress in favor of that of the white man.[20]

17 *Ibid.*
18 DuVal to commissioner in *Report* for 1849.
19 Washbourne to commissioner, in commissioners *Report*, 1854.
20 *Report* of commissioner of Indian affairs, 1858.

CHAPTER EIGHTEEN / *Emigration Resumed*

Hostilities in Florida were now a part of history. The "War" was definitely ended by the announcement of General Worth in 1843 after the surrender of Halleck Tustenuggee. The people of Georgia and Florida insisted that the war was not over and only when General Worth refused to continue feeding their militiamen would they believe him. This incitement to martial ardor abated, no more troops were offered and peace for a time rested upon the remnant of wretched Seminole Indians who hung on with the tenacity of desperation to their beloved homeland. After capturing and sending off Halleck Tustenuggee's band in 1843, General Worth estimated that there were remaining in Florida only about 300 Indians, and he sent for their headmen to meet him in council at Cedar Keys on August 14. Realizing the impossibility of capturing these resourceful and elusive people he told them that they might remain peaceably on a restricted area of swampland in the southern part of the Peninsula, the limits of which were defined by him.

Immured in the fastnesses of southern Florida, little was heard of the Seminole Indians for some years, but the Government was not permitted by the white people entirely to forget them or the desire to have them driven from the country. To consign them to death from disease or starvation in the swamps, was a challenge to the indomitable character of the Indians and it is not to be supposed that they meekly observed the restraints prescribed by General Worth, so that occasional complaints of intrusion by them into the white settlements were heard. And there were reports of depredations and murders of whites the provocations for which received scant notice.

The white people had not lost their appetite for "war" that placed numbers of troops in the field, made a market for their produce and gave employment and food to the militia. Opportunity for further military excitement and attempted removal of the Indians was revived in the early part of 1849. A party of four Seminole Indians murdered a white man named Barker on Indian River. While there was no suggestion of concerted action by the Indians, it was not long before the state was in a ferment on the subject of Seminole depredations. On January 13, 1849 the Florida legislature adopted, and the governor approved, a resolution addressed to congress presenting their parlous situation and calling for relief by the Federal Government. On the same day the legislature enacted a law forbidding the passage of any Indian across the line prescribed by General Worth.[1]

Soon negotiations were under way to send another delegation of western Seminole to exercise their influence on their eastern brothers and endeavor to secure their removal to the west. In charge of Seminole Agent Marcellus DuVal a delegation left North Fork Town October 16 for Fort Smith to take a boat down the Arkansas River. The deputation was headed by Halleck Tustenuggee, and included "Passacke Yoholo, Holatooche, Nocose Yoholo, Carbitchachuppe, Thlathlo Hadjo, Cotchar, Hothelebogeh, Cochokna Hadjo, Isipeco Chopco, Tustunnuc-cochee, with the interpreters Toney, Jim Bowlegs and Tom." They were promised $1,000 each for their service.[2]

Capt. J. T. Sprague who had much experience with the Florida Indians estimated that at this time there were only 120 in Florida capable of bearing arms, seventy Seminole, 30 Mikasuki, twelve Creeks, four Yuchi, and four Choctaw, who with their families constituted a total population of 360. They included Sam Jones (Abiaca), ninety-nine years old; also Billy Bowlegs, thirty-three years old who spoke English fluently and exercised supreme control over the Indians.

With this formidable array of 120 warriors to oppose, assuming all of them to be hostile, Col. Joseph Plympton of the Seventh Infantry at Jefferson Barracks was ordered with his command to Florida, and to report to Gen. D. E. Twiggs at Tampa Bay. The State of Florida also ordered out two companies of militia. By the next February General

1 Secretary of war to secretary of interior, March 28, 1849, enclosing letter from Maj. W. W. Morris, OIA, Seminole file, W 324.

2 But did not receive it. They left New Orleans November 6 on the steamer *Ashland* for Tampa Bay.

Twiggs was in command of a force of 1,735 officers and men at different stations in Florida.[3]

General Twiggs and his staff arrived at Tampa Bay November 17 and met a party of fifty or sixty Seminole Indians who had been waiting there "nine days with three of the murderers, and the hand of the fourth, who was killed in the attempt to capture him. Every chief and sub-chief of note in the nation was there having gone through much trouble and many trials in capturing the young men who committed the murders on Indian river. After the United States Commander-in-chief addressed the council Assunwha, the chief speaker of the nation, replied to that part of it which related to their removal from Florida:

" 'We did not expect this talk. When you began this new [removal] matter I felt as if you had shot me. I would rather be shot. I am old, and I will not leave my country. Gen. Worth said he spoke for your President, too; that he was authorized to make peace and leave us quiet in our country, and that so long as our people preserved the treaty, yours would. For many years you have had no cause to complain, and lately when a few bad men broke the law—a thing that cannot be prevented among any people—did we not hasten to make atonement? We met you as soon as we could, and promised to give ample satisfaction and from that day we have not rested. We have killed one of our people, and have brought three others to be killed by you and we will bring the fifth. There has been much trouble and grief but we have done justice and we came here confident that you would be satisfied. Now when you ask us to remove, I feel as though you had killed me too. I will not go, nor will our people. I want no time to think or talk about it, for my mind is made up. . . . . I did not expect this talk, and had I done so I would not have helped to deliver up these men to you.'

"Billy Bowlegs, who is a fine looking fellow of forty, followed with great earnestness and dignity of manner. After talking somewhat to the same effect as Assunwha, though with more wildness of phrase, but not of manner, he added: 'We have now made more stringent laws than we have ever had before, and I have brought here many young men and boys to see the terrible consequences of breaking our

3 Twiggs to secretary of war, February 2, 1850, AGO, ORD, WDF, T 4.

-{ 249 }-

peace laws. I brought them here that they might see their comrades delivered up to be killed. This business has caused many tears but we have done justice.

" 'I now pledge you my word that, if you will cease this talk of leaving the country, no other outrage shall ever be committed by my people; or, if ever hereafter the worst among my people shall cross the boundary and do any mischief to your people, you need not look for runners or appoint councils to talk. I will make up my pack and shoulder it, and my people will do the same. We will all walk down to the sea-shore, and we will ask but one question: Where is the boat to carry us to Arkansas.'

"A day was appointed for another council, but they did not promise to attend. There was an informal promise that some runner would come in to see the whites, but they often observed that they were stunned and confused by the talk, and could not promise anything."[4] However General Twiggs persevered and after much pursuasion the Indians later agreed to meet the General in a council on January 19, 1850. The council was held at the time and place proposed by Bow-legs, and General Twiggs was encouraged by the attitude of the Indians. Taking the delegation of western Seminole with them they departed for the swamps to interview their people on the subject of emigration.[5] They were offered large financial inducements to join their brothers in the West: $500 a head for each man and boy capable of bearing arms, $100 for each woman and child; the Government to subsist them for a year after their removal to the West; to pay for all cattle, hogs, crops, and other property abandoned or lost; to make presents of dresses and blankets; to furnish a physician for the journey. And in addition large sums were offered to individual Indians of influence in the tribe amounting in one case to $10,000.[6]

No such inducement was ever held out to any other tribe, but only a small part of the Seminole were influenced by it. The remainder stubbornly refused to abandon their native land. One of Twigg's posts located fourteen miles east of Fort Clinch was called Fort Ar-

4 *The Indian Advocate*, December 1849, p. 3, col. 2.

5 Twiggs to secretary of war, January 22, 1850, AGO, ORD, WDF, T 16.

6 This offer in all probability was to Billy Bowlegs as he was the Indian above all others whom it was hoped to reach. His identity was not revealed in the source from which the information was obtained.

Mikanopy. From McKenney and Hall,
INDIAN TRIBES OF NORTH AMERICA

John Bemo (Tal-a-mas-Micco, or King of the Forest)

buckle and was occupied by one company of artillery and one of infantry. Here sixty Seminole men, women, and children came and agreed to emigrate and with a few others they were taken to Manatee. On February 28 these and fourteen more Seminole emigrants headed by their chiefs Ca-pit-chu-che, and Ca-cha-fix-i-co, in charge of Maj. T. H. Holmes embarked on the steamer *Fashion* and sailed for New Orleans.[7] They were accompanied by the Arkansas delegation who were returning home. The ship arrived at New Orleans March 13, all of the party, the most of whom were children, having been very seasick.

Negotiations with the Indians had broken down. The delegation from the West having tired of their employment and departed for their homes, General Twiggs on March 11 ordered Maj. W. T. H. Brooks to proceed immediately to the western home of the Seminole and endeavor to induce Wild Cat and Jim Jumper to assemble another delegation of their people and return to Florida. Mikanopy had died a few months before and he was succeeded as chief by Jim Jumper. At the same time Twiggs directed Maj. W. H. Garrett to go to New Orleans and look after the comfort of the emigrating Indians on the *Fashion*. He was told that they had a large amount of money and he must find a comfortable boat for them on which to ascend the Mississippi, and try to induce them to put their money in the safe of the boat until they arrived at their destination.

The emigrants in charge of Major Garrett and Marcellus DuVal, their agent, were shipped from New Orleans on the steamer *Cotton-plant* which brought them to Fort Smith on April 1. Here "some of them took the steamboat *J. B. Gordon* for Fort Gibson, and the remainder traveled all the way by land, to their place of destination. . . . . They are abundantly supplied with money, and this being the first point where they have stopped since leaving New Orleans, they have been very liberal with it, and it is supposed that a large amount, the greater portion of what they had with them, has been disbursed at this town [Fort Smith]. There was a great and sudden rise in the price of horses and ponies, as many were needed by them. In fact the town has been almost entirely drained of this kind of property. It was a perfect harvest to the pony dealers and horse

7   Twiggs to secretary of war, January 19 and 29, February 11, 12, and 20, 1850, AGO, ORD, WDF, T 3, 4, 9, 13, and 17.

jockeys. The prices which the Indians, in some cases, paid for quite indifferent animals, was astonishing. The *store-keepers* or *merchants*, also, highly enjoyed themselves, *obtaining* in most cases, very *extra-vagant prices* for their wares."[8]

Twiggs reported to the secretary on March 27 that the Indians had broken off negotiations and removed from the vicinity of the troops. Bowlegs and his people, he said, had refused to emigrate and all hopes of a peaceful settlement had vanished, though no hostilities were anticipated. On May 5 Brooks arrived with Seminole Chief Jim Jumper, four subchiefs and three interpreters.[9] But this delegation had little influence with the Seminole. The latter declared they would hold no communication with them and would shoot them if they came into the Seminole country. They said they were grossly deceived by the former delegation and would have nothing to do with another.[10]

Then Luther Blake in 1851 went to Washington where he secured appointment as a special agent to the Florida Indians and received a commission to attempt their removal. He was authorized to offer $800.00 to each warrior, and $450.00 for each woman and child who would remove. But this effort also failed to induce the Seminole people to abandon their beloved homes.[11] Blake then hastened to the Indian Territory to secure another delegation to work on the Florida Indians. But he contracted the cholera near Fort Gibson and was delayed in

8 Letter written by Rev. Charles E. Pleasants dated at Fort Smith April 2, 1850, in *New York Sun*, copied in *Fort Smith Herald*, May 25, 1850, p. 2, col. 2. Rev. Mr. Pleasants was a Philadelphian temporarily residing in Fort Smith. He was a correspondent for the *Sun* and had furnished that paper with several communications describing conditions and events in the vicinity. In reply to charges that the Fort Smith merchants had imposed on the emigrant Indians Judge John F. Wheeler, editor of the *Fort Smith Herald*, wrote a sharp reply. After a rejoinder in the New York paper Wheeler again paid his compliments to Pleasants. The next time they met there was an exchange of firey epithets, whereupon Wheeler struck Pleasants with his cane and the latter in turn shot the editor in the breast with a derringer. Fortunately for both of them, Wheeler was carrying a large bundle of mail he had just taken from the post office which with the contents of a breast pocket broke the force of the bullet and saved his life.

9 Up to this time a total of eighty-five Seminole Indians had emigrated.

10 Col. J. H. Winder to secretary of war, September 20, 1851, OIA, Seminole file W 566.

11 *Report* of commissioner of Indian affairs for 1851; U. S. House *executive document* No. 2, Thirty-second Congress, first session, p. 306.

returning to his post for months. In the end he accomplished nothing.

Seminole emigration remained at a standstill for some time. And President Pierce on May 18, 1853 announced that "The manner heretofore adopted to effect the removal of the Indians from the State of Florida having failed of their object, I deem it proper and do hereby direct that the duty of removing the Indians be devolved upon the the Secretary of War" and taken away from the interior department.[12]

Nobody seemed to be getting anywhere with the removal of the handful of Indians remaining in Florida, and in November 22, 1853 Chief Chilly McIntosh of the Creek tribe offered to take a contract to remove the remainder of them.[13] But nothing came of this offer. Lieut. John Gibbons of the Fourth Artillery visited the western Seminole to secure another delegation to Florida and on December 12, 1853 the delegation joined him at Fort Smith. It was composed of John Jumper, brother of the chief, Jim Jumper, Halleck Tustenuggee who headed the delegation in 1849, "Kapitchochee," chief of the emigrant party of 1850, Toliss Hadjo, son of Sam Jones, and eleven others including Jim Factor, Indian interpreter and George Noble, a Negro interpreter. Leaving Fort Smith in wagons they descended the river until they met a boat and arrived at Tampa Bay January 5, 1854.

The Florida legislature had enacted a law prohibiting any one from trading with the Indians so that they not only would be unable to secure arms or ammunition to use against the whites, but they could not purchase food or secure ammunition with which to kill game for food or secure peltries to exchange for any of the things necessary to sustain them. It was hoped that the Indians would thus be starved out and would be willing to emigrate. Capt. J. C. Casey, who had been left in charge of the small number of troops in the country, was engaged in efforts to catch escaped slaves among the Indians and asked the aid of the latter. They declined, saying that the whites had refused to let the Indians trade with them; therefore they accepted the challenge and said, if your troops will stay on your side of the line we will stay on ours, and there will be no trouble. But Casey said their proposition could not be entertained. In March Casey wrote to Jefferson Davis, secretary of war, that there was no prospect of inducing the Indians

12 Adjutant general to Gen. Winfield Scott, May 19, 1853, AGO, ORD, WDF, A 41.
13 AGO, ORD 917 M 1853.

to leave Florida and he was going to send home the delegation of western Seminole. They took their departure April 10. The only hope of conquering the stubborn Florida Indians, he said, was to starve them out by enforcing the law against trading with the whites.

The Government was later engaged in exploring and surveying the swamps of Florida and the Indians not only did not interfere but assisted when called upon, with the pathetic plea that when the soldiers and surveyors saw how poor and worthless the country was they would agree to let them stay. But in December 1855 a company of twenty or thirty warriors burned the unoccupied blockhouses in and near Big Cypress and attacked a white man. Casey, still hopeful, asked the secretary of war to have J. W. Washbourne, Seminole agent at Fort Smith, send Ben Bruner to Florida to interpret between him and the Seminole prisoners in his custody.

In 1854 Bowlegs and some of his people visited Washington to secure some abatement of the persecution to which he and his people were subjected in Florida. Maj. J. T. Sprague later wrote the secretary of the interior concerning these unhappy Seminole: "From my long acquaintance with these people, in peace and in war, I have entertained an interest in their happiness, as well as the interests of the Government, and ultimate emigration. . . . . I have remarked, that I entertain an interest in the welfare of these Indians from the fact of my having been brought personally and intimately in contact with them—in the time of danger have been protected by their chiefs, and when in their camps been treated with the utmost kindness. During the summer of 1854, when the Seminoles were visiting Washington, Bowlegs was at my quarters on Governors Island, N. Y. when he assured me in the most positive and angry manner of his determination not to leave Florida, giving his reasons fully and freely. There are Indians in Arkansas who could be induced to exercise a beneficial influence upon the Seminoles. Bowlegs has a sister in that country in whom he has confidence; there are also many Indian Negroes once owned by himself and his father who might be used effectively at the proper time."[14]

14   Casey to Davis, March 12, 1854 and April 9, 1854, AGO, ORD, WDF, C 128.

CHAPTER NINETEEN / *Intrigues of Wild Cat*

THE Seminole Indians suffered at every turn from the injustice and ineptitude of Federal policy. Next to the thinly veiled fraud that characterized the so-called Treaty[1] of 1833 the most conspicuous of the wrongs perpetrated by the Government on these Indians was the fatuous effort to amalgamate them with the Creek tribe in the West. In the same category though of lesser possibilities for mischief was the duplicity and vacillation of the Government relating to their Negro slaves. Contention and confusion almost resulting in bloodshed and tribal demoralization were caused by the action of the Government.

To facilitate the subjugation of the Indians in Florida Gen. Thomas S. Jesup told a number of these slaves that if they would surrender and agree to emigrate they should be emancipated; and that when they arrived in the West they were to be permitted to settle in a village to themselves in the manner in which they had been accustomed to live in Florida,[2] under the protection of the United States, never to be separated or sold.[3]

1　Foreman, *Indian Removal, op. cit.*
2　The Seminole were owners of a large number of slaves who dreaded the "idea of being transferred from their present state of ease and comparative liberty to bondage and hard labor under overseers, on sugar and cotton plantations. They have always had a great influence over the Indians. They live in villages separate, and, in many cases, remote from their owners, and enjoying equal liberty with their owners, with the single exception that the slave supplies his owner annually, from the product of his little field, with corn, in proportion to the amount of the crop; and in no instance, that has come to my knowledge, exceeding ten bushels; the residue is considered the property of the slave. Many of these slaves have stocks of horses, cows, and hogs, with which the Indian owner never assumes the right to intermeddle. . . . An Indian would almost as soon sell his child as his slave, except when under the influence of

On these terms several hundred Seminole slaves surrendered and were removed to the West. Jesup was succeeded in the command of the forces in Florida by Gen. Zachary Taylor who told the Seminole Indians that those who surrendered and agreed to emigrate would be secure in their property, including their slaves. Here were conflicting elements sufficient to produce confusion and misunderstanding, but they were complicated by another. The Creek Indians who volun- teered for service against the Seminole Indians in the Florida War were promised as booty all the Seminole slaves they might capture. Expediency dictated the policy of the Government no matter how in- consistent and unjust, leading to untold evil possibilities. A conflict of policy and interest and endless contention resulted which seriously interfered with the adjustment of the immigrant Indians.

The efforts of the Creeks to sell their captive slaves to a white man were nullified by the army officers who aided the Seminole Indians in bringing them to Fort Gibson. But this was only the beginning of the trouble. The fear that the Creeks would attempt to take some of the Negroes was one of the insuperable obstacles that prevented the Seminole Indians from removing on the Creek domain set apart for them and therefore one of the influences that kept them for several years in a state of unrest, confusion and discontent living around Fort Gibson, arresting all efforts to reëstablish themselves.

After the arrival of the Seminole Indians with their slaves in the West, the confusion that arose out of the situation gave rise to con- flicting claims to certain slaves. Kidnapers were busy running some of them far away and disposing of them. Freeborn Negroes of the tribe were captured and sold into bondage. The Negroes complained to the officers at Fort Gibson and made much of the promise of General Jesup to secure them in their freedom. This situation existed for several years and when General Jesup arrived at Fort Gibson in 1845 to plan the construction of the new fort, some of the Negroes came to

---

intoxicating liquor. The almost affection of the Indian for his slave, the slave's fear of being placed in a worse condition, and the influence which the negroes have over the Indians, were used by the Government to induce their removal to the West where the continuance of this happy relation was promised them" (Wiley Thompson to secretary of war, April 27, 1835, *American State Papers* "Military Affairs" Vol. VI. 534).

3   Jesup to secretary of war, July 1, 1848, OIA, Seminole file W 244.

see him and ask for the fulfillment of his agreement. When he told them that his promise was in full force and effect and that they were entitled to their liberty, several hundred of them left their owners and some of them came to the post, where they were given sanctuary and the protection of the military against efforts to remove them. Between sixty and seventy of them were employed in the construction of the new stone fort. Subsequently the Seminole owners and Creek claimants made repeated efforts to secure the Negroes.

When the tripartite Treaty of 1845[4] was made between the United States, the Creek and Seminole nations, section three was entered into for the express purpose of settling this vexatious question, which was therein referred to the President for determination. By virtue of that article the president referred the question to the attorney general, who after long delay, rendered an elaborate opinion in the summer of 1848 in which he decided that the Negroes should be restored to the condition in which they were prior to the intervention by General Jesup. The President approved the report and gave orders for carrying the opinion into effect.

Plans were thereupon made by General Arbuckle then in command at Fort Smith to have the slaves delivered to their Seminole owners at Fort Gibson on December 22, 1848. Gen. W. G. Belknap was in command at Fort Gibson and instructions were given him for making the delivery.[5] The weather was very cold and the Seminole Indians not having become accustomed to the climate, were unable to reach the post on time so that the delivery did not take place until January 2, 1849.

What otherwise would have been a festive occasion for the Indians was made sad by the sudden death of their chief Mikanopy on the day of his arrival at the post to receive his slaves. The Seminole were greatly attached to their venerable leader who had done what he could to sustain them during their recent trials, and had made every effort to reëstablish them in the West.[6]

The Negroes delivered that day numbered 286, of whom 108 had surrendered to General Taylor in Florida; of these fifty-nine were

4 Kappler, *op. cit.*, II, 407.
5 Jones to commissioner of Indian affairs, January 30, 1849, OIA, Seminole file J 143.
6 *Indian Removal, op. cit.*

claimed by Mikanopy, six by Echo Hadjo, seventeen by Billy Bowlegs, and twenty by Nelly Factor. Of another list that were brought in to Fort Jupitor in Florida by August and Latta, twenty-seven were claimed by Nelly Factor, nineteen by Mikanopy, eleven by Holotoochee, thirteen by Billy Bowlegs, ten by Harriett Bowlegs, ten by Echo Hadjo, and the remainder by Charley Emathla and Miccopotok. Of another list that had surrendered at Pease Creek one was claimed by Harriett Bowlegs, sixteen by Billy Bowlegs, and four by Holotoochee.

The Negroes were called into the chapel where General Belknap formally turned them over to the Seminole chiefs to whom he gave some advice and instructions—that they should not sell the Negroes, and should treat them well and not punish them for things done in Florida.

The delivery was made by the military amidst sullen resentment of Creek and white claimants. The Creek chiefs disapproved of Negroes who were to enjoy a modified form of slavery and live within the limits of their country. A conspicuous one of these Negroes was Gopher John[7] who had served as guide and interpreter for the army officers in Florida. The Seminole council presided over by Mikanopy in 1843 made an order declaring him to be a free Negro.[8] He had been useful to the tribe and in 1845 for sixty days was engaged with his wagon and three yoke of oxen in removing some of the Seminole Indians and their baggage from near Fort Gibson to Little River. Being a free Negro he was in daily fear of being kidnaped and sold into bondage; he was also in danger of being killed by some of the Seminole who tried to shoot him on one occasion when they killed his horse instead. So he went to Washington to see General Jesup and secure permission to return to Florida where his life and liberty would be more secure. But he returned to the Indian Territory.

Gopher John was a smart Negro and exercised much influence over the others who looked to him for leadership. When they were turned over to the Seminole tribe he conducted them to a place to set up their town separate from the Indians in the manner in which they lived in Florida and according to the customs of the Seminole Indians. This settlement bore the name of Wewoka and was located about thirty

7 Gopher John was known to the army officers as John Warrior, John Coil, and John Cohia.
8 Gopher John to Jesup, June 10, 1848, OIA, Seminole file J 96 and 102.

miles from the Seminole agency. This arrangement was satisfactory to the Seminole Indians but not to the Creeks within whose territory the Seminole were unwittingly located. They would have had little to complain of but for the burning and deep-seated resentment of individuals at being deprived of the slaves they had captured in Florida, and of the long standing claims of some of them to slaves who many years before had fled to Florida and been protected by the Seminole.

These slaves knew as soon as they left the protection of the military at Fort Gibson they were in daily peril of being kidnaped and they armed themselves with knives, guns and pistols. This the Creeks claimed to be a violation of their laws, and said they would not tolerate it. Another difficulty and cause of trouble in the country was the fact that the Seminole agent, Marcellus DuVal, had a brother William J. DuVal, an attorney, who claimed to have performed valuable services for the Seminole Indians in securing the delivery of the Negroes to them. He professed to have had a contract with the Indians which provided that he should have one-third of the slaves recovered for his services.

There had been much friction between the Seminole and the Creeks over the Negroes, and the year before Wild Cat had cut off the ears of young Tallassee to satisfy some grievance. The Creeks were much exercised about this summary treatment of a member of their tribe and planned reprisal on the Seminole chief. A large crowd of them went to his home and held a dance during which they intended to carry out their program. But in the darkness and confusion they laid hold of the wrong man and beat him nearly to death, the wily Coacoochee easily escaping their clutches.[9] There was intense excitement and further trouble between the tribes was feared.

The agent was very bitter at General Arbuckle for holding that the Seminole Indians were obligated not to sell their slaves by the promise made them in Florida by Jesup. DuVal wrote numerous letters complaining of the attitude of the military which interfered with the performance of the contract with his brother. The Indians had been told also that no contracts for sale of any of the slaves made prior to the delivery of the Negroes could be executed. DuVal called on Arbuckle

9 *Cherokee Advocate*, June 5, 1848.

for a force to disarm the Negroes for the apparent purpose of carrying out the contract made with his brother and taking possession of them. Arbuckle told him that it was impossible to send a force for this purpose as there were 180 cases of cholera in his command of 193 men at Fort Smith, and the eighty-six soldiers at Fort Washita were busily engaged in erecting quarters for themselves and troops coming to that post from New Mexico.[10]

At this point Coacoochee entered the controversy. He came with some of the Seminole chiefs and warriors to Fort Smith to see General Arbuckle and protest against the delivery of the Negroes to DuVal's brother as he said the owners of the salves were not consulted about the contract which was made by Jim Jumper before he became chief.[11]

Coacoochee or Wild Cat was a remarkable man of conspicuous intellect, easily the shrewdest man in the tribe. He was the son of King Philip, an influential chief in Florida. When he went to Washington in 1844 he was greatly impressed by the power of the United States and he returned home correspondingly impressed with his own importance and that of his people who had been able through six years to defy ten times as many well trained and provisioned soldiers of the great Republic. The army officers regarded him as a man of great force and predicted that he would some day become chief. However on the death of chief Mikanopy he was succeeded as chief by Jim Jumper (Micco-nut-char-sar), probably the son of the Chief Jumper who died at New Orleans during the removal. Whether Wild Cat was disappointed at not being made chief to succeed Mikanopy does not appear from available records but that was probably the case. At any rate after Jumper became chief and sought to commit the slave-holding members of the tribe to a deal whereby the agent's brother would obtain a large part of their slaves, Wild Cat began to make plans to leave the Indian Territory for another home, and sought to influence some of the Seminole Indians to accompany him.

He was a resourceful and ambitious man and his efforts excited considerable interest and apprehension among the Indians and the officers of the Government. He had engaged in trading expeditions among the prairie Indians[12] and the Comanche especially looked up to him as a

10   Flint to Drennan, August 13, 1849, AGO, OFD, 238 D 49.
11   Ibid., September 10, 1849.
12   In the autumn of 1846 about 650 Indians crossed the Red River on their way

man to be respected and cultivated. He had become familiar with the southwestern country far toward the Mexican border and entertained a scheme for setting up an Indian colony in that region of which he would be the head. The injustice to which he and his people had been subjected by the Government burned deep into his soul and he had never forgiven the authors of those wrongs. Brought a prisoner from the home of his birth he had never reconciled himself to the change as some of his people had, and consistently refused to conform to the plans of the Government, settle on the lands of the Creeks and become subject to their domination.

Before the Seminole delegation left North Fork Town in October, 1849, for Florida, Wild Cat conferred with them and their agent. He made a proposition to DuVal which he wished conveyed to the President. He said that his people were dissatisfied with their present situation with the Creeks and desired to remove with him to Mexico; and if the President would favor the enterprise he would get Bowlegs and the remainder of the Seminole in Florida to remove to that country, whereas they would never willingly locate in the Creek country. But, DuVal said, Wild Cat secretly told memebers of the delegation to advise Bowlegs and his people to hold on until he could induce the Government to make a treaty by which they could remove with him to the Rio Grande. Wild Cat was not hostile to the Government said DuVal, "but he is ambitious and would want to cut a figure in the world; would wish the Govt. to believe *he* is controlling and holding in check the Wild Indians of the Prairies & would at the same time convince the Indians that he was only playing the part of a skillful diplomatist in deceiving Govt. for their benefit."[13]

The Creek leaders played into Coacoochee's hands by their determination to possess the slaves of the Seminole. They had declared that no town of free Negroes or Negroes in a form of qualified slavery such as those of the Seminole, should be permitted to exist within the limits of their nation. They passed a law prohibiting any free Negro living among them and prohibiting any Negro from possessing arms.

to the Colorado where they planned to spend the winter hunting. One company of 150 was commanded by Wild Cat who said he was going to hunt and treat with the Comanche Indians (Upshaw to Armstrong, October 6, 1846, OIA, "I. T. Misc. Upshaw").

13   DuVal to Brown, November 5, 1849, OIA, "Florida" file D 251.

An incredible amount of controversy and disturbing contention revolved around this situation. And Wild Cat had no trouble in inducing some of the Negroes to accompany him on his adventure to Mexico where they would be free. With twenty or twenty-five warriors and their families and a large number of Negroes headed by Gopher John, some Creeks and Cherokee, he set out early in the winter of 1849-50 and made a temporary stopping place on Cow Bayou, a branch of the Brazos River, in the vicinity of the residence of a number of Kickapoo Indians. Here they were to remain and make a crop while Wild Cat cultivated the Indians in the neighborhood and attached them to his enterprise. Wild Cat had left word that any whites or Creeks who undertook to follow him would be killed.[14] He was "determined to entice away as many Indians as possible and settle in Mexico where he will not have to contend with rival chiefs. He is a cunning, ambitious man, and is not willing to be less than head of the tribe."[15] According to the *San Antonio Western Texas* of June 6, there were 700 or 800 "Seminole, Lipan, Wago and Tankawah Indians under the command of Wild Cat encamped on the Llano."[16] Some Cherokee and Creek slaves accompanied him and it was thought they were to learn the route and then act as guides in running off others to join his colony.

The Creeks determined to take a number of the Seminole Negroes remaining in the Negro town and on June 24 a party of them accompanied by several white citizens and a few Cherokee "arrived in the vicinity of Wewoka, Seminole Nation, manned and equipped. I soon learned their object was to take forcible possession of a number of Negroes at that time residing in the Seminole nation known as the Seminole Negroes, but claimed by some of the leaders of the aforesaid party. Much excitement was produced among the Seminole people in the vicinity, as the object of these men was not clearly known to them, and when they did learn that it was their intention to attack the Negro town, many of them painted themselves for war and asserted their firm determination to assist the Negroes in defending themselves." The military authorities at Fort Smith under Capt. Frederick T. Dent then interposed and warned Agent DuVal and Chief McIntosh of the Creeks to use their authority to prevent what might bring on a war

14 DuVal to Brown, May 30, 1850, OIA, "Seminole" file D 392.
15 *Fort Smith Herald*, March 2, 1850, p. 2, col. 2.
16 *Idem.*

between the two tribes. Under this pressure the Creek force withdrew to the north side of the North Fork River. A council was then held between the leaders of the two tribes and it was agreed that the Creeks might take a number of Negroes claimed by them. About 180 Negroes accordingly were taken to the Seminole agency where they were held to prevent their flight to join Wild Cat in Texas and from giving information to him and support to that many more who had fled and planned to join him. The fugitives were led by Jim Bowlegs, a slave of Billy Bowlegs of Florida. The leaders of the Creeks and the individual white men and Cherokee who were engaged in this effort to capture these slaves were "Nunin" McIntosh, Siah Hardage, Tom Carr, Joe Smith and John Lilly, Creeks; William Drew, Dick Drew, and Martin Vann, Cherokee; P. H. White of Van Buren, I. M. Smith of Fort Smith, one Matthews a trader near the Creek agency and Gabriel DuVal, a brother of the agent, from Montgomery, Alabama, white men.[17]

Wewoka was within the limits of the Creek Nation as then defined. The Creek authorities were determined that its law forbidding free Negroes from residing within the Nation should be respected, and enforced, even if they were obliged to resort to force of arms to bring it about. The Creeks said that if the Negroes were free they should not remain in the Creek Nation: on the other hand if they were slaves they must be under the control, care and custody of their owners in accordance with the established custom of the tribe. The Creeks refused to recognize the custom that had prevailed between Seminole Indians and their slaves of permitting them to reside in separate towns. "On more than one occasion the Creek people as one man, had determined to take the matter in hand and with rifle and ball disarm the Negroes and turn them over to their masters, or drive them from the country," said Philip N. Raiford and John Drennan, Indian officials, though their real purpose was to secure the slaves for themselves.[18]

Wild Cat returned to the Seminole Nation in September, 1850 and held a council with the chiefs and headmen of his tribe. His visit caused much excitement among the Creeks, who greatly feared the enterprise and resourcefulness of the chief. Having opened a route to the Spanish country and familiarized the Negroes with it the Creeks were fearful that he would be the cause of many of their slaves running off to free

17 Dent to Arbuckle, July 15, 1850, AGO, OFD, 135 A 50.
18 Drennan and Raiford to Lea, August 24, 1850, OIA, Seminole.

Mexico. At the Seminole council Wild Cat endeavored to induce the tribe to follow him to Texas but the opposition of the authorities prevented many from going. He had succeeded in enlisting nearly a thousand Kickapoo Indians under his command and represented himself to be in a position where the combination of Indians could maintain themselves and set up a little Indian state in Mexico.[19] The Kickapoo allies of Wild Cat had purchased their powder and lead from the merchants at Little River, and Echo Hadjo, Creek head chief and Billy Hadjo second chief, ordered these merchants not to sell them any more ammunition.

The Creeks were greatly exercised and Chief McIntosh gave orders to arrest Wild Cat because of his threat to overturn the established order of affairs. When Wild Cat heard of the order for his arrest he called on DuVal and told him that he had a large force of Tawakoni, Kickapoo, and other Indians who were prepared to fight for him; that he was going to remain with his warriors on the south side of the Canadian River, prepared to fight McIntosh and the Lower Creeks; but he did not wish to have any trouble with the whites or the Upper Creeks.[20] The Creeks then abandoned their warlike demonstrations.

"It appears that the return of Wild Cat to the Seminole country has produced a great deal of excitement in the Creek Nation. Five or six hundred Creeks started off a few days ago from the Creek Nation to arrest him, but from some cause they turned back when within forty miles of him. He has free intercourse with all the roving bands of the prairies, and wields a powerful influence wherever he goes. He is a proud ambitious fellow, and prides himself on his cunning and sagacity. What his present visit will amount to we shall soon find out.[21]

Before the end of the month Wild Cat set out for the Rio Grande with a few Seminole and about 100 Negroes. A large number of Creek warriors pursued but before they could overtake them the Negroes were attacked and captured by the Comanche Indians. When the

19 DuVal to Lea, September 30, 1850, ibid., D 392.
20 DuVal to Brooke, October 20, 1850, ibid., D 481.
21 *Fort Smith Herald*, October 11, 1850, p. 2, col. 3. Wild Cat was said to have been accompanied by a large number of allies from the prairies. The Creeks were much alarmed and a council of chiefs was called who ordered twenty-five men from each Creek town to report for service against Wild Cat and his allies (*Indian Advocate*, October 1850, p. 3).

Billy Bowlegs, Seminole Chief

Seminole Council House

Creeks came up with them they demanded possession of the captives who were delivered up only on the payment of ransom to the Comanche Indians. When the Creeks started to return to the Indian Territory with the Negroes the latter resisted and made an abortive effort to escape. A bloody encounter resulted in which a number of Negroes were wounded. On their return there were sixty captive Negroes in possession of the Creeks when on October 23, 1850 they passed Camp Arbuckle, where Dr. Rodney Glisan noted the number of wounded prisoners.[22] Wild Cat was not present when the capture of the Negroes was effected or the result of the encounter might have been different.

Other Seminole Negroes attempting to cross the plains and join Wild Cat on the Rio Grande, were massacred by the Comanche Indians. In one party every Negro except two girls was put to death. These girls were taken to the camp where the Indians perpetrated the most inhuman barbarities upon them; among other fiendish atrocities the savages scraped through their skins into the flesh believing that beneath the cuticle the flesh was black like the color upon the exterior. They burned them with live coals to ascertain whether fire produced the same sensations of pain as with their own people, and tried various other experiments which were attended with most acute torture. The poor girls were most shockingly scarred and mutilated when Captain Marcy saw them in 1850. A Delaware trader had secured them from their captors and brought them to the Little River settlement when Marcy was there.[23]

Upon inquiring of the Indians the cause of their hostility to the blacks they told Captain Marcy, with sardonic humor perhaps, that it was because they were slaves to the Creeks and the Indians were so sorry for them that they killed them to send them to a better world and release them from the fetters of bondage. But Captain Marcy thought their real motive was the fear that the Negroes would aid Wild Cat in building up a force on the Rio Grande that would interfere with the marauding operations of the Indians along the Mexican borders.

The Kickapoo Indians to the number of 500 emigrated from Missouri to the Canadian River where they remained for some years upon the land of the Creek Indians, after which they removed to the site upon

22   *Fort Smith Herald*, November 1, 1850, p. 2, col. 2; *Cherokee Advocate*, November 19, 1850, p. 2, col. 5; Dr. Rodney Glisan, *Journal of Army Life*, 65.
23   Col. R. B. Marcy, *Thirty Years' of Army Life on the Border*, 55.

which Fort Arbuckle was afterwards built. Here they remained until the winter of 1850-51 when they all left for the Rio Grande and joined Wild Cat's colony.[24]

Wild Cat's operations and his undoubted astuteness and influence with other Indians made him a figure to be reckoned with by the Government and in March, 1851 a commission was sent out to have a talk with him and other Indians in Texas. It was hoped to discover Wild Cat's real purpose and to determine the extent of mischief or of good he was capable of doing. The commission found the Seminole chief at Eagle Pass, Texas. He was temporarily staying in Mexico with his colony but denied that he was a permanent resident of that country. He said "his great father had given him land in Arkansas as a home and a burying ground for him and his people, on which they might hunt and raise corn and live in peace with their brothers, the Whites. But, he said, the Creek Indians had come upon his land and tried to involve him in difficulties; had stolen from him his Negroes, and to avoid a war he had left that place and started to search for a new home in Texas." And that when he had found it all his people in Arkansas would follow him. "He seemed," as he stated, "pressed down with care and anxiety on account of his people, and troubled because of the difficulties and doubts that surrounded him. He spoke with feeling, and his countenance gave proof of it. His manner was entirely respectful and kind; there was no insolence—no threats, no unkind reproaches, but expressions of deep friendship."[25]

24   Marcy to Jones, November 25, 1851, AGO, OFD, 489 M 51.
25   "Memorandum of a conversation between Wild Cat or Coachoochee and Cols. Cooper and Temple, Eagle Pass, Texas, March 27, 1851," OIA "Misc. File" T 463.

CHAPTER TWENTY / *Justice to the Indians*

ORE than a decade had now passed since the removal of the great body of Seminole Indians; they were far behind the other four immigrant tribes in the scale of progress and adaptation to their new environment. There were several reasons for this situation, none of which reflected on the character of the Seminole who were its innocent and helpless victims.

The country they left in Florida encouraged a life of idleness, for abounding in fish, game and fruits much of the time, it gave little incentive to labor, and most of the Seminoles' work was done by their slaves. The climate required little clothing and shelter. The change therefore was most difficult for these people. Removed to a colder climate, obliged to clothe themselves, build houses and till the soil it was harder for them to adapt themselves to their new environment than for the other tribes. They did not all apply themselves to farming and were restless and discontented, some of them pushing farther west where there was better hunting.

The principal reason for their tardy recovery was the stupid and vicious policy conceived by the Government to force these people to become subjects to the Creeks. The latter outnumbered them ten to one, yet with no thought of their history or of the consequences, it was proposed to amalgamate the tribes, an obviously impossible thing. Fear of this scheme kept nearly half of the tribe hanging around Fort Gibson for years, idle, purposeless, destitute and deteriorating; and other hundreds remained secreted in the Everglades of Florida rather than submit to the domination of their traditional and only enemies, the Creeks.

It was this foolish and unjust policy more than all other influences that prevented the Seminole tribe from settling down and taking root as the other tribes had done, retarding their development many years and inflicting damage from which as a tribe they never recovered. But a better day was coming to them. Even officers of the Government after unhappy, futile years of coercion began to understand and appreciate the feelings of these friendless and helpless Seminole people, their high spirited and unyielding resistance to Creek domination.

"It was this indisposition to submit to Creek laws, innovation on their old customs or to the administration of them which induced them to leave the 'Country of their fathers.' This separation involving as it does very frequently the right to certain property, has always been the cause of much jealousy between the two nations. Frequent wars or incursions by the Creeks after slaves whom they took by force or stealth widened the breach between them; and in each of our campaigns against the Florida Indians, Creeks have been our allies, caused, no doubt, more by their hostility to the Seminoles than for any love for the whites.

"These things the Seminoles knew; and further, they look upon their operations under General Jesup in the Florida War of 1835, 1836, &c., as a direct effort on the part of the Creeks to subjugate them, as an independent Indian tribe, to make them dependent on the Creeks, subject to their laws, and under which they would be deprived, not only of their position as a nation, but also of their property as individuals."[1]

The Seminole felt denationalized and humiliated by subjection to the laws of the Creeks, which discouraged them from efforts at improvement and engendered a reckless attitude threatening serious consequences. Because the Creeks had stringent laws against the introduction of liquor into their country, some of the Seminole entered with whole-hearted enthusiasm into persistent and successful violation of that law; and in flat boats and large canoes they brought from Fort Smith up the Arkansas and Canadian rivers to North Fork Town large quantities of liquor which they retailed throughout the Creek country. In this and various other ways they made the anamolous relation of the tribes difficult and obnoxious to the Creeks as well as to themselves.[2]

1 *Report* of commissioner of Indian affairs for 1851.
2 Drennan to Lea, October 15, 1852: *ibid* for 1852; *ibid* for 1856.

Finally their agent, J. W. Washbourne, reached the conclusion that there must be a separation of the tribes and in the summer of 1855 convened the Seminole in council where they formulated a statement of their complaints, demands, and desires to be communicated in a friendly letter to the Creek council. They declared that they were a separate and independent people; that the Government unjustly and arbitrarily compelled them to merge their tribal organization into that of the Creeks; that the Creek laws over them were oppressive and unjust; that they were passed by councils in which they had no voice, the Seminole refusing to participate in the Creek councils and thus admit the right of the Creeks to govern them. Some Seminole who had merged themselves with the Creeks renounced them and rejoined their tribe.

They said that though they were induced to pledge themselves to abide the Treaty of Fort Gibson in 1845 and to conform to all its provisions, yet they unanimously protested against that treaty as operating unjustly and injuriously to their people; that there was no prospect of their ever becoming an amicable, integral part of the Creek tribe, and consequently no improvement could be achieved among them while that condition and feeling lasted. And they earnestly prayed for a separation from that tribe, and that they might be permitted to send a delegation to Washington during the succeeding session of Congress so that all their grievances, claims and desires could be presented to the Government. The agent in communicating these proceedings to his superiors in Washington testified to the reasonableness of the request of the Indians.

The Seminole people were sadly neglected by the Government, said their agent, and there was no indication of improvement during the year, but nothing else could be expected. "Possessing no means of schools whatever, totally destitute of any kinds of instruction save the little afforded by benevolence, believing themselves neglected, how can it be supposed that they should improve? Were these means and instructions provided, I am confident, from my own judgment and from the desire evinced by the people to possess means of improvement, that the Seminoles would advance equally with their more favored brethren, the Creeks and Choctaws. It seems palpably prominent to my mind that the Seminoles, no matter how provocative their wars in Florida were, have been treated with neglect and injustice. Compelled to merge their tribal organization into that of the Creeks—an act which the larger portion of the tribe regard as arbitrary, unjust, and detrimental—it is strange that no facilities were furnished them for education and improvement. Possessing their own annuities, scant though they are, they should also have had their own school, farming, and blacksmith fund. They will not share with the Creeks in these, even were they invited so to do; and if any improvement is expected from them it will only be attained after a separation from the Creeks is effected, and the means of culture furnished them by the government."[3]

An enlightened Indian administration under the newly created department of the interior had at last recognized the necessity of undoing the great mistake of trying to unite the Choctaw and Chickasaw tribes and had effected that measure of reparation by the Treaty of 1855.[4] It now realized the justice and greater necessity of doing as much for the Creeks and Seminole. Though behind that gesture of restitution was the bargain for the assistance of the western Seminole in effecting the removal of their people remaining in Florida. A treaty was thereupon entered into in Washington, August 7, 1856,[5] by and between the delegations of the Creek and Seminole tribes and the United States, by which the Seminole Indians were given a separate tract of land lying west of and adjoining the country secured to the Creeks; the latter making a formal cession to the Seminole of the lands described, and the United States guaranteeing the title. The land conveyed to the Seminole was a long narrow strip lying between the Canadian River and the North Fork of the Canadian River and extending from about the middle of what is now Pottawatomie County, Oklahoma, northwestward to the One Hundredth parallel, or the present western boundary of Oklahoma, and estimated to embrace 2,169,000 acres.

It was provided that as soon as the Seminole should remove from the Creek lands where they were then living to the country conveyed to them, the laws of the Creek Nation should have no further effect within those boundaries. Separation of the Creeks and Seminole was thus made effective by the terms of the treaty and the Government agreed further that payment would be made to the Seminole for the improvements they would be obliged to abandon in the Creek country on their removal; and that as soon as they had removed to their new

3 *Ibid.* for 1855.
4 *Kappler*, II, 531. The department of the interior was created in 1849.
5 *Idem*, II, 569.

home necessary buildings for an agency[6] and for a tribal council house would be erected. The Government expressed its solicitude for the removal of the Seminole in Florida to the new Seminole country and liberal inducements were made to them to leave Florida. Rifles, blankets, ammunition, hunting shirts, shoes, and tobacco were promised them; $20,000 for improvements and other sums for plows, axes, seed, looms, cards, and wheels.

The leaders of the western Seminole saw in the embarrassment of the Government in its efforts to remove the Florida Indians an opportunity for profitable bargaining. They knew that forcible removal of the Seminole was out of the question and that the Government must have their assistance to bring about what it so ardently desired. Astute to learn how much the Government needed their help and knowing that large sums of money vainly had been offered to the Florida Seminole to remove, besides the vast sums expended in the war for their conquest, they adroitly held the Government to terms highly advantageous and just to themselves; severed the bonds with which a foolish governmental policy sought to hold them in subjection to the Creeks; located them where they could live in peace by themselves, under their own laws;[7] where they and the Creeks would be at peace with each other; made provision for the education of their children, and for the encouragement of agriculture. The wonder is that a government so long could have ignored the evils of this situation, and continued a stupid unjust policy towards these people.

The Seminole agreed in the treaty to send to Florida a large delegation under an agent of the Government to render such service as they could in securing the consent of the members of the tribe there to emigrate. Besides the separation from the Creeks, the Government agreed to pay the Seminole $90,000 in lieu of their improvements, and to defray the expense of their removal; to pay them $3,000 annually for ten years for the support of their schools; other sums for agriculture and blacksmiths; and to set aside the sum of $250,000 the interest of

6 A contract was made with Henry Pope of Sebastian County, Arkansas, October 30, 1858, for a Seminole agency building, thirty-two by forty-four feet in size and a log kitchen sixteen feet square (OIA).

7 The Seminole Indians were practically penniless, having no tribal funds or annuities as the other emigrant tribes had; they had received nothing on their removal to the West.

which at 5 per cent annually was to be paid them as an annuity, and as much more when they were joined in their new home by the Seminole of Florida.

And thus at this very late day the Government for the first time appeared to give thought to the welfare of this tribe of Indians; neglected as to schools and everything else necessary to their development and progress, retarded by the inertia of their own backwardness, they had been allowed to drop far behind the other immigrant tribes, the Government making little effort to improve their condition. And what they had accomplished had been largely in spite of, and not by the help of, the Government.

The Seminole Indians were well satisfied with the terms of the new treaty but when some of them went to their new country to select sites for their homes they found themselves menaced by the roving tribes of the prairies. To meet these Indians on their trading and hunting expeditions was one thing, but the prospect of trespass and depredations by these restless freebooters on the homes and herds of the immigrants was disquieting and they asked that the Government give them some protection. Only a few located in their western home for more than a year after the execution of the treaty. The Government postponed the payment of the funds promised until the emigration of the Florida Indians and the immigrants anxiously looked forward to the realization of these terms. The population of the tribe had now diminished to 1907 of which 1,000 were females.[8] The immigrants were anxious to engage in the emigration of their people in Florida in order not only to receive the consideration promised them; but they very much desired to add to their population now much depleted by deaths, so as to increase their importance and influence.

On March 17, 1857, Elias Rector was commissioned superintendent of Indian affairs for the Southern Superintendency and in November S. M. Rutherford, the Seminole agent, notified the tribe to select the delegation that was to go to Florida. An abortive effort had been made the preceding winter by the officers at Fort Gibson to handle the matter. Second-lieut. Edgar O'Connor of the Seventh Infantry, had been selected to accompany and take charge of the delegation consisting of both Seminole and Creeks; but when the Indians arrived at Fort Gibson

8 *Report* of commissioner of Indian affairs for 1857.

they learned that no provision had been made for paying them and they refused to go. They said also that if the military had anything to do with the removal it was doomed to failure. The first of the January following, Rector and Rutherford and W. H. Garrett, Creek agent, left Fort Smith for Florida with a delegation of forty Seminole and six Creeks.

On their arrival in Florida, they spent nearly three months in coöperation with the Federal troops searching through the Ever-glades, counselling with Indians they could reach, and endeavoring to persuade them to emigrate. All was not peaceful negotiation however if one may judge from Colonel Rector's letter from Fort Myers: "Col. Rutherford has taken with him a niece of Billy Bowlegs who was a prisoner at Egmont Key, as a guide; she says that Bowlegs is disposed to negotiate, which statement is confirmed by the last prisoner taken, who is an Indian of Bowleg's Band, and now in the hospital at this place, having been shot in the leg in being captured."[9] It was several weeks later (March 15) that Rector succeeded in holding a council thirty-five miles southwest of Fort Myers, with representatives of the bands in Florida. Upon offering them large sums of money and other inducements, Bowlegs and his principal men agreed to emigrate their families; and soon after, Nocus Hadjo reported that his chief Assoou-wah (Assunwha) had already begun moving his women and children out of the swamp to a point where wagons could be sent to assist them in reaching Rector's camp. Bowlegs brought the twenty-three members of his family to the camp of the delegation from the West and then went in search of a part of his band who were living in boats whom he agreed to remove. Rutherford and Jumper had gone to look for a small remnant of Tallahassee Indians seventy miles back of Tampa Bay.

Rector was enthusiastic over the prospect of bringing to an end the "war" in Florida. The only doubt he entertained was based upon an almost incredible situation in that state: the sordid interest of the people in continuing the "war." "The greatest obstickle in the way of successful removal of the Indians is to be aprehended from the volun-teers and disapointed citizens of Florida, who, I am sorry to say would dislike this war to be ended."[10] Hunting and killing the Indians was

9 Rector to Mix, February 10, 1858, OIA, Seminole R 481.
10 Ibid., March 29, 1859, OIA, Seminole R 526.

-[273]-

more than a sport for these people. For years the provisioning of expensive and usually futile expeditions into the retreats of the Indians brought financial returns to those who had supplies for sale, and the "volunteers" enjoyed employment and subsistence at public expense. This shameful and cruel motive mentioned also by other Federal officials, contributed not only to the misery of these unhappy people but to the ineffective character of the campaigns waged against them.

At last Colonel Rector, Rutherford, and Garrett sailed from Fort Myers May 4, on the steamer *Grey Cloud*, with 125 Indians and proceeded to Egmont Key where they took on board forty more who had been captured by the Florida volunteers. Of the total of 165 hostiles, thirty-nine were warriors and 126 women and children. The warriors included Billy Bowlegs,[11] principal chief of the Florida Indians, Assoonwah second chief, Nocose Emathla, Foos Hadjo, subchiefs, Nokus Hadjo, inspector general, and Fushutchee Emathla. This contingent included ten of the Mikasuki or Sam Jones band, leaving with Sam Jones twelve warriors who refused to desert their venerable and implacable chief then 108 years old. They said they would stay until his death and then they also would emigrate. There remained in Florida two small parties of "Boatmen" Indians who included twelve warriors, and a small party of Tallahassee. But these Indians were so successfully concealed in the Everglades, the Indians guides themselves had been unable in several months search to find them. Rector had promised five of the chiefs $1,000 each in addition to large sums paid Billy Bowlegs and the warriors, women and children.

Rector and his people transferred at New Orleans on the Steamer *Quapaw*, and arrived at Fort Smith May 26. The Creek and Seminole delegations in charge of Agent Garrett left New Orleans on the steamer *Arkansas*, and arrived at Fort Smith May 28. On June 1, Bowlegs and his party of 164 Seminole Indians were placed in charge of Colonel Rutherford who started with them for their new home on the third. They were thirteen days on the road contending with bad weather, worse roads and high water. Many of his people were sick, four of them died on the road and more died after their arrival at their

11   Bowlegs died in the West and his remains are interred in the National cemetery at Fort Gibson. "Bowlegs" was a corruption of "Bolek." His death was reported in *Report* of commissioner of Indian affairs for 1859, p. 529.

destination from an ailment that assumed the character of typhoid fever, said Rutherford.

There was more work for Rector in Florida and in the autumn he sought another delegation to accompany him. He was obliged to agree to Bowlegs's demand for $200 for his service as head of a party of eight Seminole Indians. They set out from Fort Smith in December 1858. Of the remnant of the tribe left in Florida many were now willing and anxious to leave and join their friends and relatives in the West, though influences were at work to interfere with the movement, said Rector: "There are many unprincipled white men in the country, men ready for the worst and lowest crimes, who for a temporary and precarious livelihood furnish the Indians with small quantities of such supplies as they need, and hold out false promises of future assistance. There is another class more villainous then the other, who are endeavoring to retain the Indians here until my present effort shall have been made, in the hope of raising fresh disturbances and of inducing the Government to again send troops into the country.

"Besides such opposition as this I have had no means of travel. I could not make deposits of provisions for my delegation at convenient points; they have had to overload themselves with supplies of food and blankets, and their movements in the jungles and among the palmettos have necessarily been very laborious and slow. No steamer has been at my disposal—nothing that could facilitate my movements except wretched sailboats, and these have rather retarded than advanced them.

"Besides the Boat Party I have had an interview with another band, scarcely known in this country—a band which Bowlegs thought had been killed in the last war. It was fortuitous that I saw them, as their existence in the country might not have been known except from depredations and murders. They were under the lead of the celebrated Black Warrior. Some of them appear favorable to emigration."

Rector arrived on the steamer *Magnolia* with seventy-five Seminole warriors, women and children off St. Marks February 15 ready to depart for New Orleans. The remainder of these wretched people he consigned to the "mercies of the Florida troops which Governor Perry in his recent message proposed to visit them with."[12]

12 Rector to Denver, November 22, 1858, January 22, 1859, February 15, 1859, OIA.

Agent Rutherford urged that the Government comply with its promise to erect buildings for an agency and a council house and black-smith shops for the Seminole immigrants. The Indians said that as soon as these buildings were started they would select sites for their homes.[13] By 1859 only about a third of the tribe had removed to the land set apart for them in the Treaty of 1856, but others were preparing to remove as soon as their crops were gathered. The Florida immigrants lately brought as prisoners were much dissatisfied and restless and showed little inclination to settle down and build homes. The number in the tribe, according to a recent census was 2,254 of which 1,009 were females. The Seminole Indians had been reduced in population nearly 40 per cent in thirty years, by the war of extermination waged against them and the fugitive manner in which they had lived in the swamps to escape capture. As usual, none of the $2,000 promised in the Treaty of 1856 for agricultural assistance had been advanced to the Indians who were becoming restless for a fulfillment of that engagement; and Rutherford urged that the Government comply with this promise. There was no school in the Seminole Nation but a few of the leading members of the tribe were anxious that the treaty stipulation on the subject be carried into effect.

The Seminole people held a general council in the summer of 1859 where they discussed the project of setting up a government such as was enjoyed by the other immigrant tribes. They desired the Federal officials to withhold from their annuities and turn over to the officers of the nation a sum sufficient to meet the expenses of their proposed government. They wished to create a light-horse to execute their laws, and to set up other officials for the administration of their national government. Their chiefs and law makers expected to be paid for their services also.

The Seminole agency building was erected in 1859 about sixty miles west of the former agency one mile west of the eastern boundary of the Seminole country and two miles north of the California road laid out by Lieutenant Beale. And the next year a council house thirty-six by twenty feet containing two rooms with a fire place in each, had been constructed for them eight miles northwest of the agency.[14]

The Civil War had now begun. Agent Rutherford and the Indians

13 *Report* of commissioner of Indian affairs for 1858.
14 *Ibid.*, 1860.

-{ 276 }-

were still urging that schools be set up in the Seminole country as promised in the treaty. "The greatest clog upon the advancement of civilization, and the general diffusion of national pride and spirit among this people, is the want of schools. Since moving up to their new country they have been deprived of the only one which heretofore they could avail themselves, to wit, Oak Ridge Mission, in the Creek country. They are very anxious to have the fund for educational purposes provided by the Treaty of 1856, applied in establishing a manual labor school, of like character and upon similar conditions to those in the Creek country. . . . . This is a subject that has been referred to in each of my reports; and, in view of its importance to these people, I cannot refrain from again calling the attention of the department to it through you.

"By improving their educational facilities, all the ignorance and superstition which now characterize them as a tribe will vanish, and a few years will find the Seminoles an intelligent race, worthy to be considered a part of our common country, and fully competent to aid in sustaining its reputation for intelligence and Christian philanthropy; for the Seminoles are by no means deficient in native force of character and keenness of wit. It wants only cultivation, a knowledge of letters, and the excellencies of moral and mental discipline; and I ask you to consider the importance of this matter and place it in a true light before the department. There seems to be among them a preference for the original customs and habits of their tribes; it is only the progress of civilization that can remove these absurdities, and render them a happy and contented race.

"The Seminoles have been trying to organize their government, but have not succeeded in perfecting it. A good many prefer adopting their former habits and customs, while others desire to place themselves under laws similar to those by which the Creeks and other tribes are governed. It is doubtful however, which party will succeed. They have no funds set apart for the support of their government, and this cir- cumstance will make much in favor of those who favor adopting their former habits and customs."[15]

Before the surveyors could run the boundaries of the new grant to the Seminole tribe, they were compelled to abandon their work

15 Rutherford to Rector, August 15, 1860, report of commissioner of Indian affairs, for 1860.

by the hostilities of the Comanche, Kiowa, and Cheyenne Indians in the vicinity. They committed depredations also on the immigrant Seminole who complained for several years of the loss of their live stock.

The Indians were slowly improving; moving on to the land assigned them, adapting themselves to the change from their former home in Florida, building homes and making their little farms. They were still crying in vain for the schools promised them years before when the Civil War began and they were obliged to flee from the country. After the war most of them were for a time again located near Fort Gibson, all of their improvements and stock having been swept away by that conflict. A new treaty was made in 1866[16] by which the Seminole tribe ceded their land back to the United States and received in place of it the very much diminished tract of 200,000 acres that has since been their home, co-extensive with the present county of Seminole, Oklahoma. And thus nearly thirty-five years after the Government by devious means secured the execution of the so-called treaty with the Seminole which drove them from their homes in Florida, they became fixed upon a tract of land of their own. Here they applied themselves industriously to farming, built cabins and fenced their lands; schools were erected, and these neglected Indians though much behind, caught step with the other tribes, and exhibited a commendable zeal for improvement.

16 Kappler, *op. cit.*

BOOK FIVE / Cherokee

CHAPTER TWENTY-ONE / *Readjustment*

THE Cherokee Indians exchanged their residence in the East for a home in the West at different times and under different conditions. More than two thousand of them came voluntarily in the early part of the nineteenth century to Arkansas and afterwards in 1828 exchanged their holdings there for what became the permanent domain of the Cherokee Nation in the present Oklahoma.[1] After the enactment of the Indian Removal bill in 1830 several thousand more were induced to remove under Government supervision to their new western home. But the greater part of the tribe, refusing to remove voluntarily, were driven from their homes at the point of the bayonet, herded into concentration camps, and forced out of the country. A few thousand were taken west as prisoners on steamboats, but the great body of the tribe numbering more than 13,000 was brought in thirteen parties on overland journeys of from three to five months through Tennessee, Kentucky, Illinois, Missouri, and Arkansas to the Indian Territory.[2] The hardship, suffering, and mortality to which these unhappy people were subjected were appalling.

No report was made of the number of Cherokee who died as the result of the removal. It was as if the Government did not wish to preserve any information touching the fearful cost to the helpless Indians of that tragic enterprise, and was but little interested in that phase of the subject. From the fragmentary official figures it appeared that more than 1,600 of those alone who removed under the direction of John Ross died on the journey. It is known that the rate of mortality

1 For an account of these migrations see Grant Foreman, *Indians and Pioneers*.
2 This tragic migration is described in *Indian Removal* by Grant Foreman.

-{ 281 }-

was higher among the previously removed parties, whose suffering led to the proposition that the Cherokee officers be permitted to manage the remainder of the emigration. Hundreds died in the stockades, and the concentration camps, chiefly by reason of the confinement and the rations furnished them, flour and other provisions to which they were unaccustomed, and which they did not know how to prepare. Hundreds of others died soon after their arrival in the Indian Territory from sickness and exposure on the journey. A very small percentage of the old and infirm, and the very young survived the hardships of that ghastly undertaking. It has been stated upon good authority based upon all available data, that over 4,000 Cherokee Indians died as the result of the removal.[3]

On arriving at the end of their journey, the misery of the expatriates was somewhat diverted by the task of preparing for their immediate needs, building shelters and homes, planting crops, and other employment of a thrifty people bereft of their homes and belongings.

Many of these people who lived in comfortable circumstances in their old homes arrived in the West destitute of every convenience and comfort. Fortunate were those able to bring with them some of their cherished household possessions. Too often as they pursued their sad journey, the wagons that carried their little children and meager personal belongings were requisitioned by the conductors, and the loved spinning wheel, the mortar and pestle with which they prepared their corn for food and other essentials of their home life were thrown by the wayside to make room for the sick and dying who at times filled to overflowing every wagon.

These unhappy people were delivered here upon the raw virgin soil, destitute, possessed of little besides the primitive instinct to live and protect the lives of their helpless children. They were compelled to start life anew, many of them fortunate to possess an axe with which to construct wherewith to shelter them against the storm and sun. One old woman who remembered that experience told the

3 James Mooney, *Myths of the Cherokee*. Nineteenth annual Report, Bureau of American Ethnology; "Dr. Butler, one of the physicians of the emigrating Cherokees, computes that 2,000 out of 16,000, or one-eighth of the whole number, have died since they left their houses, and began to encamp for emigration in June last" (*New Orleans Bee*, copied in *Army and Navy Chronicle*, January 3, 1839, VIII, 12; *Arkansas State Gazette*, December 19, 1838, from the *Jackson* (Mo.) *Advertiser*).

Author of her recollection:[4] "Very few of the Indians," she said, "had been able to bring any of their household effects or kitchen utensils with them and the old people who knew how, made what they called dirt pots and dirt bowls. To make them they took clay and formed it in the shape desired and turned these bowls over the fire and smoked them and when they were done they would hold water and were very useful. We could cook in them and use them to hold food. In the same way they made dishes to eat out of and then they made wooden spoons and for a number of years after we arrived we had to use these crude utensils. After awhile as we were able, we gradually picked up glazed china ware until we had enough to take the place of the substitutes. We had no shoes and those that wore anything wore moccasins made out of deer hide and the men wore leggins made of deer hide. Many of them went bare headed but when it was cold they made things out of coon skins and other kinds of hides to cover their heads.

"I learned to spin when I was a very little girl and I could make cloth and jeans for dresses and such other garments as we wore. We never any of us wore store clothes and manufactured cloth until after the Civil War. To color the cloth we used different kinds of dyes. We raised our indigo which we cut in the morning while the dew was on it; then we put it in a tub and soaked it over night and the next day we foamed it up by beating it with a gourd; we let it stand over night again, and the next day rubbed tallow on our hands to kill the foam; afterwards we poured the water off and the sediment left in the bottom we would pour into a pitcher or crock to let it get dry, and then we would put it into a poke made of cloth and then when we wanted any of it to dye with we would take the dry indigo. We raised the indigo for many years and then when I moved away from Barren Fork I lost my seed and was never able to raise any more; we always thought the indigo we raised was better than any we could buy in later years.

"If we wanted to dye cloth black we used walnut bark and when we wanted to dye purple we used maple bark and if mixed with

4 Mrs. Rebecca Neugin, who died near Hulbert, Oklahoma, in the summer of 1932 at the age of nearly a hundred years. Mrs. Neugin, who was a small child when her people removed from the east, could recall only one incident of that experience and that was of her pet duck that she cherished and would not leave behind. She carried it in her little arms until she squeezed the life out of it and grieved to see it thrown by the road side. The poignant memory of that childish love and grief remained with her more than ninety years.

hickory bark it made yellow. Hickory bark by itself made green dye. To make red we mixed madder and alum. We used to find alum in caves. We used sumac berries to make red dye. When we wanted salt we drove to a salt lick on the west side of Grand River."

While the great majority of the tribe was forced to this country in a destitute condition there were some parties containing a considerable admixture of white blood who were more fortunate, such as those who were known as the treaty party who came voluntarily ahead of the great movement of 1838, and arrived in the West in a state of some affluence. By reason of their compliance with the wishes of the Government they were able to dispose of their property in their old home to good advantage and a number including the Ridges settled on Honey Creek in the northeastern part of their new domain possessed of considerable money so that they were able at once to embark in merchandising, agriculture and traffic in live stock.[5]

The immigration of the Cherokee Indians effected a marked change in the country and a large number of traders came to barter with the Indians. Gov. Montfort Stokes, Cherokee agent, explained the large number of licenses granted by him to traders in the Cherokee country in 1838, by the fact that numbers of emigrants like the Ridges had arrived with considerable money which they desired to invest in trade with the Indians. Besides there were white merchants lately come into the country attracted by the immigration of Indians who had money they must exchange for supplies in order to set themselves up in their new home. Some of the traders were driven from New Orleans and other cities to the Indian country by the panic of 1837 and the fact that the currency that circulated in their states was of such uncertain value that they brought their goods to the Indian Territory where payment was made to the Indians in silver which the merchants preferred to paper issues of the states.[6]

As if the Cherokee Indians had not suffered enough from the rapacity of the white man and the hardships of the tragic removal, their cup of misery was filled to overflowing by the neglect and extortion of the contractors in their new home, the same contractors who added to the misery of the Creek and Seminole immigrants.

5   "The Cherokee War Path" edited by Carolyn Thomas Foreman, *Chronicles of Oklahoma*, IX, 262.
6   Stokes to Armstrong, August 8, 1838, OIA, Cherokee file.

A contract was made with Glasgow and Harrison to ration the help-less and destitute immigrants upon arrival at their destination. Several places for issue of rations were established: one at Skin Bayou ten or fifteen miles from Fort Smith; another at the former home of Mrs. Webber, widow of Walter Webber, where W. A. Adair was living, near the present Stillwell, Oklahoma; another at the home of Rev. Jesse Bushyhead, which he called Pleasant Hill, a short distance north of the present Westville; because rations were issued here it became known as Breadtown; it was later called Baptist Mission from the mission that was established there. Another place of issue was near the home of the Ridges on Honey Creek; another at McCoy's afterward removed to Kesse's on the Illinois River near Park Hill.

Four of the issuing agents were discharged soldiers, all but one of whom were dissipated men who neglected their duties. The exception was named Daninburgh who was "a man of steady habits—a man of intelligence, and of business habits. He married a Cherokee woman, and now lives on a farm on the line dividing the Arkansas State from the Cherokee nation, his farm being partly in the State and partly in the nation," reported Benjamin F. Thompson of Beattie's Prairie, to Maj. E. A. Hitchcock.[7]

Thompson said he saw many issues made and that the ignorant Indians were much imposed upon. He had seen cattle of all descriptions delivered to the Indians varying from good to those that were entirely worthless, such as old bulls and poor old worn out oxen, some so poor that they could hardly stand. They were issued to Indians who did not know how to protect themselves, at from a fourth to a third more than their actual weight. Much complaint was made of this imposition, by the more intelligent Indians. To circumvent exposure of their tactics, Thompson said, the agents Williams and Tree began issuing to the "common Indians" at the depot at daylight before the arrival of the more intelligent Indians who had been trying to protect their less fortunate brothers. During all the months the issues were being made, Thompson said, he never saw or heard of an officer of the Government attending to see that the Indians were justly treated.

7 U. S. House *Executive Document*, No. 219, Twenty-seventh Congress, third session: "Right of President to withold papers—Frauds on Indians. Message from the President of the United States, transmitting the report of Lieutenant colonel Hitch-cock, respecting the affairs of the Cherokee Indians, &c."

Thompson kept a public house for the entertainment of travelers near this place of issue; he knew the superintendent and Indian agent well and he said that neither ever came to the neighborhood. The detachments that came in here on their arrival from the east were Sittewakie's, Jesse Bushyhead's, George Hicks's, and Wofford's. The three detachments that came in at Fort Wayne were John Benge's, John A. Bell's and Richard Taylor's. Many witnesses testified to Hitchcock of short measures of corn and unwholesome or unpalatable meat. The most common form of fraud arose out of the custom the contractors evolved of issuing to the Indians certificates entitling them to certain amounts of rations. Their hirelings then purchased these certificates for a fraction of their face value and using them as evidence of satisfaction of the claim of the Indians they hugely increased their profits and the Indians were deprived of their just claims on the Government.

The Cherokee immigrants had been in their new country only a few weeks when their chief, John Ross, addressed a communication to General Arbuckle protesting against the impositions and neglect to which they were subjected. It was a formal and impressive appeal, said Major Hitchcock, dated April 23, 1839, accompanied by three papers from different sections of the country numerously signed by the principal men of the Cherokee Nation; all representing in simple but impressive language specified grievances suffered by them, growing out of the manner in which the contract of Glasgow and Harrison was executed. Their contract was dated January 15, 1839 and was to take effect March 1 following. The complaints arose almost immediately after the issue of the rations began, Hitchcock said.

"During the two years immediately preceding this period, the Creeks and some other Indians had arrived in the country," said Hitchcock," and had suffered under the issue of provisions made by the identical contractors of whom John Ross, the Cherokee chief, complains to General Arbuckle. The outrages practiced upon the Indians, especially the Creeks and Seminoles, were so notorious in the country, that I have never met with a single individual in their vicinity, at the time, who did not appear to be perfectly aware of them. Many of the officers at Fort Gibson have spoken without reserve of the injuries inflicted upon the Indians, as if those injuries were within the knowledge or belief of every one. Two years of fraud having passed by among the Creeks and other Indians, a third year is commenced among the Cherokees; but, at the very threshold, formal complaints were made by the Cherokees to their principal chief, who made a respectful and earnest appeal to the general in command for the correction of the alleged abuses.

"In this stage of the business, General Arbuckle appears to have handed the papers, representing the complaints of the Cherokees to Captain Armstrong, the acting superintendent of Indian affairs; and, beyond this, there is no trace of his having taken any steps to give effect to the appeal made to him by the Cherokee chief. On the part of Captain Armstrong, there is no evidence of his having taken any remedial measures beyond his stating, in his letter of the 25th of April that he will 'see Captain Stephenson, and represent to him that the Cherokees complain of not receiving their ration of corn'; and, at that point, all intervention by the Government agents, for the correction of the grievances complained of, seems to have terminated, so far as these papers show."

In due course the contractors were paid, their accounts closed, and their iniquity was thus protected against inquiry except for the belated, and as it developed, futile investigation by Major Hitchcock, ordered by the secretary of war when it was too late to be effective. When Hitchcock's report was filed the secretary of war delivered it to the solicitor of the treasury for an opinion as to the possibility of proceeding against the contractors criminally and for recovery of some of their loot. As if solicitous for the feelings of the culprits, the secretary wrote the solicitor "This report of Lieutenant Colonel Hitchcock is strictly confidential—is not to be exhibited to any one; nor are its contents to be made known without the authority of this department; and it is to be returned as soon as you have become familiar with it. Although not officially bound to give it, yet I should be glad of your opinion respecting the conduct of Captain Armstrong."

Solicitor Charles B. Penrose reported that the contractors did not faithfully perform their contract but as the department had ignored the complaints against them and had approved their accounts it was now too late to do any thing about it. As they had delegated their subordinates to do the work that brought on the criticism, there was no tangible evidence of conspiracy and no criminal action would lie against the principals. It was significant, said the solicitor, that few of the agents involved in the business could be found by Hitchcock, "and from those to whom Colonel Hitchcock had access, but little information of a positive nature could be obtained, as 'delicacy,' or 'unsettled accounts with the contractors,' were stringent reasons for silence." The solicitor evidently gave the secretary the kind of report that was desired as he recommended against any action either criminal or civil. Colonel Hitchcock concurred in the opinion as to the futility of an action against the contractors but he recommended the dismissal from public service of all the agents responsible for or having knowledge of the "abominations practiced" on the Indians, who he said, were "grievously and barbarously abused."[8]

The occupation of the Indians in reëstablishing themselves in their new home demanded much of their attention, but could not entirely beguile them from their sorrows or soften their feelings against the persons and elements that had brought upon them so much wrong, suffering and unhappiness. And it would have been surprising if adjustment to their new surroundings had been accomplished in a tranquil spirit. But among them was no spirit of reprisal such as some of the officials were ready to ascribe to them.

Evilly disposed persons seeking to injure the newly arrived Cherokee immigrants caused a report to reach General Arbuckle that they planned an attack on Fort Wayne. General Arbuckle, surprisingly gullible at times, was sufficiently impressed that he called on Chief John Ross at Park Hill to assist in investigating and explaining the rumor. Capt. George A. McCall was sent from Fort Gibson to see Ross and then on to the Arkansas line. On his return he reported to General Arbuckle that everywhere he noted the Cherokee people engaged in building houses, clearing and fencing land, and planting. And the only meeting he could hear of among them was assembled to discuss the suppression of the sale of whisky. One was held at the home of Bushyhead, where resolutions against the introduction and sale of whisky in their country were signed by about 100 members of the tribe; and the same week another meeting at Judge W. A. Adair's was attended by 62 members, who signed similar resolutions.[9]

A considerable number of the Treaty Party had previously arrived in the West in 1838 where their leaders alarmed and excited the Old

8 Hitchcock to Spencer, August 4, 1842, AGO, ORD, WDF, "H.244."
9 U. S. House *Documents*, No. 129, Twenty-sixth Congress, first session, p. 42.

Settlers: "Another matter which has produced much uneasiness among the Cherokees of this part of the country is, that a report is in circulation among them, and believed by many of the ignorant Indians, that Ridge and Boudinot have an idea of selling a part of the country to the United States, to be annexed to Arkansas, and that Ridge has actually gone to Washington City for the purpose of making the sale. In event that this report be true, or even that Ridge has made a proposition of the kind to the U. S., the Cherokees will kill him and Boudinot both, and all other individuals connected with them, that they may find in the nation, and it is to be presumed that no honest man could blame them for so doing. I do not think that it is the intention of this part of the Cherokee Nation to molest either of those men, for what is known to have passed, but only in event of their doing what I presume there is no probability that they will attempt."[10] The letter of Capt. John Stuart is significant; it reveals that what actually befell Boudinot and the Ridges the next year was under consideration by their allies, the "Old Settlers," in 1838; and that the unauthorized effort to sell their land by any member was held by all the tribe to be treason punishable by death.

While preparations for removal were going forward in the East, the Western Cherokee, through John Jolly and other chiefs, called a conference of Indians to be held at Takatokah or Double Springs. This meeting which began on September 15, 1838, was attended by representatives of the Cherokee, Creek, Seminole, Seneca, Delaware, Shawnee, Quapaw, and Sauk tribes; the purpose as expressed in the invitations prepared with the help of their agent Governor Stokes, was to renew "the friendship once existing among their forefathers."

A tremendous uproar was made by Col. R. B. Mason and Gen. Edmund Pendleton Gaines, when they heard of this proposed conference; Mason then at Fort Leavenworth, wrote Gaines that the Cherokee had erected a council house larger than any theretofore erected, and that the meeting was to plan a concerted attack in the spring by the western Indians on the white "settlements of Arkansas and Missouri from Red River to the Upper Mississippi." This report seemed to throw Gaines completely off his balance, and he elaborated on the news in a letter to the governor of Tennessee in which he conjectured that the Cherokee were "instigated by agents of Mexico and are planning to bring into

10   Stuart to Jones, June 9, 1838, OIA, "Fort Coffee."

the field 20,000 warriors to lay waste all the settlements from the mouth of the Sabine to the Falls of St. Anthony." He associated this proposed council with efforts that had been exerted for two years by emissaries of Mexico to array the Cherokee Indians of Texas with all the Indians west of Arkansas in a force sufficient to destroy all the frontier white settlements. General Gaines simultaneously on August 8 wrote the secretary of war, and the governors of Tennessee and Kentucky, saying that he desired 10,000 troops with which to attend the council of Takatokah and cope with the threatened uprising. He induced the governor of Arkansas to issue a call for troops. For a few weeks the pages of the press bristled with news of imminent hostilities.[11] In compliance with his orders General Arbuckle had 350 muskets, cleaned and oiled, transported overland to Fayetteville, Arkansas, and delivered to I. Meek, designated as military storekeeper who was to hold them for use against the Cherokee.[12]

Then in deep mortification and exasperation, the local agents for the tribes in the West reported that there was not the slightest foundation for the extravagant rumors concerning the Indian council, which was attended by Governor Stokes, General Arbuckle and Colonel Logan, the Creek Agent. William Armstrong, acting superintendent for the Indians in the West, reported that he was too ill to attend the meeting; that ". . . . the Indians are quiet, no organization, no hostile movements, or even appearances of it, can be seen amongst them; numbers are sick—fully one third of the new emigrants; a great drought had prevailed through the whole Indian country."[13]

As the truth became known, Gaines was discovered in a ridiculous position where his sanity almost was in question; the *Louisville Journal* wrote that "the extraordinary operations in which he is now engaged, are at least sufficient to create a strong apprehension that the day of his usefulness is well nigh past."[14]

11 *Louisville Public Advertiser*, August 24, 1838, p. 2, col. 2; *Missouri Saturday News*, September 1, 1838, p. 3, col. 3; *New York Observer*, September 8, 1838, p. 3, col. 3.

12 AGO. ORD. Headquarters second department Western Division, *Order Book* No. 24 order No. 72 August 15, 1838.

13 Armstrong to Harris, September 28, 1838, OIA.; *The Daily National Intelligencer*, October 27, 1838, p. 3, col. 4.

14 *New York Observer*, September 29, 1838, p. 3, col. 4; General Gaines died of cholera at the St. Charles Hotel, New Orleans, June 6, 1849.

John Jolly, the principal chief of the Western Cherokee died in December, 1838. The second chief, John Brown, having resigned, the chieftainship devolved upon the next in succession, John Looney, whose tenure of office was to terminate the next October. After the arrival of the late emigrants, the Western Cherokee decided to strengthen their separate organization and called an informal council for April 22. On this occasion John Brown was elected principal chief in place of John Jolly, and John Looney, and John Rogers were selected to serve with him until October.[15]

The large body of more than 13,000 Cherokee having arrived in the spring of 1839, both factions found themselves in a peculiar and difficult situation. The late emigrants numbered more than twice as many as the remainder of the tribe, and they had a code of laws for their government. So had the western faction or "Old Settlers." Each faction was accustomed to looking to their respective chiefs and officers for advice and guidance in their tribal affairs; neither could have been expected to abandon their laws and chiefs for those of the other. Embodied within the same territory as both factions then were, it soon became apparent that serious contention and difficulty would arise unless steps were taken to effect an understanding for their future guidance.

The Western Cherokee occupied a position of strategic advantage, of which they proceeded to make use. They arranged a meeting for the purpose of welcoming the late emigrants. On Monday the third of June the meeting began at Takatokah[16] that grew in numbers until five or six thousand Indians were in attendance. After several days of visiting, the business of the conference was begun by an inquiry from the western chiefs as to the object and wishes of the late emigrants. On the tenth of the month the answer was made in a message over the signature of John Ross inviting the Western Cherokee to join them in setting up a government. The western chiefs the next day, pretended not to understand the request, and asked for a more definite statement of their purpose.

15 Jones to Payne, July 25, 1839, *Payne Manuscripts*, Ayer Collection, Newberry Library, Chicago.

16 In the south half of the northwest quarter of the northeast quarter of section twelve, township seventeen north, range twenty-one east, where the Cherokee Negro Seminary was afterwards located.

Two days later, the late emigrants adopted and submitted to the resident faction a set of resolutions proposing that each select three men and that the six should select three more, the nine to draft a code of laws under which the tribe could unite, which should be submitted for consideration and approval to a general council of the tribe to be held at a time to be agreed upon; but pending the adoption of the new code, the members of the tribe were to be governed by their respective laws as theretofore. The next day this proposition was rejected in a message from the chiefs of the western Cherokee, saying that the tribe was already united by the welcome of their western brothers whose laws must be accepted by the late emigrants as the law of the land. Though the latter asked the western chiefs to submit the proposition to their followers, the chiefs remained obdurate; John Brown, John Looney and John Rogers as chiefs of the western Cherokee, determined these matters without consulting the common people, but it was said that some of the leaders of the "Treaty Party" or Ridge faction attended for a short time and advised against accepting the proposition of the Ross faction.

On the twentieth, John Brown, first chief of the Western Cherokee declared that the general council was dissolved. Soon it became generally known by the people assembled that the western chiefs had prevented the measures for which they had attended, and there was great excitement and indignation. George Guess or Sequoyah, presiding in behalf of the Western Cherokee, and Captain Bushyhead for the late emigrants, immediately assembled the people in attendance, who adopted a resolution calling a general council to meet on July 1 for the formation of a government for the whole nation. The gathering then adjourned on the twenty-first.

The next day the whole country was thrown into great excitement by the brutal murder of Major Ridge, his son John Ridge, and Elias Boudinot.[17] A party of Cherokee Indians proceeded to the home of John Ridge on Honey Creek in the northeastern part of the Cherokee

17   Elias Boudinot (native name Galagina, 'male deer' or 'turkey'). A Cherokee Indian educated in the foreign mission school at Cornwall, Conn., founded by the American Board of Commissioners for Foreign Missions, which he entered with two other Cherokee youths in 1818 at the instance of the philanthropist whose name he was allowed to adopt. In 1827 the Cherokee council formally resolved to establish a national paper, and the following year the *Cherokee Phoenix* appeared under Boudinot's editorship. After a precarious existence of six years, the paper was discontinued,

Nation "and having surrounded the house with their rifles, three of them forced his doors, drew him from his bed midst the screams of his wife and children, and having given him twenty-five stabs in his body, left him dead in his yard." Major Ridge, the father of John, had "started the previous day, to Vineyard in Washington county Arkansas. He stayed on Friday night at the home of Mr. Ambrose Harnage, forty miles south of his son's residence. He was waylaid about ten o'clock on the same morning, by a party of Indians five miles west of Cane Hill and shot from a high precipice which commanded the road. It is reported that ten or twelve guns were fired at him; only five balls, however penetrated his body and head."[18]

At about the same hour while Boudinot was engaged in building his house at Park Hill, he left with three men for the home of Doctor Worcester to secure medicine for them; about half way there his companions seized and killed him, and cut him in pieces with knives and tomahawks. There was no evidence that John Ross had anything to do with the killings, but it was obvious that they were committed by some of the recent emigrants. The bitterness against the signers of the Schermerhorn treaty, an act for which their laws prescribed the penalty of death, and the reported aid which the Ridge faction had contributed to the failure of the recent meeting to effect a union under a new government, furnished provocation if not justification for the bloody deeds that shocked the Nation.

---

and was not resumed until after the removal of the Cherokee to Indian Territory, when its place was finally taken by the *Cherokee Advocate*, established in 1844. In 1833 Boudinot wrote *Poor Sarah; or the Indian Woman* in Cherokee characters, published at New Echota by the United Brethren's Missionary Society, another edition of which was printed at Park Hill in 1843; and from 1823 to the time of his death he was joint translator with Rev. S. A. Worcester of a number of the Gospels, some of which passed through several editions. Boudinot joined an insignificant minority in support of the Ridge treaty and the subsequent treaty of New Echota, by the terms of which the Cherokee Nation surrendered its lands and removed to Indian Territory. This attitude made him so unpopular that on June 22, 1839, he was set upon and murdered, although not with the knowledge or connivance of the tribal officers (*Handbook of American Indians*, I, 162.)

18   Account by John A. Bell and Stand Watie in *Arkansas Gazette*, August 21, 1839, p. 2, col. 4. Stand Watie lived four or five miles from Park Hill (Arbuckle to Jones November 24, 1839, AGO. ORD. Ft. Gibson *Letter Book* VI, p. 154); Sarah Paschal, daughter of Major Ridge, wrote an account of the killing December 21, 1839 that appeared in the *Arkansas Gazette*, January 15, 1840.

John Ross, as chief of the majority faction, was therefore held responsible by the military authorities and General Arbuckle undoubtedly would have arrested him if he had been able to do so without inevitable bloodshed and further disorder in the tribe. But, as evidence of the murder was fastened upon three other men of the tribe, they were held to be the guilty ones and John Ross was reserved for the bitter vindictiveness of the authorities. Ross reported the murder to General Arbuckle the day it happened; he reported also that Stand Waitie,[19] the half brother of Boudinot, had determined on raising a company to take Ross's life as punishment for what Stand Waitie declared was his responsibility for the murder. Ross said that his friends to the number of several hundred had surrounded his home for his protection and

19 Stand Waitie (native name De gata ga, conveying the meaning that two persons are standing together so closely united in sympathy as to form but one human body) noted Cherokee Indian, son of Uweti and after the death of Boudinot a leader of the party which had signed the removal Treaty of New Echota. On the outbreak of the Civil War he and his party were the first to ally themselves with the South, and he was given command of one of two Cherokee regiments which joined the Confederate forces and participated in the battle of Pea Ridge and in other actions. Later he led his regiment back to Indian Territory and in conjunction with Confederate sympathizers from other tribes laid waste the fields and destroyed the property of the Indians who espoused the Federal cause. In revenge for the death of his brother he burned Rose Cottage, the handsome home of John Ross, the head chief. He is further noted as one of the principal authorities for the legends and other material collected by Schoolcraft among the Cherokee (Handbook of American Indians, II, 634).

Stand Watie had married before his removal to the West. His wife, Betsey, died in childbirth late in March 1836 (Lavender to Ridge, May 3, 1836, OIA, "Cherokee file"). The child died also. Stand Watie emigrated by water in 1837 with the Ridge's and the journal kept by Dr. C. Lillybridge, who accompanied that party, mentions his ministering to Mrs. Watie. There was also another wife. The files of the Indian office contain a letter written by K. W. Hargrove of Rome, Georgia, in behalf of Isabella Watie, wife of Stand Watie from whom he separated when he left for the West. She was formerly the wife of Eli Hicks by whom she had a child named Henderson Hicks. She afterward married Stand Watie and when he left her she and her child were "in a destitute situation having been forced out of a comfortable home with the usual means of living, through the cruel policy of the Georgia laws and the ill treatment of her husband," Stand Watie. She had been awarded $1,660 for her improvements and the writer of the letter who was trying to secure it for her learned that the warrant had been sent to the agent for the Cherokee Indian in the West where Stand Watie had gone (Hargrove to commissioner of Indian affairs, November 1, 1837, OIA).

asked General Arbuckle to send a force to prevent the bloodshed that would undoubtedly result if Stand Waitie attempted to make good his threat.

General Arbuckle invited Ross to come to Fort Gibson for protection, but the latter was too wily to chance either the loss of life the visit might entail or the arrest General Arbuckle would undoubtedly have imposed on him if he had gone to the army post; he replied that he was surrounded by a sufficient force for his protection and would remain at home. Arbuckle then requested Ross and other principal men of the tribe to meet at Fort Gibson on the twenty-fifth, so that the killing might be discussed and measures adopted to prevent further violence. Ross, however, was not to be beguiled from his position and the meeting was not attended by him. A few days later John Brown, John Looney, John Rogers[20] and John Smith, as chiefs of the Western Cherokee, were at Fort Gibson and at the apparent suggestion of General Arbuckle wrote a letter to Ross and his associates urging them to meet there on the twenty-fifth and abandon the meeting called for July 1, 1839; they suggested further that instead of meeting in a body proportioned to their numbers, each party send sixteen men to negotiate an agreement. At the same time, with the apparent purpose of forestalling the meeting called by Ross for July 1, General Arbuckle and Governor Stokes sent Ross a letter warning him that the eastern Cherokee must accept the terms offered them by the western Cherokee as a basis for union or accept responsibility for serious difficulties and disturbances.

20 "After the arrival of the late emigrants, the old settlers had a council on the 22nd of April, of which John Brown was made Principal Chief of Western Cherokee, in place of Jolly deceased, by vote of eight members of Council" (Evan Jones, Park Hill, July 25, 1839, to John Howard Payne, *Ayer Collection*, Newberry Library, Chicago.)

CHAPTER TWENTY-TWO / *The Act of Union*

THE action of Ridge and his associates who signed the Treaty of 1835 became a bitter controversial subject.[1] It was a violation of their laws and upon the face of it was treason to the tribe. They acted as irresponsible members with no authority whatever to bind the Nation, a fact that was well known to the Federal Government. And Rev. John Schermerhorn who inveigled them into thus compromising themselves was in no small degree responsible for their tragic death. It was said, and no doubt truthfully, that their motives were consideration for the best interests of the tribe, which led them to pursue the line of least resistance. Schermerhorn himself acting as the Government negotiator, who knew full well that these men were wholly unauthorized to sign the treaty he tendered them, testifies to their good intentions and guilelessness and so compromises and convicts himself of guilt for their summary execution:

"These men before they entered upon their business, knew they were running a dreadful risk; for it was death by their laws for any person to enter into a treaty with the United States—a law which Ridge himself, in October, 1829 had drawn up, and was enacted while he was a member of the National Committee Council. But Ridge, Boudinot, Bell, Rogers, and others, their associates who finally united in making the New Echota treaty, had counted the cost, and had deliberately made up their minds, if need be, to offer up their lives as a sacrifice, to save, if possible, their nation from inevitable extermination and ruin if they continued where they were. . . . . I consider Ridge, Boudinot, and Bell and their associates as having acted on the

1 An excoriating arraignment of John Ross by Stand Watie and John A. Bell appeared in the *Arkansas Gazette*, August 21, 1839, p. 2, cols. 1 and 2.

purest principles of patriotism in negotiating the New Echota treaty; their object was to save their country from a war of extermination and ruin, and to provide for them a quiet and peaceable home, which they had no longer, and could not obtain in the land of their fathers."[2]

It mattered little to the unctuous Reverend Schermerhorn what the cost to others, he was out to do the servile bidding of his masters. President Jackson, at the instance of the whites, had determined that he would not, confessing that he could not, enforce the laws of his Government for the protection of the Indians. Any artifice, no matter how fraudulent, that would drive the Indians from the country, relieve him from importunities for their legal rights, abate the intolerable condition caused by the lawless action of the whites and put them in undisputed possession of the lands of the Indians, was what the subservient reverend gentleman was bent on securing. And he induced these unauthorized Cherokee individuals to sign their death warrant by agreeing to what purported to be a treaty of removal, but which was not a treaty because it was not the action of the tribe. However Schermerhorn took this fraudulent document to the President who, knowing full well that it was not a treaty, asked for its ratification by the Senate. And the Senate in the face of protests by 90 per cent of the tribe ratified it by a close vote.

An interesting light on that tragic situation appears in a letter written by the Rev. S. A. Worcester at Park Hill after the arrival of the Ridge and Boudinot parties and before the emigration of the great majority of the tribe: "The great trial we have at present is in relation to my translator. Mr. Boudinot whom I employed in the old nation arrived late last fall, and returned to his labor with me here. But in the mean time his extreme anxiety to save his people from threatening ruin had led him to unite with a small minority of the Nation in forming a treaty with the United States, an act, in my view, entirely unjustifiable; yet in his case dictated by good motives. This has rendered him so unpopular in the Nation that they will hardly suffer me to continue him in my employment." Mr. Worcester greatly needed the service of Boudinot but the feeling of the old settlers was so strong against the man they regarded as the betrayer of his people that the mis-

2 From a letter from Rev. John Schermerhorn to the *Utica Observer* published in his home town, July 17, 1839, and copied in the *Little Rock Observer*, October 2, 1839, p. 2, col. 3.

sionary was fearful the Cherokee people would not permit him to continue his mission and printing press in their country.[3] However as
subsequent events showed, the members of the "Treaty Party" and
most of the "Old Settlers" later found a common ground on which
they stood against the members of Ross faction with their threat to
dominate the Cherokee government.

The July 1 meeting was appointed to be held at Illinois Camp Ground
about ten miles from Takatokah, one mile from the Illinois River, a mile
and a half down the creek from Tahlequah and about as far north of
the present Park Hill; this was in a little valley containing some fine
springs; it was shut in on two sides by hills running east and west,
so that it easily could be guarded at each end. Here were gathered two
thousand Cherokee, and, while the western chiefs refused to attend,
many individuals of their faction were present taking part in the deliberations. On July 2 Sequoyah, who was one of the presidents of the
conference, and a number of other Western Cherokee at the meeting,
joined with John Ross in a communication to the chiefs, Brown,
Looney, and Rogers at Fort Gibson, requesting them to come to the
meeting and help work out a solution of their difficulties. This the
latter refused and countered with the information that they were
going to have a convention at the old "Tahlontuskey" council house at
the mouth of Illinois River on the twenty-second and invited "such
others as choose to attend."

One of the first actions at Illinois Camp Ground was the preparation of a joint letter by several of the leading men to the chiefs of the
Creek Nation concerning the excitement resulting from the killing of
the Ridges and Boudinot and the resort to arms of their followers;
assuring the Creeks that they did not wish to make war and warning
them against believing false reports regarding their intentions circulated
by their enemies. Later in the month they addressed a letter to the
Seneca, Shawnee, Delaware and Quapaw Indians inviting them to send
some of their number to the council so that they could observe the
pacific proceedings there and "would be able to detect false reports that
may have reached you."[4]

On July 8 General Arbuckle addressed John Ross "and others,"

3 Worcester to Samuel Chandler (his brother-in-law) June 14, 1838 property of
his grand-daughter Mrs. N. B. Moore, Haskell, Oklahoma.
4 United States House *Document* No. 222, Twenty-sixth Congress, first session.

at Illinois Camp Ground, in a truculent vein, demanding of them that they remove the cause for anxiety in the minds of the inhabitants of Arkansas who were reported to be leaving their homes from fear of Cherokee disorders. General Arbuckle had more than met his match in the adroit John Ross and he was enraged that his orders had been ignored and his plans thwarted. "In consequence of my efforts to restore peace to the Cherokee people, not having received from you the attention they merit, I determined to have no further concern with the present difficulties in the Cherokee Nation, unless my duty should imperiously require it; and I much regret that the information I have received does not justify me in remaining longer silent." Ross had not only held his convention, but he had secured the coöperation of influential men of the Western Cherokee like Sequoyah, who called on the chiefs Brown, Looney and Rogers to come and attend to the important business in hand and had put them in the position of recalcitrants, guilty of dereliction of duty—men on whom Arbuckle was depending to compel the surrender of Ross to his views.

Sequoyah wrote to the chiefs: "We, the old settlers, are here in council with the late emigrants, and we want you to come up without delay, that we may talk matters over like friends and brothers. These people are here in great multitudes, and they are perfectly friendly towards us. They have said, over and over again, that they will be glad to see you, and we have full confidence that they will receive you with all friendship. There is no drinking here to disturb the peace, though there are upward of two thousand people on the ground. We send you these few lines as friends, and we want you to come on without delay, and bring as many of the old settlers as are with you; and we have no doubt but we can have all things amicably and satisfactorily settled.[5]

The constructive efforts of Ross and his followers were successful in spite of the opposition of General Arbuckle, and out of the difficulties an act of union was adopted on July 12, 1839, by which the two parties were declared "one body politic, under the style and title of the Cherokee Nation." John Looney, of the Western Cherokee realizing the futility of further opposing, joined the union; his former associates, chiefs John Brown and John Rogers, however, proceeded with their meeting at Tahlontuskey. A delegation from the Ross convention went

5   United States House *Document* No. 188, Twenty-sixth Congress, first session.

to visit and confer with them on the subject of reunion, but they were driven away by threats of violence by Bell, Starr and other armed men on the ground. Brown and Rogers then on August 2 attempted the plan that had once been rejected by them, of having each faction appoint a committee to meet, this time at Fort Gibson. But, they added, "Old Settlers on your part of the committee will be rejected; that is, no old settler must be appointed to serve on your part of the committee, as the old settlers have refused to meet them." By this they repudiated men of their own faction such as Sequoyah who had already agreed to the union effected on the twelfth. Naturally the proposition was declined.

This declaration of union between the two factions of the tribe written by William Shorey Coodey, was preserved and published in the authorized printed editions of the constitution and laws of the Cherokee Nation, through the years that followed. And the union thus achieved by Ross was the foundation upon which all Cherokee national unity, prosperity and progress was constructed.

The convention at Illinois Camp Ground continued in session for several weeks and in the depth of their bitterness and sense of wrong, and determination in the new environment to vindicate their views and exercise the rights of a free people, the members permitted themselves to advocate and adopt futile measures calculated to do more harm than good. They went so far before the constitution was adopted as to enact a decree declaring that according to the laws of the tribe, the three men killed had rendered themselves outlaws by their own conduct, extending amnesty on certain stringent terms to their confederates, and declaring their slayers guiltless of murder and fully restored to the confidence of the community. This decree provided for the organization of eight auxiliary police companies to keep the peace. They were to be made up of volunteers each commanded by a captain and a lieutenant and the whole organization to be commanded by Jesse Bushyhead, with Looney Price second in command.[6] This was followed by another decree in August, made by another council, declaring the Treaty of New Echota void, and reasserting the title of the Cherokee to their old country. Three weeks later they adopted another decree summoning the signers of the treaty to appear and answer for their conduct under penalty of outlawry.

6   *Arkansas Gazette*, August 21, 1839, p. 2.

These extreme actions of the council were considered by the authorities as a menace to the peace of the country, and as the council had
condoned the murder of the Ridges and Boudinot, John Ross was
threatened with arrest as an accessory. Arbuckle demanded of Ross
that the murderers be delivered to him,[7] under threat that otherwise
he would send a military force into the Nation to make the arrest.
Ross defied him on the ground that the offense was one with which
the Cherokee Nation alone was competent to deal, and, as it had already acted in the matter, the Government under the treaties was
powerless to proceed further. Ross's reply to Arbuckle written November 4, 1839, was a skillfully worded document beyond Arbuckle's
ability to answer, and in cogent language exposed Arbuckle's illegal
position in interfering in the local political affairs of the Cherokee
Nation.

During the weeks the convention was in session considerable correspondence ensued between that body of men and General Arbuckle.
The communications from the convention were signed by George
Lowrey and George Guess (Sequoyah), Presidents, and John Ross and
other members. But General Arbuckle persisted in addressing his
replies solely to John Ross as Principal Chief of the eastern Cherokee,[8]
ignoring the existence of the officers of an orderly meeting. He gravely
repeated the most extravagant rumors of violence advocated by the
meeting; he would send no one to the meeting to learn from first hand
what was being discussed and what the members were trying to accomplish; but pursued what, in such an experienced officer, was the
amazing course of receiving fantastic rumors to damn the meeting and
its officers, such as that "Young Mr. Dillard was at Webbers Falls
where he heard several individuals (Cherokees as I understand him) say

7 Arbuckle charged that Daniel Colston, Joseph Spear, James Spear, Archibald
Spear, and Hunter and twenty-five others murdered John Ridge; that James Foreman,
two of the Springstons, Bird Doublehead, Jefferson Hair, and James Hair, killed Major
Ridge; and Soft Shell Turtle, Money Taker (or Money Striker) Johnston, Car-soo-
taw-dy, Cherokee (or Joseph Beanstalk) and Duck-wa were guilty of the murder of
Boudinot (United States House *Document* No. 188, Twenty-sixth Congress, first
session).

8 In contrast to this was the attitude of the courteous and dignified Governor
Stokes, the Cherokee agent, who refused to depart from his uniformly correct manner;
in addressing the meeting, he named the officers according to the manner in which their
names and titles were signed to the communications to him.

that information had been received there, that it was the intention of your convention to send an armed force to the council of the Old Settlers, with the object of seizing the chiefs and taking them before you."

Largely upon such rumors, and somewhat from fear of the result of radical acts of the convention, General Arbuckle called on the governors of Arkansas and Missouri to raise and equip a brigade of volunteers to concentrate near the Cherokee boundary, for the protection of the frontier from an imaginary uprising of the Cherokee tribe; and he made a requisition upon the military storekeeper at Fayetteville for 132 muskets for Fort Gibson and for Fort Wayne 100 muskets with bayonets, 100 cartridge boxes and belts, 100 bayonet scabbards and belts, 10,000 musket cartridges, and 10,000 flints to be supplied to the citizens of Arkansas.[9]

Realizing his defeat, General Arbuckle advised Brown, Looney and Rogers, whom he addressed as the Cherokee chiefs, to yield to the majority. It must be said to his credit, however, that he did so in the belief that that was the way of peace, for it must have been distasteful in the extreme to concede that Ross had carried his program against the stern hostility and opposition of the doughty old General, a course in which the latter had gone to the extreme in trying to control the internal affairs of the Cherokee Nation. But while General Arbuckle advised this course, he ignored to the last the fact that many of the Old Settlers had already joined the eastern Cherokee, and while manifestoes were issued from the convention in the name of both factions, Arbuckle persisted in addressing them merely as John Ross and the Eastern Cherokee.

After the adoption of the act of union of the tribe, a convention

9 *Army and Navy Chronicle*, November 14, 1839, p. 316. "A detachment of two hundred and fifty men of the First Regiment of Dragoons under command of Colonel S. W. Kearney, have just returned to Fort Leavenworth, from a march from that post along the Missouri frontier, and into the Cherokee country as far as Fort Wayne on the Illinois River near Fort Gibson. On reaching Fort Wayne he learned from authority to be relied upon that the reports of intended hostilities, on the part of the Cherokees were utterly groundless, and that the whole country was entirely quiet. The command remained three days at Fort Wayne, during which Colonel Kearney corresponded with General Arbuckle at Fort Gibson, distant sixty miles, by express. He then marched his command back to Fort Leavenworth" (*Army and Navy Chronicle*, December 12, 1839.)

was held at Tahlequah where on September 6, the assembled Cherokee adopted the constitution which has been preserved throughout the tribal existence of that Nation as the basis of their government and laws. This document was signed by George Lowrey[10] as president of the convention and forty-six others, including Sequoyah. They then proceeded to organize their government according to its provisions, elected their officers, established courts of justice, passed all the regulations to put the new government into operation, and closed their proceedings on October 13 by appointing a delegation, with John Ross, their principal chief, at the head, to proceed to Washington to secure the adjustment of all unsettled claims and other questions pending between them and the United States. Ross and William Shorey Coodey left soon after for Washington, but the remainder of the delegation composed of Joseph M. Lynch, Elijah Hicks, Edward Gunter, Archibald Campbell, and Looney Price, did not depart until November 15.

Though Ross had been elected by an overwhelming majority of the tribe as chief of the Nation, the secretary of war refused to see him or Coodey, agreeing, however, to see the remainder of the delegation; they declined the offer and demanded to know who was the accuser and what proof the secretary had of Ross's complicity in the killing of Ridge and Boudinot which the secretary gave as his reason for not receiving Ross.[11] Boudinot's half brother, Stand Waitie, who was then

10 Maj. George Lowrey, one of the most distinguished citizens of the Cherokee Nation was born at Tohskeege on the Tennessee River near Tellico Block-house about 1770. He was one of the Cherokee delegation headed by John Watts who visited President Washington at Philadelphia in 1791 or 1792. He was captain of one of the Light Horse companies appointed to enforce the laws of the Nation in 1808 and 1810; a member of the National Committee organized in 1814, and one of the delegation that negotiated the treaty of 1819 in Washington. He was a member of the conventions that framed the constitutions of 1827 and 1839 and was elected assistant principal chief under the latter, an office he held for many years. At the time of his death he was a member of the Executive Council. He died October 20, 1852 at the age of eighty-two. The National Council being in session at the time, on hearing of his death, passed resolutions providing for his interment in a burying ground near Tahlequah and for funeral services on the occasion, then adjourned to Friday. His funeral services were preached on Thursday by the Rev. S. A. Worcester. His passing brought sorrow throughout the Cherokee Nation (From an account prepared by Rev. S. A. Worcester on information obtained from Chief John Ross: *Indian Advocate*, January, 1853, p. 3, col. 1.)

11 Cherokee Delegation to Poinsett, secretary of war, January 3, 1840, *OIA.* Cherokee L, 902.

in Washington with John A. Bell, had made the charge of Ross's guilt.

After the government of the majority faction had been launched, a small and irregular council of the opposing Old Settlers was held for the purpose of closing up their depleted ranks. At this meeting on October 10, John Rogers was elected first chief, John Smith second chief, Dutch third chief, Will Rogers treasurer, James Starr and John Huss executive council, and John A. Bell chief justice of the supreme court.[12] A law was passed expelling all white men who were favorable to John Ross; a fine of $500 was prescribed for any person attempting to enforce the laws passed by the Ross government. "Sheriffs and light horse were appointed to each district authorized to press as many men as they shall require to enforce *our* laws."[13] The Treaty Party and this part of the Old Settlers entertained such implacable hostility toward the majority faction that Stand Watie, John A. Bell and William Rogers, then in Washington, joined in a communication to Secretary of War Poinsett, suggesting that the Cherokee Nation and their annuities be divided between the Old Settlers and Treaty Party on one side and the Ross faction on the other; and asked that Arbuckle and Armstrong be entrusted to make the division.[14]

The Treaty Party, the followers of Boudinot and Ridge, held a meeting at Price's Prairie on August 20, and adopted a resolution and

12 John Brown deserted however, and left the Cherokee Nation for Mexico; on June 20, 1840, Almonte, secretary of war for Mexico, gave Brown and the families with him permission to settle in Chihuahua, Nueva Leon, Coahauila and Tamaulipas (OIA. Cherokee File B. 1087).

13 Stand Watie to Crawford, January 8, 1840, OIA. Cherokee File B. 856.

14 Stand Watie, Rogers, and Bell to Poinsett, January 22, 1840, ibid., R 454. On their arrival in Washington Stand Watie and Bell proceeded to deck themselves out in the prevailing hues and fashions. They went shopping together and bought each a "superfine" frock coat, the former selecting green, Bell preferring mulberry color. These garments cost $32 each; Bell's beaver overcoat was $43 and his companion's brown cloth coat cost $38. Cassimere pantaloons, velvet and "superfine" vests, stocks, cloaks, handkerchiefs and other items completed the gaudy raiment these Indians wore to standardize themselves with the white men with whom they associated. Bell departed for the Indian Territory March 16, 1840 and Stand Watie May 3. Just before leaving, the latter settled their account at the Globe Hotel amounting to $333.75. One of the bills for clothing purchased by both, amounting to $156, he paid with a draft on Glasgow and Harrison, though the character of his relation with these contractors is not disclosed. Half a dozen bills for the clothing purchased by them were filed with the commissioner by Stand Watie with the view to being reimbursed.

an address to the secretary of war representing that their lives were in danger; that they would not submit to the authority or dictation of John Ross and his partisans; that the only alternative left was to appeal to the United States for protection; that a delegation consisting of Bell and Stand Watie would proceed to Washington to represent their wishes to the secretary of war.

The Eastern Cherokee were winning over more of the Old Settlers, until both factions, well amalgamated, were meeting and discussing measures for their common good. The western chiefs, Brown and Rogers, on August 9 appealed to the Government of the United States to be sustained in the enforcement of their laws, and the protection of their lives. They and their following were the objects of a resolution adopted August 23, by a council of the Old Settlers including John Looney declaring that ". . . . . in identifying themselves with those individuals known as the Ridge party, who by their conduct had rendered themselves odious to the Cherokee people, they had acted in opposition to the known sentiments and feelings of that portion of this Nation known as the Old Settlers, frequently and variously expressed." And at the same time these offending chiefs of the Old Settlers, who had remained at Fort Gibson with General Arbuckle and had refused to attend the council with the late emigrants, were deposed from all authority; and their appeal to Washington in support of their laws was declared to be without the sanction of the Old Settlers they claimed to represent. This document was signed by 200 persons, including Sequoyah, who signed as vice-president.

For answer some of the Western Cherokee held a meeting at "Takat-tokah" on November 5 where they resolved that Ross and his party were illegally attempting to annul the laws of the Cherokee Nation and declared all of their proceedings "unlawful, unauthorized, and made by this null and void;" protested against John Ross and his delegation doing any thing to bind the tribe in Washington, and declared that the Old Settlers who had joined the Ross faction were unauthorized in their acts.[15]

Two days later they made an ingenious suggestion to Arbuckle: that an office be opened at the agency where the late arrivals should be invited to come in and enroll and pledge themselves to acknowledge

15   United States House *Document* No. 188, Twenty-sixth Congress, first session.

the laws of the Western Cherokee, with the promise that the money due them by treaty would be paid them. "We believe when the plan would be made known to them throughout the nation, they would come in crowds to those offices, as numbers now come, and inquire how they can become citizens, in order that they may get their money and have the benefit of the law &c."[16]

In reply to the letter and "decree" Arbuckle wrote John Rogers, John Smith and Dutch, November 10, "I have no hesitation in saying that the government the late emigrants found here is the only lawful government in the Cherokee Nation." Governor Stokes however hastened to assure all the Cherokee by a formal writing that he held himself neutral between the partisans, though he said he would continue to recognize the old government of the Western Cherokee as the only government of that tribe until directed to follow some other course.[17]

In November John Ross and his delegation departed for Washington; in order further to prejudice him with the secretary of war, Arbuckle wrote the latter on November 24, enumerating all the particulars he could think of calculated to involve him in the killing of the Ridges. Arbuckle said that if he had not "been prepared to start to Washington on business of much interest as it was understood, to the late emigrants, I would have caused him to be arrested and placed in confinement until the pleasure of the Government was known."[18] Another effort was made to embarrass them by arresting Lewis Ross in Wheeling, West Virginia on an alleged account for $9,000 growing out of the purchase of supplies for the emigrating Indians. Upon showing to the Court that these accounts were still pending in Washington, Ross was released.[19]

The three chiefs of the Western Cherokee then on November 22 petitioned for authority to send a delegation of five to Washington; but on January 2, 1840 the secretary of war said that as Bell and others were then in Washington, it was unnecessary for any more representatives of the Western Cherokee to be in the city.

While union of the factions of the tribe was an accomplished fact, hostile influences persisted to prevent general acknowledgment and

16   *Idem.*
17   *Idem.*
18   *Idem.*
19   *Wheeling Gazette*, copied in *Arkansas Gazette*, February 5, 1840, p. 3, col. 4.

understanding of that fact. But the tact of the patient Governor Stokes did much to remove further open opposition and made it possible to announce a complete amalgamation of the factions. The veteran Cherokee agent met with the Ross organization at Tahlequah December 20, 1839, and requested the members to make certain concessions to the few Old Settlers who continued to stand against them, and to meet at Fort Gibson for a general conference. The members present would not agree to the Fort Gibson meeting, but did agree to hold a meeting at which, as on former occasions, all members of the tribe were invited to be present. Accordingly an invitation was extended to all Cherokee people to meet at Tahlequah January 15, 1840. At that meeting the 1,700 members present voted unanimously to rescind the decree of outlawry enacted against the members of the Treaty Party in the July preceding.

Under the new constitution John Ross was elected principal chief, and Joseph Vann for many years a chief of the Western Cherokee, second chief. Six executive counsellors including John Looney, Aaron Price and Dutch, Western Cherokee. Dutch however refused to serve, "and went over to the agitators." The national committee was composed of forty members of the two branches: a committee of sixteen and a council of twenty-four. William Shorey Coodey was president of the national committee which included also John Drew, Thomas Thumb, John Spears, Bluford West, Joseph M. Lynch, Joshua Buffington, Thomas Taylor, and Turtle Fields, the latter four of whom emigrated in 1837.

Of the council Young Wolf was speaker and David Carter was clerk. The five members of the supreme court included Looney Price, an old settler, and John Martin who emigrated in 1837. The two circuit judges were John Thom, an old settler and Daniel McCoy, emigrants of 1837. There were four district judges including Looney Riley, an old settler, and John Brewer who came west in 1837.[20]

From February 2 to 8, 1840, another council of the Ridge faction was held at Fort Gibson, where was effected a union of Old Settlers and the Treaty Party. On the seventh the meeting adopted a resolution reported by a special committee, declaring that they were a sovereign and independent people; that John Ross and his partisans would not be permitted to participate in their government except by conquest or

20 United States House *Document* No. 222, Twenty-sixth Congress, first session.

by their consent, and that they had no intention of yielding to Ross and they declared his conduct and that of his partisans to be an "unprecedented act of usurpation—we will never acknowledge his government"; they resolved further "that the only legitimate government of this nation is the one handed down to us by the original settlers of the Cherokee Nation West, and we will to the utmost of our power and ability uphold and defend the same." They then appointed a delegation composed of Dutch, William Rogers, George Adair, James Carey, Alexander Foreman, Moses Smith, John Huss, and William Holt to carry the resolutions to Washington and urge their claims before the officials there.[21]

After the meeting adjourned, Governor Stokes wrote the secretary of war what had been done there, and that the Old Settlers and Ridge party claimed to own all the land of the Cherokee Nation in the West.[22] He called attention to the fact that the Cherokee council at his request had repealed the decree of outlawry enacted the July before; that the western Cherokee, including the Ridge party, numbered about six thousand as against sixteen thousand of the majority faction, and that the latter were bound to prevail by force of their number; and suggested that concessions from both sides be requested which would result in peace. Governor Stokes also sought to aid the department to attain a correct perspective of the situation by vouching for the character of John Ross whom he had known for twenty-five years. But in response, soon after the arrival of the Ridge delegation in Washington, the secretary of war suspended Governor Stokes from his office as Cherokee agent, and committed the regulation of Cherokee affairs to the military under General Arbuckle.

There were now two opposing delegations in Washington; that of the Ross faction composed of John Ross, John Looney, E. Hicks, Archibald Campbell, Joseph M. Lynch, Edward Gunter, Looney Price, and George Hicks, on February 28, 1840, prepared a memorial to Congress[23] giving an account of their removal, the steps taken to reëstablish themselves and their government in their new home, and the diffi-

21 Stokes to secretary of war, February 13, 1840, *OIA*, Cherokee File, S. 1717.
22 *Ibid.*, Stokes to Poinsett, February 12, 1840.
23 United States House *Document* No. 129, Twenty-sixth Congress, first session.

culties created by opposing forces, including the policy of the administration through the military at Fort Gibson.

The House responded on March 23 by adopting a resolution calling on the secretary of war for "copies of all orders and instructions issued from the department to any officer of the army, or to any agent of the Government, requiring his interference with the Cherokee Indians in the formation of a government for the regulation of their own internal affairs," together with copies of instructions prescribing any particular form of government.

Before the secretary of war complied with this request, the opposing Cherokee delegation[24] submitted a counter memorial which was introduced in the House April 1.[25] In this the memorialists detailed at length the wrongs alleged to have been committed upon them by the majority faction, and the tyranny of their laws, and prayed that Congress intercede to protect them in the independent government they had enjoyed before the removal of the majority of the Cherokee tribe from the East. By the middle of the month the secretary complied with the request made on him, and filed with the House a report with many interesting letters and orders attached. A few days later the Ross faction filed an additional statement of their contentions attaching copies of the proceedings creating their new government in the West.[26] These documents were all referred to the committee on Indian affairs.

Part of the Old Settlers claimed that those of their faction who participated in the union of the tribe of 1839 were but a minority without authority to bind the remainder; moved by this contention, the secretary of war on March 7, directed General Arbuckle to call a meeting of representatives of the factions at Fort Gibson where the union of 1839 would be ignored and a new one formed, under which all should have equal rights, but John Ross and William Shorey Coodey, who would not be permitted to have any voice in the new government. He was instructed to say further that the government of the western Cherokee was recognized as the only legitimate government in the tribe. This meeting was held at Fort Gibson on April 21, 1840, when General Arbuckle made a speech in which he gave the information directed by the secretary, and said that John Ross would not be per-

24 Representing the Old Settlers and Treaty parties.
25 United States House *Document* No. 162, Twenty-sixth Congress, first session.
26 This was filed by the secretary with the Senate in response to a resolution of that body of March 12.

mitted to hold any office in the Cherokee Nation. The administration was determined to maintain a hostile attitude toward any form of government achieved by the majority of the tribe under the leadership of John Ross. It is not surprising that the meeting broke up with nothing accomplished.

However, Arbuckle tried again and assembled another meeting of members of the factions at Fort Gibson in June, when he was more successful. To that meeting he invited twelve men from each of the two factions and induced them to agree to a new act of union prepared by him, and required those members claiming to represent the Ross government to surrender a third of the offices held by them, to be filled by the Old Settlers. A majority of those participating signed this so-called act of union, but later, when testifying before General Jones's commission, most of the signers belonging to the Old Settlers disclaimed having any authority to bind any one but themselves.[27] In fact, John Rogers, chief of the Old Settlers, refused to sign the agreement prepared by Arbuckle, and left for Mexico City to avoid taking part in carrying it into effect. Under the martial law imposed upon the Cherokee Nation, the so-called government dictated by Arbuckle, was enforced for some time, and the government established by the great majority of the tribe in 1839 was suspended.[28]

27 United States House *Document* No. 222, Twenty-sixth Congress, first session.
28 United States Senate *Document* No. 140, Twenty-eighth Congress, second session.

THE continued interference by the secretary of war in the affairs of the tribe, preventing a government by majority, finally impelled Congress to take notice of the situation; and the committee on Indian affairs of the House made an investigation of the matters presented by the various memorials and reports referred to them.[1] Testimony was taken and an exhaustive report[2] was prepared with recommendations; the substance of the finding was that the war department had pursued a vicious and dangerous course in the Cherokee country, keeping alive the rancor and unrest in that nation instead of allaying it.

At one stage the report said, the department had announced that majority rule should control, but when the factions had finally united so that four-fifths of the tribe had committed themselves in favor of a new government, had elected John Ross chief and the situation was in a fair way to produce the peace so much desired, at the instance of the remaining one-fifth and General Arbuckle who was moved by bitter animosity against Ross, the department reversed its position, and issued an order purporting to nullify the action of the nation in adopting and putting in operation the constitution, and put the whole Cherokee Nation under the military control of General Arbuckle. This for reasons assigned, that reports had been received that the majority had been guilty of tyrannical and oppressive acts toward the minority. And this in the face of reports from the constituted representatives of the govern-

1   *U. S. House Document* No. 129, Twenty-sixth Congress, first session.

2   The committee on Indian affairs to which these matters were referred, prepared a report which according to John Bell of Tennessee, a member, was adopted by a majority of the committee, but the House refused to permit it to be filed. Bell gave it to the press on July 27, 1840, and it became known as *Bell's Suppressed Report.*

ment on the ground, Superintendent Armstrong and Governor Stokes, that the great majority of the tribe had adopted the new constitution and that peace at last was in sight.

In considering this phase of the matter the report said that "Instead of the arrival of the period which called for the active interference of the Government to protect the Cherokee from 'domestic strife,' the committee recognize in the order of the secretary of war of the 6th of March, a revival of the practice of government interference in the internal affairs of the Cherokees which had recently been suspended; and, instead of an interference of the Government for the prevention of domestic strife, the order of the 6th of March ushered in a period of unrest, dissension and anarchy, by the undisguised attempt to control a majority of four-fifths of the Cherokee Nation, and compel them to yield obedience to a government dictated by the wishes and interests of the remaining one-fifth."

The sum of $800,000 was due the emigrant Cherokee on their arrival in the West to pay for spoliation and abandoned improvements, and to enable them to establish themselves in their new home; but the administration at Washington in furtherance of plans advocated by General Arbuckle and the small body of recalcitrant Treaty and Old Settler factions, decided to withhold payment of these funds of which they were in desperate need, until such time as they should agree to abandon the government recently set up by them and acknowledge the rule of the Old Settlers as the only valid government in the Cherokee Nation. The report continued: "The Committee are reluctantly compelled to believe, that upon no better or higher suggestions than the hope of operating upon the necessities and avarice of the Indians has the Executive of the United States been influenced in withholding the large sums of money long since due by treaty."

The report held that interference by the Executive in the affairs of the Cherokee Indians by prescribing any particular form of government or interdicting any system of laws already adopted by the majority, was unconstitutional and that the exercise of such power through military authority was dangerous to the peace of the country, and was an abandonment of long established policy of the Government which, if persisted in, would probably lead to disorder and war; that the peace and security of the western frontier could be maintained only by justice and good faith of the Government toward the large and wealthy tribes recently removed there.

In the latter part of August, 1840, John Ross and John Howard Payne left Washington for the Indian Territory. Others in the party were Lewis Ross, Elijah Hicks, John Looney, Archibald Campbell, and J. Parker Ridgeway. Going by way of New Orleans where they arrived about the middle of September, they proceeded up the Arkansas River and reached Park Hill in the Cherokee Nation in the early part of October.

The Cherokee council under the new constitution was to hold its first session in the autumn of 1840 and Ross's return was so timed that he would be present to report on his negotiations in Washington. Payne had secured from the war department a passport permitting him to visit in the Cherokee Nation so that he could continue his study of the Indians with a view to writing their history. He spent four months at Park Hill and wrote a series of articles for eastern newspapers describing conditions in the Indian country and the difficulties in the Cherokee tribe. What took place at that session of the new Cherokee council is best related in the words of this eye witness:

"*From the reports of the feverish state of this country, which prevailed not long ago, I presume you will not be reluctant to learn its real condition. Being upon the spot, I will acquaint you with what I have myself observed. But, to make my story plain, I shall have to revert to what passed a few months preceding my arrival.*

"*Sometime last summer, I understand, a meeting of leading men among the Cherokees was called at Fort Gibson by General Arbuckle. The real object was, by many, conjectured to be this: to obtain some expression of acquiescence in a declaration by Government agents that the lately adopted act of union, constitution, laws, and rulers of the Cherokees, were not the people's choice, but forced upon them by certain ambitious demagogues among the late emigrants from the East who had usurpingly excluded the old settlers from the Councils and power of the Nation; inasmuch as, although these last were nominally eligible to more than a fair participation in the public offices and representation, the arrangement was rendered nugatory by intrigues which had only permitted the admission of those who were previously ascertained to be friendly to the cause of John Ross.*

"The convention thus called by General Arbuckle to set all right, came to the following conclusion:

"They would not venture to disturb the decision regarding the Act of Union between the Eastern and Western Cherokees and the Constitution and Laws which followed it. Upon these the people's will had been so unequivocally spoken that it would be dangerous to thwart it. These must stand; so must all the elections under them, of that portion of the public officers which had been chosen from among the new emigrants, the Principal Chief included. But to prevent cavil, it was suggested (and, I think, by the Ross party) that, if those public functionaries who had been already chosen from among the old settlers would tender their resignation, that part of the Convention consisting exclusively of the party of old settlers might nominate substitutes, provided such a measure would be regarded as extinguishing all objections and as finally composing the troubles of the Nation. On this being agreed to, I learn that the functionaries in question immediately resigned, and substitutes were chosen by the part of the Convention formed of old settlers.

"The first annual National Council following this compromise had already commenced its session, when John Ross returned from Washington with the delegation. Among the members of the new Council were the most prominent of those called the "Treaty Party," who memorialized Congress against John Ross last session. Upon hearing of the Chief's arrival, runners were sent to gather the Nation at the Council Ground, that the measures of their embassy and the communications of their Chief might be presented without delay for the opinion of the entire people.

"In the last week of October the people had all assembled, and the message of their Chief, after being presented to the Committee (Senate) and the Council (Representatives) was ordered to be produced before them. John Ross accordingly appeared at a sort of rustic forum set up in the open square, with the written message in his hand, which he read, sentence by sentence, in English, pausing at every period for an interpreter, who stood by his side to repeat his words, in Cherokee, to the multitude. The Chief, I am told, could always very readily do this himself, but the people here, on such occasions, like the citizens of London in the time of Richard the Third, are, as Shakespeare says, 'used to be spoken to only through the Recorder.' The Cherokee custom probably arose from the desire to show that there were no alterations or suppressions in the public documents, so few of which—owing to the Indian relations with the United States—can be originally expressed in their own language.

"The message was long, but perfectly temperate throughout. It commended the people for having shown so much moderation under their trials, and for having displayed their unanimity in a manner so unquestionable, as must entirely destroy the misconception under which the United States continue to withhold their dues. The Chief explained that the Delegation to Washington had failed in all its objects, because the Government there had been taught to consider the Cherokee nation as disunited; but he exhorted them not to lose patience, for the truth concerning them must speedily be known; and, doubtless, as soon as it should be so, the declaration of the Secretary of War that the voice of the majority would be respected in his dealings with their country must be acted upon; and they asked no more. He urged their attention to the subject of education, for which the Nation had ample funds in the hands of the President that had never been brought into use, although complaints arose on every side of the want of schools. He referred to the numerous subjects which still called loudly for adjustment with the United States; and among them, the unsettled claim for the balance of the Emigration expenses, that so many of the people are interested in so deeply. He exhorted them not to suffer the inconveniences of this delay to weaken their confidence in ultimate justice from the Executive at Washington, but to continue more scrupulously observant than ever of all their treaty obligations, as the surest means of securing a punctilious regard for their own rights in return. He reminded the people, incidentally, that he himself was only interested in the Emigration claim in common with them—having enrolled himself, like the rest; and that he and his family had made the journey under a conductor of his own appointment, and without being in any way a sharer in the emoluments; for although superintendent of the whole, he freely gave the Nation both his time and services. He also mentioned that the disregard of all their claims by the United States Government at Washington might have been yet more injurious, had he not demanded, under a protest, the proceeds of a partial valuation of improvements taken from him in their late country, and thus obtained means to discharge the expenses of the National Delegation.

"The multitude appeared highly pleased with the Principal Chief's address. It was followed by speeches among them, and the whole wound up with a series of resolutions which were adopted unanimously and enthusiastically. They expressed the delight of the Cherokees that the Secretary of War had declared that he would regard the will of their majority in dealing with them; they avowed their desire to accommodate themselves, as far as possible, to the wishes of the United States Executive, and that they would prove it by waiving their own inclinations to any extent short of a sacrifice of the right of self-government and of the rulers of their choice, which nothing would induce them to abandon. They instructed their committee and council (Senate and Representatives) to carry out this principle and to convey their expression of it, through Gen. Arbuckle to the War Department.

"This last measure has already, I understand, been taken. The Gen. answered the Council very courteously, but reiterated the purpose of the Secretary of War not to recognize John Ross as Principal Chief and William S. Coodey as President of the National Committee. This indiscretion would, I have reason to think, have disturbed the progress of good will, had it not been for the discovery of qualified expressions in sentences of the General's letter, whence it might be inferred that when the entire truth came to be known at Washington, the policy there would change; so the proposed argument with the General was abandoned, and the Council closed its session, leaving the people under a strong expectation of better times ere long.

"A delegation was appointed by this National Council to visit Washington on the general business of the country. It consists of John Ross, John Benge, and David Vann. Resolutions were also passed approving the course of John Ross in reference to the emigration claim, and directing him to pursue it to a final settlement. The resolutions go at large into a statement of this claim, which may be summed up as follows: For the expenses of subsistence, horse and wagon hire, physicians and physic, ferries and steam boats, and all the endless et ceteras. General Scott had agreed with the Nation that the United States would pay at the rate of a fraction above eighty-two cents per day per head. Soap was to be paid for extra at fifteen cents a pound. It was supposed that the emigration could be brought within eighty days, but no time could be covenanted for; and, owing to a prevailing drought, and fatal sickness, when it had begun, the General himself ordered a halt; so that, the journey thus covering several weeks more than was expected, the account of its expenses became augmented in proportion. It is from this augmentation that misconceptions have arisen, which will doubtless be properly removed, and with them this deep source of discord and distress among the Cherokees.

"And now, gentlemen, it really appears to me, as I trust it will to you, that the various mistakes which have so long embarrassed the Cherokee question are so nearly disentangled that we have a right at length to look for, as the British Alderman so gravely said in his toast, 'a speedy peace and soon.'"[3]

Payne wrote other accounts for the New York Journal of Commerce describing the sessions of the Cherokee Council at Tahlequah; and showed how the large gathering of Indians was striving earnestly to achieve a peaceful settlement of their difficulties; but at the same time affirmed in well chosen words their prerogative as a people to govern themselves under a system providing for majority rule and adhered to their right to select a chief of their choice by majority vote. While never disrespectful to the authorities at Washington they made it clear that the efforts of the war department to interfere with their domestic affairs and upset the action of the majority was a violation of their rights under their treaties, and that the secretary was dealing with men quite as capable as he of judging of their rights and defending them in debate.

Payne's letters were detailed and threw a strong light on the situation that helps to visualize the tyranny the secretary of war sought to impose upon them. Shortly after the cruel massacre of Boudinot and Ridge, Evan Jones, the venerable missionary, wrote a number of letters to Payne which have been preserved and help to illuminate the situation. Jones's language was less restrained than Payne's and he expressed the opinion that Ridge and Boudinot had been killed because of their interference with the efforts of the immigrant Cherokee to set up a government. He charged that Ridge advised the western chiefs not to come to an agreement with recent arrivals and as a result their first conference broke up in failure.[4]

"Threats have been made by some of the last remains of the Treaty party," said Mr. Payne, "that John Ross shall never reach Washington, but it is likely enough you will hear of him there soon after the new

3 National Intelligencer (Washington, D. C.), December, 1840.
4 Evan Jones to John Howard Payne July 22, 1839, Ayer Collection, Newberry Library.

year."[5] In company with the delegation in February, 1841, Payne left Park Hill for Washington where they arrived on the twenty-first. There the delegation had the benefit of Payne's study of their situation, and his advice.

A new day seemed to be dawning for the Cherokee Nation. After President Harrison's brief incumbency, John Tyler became president on April 4, 1841. Gen. Matthew Arbuckle was ordered from Fort Gibson to an obscure post at Baton Rouge, to the indignation of his friends in Arkansas and the Indian Territory. He was undoubtedly a conscientious officer and executive but his prejudice and vindictiveness had carried him to unreasonable and unnecessary lengths in opposing John Ross and his undertakings. Ross was probably the most talented man in the Indian Territory and his ability and success in his controversies with Arbuckle had earned the bitter animosity of the latter who pursued injudicious and harmful efforts at reprisal. There was not room in the Indian Territory for two men of their conflicting views and influence, and Arbuckle had to go.

Payne was employed by the secretary of war to study the so-called Cherokee Treaty of 1835 and report his views concerning the claims of the Cherokee Indians and the obligations of the Government growing out of the treaty. He prepared an interesting memorandum[6] based on his observations of the Indians, their proceedings and arguments in council, and statements made in his presence.

The Cherokee people had claims against the Government growing out of their enforced removal; and the failure to adjust these as promised, kept them in state of dissatisfaction and rancor. A new treaty was much desired by them and Mr. Payne gave several reasons why it should be entered into. There were but few who would acknowledge the compact maneuvered by the Reverend Schermerhorn in 1835. The Cherokee people would not have moved except by force, said Mr. Payne, if the validity of that so-called treaty had not been waived; and they had since felt that that document would be superseded by a genuine treaty, which he urged, was the only means by which the

5 Payne wrote a long letter that appeared in the *New York Journal of Commerce*, January 22, 1841; he described the meetings of the Cherokee council, quoted speeches delivered, and resolutions adopted there.

6 Memoranda by John Howard Payne, Washington City, Saturday, July 10, 1841, *Ethan Allen Hitchcock Manuscript Collection*, Library of Congress.

William Shorey Coodey, who wrote the Act of Union between the factions of the Cherokee Nation in 1839, from an ivory miniature painted while he was in Washington, now the property of Mrs. Ella Coodey Robinson of Muskogee

Rose Cottage, home of Chief John Ross at Park Hill

honor of the Government could be purged of the stain resting upon it.

"Conditions have changed fundamentally since the 'treaty' of 1835 was made so that many new problems had arisen to demand adjustment. A new treaty would restore the Government in the confidence of the Cherokee people whose favorable influence with the wild Indians was worth having." In the third place, he said, the Cherokee had "a man [[John Ross]] at their head, of great energy, untiring perseverance, and far reaching views. By strengthening him with his people and with his neighbors, we enable him to carry out plans of civilization and improvement vastly important in their future action upon our Indian relations; and which there appears no other person among all the tribes equally competent with him to manage. He has thus far kept his people quiet by assuring them that they may rely upon the ultimate justice of the United States. The time has come when that assurance can be fulfilled. If it is not, John Ross will be regarded by the Cherokees as their deluder; his sway over them will be lost; and should this misfortune arrive, we may look for long and costly troubles, to which the Seminole war will be a bagatelle."

The Cherokee people themselves felt that a new treaty was necessary, said Mr. Payne, because "they have been captured; an act of war has been committed against them without any provocation but that of desiring their property; and under that capture, they have been removed to a new and strange region. To atone for this wrong, and to avert resistance, they have been promised payment for what has been taken from them; with security in the place whither they are removed. Neither of these promises are [sic] yet kept. Swarms of persons have claims which we have never answered. Although large sums of money have been appropriated, no one seems to know what has become of it. The country east of the Mississippi yet remains unpaid for. In the country west of the Mississippi—although nominally theirs in return for former cessions of territory long prior to the removal thither of the entire nation, they are no safer now than they were in the region whence they have just been ejected. They feel that the miseries so lately endured, may, at any moment, be brought back upon them. That this apprehension is no chimera, is evident from some of the recent debates in Congress" where it was asserted that there was no constitutional guarantee of the title of the Cherokee Nation in the lands occupied by it. The Cherokee people desired this point satisfied by a treaty and grant of their lands. If the Cherokee were secured in this boon, said Mr. Payne, "the foundations would be firmly laid of perpetual peace and good will between the red man and the white. But the longer a legal guarantee to this effect is omitted or delayed, the more distrustful will this people become of our sincerity. . . . . They have been kept so long in suspense, that, whatever their fate is to be, they desire to know at once. They will look upon further silence as confirmatory of their worst doubts; as mere craft and evasion. Hope deferred, which makes the civilized man sick, makes the less civilized ferocious. Under these circumstances, they do not feel secure in opening farms, in building houses, in establishing schools nor churches; for ere these are half finished, they may be captured again."

CHAPTER TWENTY-FOUR / Civil Disorders

THE Cherokee delegation returned from Washington in the autumn in time to participate in the council which was attended and described by Maj. Ethan Allen Hitchcock.[1] It was the first day of December, 1841 that Chief Ross appeared "and rode into the middle of the council ground and tied his horse to a tree. Great numbers of the people were standing around but Indian-like no one approached him. I was the first to go up and speak to him. We shook hands and several questions of civility passed and we separated. He walked a short distance and then began a general greeting. It was nearly an hour after his arrival before he took his place in a sort of pulpit under a large shed and the Committee and Council and people assembled promiscuously so far as I could observe to hear the message. . . . . Mr. Ross took with him Bushyhead, the Chief Justice, a good looking rather portly man some 35 or 40 years of age. Mr. Ross then read in English from a written paper his message, which was sentence by sentence translated into Cherokee by the Chief Justice, both standing.

"The auditors were seated or standing at pleasure with their hats on and some were smoking but all was perfect order and silence. The council shed was merely a roof sustained by uprights. The seats were split logs or hewn logs supported by pins like a common farmer's stool, but long, each seat holding 12 or 15. In the message Mr. Ross gave an account of his mission to Washington from which he had just returned. He dwelt particularly upon his efforts to obtain a new treaty for the Cherokees, concluding his message by detailing almost the whole of a letter to the delegation from President Tyler, dated last August which

1 Grant Foreman, A Traveler in Indian Territory.

seems to promise a new treaty with full indemnity to the Cherokees for all their losses and 'wrongs'."[2]

Major Hitchcock details some interesting proceedings witnessed by him at the council during several days of his attendance there. The council appointed another delegation of five members to return to Washington and make further efforts to obtain a treaty and adjustment of their claims against the Government. The delegation included Chief Ross, Jesse Bushyhead, David Vann, Captain Benge and William Shorey Coodey.

Major Hitchcock was engaged on an official mission of investigation in the Indian Territory and he reported to the secretary of war the result of his study of John Ross, and the Cherokee people, their grievances and demands. Of John Ross, he said, "like other conspicuous men, he has been variously spoken of, in terms of great praise and great censure. He resides five miles from this place on a beautiful prairie in sight of Park Hill—is of mixed blood between 45 and 50 years of age— is under size and his manners, unless excited, have a dash of diffidence in them—is not of ready speech—speaks English principally and will not trust himself to address his own people in Cherokee—is a man of strong passions and settled purposes which he pursues with untiring zeal; is of undoubted courage unless it be that he fears the defeat of his plans more than the loss of life and would preserve the latter to execute the former. After much attentive observation I am of opinion that John Ross is an honest man and a patriot laboring for the good of his people. In the recent trouble of his nation, including several years, with almost unlimited opportunities he has not enriched himself. . . . . It would be strange if there was not ambition with the patriotism of Jno Ross, but he seeks the fame of establishing his nation and heaping benefits upon his people. Though not a fluent speaker, even in conversation, he is a clear-minded, accurate thinker of very far-reaching views."[3]

The matters the delegation would present for adjustment, Major Hitchcock said, included a demand for a fee simple title to their land in the West; the withdrawal of the United States troops from Fort Gib-

2 President Tyler wrote this letter September 20, 1841 (*Cherokee Advocate*, November 28, 1844, p. 1, col. 3). See Butler to Taylor with Taylor to adjutant general April 27, 1842, AGO, OFD, 133 T 42.

3 Grant Foreman, *A Traveler in Indian Territory*, 38.

son and Fort Wayne, in the Cherokee Nation on the ground of the introduction of whisky and demoralization of the country adjacent to them; losses of cattle, horses and other property occasioned by the forced removal of the Cherokee from their homes; payment for their country and improvements necessarily abandoned by them and remuneration for the wrongs and suffering occasioned by their forced removal; the execution of a new treaty to incorporate the matters presented by them and as a vindication of their refusal to recognize the spurious Treaty of 1835 as binding on them.[4] The Cherokee Nation now numbered 12,000 members of the Ross faction, 4,000 of the Ridge or Treaty Party, and 2,000 Old Settlers.[5]

Colonel Hitchcock returned to Washington in April, 1842, and made an extended report to the secretary of war which included 100 exhibits compiled by him in four months of searching investigation. Hitchcock was an honest and fearless investigator and his report corroborated in unequivocal language the charges of fraud committed by remorseless contractors on the helpless Indian immigrants. In the ordinary course the President would have transmitted Hitchcock's report to the House with no unnecessary delay. But that was not done in this instance. During Hitchcock's absence in the West John Bell of Tennessee was succeeded as secretary of war by John C. Spencer of New York. When Hitchcock delivered his report to the new secretary he found himself in a decidedly hostile atmosphere.

Members of the House of Representatives, aroused by charges that for years had been dinned into their ears, desired the report delivered to them so that appropriate action could be taken. It was said that friends of the administration were involved in the turpitude discovered and exposed by Hitchcock and the secretary was determined at all hazards to protect them. Confirmation was seen in his attitude when he said that the House should not see the report except over his dead body. He claimed that Hitchcock's investigation was *ex parte;* but the fact was that Hitchcock invited any one interested to appear and make such charges or defense and explanation as he chose. The contractors and their agents not only declined the invitation but those still there

4 Ibid., 234.
5 Butler to Taylor, April 16, 1842, with Taylor to Jones, April 27, 1842, AGO, OFD, 133 T 42.

fled the country when the investigator came to the Indian Territory so that Hitchcock was unable to interview them.

After waiting in vain for the report a resolution was adopted May 18, 1842, calling on the secretary of war to communicate to the House the several reports made to the war department by Colonel Hitchcock, together with all information communicated by him concerning the frauds he was charged to investigate; also all facts in possession of the Executive relating to the subject. By direction of President Tyler the secretary refused to comply with the request on the ground that the nature and subject of the report rendered its publication at that time inconsistent with the public interest, referring particularly to Hitchcock's letters relating to negotiations with the Cherokee people then pending.

The House declined to accept the reply and explanation of the secretary which effectually barred the revelation of Hitchcock's investigation and action on it, and subsequently adopted another resolution to the same effect. To this President Tyler replied on January 31, 1843 in a special message which was in the main a demonstration of the right of the Executive to deny the demand of the House for the documents in question. While he decided the matter in his own favor, he did transmit a part of Hitchcock's report, including his 100 exhibits. Papers relating to Cherokee negotiations and parts of others he refused to submit. Of particular significance was a long letter written by Hitchcock at Tahlequah, December 21, 1841, to the secretary of war, in which he described the condition of the Cherokee people and the character and aspirations of some of the leading men of the Ross faction. Several pages of this letter including that part in which Hitchcock described John Ross as an honest man and a patriot, he deleted and submitted the remainder.[6]

In the spring of 1842, an event occurred which again threw the whole nation into a state of the wildest excitement. The friends of the murdered Ridges and Boudinot had never forgiven the act, nor had time softened their resentment against the perpetrators and their supposed abettors. On the ninth of May, Anderson Springston, one of the Ross faction, was shot by a white man at a grocery store on the Arkansas side of the line, and a few days later, at the same place, Stand Watie

6 United States House *Executive Document* No. 219, Twenty-seventh Congress, third session.

killed James Foreman, a member of the Ross party whom Stand Watie charged with being a participant in the murders. Stand Watie was subsequently tried in Arkansas and acquitted on his plea of self-defense. Armed guards gathered for the protection of Ross adherents, and as the attacks were understood to be a renewal of the feud, they destroyed all hopes, for the time, of reconciliation of the tribal factions.[7] In February, Moses Alberty, Jr., killed in the Cherokee Nation a white man named George Long from Arkansas, and the governor of that state ordered the organization and rendezvous of a regiment of volunteers in Washington County. A messenger from Fort Smith was found hanging to a tree near Fort Gibson; Indians were suspected of the murder.[8]

It was claimed that Alberty murdered Long in Madison County, Arkansas,[9] and Gov. Archibald Yell of that state wrote a petulant and abusive letter to the secretary of war saying that if the Federal Government would not protect the state he would call out the militia to do it. The secretary replied that there were plenty of Federal troops near to give the whites of the state all the protection necessary; but that the Cherokee Indians were peaceful and were not guilty of the disorders charged against them.[10]

Pierce M. Butler, the Cherokee agent, said the Indians were much abused by being taken from their own country for minor offenses committed on white men having no business in the Cherokee country. Such broils were "eight times out of ten provoked on the part of itinerant persons from all parts of the United States, tempted or induced there by gain. It is too much the habit abroad to cry out 'Indian outrage,' without a just knowledge of facts.

"All persons familiar with that portion of the Cherokees bordering on Crawford and Washington counties, in Arkansas, know that they are industrious, intelligent, and neighborly disposed. The inhabitants of those two populous counties are distinguished as a laboring, intelligent, high-minded, and judicious people. It is not from them the difficulties occur, or complaints are made, but from a plundering predatory

7   Charles C. Royce, op. cit., p. 297-8; J. M. Lynch and others to P. M. Butler, May 17, 1842, OIA.
8   Taylor to adjutant general, February 14, 1842, AGO, OFD, 58 T 42.
9   Daily National Intelligencer, January 31, 1842, p. 4, col. 2.
10 Ibid., April 4, 1842, p. 4, col. 3 and p. 3, col. 2.

class, upon whose oath before a magistrate the Cherokees are hunted down by the military, and taken a distance of 200 miles to Little Rock, for trial; there lodged in jail, to await slow justice. These are evils of no small import, and of every day's occurrence, and which produce angry and embittered feelings.[11]

An amusing illustration of the peculiar conception entertained by some of the white people of Arkansas regarding the Indian country west of them was furnished in connection with the efforts of Gen. W. G. Belknap, when he was in command of Fort Gibson, to preserve the peace of that community. He had made an order intended to suppress the activities of a gang of lawless horse racers and gamblers who infested the country and had a demoralizing influence on the post and the country round about. A particularly conspicuous offender was one Goggle-Eyed Williams who was removed from the country by the orders of the post commander at Fort Gibson. He seemed to have friends in high places, for one Senator Clarke of the Arkansas legislature introduced in the Senate a resolution reciting that General Belknap at Fort Gibson had perpetrated "unlawful tyranny and unjustifiable outrages upon citizens of Arkansas" and demanding that Congress define the rights of citizens in the Indian country beyond the limits of the state.[12]

The constitution of the Cherokee tribe adopted at Tahlequah on September 6, 1839 provided that the chief and most of the other officers should hold office for four years. The first election was held in 1839 under the protection of the large body of Ross adherents during the convention at Tahlequah in 1839. The subsequent change in office holders was made under the influence of the martial law enforced in the Cherokee Nation by General Arbuckle; the election on August 7, 1843[13] then, was to be the first test of a popular ballot under the constitution of the Cherokee Nation. A lawless element that was opposed to the government proceeded to terrorize the voters and

11   Butler to commissioner, *Report* of commissioner of Indian affairs for 1842.
12   *Cherokee Advocate*, November 26, 1851, p. 2, col. 1, copied from *Arkansas Banner*.
13   In this election John Ross was reëlected chief by a handsome majority, defeating Joseph Vann, the candidate of the "western Cherokees" (United States Senate *Document* No. 140, Twenty-eighth Congress, second session, p. 35). Vann had been elected assistant principal chief in 1839 and served until the revision of the government, June 26, 1840, when he resigned and the office was filled by Andrew M. Vann, who served until his death in 1842 (*ibid.*, 41).

election officials in some of the precincts; they were particularly active in Saline District, where they destroyed the election papers, attacked and killed Isaac Bushyhead at the polls and severely wounded David Vann and Elijah Hicks. Six persons were involved in the affair, four of whom were at once arrested and placed in irons.[14] Two of them escaped and fled with the Starr boys, who were engaged in similar efforts to nullify the election. One of the murderers who was taken was Jacob West, a white man from Virginia, who had lived with the Cherokee for thirty years and had a Cherokee wife and children. Though he had long exercised all the rights and privileges of a member of the tribe, when he was arrested, claiming the immunity of a white man from the processes of the Cherokee courts, he applied to the judge of the United States Court in Arkansas for a writ of habeas corpus, which was denied. He was accordingly tried, convicted and executed by the Cherokee authorities. During this disturbance Gen. Zachary Taylor came to Fort Gibson, but when the United States court refused to intervene, he satisfied himself that the Cherokee government could handle the situation without his assistance, and he returned to Fort Smith.[15]

This same element continued their lawless course to show their contempt for the Cherokee government, and the next month the country was shocked by an outrage more than usually atrocious; on September 15, after killing a white man named Kelly, Thomas Starr, Bean Starr, Ellis Starr, and Arch Sanders killed old Mr. and Mrs. Benjamin Vore. ". . . . about thirty miles from this post,[16] on the military road leading to Fort Gibson. Mr. Vore, a white man and licensed trader in the nation, was killed together with his wife & a stranger stopping for the night in the house. After robbing the premises the villains set fire to the house which was entirely consumed with the bodies of the unfortunate victims."[17] General Taylor sent a company of dragoons after them, and the murderers were pursued across the line into Arkansas, where they were captured, but the state officer in whose

14 General Taylor to adjutant general, August 15, 1843, AGO. OFD. 223, T 43. The same summer the Starrs killed David Buffington.

15 United States Senate Document No. 138, Twenty-eighth Congress, second session, p. 123; Taylor to Adjutant General, ibid.

16 The home of the Vores was near Dwight Mission.

17 General Taylor to adjutant general, October 8, 1843, AGO. OFD. 265, T 43.

custody they were, permitted them to escape.[18] Most of the difficulty in the Cherokee Nation, General Taylor continued, was fomented by white people along the line in Arkansas.

By authority of the National Council, John Ross offered a reward of one thousand dollars each for the apprehension of Thomas Starr, Ellis Starr, and Bean Starr, who ". . . . .besides other deeds of blood and robbery, murdered, robbed and burnt in September, 1843, Mr. Vore, a licensed trader, his wife and a traveler." Thomas Starr was described as twenty-eight years old, six feet five inches tall, straight, well built, broad forehead, black hair, grey eyes, generally with the lashes plucked out, large feet, of great muscular strength and smiles when talking. Ellis Starr was but five feet ten inches or six feet tall, two hundred pounds in weight, with large neck, dark auburn hair, and blue eyes.[19]

The grand jury of Washington County, Arkansas, returned into the circuit court an indictment against Isaac Springston and one Shell, charging them with the murder of Major Ridge, and on December 28, 1843, Governor Yell of Arkansas addressed a requisition to Gov. P. M. Butler, Cherokee agent, for the arrest and delivery of the persons named therein. Butler referred the matter to the military authorities, and on February 2, Gen. Zachary Taylor wrote to Loomis, in command at Fort Gibson, saying that he would not assist in delivering these Indians to Arkansas, as to do so would cause great excitement in the Cherokee Nation. ". . . . I have little doubt from many circumstances, that the present case is connected with the systematic efforts which are making by certain citizens of Arkansas, to revive and keep up a political

18 The next autumn Bean Starr, Tom Starr and Ellis Starr were making their escape to the Texas border with stolen horses, when they were overtaken at a Cherokee settlement on the Washita River twenty-five miles above Fort Washita by a volunteer company of Cherokee commanded by Daniel R. Coodey; a fight ensued in which Bean Starr was wounded, and a number of horses and mules stolen from Cherokee citizens were recovered. Colonel Harney at Fort Washita, assisted in holding the prisoners. Bean Starr died of his wounds in the hospital at Fort Washita. Relatives of the Starrs organized to waylay Coodey and his company on their return, and early in December, 1844, the Cherokee police started southwest from Webbers Falls to meet and protect them (United States Senate *Document* No. 140, Twenty-eighth Congress, second session, p. 141; *Cherokee Advocate*, December 26, 1844, p. 3, cols. 2, 3, and 4).

19 *Cherokee Advocate*, January 23, 1845, p. 1, col. 5; *ibid.*, March 20, 1845, p. 4, col. 6. Tom Starr emigrated to the west in 1829 or 1830 (*Documents* II, 171).

excitement in the Cherokee Nation in the internal affairs of which they have no legitimate interest whatever."[20]

John Ross headed another delegation that arrived in Washington April 20, 1844; the other members were John Benge, David Vann, Elijah Hicks, and William P. Ross, secretary. William Wilkins of Pennsylvania had assumed the duties of secretary of war on February 15 and the delegates hopefully approached him on the subject of the much desired new treaty which they claimed had been promised them by President Tyler whose letter of September 20, 1841 they exhibited to him.[21] Secretary Wilkins treated them with much consideration and told them to put their propositions in writing; but he informed them also that the negotiations must include the complaints and grievances[22] presented to him May 6 by John Rogers, James Carey, and Thomas L. Rogers of the Old Settlers, and John A. Bell, Ezekiel Starr, and Bluford West of the Treaty Party. These men demanded a separate part of the Cherokee Nation for their exclusive use, a readjustment of the annuities growing out of the treaties of 1819, 1828, and 1833 so as to give the Old Settlers a larger share; and the Treaty Party demanded a per capita payment which they claimed to be due them under the terms of the treaty entered into by them in 1835. The Ross delegation replied that as theirs was a republican government representing the whole Cherokee Nation, they could not admit the necessity or propriety of negotiating with a faction of the tribe.

The secretary addressed a long communication to the delegation on July 8, giving them little comfort and advising them that he would ask the President to authorize the sending of a commission to the Cherokee country to investigate the charges brought by the minority faction of the tribe. To this the delegation replied that the difficulty was caused in a large part by the encouragement given to the complaining delegations by the Government. That the difficulty was created in the beginning by the Government in countenancing the fraudulent execution of a pretended treaty with a small part of the tribe. "Nothing was more natural nor more to be anticipated than excitements and divisions between the different portions of the Cherokee people on their being

20 Taylor to adjutant general, February 14, 1844, AGO. OFD. 46 T 44.
21 *Cherokee Advocate*, November 28, 1844, pp. 1, 2 and 3.
22 Dated April 13, 1844. United States House *Document* No. 234, Twenty-eighth Congress, first session.

brought together west of the Mississippi. A very small portion, not more than one-fiftieth of the population had undertaken to cede away the whole country of the Cherokees. The great mass of our people were in consequence of this 'Treaty' expelled at the point of the bayonet from their native country—from the country where reposed the bones of their ancestors for countless generations, and where they had pleasant homes, good farms and all the comforts which their constant advances in civilization had secured for them—and removed under circumstances of varied and complicated sufferings and hardships, disease and death, when they found themselves re-united with those who had entailed all this misery upon them, and who were still striving to prevent the re-union between the Eastern and Western Cherokees, and the mutual adoption of a more regular and wiser constitution and laws for the government of the whole people; what was more natural ever with a people in the highest degree civilized, than occasional ebulitions of passion and acts of violence?"[23]

The delegation argued to the secretary that no commission sent to the country could possibly learn more about conditions than was known by Gov. Pierce M. Butler and Gen. Zachary Taylor, representatives of the Government already living there. Concerning the secretary's rejection of their claim for indemnity for property lost on the removal they said that "as to the sacrifice of the personal effects of the Cherokees by the troops and citizens of the United States; a sacrifice which stripped hundreds of their all at that most gloomy epoch of our nation's history—we would gladly obliterate if we could, from our memory every thing connected with it. It was a scene not often witnessed, and which, we trust in a righteous God, will never be repeated—of a people, a civilized and unoffending people, driven from their country and their homes, for no other reason than that another and more powerful people wished to possess that country.

"If the government of the United States had taken that country by force, open and direct, under a state of circumstances creating a necessity, real or supposed, a just regard for their own character, for the opinion of the world, would have suggested the most liberal indemnity both to the Nation and individuals suffering. We cannot perceive that the moral force of these considerations is diminished by this pretended Treaty; to which we do not choose to apply the terms

23 *Cherokee Advocate*, December 5, 1844, p. 2.

which we deem it merits, which we perhaps could not do without giving offence. We cannot therefore believe that the Cherokees, for indulging that patriotism which is inherent in the human heart, and which is universally esteemed honorable, and for clinging to their country with fervid and continual devotion, until 'the steps that were finally adopted' forced them to remove, have, thereby, forfeited their just claims to indemnity for 'any spoliations upon personal property prior or *subsequent* to the Treaty of 1835'."[24]

With scant comfort to take home with them, the delegation returned in the summer to the Cherokee Nation; one of them however tarried in the East as romance took a hand in the affairs of the Cherokee Nation, and on September 2, 1844 Chief John Ross was married in Philadelphia to Miss Mary B. Stapler of Wilmington, Delaware.[25] He did not return to the Nation in time to attend the session of the council in October, and it was not until November 13 that he appeared before the council and made a full report of his mission to Washington and read all of the correspondence that passed between the delegation and the secretary of war.

Much dissatisfaction was caused by the enactment by the tribal council on October 30, 1843 of a measure[26] declaring all salines in the Cherokee Nation but one, to be the property of the Nation; that exception was the one granted to Sequoyah by the Treaty of 1828. In this they followed the theory that controlled in the Government of the United States with reference to salines on the public land. Unfortunately, a number of Old Settlers had expended considerable money in fitting up plants for the operation of works where a number of them for some years had been engaged in a small way in the manufacture of salt. This law operated to deprive them of their property, and there was loud complaint. Among those who suffered from the law was Capt. John Rogers, a chief of the Old Settlers, who had for many years operated what was known as The Grand Saline, near where is now Salina, Oklahoma. His bitter hostility toward the government of the tribe had caused him to remove to Fort Smith. In September, 1844, he and others circulated a call for a meeting on the sixteenth of the month at Tahlontuskee, at the mouth of the Illinois River, where they planned

24 *Ibid.*
25 *Ibid.*, October 5, 1844, p. 3, col. 1.
26 *Laws of the Cherokee Nation*, Edition of 1868.

to memorialize the Government for relief. This meeting was decided upon at a conference near Fort Smith of 160 Old Settlers soon after the return from Washington of their delegation. On hearing of the proposed meeting the authorities of the nation took steps to prevent it, alleging that it was the intention at the meeting to agitate measures looking to the division of the Cherokee people and the overthrow of the government. Major Armstrong, fearing a renewal of bloodshed, prevailed on the Old Settlers to abandon their meeting.[27]

In response to the recommendation of the sceretary of war, William Wilkins, to send a commission to the Cherokee Nation to investigate the situation, and ascertain whether their government was opposed by a considerable part of the tribe, and whether the laws were enforced equally on all factions, President Tyler named a commission composed of Roger Jones, adjutant general of the Army, Col. R. B. Mason, and Gov. Pierce M. Butler, Cherokee Agent. After organizing at Fort Gibson on November 15 and giving notice of the meeting[28] the commission began its inquiry on December 4, at Tahlontuskee.[29]

The conference continued there in session four days, and it was attended by 546 Old Settlers and 362 of the Treaty Party; 155 of these, however, were ascertained to be white men who were found by the commission to include most of the individual complainants.[30] The Indians assembled under an open arbor, where speeches were made by deputations who represented them. The regularly constituted Cherokee government refused to send a delegation to the meeting; they informed the commission that if it would come to Tahlequah, the

27 Arbuckle to Jones, September 14, 1844, AGO. OFD., 149, 1 A. 44.

28 *Cherokee Advocate*, November 28, 1844, p. 3, col. 6.

29 This was the council ground of the Old Settlers, near the mouth of the Illinois River; it was on the east bank of the stream near the home of John Jolly, and was named for his brother, former chief of the Cherokee who lived in Arkansas. The investigation was based largely on charges made by Capt. John Rogers, Thomas L. Rogers, John A. Bell, Ezekiel Starr and Bluford West.

30 Report of Commission—United States Senate *Document* No. 24, p. 5, Twenty-eighth Congress, second session. Ross's delegation had informed Wilkins that the agitation was fomented and kept alive by white men. "Colonel Armistead, an old, white haired gentleman, and Col. George C. Washington, who had been among the Cherokee," descended the Arkansas in the steamboat *Lucy Long* which on April 10, 1845, went aground about sixty miles above Little Rock. "Colonel Hunter," also was on board (*Autobiography of William Wood*, Vol. II, 34).

seat of the Cherokee government, they would be glad to participate, and furnish all the information possible; but they took the position that for the commission to meet a faction of the tribe in a remote part of the nation was a slight to the tribe as a whole, and was an unlawful meddling in the affairs of the nation. There were, however, a few individual members from the Ross faction who attended and cross-examined witnesses.

A few log cabins encircled the arbor, and as the weather was cold, the people were gathered in groups around the fires, warming themselves and cooking food. Before the meeting was over, it snowed, and many thinly clad people suffered from the cold. During the meeting, the police of the nation appeared on the ground, and as the people appeared to be in fear of them, the commission ordered them away. The commission was attended by a company of Dragoons to preserve order. The meeting was opened with a speech delivered by General Jones to which Dutch made a short response in behalf of the complaining Indians. Little was accomplished at Tahlontuskee, and the commission adjourned on the seventh to meet at the old Cherokee Agency, seven miles east of Fort Gibson; here was taken the testimony of Governor Stokes and of General Arbuckle who had been returned to the command of Fort Gibson. The former testified to the regularity of the proceedings of the new government. The sessions were continued at Fort Gibson until December 14, when they were adjourned and resumed on the sixteenth;[31] after a few days in Tahlequah, the commission concluded its work at Fort Gibson on January 17, 1845.

The commission reported in detail on its investigation of the charges January 17. It found that the complainants were not deprived of their property. And that they had "not shown in any case that life has been taken or endangered by the Cherokee authorities since the 'act of union,' except in the administration of wholesome laws. It cannot be denied that human life in the Cherokee country is in danger—great danger. But the danger lies in the frequent and stealthy incursions of a desperate gang of banditti—'half breeds' notorious in the nation as wanton murderers, house burners, and horse stealers, but whose fraternity is not of the dominant party; nor are the dangers from these

31 *Cherokee Advocate*, December 26, 1844, p. 3, cols. 1 and 2; AGO., OFD., 366 C 44.

outlaws most dreaded by the parties who send up their complaints of the insecurity of life. . . . . All the complaints admit the forms of law were duly observed. But in what community, even the most enlightened, do parties defeated or convicted, including sympathizing friends, feel satisfied with the judgment of the court or of a jury? . . . . The ample share in the offices of the nation by the Western Cherokees, especially in the judiciary (for the bench has been filled chiefly from among them) ought to lull suspicion of partial administration of the laws, and at least encourage them in the reasonable hope of equal security in life, liberty, and property.

"In view of all these ascertained facts, the allegation 'that they cannot live in peace in the same community with their alleged oppressors' is of little weight, and ought not, in the opinion of the commissioners, to be entertained. The commissioners have discovered, that even while present on the spot, where they are able in most cases to elicit the truth, complaints have come up, either frivolous in the extreme, or not true. And it is believed that the 'old settlers' and 'treaty party' enjoy, under the 'act of union' and the constitution of the Cherokee nation, liberty, property, and life, in as much security as the rest of the Cherokees.

"The commissioners do not believe that any 'considerable portion of the Cherokee people are arrayed in hostile feeling and action against those who are in the rule of the nation.' The 'bitterness of hostility to the dominant party,' whatever it may be, it is believed, is confined only to a few. In the same relative proportion, probably in a less degree, like feelings and corresponding dispositions prevail in the majority toward the minority. But the masses, on either side, it is thought, are as well disposed to each other as in most communities divided into political parties, due allowance being made for the peculiar people."

The continuation of disorder in the country or the restoration of peace the commission believed, depended on the course which the Government thereafter would pursue towards the parts— "the few, who, irrespective of the whole nation, come forward to represent the fraction of these parts at the seat of government. Nothing is more calculated to keep alive the flame of discord in the Cherokee nation, than the belief that the restless or discontented, though comparatively few in number, will always find a ready audience at Washington, and the hope that complaints of oppression, and the like, may enlist the sympathies of the Government and the community. It is far from the intention or wish of the commissioners to intimate that complaints of alleged wrongs and grievances of any portion of the Indian families should not distinctly come up to the ear of the President. But on the mode and manner in which these complaints are made and entertained, may depend the harmony, if not the integrity of the government of the Cherokee nation."

As a means of restoring peace and harmony and promoting the improvement of the whole Cherokee people, the commission recommended that "their authorities be heard in support of their claims on the United States, and that a new treaty be concluded on the just and liberal basis set forth and promised in the letter of his excellency President Tyler, September 20, 1841. By such a measure, it is believed, not only will the good faith of the United States be triumphantly shown, but they will be more than repaid for this liberal policy in the beneficial results to the Cherokee nation, and its rapid progress to the position of an enlightened well ordered community."[32]

Came a new administration. James K. Polk of Tennessee was inaugurated President March 4, 1845 and two days later William M. Marcy became secretary of war. The "Treaty Party" sent another delegation to Washington composed of Ezekiel Starr, J. L. Thompson and J. V. McNair, who proceeded to demonstrate the truth of the report made by the recent commission to the Cherokee Nation: that the administration at Washington was greatly responsible for keeping alive the unrest and resistance to constituted authority in that nation by the encouragement it gave to frivolous complaints of irresponsible individuals.[33] Notwithstanding the charges had been found baseless

32 United States Senate *Document* No. 140, Twenty-eighth Congress, second session.

33 A scholarly study of this unhappy phase of Cherokee history is that of Thomas Valentine Parker, *The Cherokee Indians, with Special Reference to their relations with the United States Government* (New York, 1907). Concerning this stage of Federal ineptitude he says: "After this investigation one would think that sufficient time had been given to discussion, and that the time for action had arrived. If the United States authorities had at once fully recognized and acknowledged the Ross government as the only legitimate one, and had discountenanced factional attempts to overthrow it, a disgraceful page of Cherokee history probably never would have been written. But no such course was pursued. . . . Instead Commissioner Medill sent to President Polk, who had succeeded Tyler, a communication which, after the clear

by the president's commission, Secretary Marcy addressed a communication April 24, 1845, to the delegation containing a threat of military intervention in the Cherokee Nation if the authorities there neglected to "strictly regard the wishes of" the war department and committed further "outrages" on any individuals in the nation.[34] On May 15 next the secretary transmitted the correspondence on the subject with a letter to John Rogers as "principal chief of the Western Cherokees" thereby perpetuating and encouraging the schism in the tribe created by the defection of the small and jealous body of malcontents who were still striving to break down the Cherokee government and discredit its constituted leaders.

The Cherokee council named another delegation to Washington composed of John Ross, Richard Taylor, Joseph Vann, John Looney, Aaron Price, David Vann, Joseph Spears and Thigh Walker. They were directed to continue their efforts to secure an adjustment of the claims and other unsettled business of the Cherokee Nation. They left Park Hill for Washington on April 1, 1845.[35]

Receiving little comfort from the commission sent to investigate their complaints, in the summer of 1845 a part of the Old Settler and Treaty parties feeling that they could not be happy under a government dominated by John Ross, determined to seek a home on the borders of Mexico. Conferences were held near the Arkansas line where members were selected to explore the country to which it was proposed to move. A delegation left Evansville Arkansas, about September 1 for that purpose. Among them were Charles Reece, Tessee Guess, the son of George Guess, James Starr, Ezekiel Starr, Joseph M. Lynch, Dr. J. L. Thompson, Matthew Moore, John Harnage, Jess Mayfield and John A. Bell; beside W. Quesenbury who went along out of curio-

---

and illuminating report of the commission, is more than disappointing. In it Medill showed a factional spirit, in all things championing the cause of the Old Settlers, and saying that the act of union was of no binding force. In accordance with Medill's suggestion Polk recommended in his message to Congress a separation of the two parties in the nation, both in territory and government, and the extension of the United States laws over the Indians. This project of separation was not put into effect, but served to keep alive the feud among the Cherokees and to resuscitate the hope among the Old Settlers that the United States would interfere in their behalf."

34 *Cherokee Advocate*, July 17, 1845, p. 1, col. 3.
35 *Cherokee Advocate*, April 3, 1845, p. 3, col. 1.

sity. They were equipped with horses and pack mules.[36] The party consisting of forty-three members of the Treaty and eleven of the Old Settler party, met at the forks of the Canadian and Arkansas rivers and after electing a captain proceeded by Fort Washita, crossing the Red River at Coffee's trading house, and followed the ridge dividing the waters of the Trinity and Brazos to the latter river, which they crossed at Basky Creek. Here they found a small settlement of sixty-three Cherokee, who had moved in the preceding June from a place called by them Mount Clover, in Mexico.[37]

Leaving the Brazos River the explorers traveled westward to the Colorado, reaching it at the mouth of Stone Fork Creek, beyond which they proceeded in a southwesterly direction to the San Saba Creek, at a point about forty or fifty miles above its mouth. They returned on a route some sixty miles south of their outgoing trip, by way of Fort Towson, where they arrived early in January.[38] On their return to the Cherokee Nation they held a council with their partisans, at which it was decided to ask the United States to provide them a home in Texas upon their relinquishment of all interest in the Cherokee Nation, or in case of the refusal of this request that the territory of the nation be divided into two parts, and their share be assigned to them with the privilege of setting up their own government and living under it.

36 *Arkansas Intelligencer*, August 30, 1845, p. 2, col. 2.
37 Charles C. Royce "The Cherokee Nation of Indians": *Report of the Bureau of American Ethnology* for 1887, p. 302.
38 Royce, ibid.; *Arkansas Intelligencer*, January 10, 1846, p. 2, col. 1.

CHAPTER TWENTY-FIVE / *The Treaty of 1846*

OMPARATIVE quiet rested on the Cherokee Nation through the spring and summer of 1845, but in the autumn there was a recrudescense of outlawry that shocked the people. November 2 a party of armed and disguised bandits came to the home of R. J. Meigs whom they tried to kill; he escaped however and after they plundered his home, a substantial brick house near Park Hill, they fired and burned it with its contents. Then in the neighborhood they killed two full-blood Indians who had recognized and might have reported the bandits.[1] Meigs identified the outlaws as Tom Starr, Washington Starr, Ellis Starr, Suel Rider, and Ellis West. The term of the light horse or mounted police had expired by operation of law so that there was no force but that of the sheriff to cope with lawbreakers, a state of affairs that was doubtless counted on by the miscreants. A posse of citizens then armed themselves and went to Flint District to the home of James Starr, the father of the notorious sons. The posse killed the elder Starr and wounded his four-teen-year-old son Washington, and another son William. Then they proceeded half a mile to the home of Suel Rider whom they killed.

A standing reward for the capture of each of the Starrs had failed to secure them. Through fear and friendship they were harbored in the Cherokee Nation. One man who was suspected said he was more afraid not to take them in than he was to act as their host. But their particular sanctuary was over the line in Arkansas among the white people who had been said by both General Taylor and General Arbuckle to be engaged in officious interference in the affairs of the Cherokee people.

1 *Cherokee Advocate*, November 6, 1845, p. 3, col. 1. Meigs was married to Jane the daughter of Chief John Ross.

While it was not charged by the Cherokee government that the lawlessness by the bandits was incited by the faction that called itself the "Treaty Party," the Starrs were of that "party" and most of the outrages committed by them were directed against the regular government and those who were in sympathy with it. A man who was both a lawyer and newspaper man in Van Buren, and who had married a member of the "Treaty Party," was a leader in spreading the alarm that the members of that faction were in peril of their lives with the result that a large number of them fled across the line into Arkansas. It was charged by the *Cherokee Advocate* that this lawyer was interested in creating and keeping alive excitement and disorder so that the Government might be induced to award large compensation to members of the Treaty Party in the new treaty that all felt was soon to be negotiated. The Starrs were treated as martyrs and through the efforts of the whites and disgruntled Indians they succeeded in building up a tradition that the killing of these and other outlaws were "political" reprisals.

The Cherokee council was in session within three miles of the scene of the attack on Meigs and the burning of his home, an act designed to exhibit the contempt of government and law by the bandits. The council promptly met the challenge and enacted a measure organizing a light horse company "to pursue and arrest all fugitives from justice."[2] This arm of the government entered vigorously into the discharge of its duties. Persons who had been harboring the Starrs realizing that they were suspected and subject to the penalties of the law, fled to Arkansas to reside among the whites who were friends of their faction and engaged in making trouble for the established Cherokee government.

The situation was explained by the *Cherokee Advocate* as resulting from "the infamous cowardly horse thieves, robbers and murderers, whose infernal deeds recently roused to madness an honest, patient, orderly and law-abiding number of men." But the responsibility rested mainly on white people whose "interests and aims are somewhat different, though they unite in a common effort for their accomplishment. Our comfortable cabins, productive farms, valuable mineral resources, clear streams and beautiful prairies excite the cupidity and moisten the lips of those who have not failed to filch by fraud, or rob

2 *Ibid.*, November 13, 1845, p. 3, col. 1.

-{ 339 }-

by superior power of their native inheritance, every Indian community with whom they have come in contact. This is one class and is found among every border population. Merchants, speculators, and Lawyers complete the cabal. The first two species include both whites and Cherokees. In the state of Arkansas and especially about Fort Smith both may be found. There are men who have sold goods, lent money, and given board, until certain so-called 'chiefs' are now indebted to them thousands of Dollars. Their only chance of getting a copper is to foment difficulties, creating dissentions to bedevil the Cherokees until by a regular system of interference, slander, falsehood and misrepresentation, they can cajole the United States Government and create an apparent necessity for the adoption of some measures that will destroy our integrity and throw a few millions of dollars into the hands of those 'Chiefs,' as indemnity for the supposed grievances they have sustained. There are several Lawyers engaged in this scheme of acquisition, besides a few pettifoggers. The former are well known; and as a specimen of the latter we would mention one George W. Paschall, known from the fact that he married a daughter of the late Major Ridge but principally from the fact that he at one time, held the distinguished station of corporal or lieutenant in a company of Georgia militia, that was called into service to expel the Eastern Cherokees from their native homes. . . . he carries on a subterranean system of officiousness and. . . . misrepresentation which no denunciation however galling and destructive to an honest man's feelings and veracity, can force him openly to avow and maintain."[3]

White people of Arkansas aided industriously in spreading the report that the killing of James Starr and Rider was but the beginning of a contemplated series of bloody reprisals to be visited on the Treaty Party. An article in the *Arkansas Intelligencer* published at Van Buren said that an indiscriminate massacre of all the Treaty Party had been determined on; and that it was planned to kill all the Starrs from two years of age up. These extravagant statements had the effect as it was planned to create a panic in the minds of many who were of the Treaty Party, and they fled across the line into Arkansas.

No time was lost by the whites in sending in its most sensational form news of the situation in Flint District and the adjoining Arkansas

3 *Ibid.*, November 27, 1845, p. 3, col. 1.

to General Arbuckle. To investigate he sent Major Bonneville who reported that 100 men and their families had fled to Arkansas in fear of their lives. "They fear and I think very justly, to return, having no guarantee, however innocent they may be, that they may not fall victims like their friends, to the illegal and savage acts of an armed and irregular body."

General Arbuckle, still cherishing a grudge against John Ross and the successful government headed by him, willing to believe the most extravagant charges against that government if not to welcome the infirmities that would presage its collapse, wrote on November 15 a truculent letter to Maj. George Lowrey, acting chief. Chief John Ross was then in Washington with the Cherokee delegation. Arbuckle without making any inquiry of Lowrey as to the facts, with supreme effrontery informed the chief that "the Light Horse must be disbanded at once, and the persons concerned in the murder of James Starr and Rider arrested."[4] And without consulting the Cherokee authorities he ordered a company of dragoons under Capt. Nathan Boone to the "scene of the disorders."[5] The Cherokee Nation was jealous of its prerogatives and bitterly denied the right of the military to invade its territory or to interfere in its domestic affairs. Chief Lowrey sent to the Cherokee agent Arbuckle's communication with a letter explaining the situation and saying that he recognized the agent as the only proper officer of the Government to whom he was accountable. The Chief then dispatched a delegation to Flint District for the purpose of securing information relative to the condition of affairs there. This delegation was composed of the most conservative and responsible men of the Nation: George Hicks, Rev. Stephen Foreman, John Thorn and William Shorey Coodey. On their return November 25 they reported to the chief. They and the Cherokee agent met a number of the fugitives at the home of the W. S. Adair near the line; all endeavored to persuade the alarmed Cherokee citizens who had fled that they might safely return to their homes, but such was the fear created in their minds by the rumors circulated by the white people that they would not be convinced and insisted on remaining in Arkansas. James McKissick, the agent, informed the delegation that the dragoons had been

4 United States Senate *Document* No. 298, Twenty-ninth Congress, first session, p. 166.
5 Boone to Arbuckle, *Report*, November 27, 1845, AGO, OFD.., 193 A 45.

sent from Fort Gibson not on his request but on that of white residents of Evansville, Arkansas. The delegation returned to Tahlequah and reported November 25 to the chief that the fugitives "were determined not to be convinced of their safety at home; and they were striving to give the affair a party aspect; they were invoking the sympathy and aid of the white people by false statements, and endeavoring to seduce by false reports as many Cherokee citizens as possible to leave their homes and join them for the purpose of giving some plausibility to their denunciations of the Cherokee authorities," and denying the representative capacity of the delegation.[6]

The excitement began to abate somewhat in December, but General Arbuckle said there was still a band of men on the mountain near Evansville committing depredations, "killing stock, hauling off corn, and plundering the houses of those who have been forced to leave their homes."[7] Stand Watie with sixty men had assumed a belligerent attitude: at Fort Wayne were congregated "a mongrel set of Cherokees, white men with Indian wives, citizens of the United States and one or two mulattoes under the command of Stand Watie. . . . . The manner in which they have fortified themselves, the attempt at military discipline, the inducments held out to increase their number, threats that some of them have made, the burial of the dead with 'the honors of war,' and their persisting in these things are highly censurable. They smack of a rebellious spirit and show conclusively that the company have some latent object in view inimical to the peace of the country."[8]

To prevent violence threatened by these manifestations, General Arbuckle ordered to the border two more companies of dragoons from Fort Washita, Company D under Lieutenant Johnson, and Capt. Enoch Steen's Company E. This force and the persuasion of Captain Boone and G. W. Adair prevented other recruits from joining Stand Watie at Fort Wayne and organizing for a threatened aggressive movement against the established Cherokee officers. Johnson who was stationed near Fort Wayne advised Stand Watie to disband his force. The evidence finally convinced General Arbuckle, and he was reluctantly forced to join Captain Boone in the opinion that the white people

6 *Cherokee Advocate*, November 27, 1845, p. 3, col. 5.
7 Arbuckle to adjutant general, December 12, 1845, AGO, OFD, 203 A 45.
8 *Cherokee Advocate*, January 29, 1846, p. 3, col. 2.

of Arkansas were encouraging Stand Watie and other Cherokee to acts of violence.[9]

The determination of General Arbuckle to maintain a censorious and hostile attitude toward the established Cherokee government, discrediting its pretentions, and weakening its authority to prevent disorder, is in sharp contrast to the report recently made by his superior, General Jones, Colonel Mason and Governor Butler vindicating the officials of the charges so hastily accepted by Arbuckle as true. It is explicable only in the light of his advanced age, the controversy with John Ross in which he came out second best, and his rebuke by being sent to the little post of Baton Rouge; this left a deep resentment that lasted as long as he lived. After a study of all the evidence one cannot escape the conviction that Arbuckle hindered and delayed the establishment of law and order. His interference with the functioning of the established Cherokee government, his sympathy for and protection of the Starrs not only actively hindered the application of wholesome Cherokee laws, but perpetuated the fiction that these outlaws were innocent victims of an oppressive government, and aided in misleading the federal officials in Washington, thereby inducing them to lend their countenance to the plans of Stand Watie and Bell, which, if they had succeeded, would have wrecked the Cherokee Nation. One reads with amazement some of Arbuckle's misstatement of facts showing his prejudice and willingness to believe reports to the prejudice of the Cherokee government.[10]

A spirit of reprisal pervaded the land. Murders were of frequent occurrence. Among those was that of Granville Rogers, son of Capt. John Rogers, at Beattie's Prairie in January, by Braxton Nicholson and his partner Pitner, a white man married to a Cherokee.[11] Charles Smith was a son of Archilla Smith who was tried and convicted of murder and executed on January 1, 1841.[12] Charles Smith stabbed and killed a young man named John M. Brown because he was of the party which pursued and killed Smith's friend, Bean Starr at Fort Washita. When

9 Arbuckle to adjutant general, January 14, 1846, AGO, OFD., 19 A 46.
10 United States Senate *Document* No. 301, Twenty-ninth Congress, first session, p. 7.
11 *Arkansas Intelligencer*, January 17, 1846, p. 2, col. 1.
12 The trial of Archilla Smith as reported by John Howard Payne was recently published; see Grant Foreman, *Indian Justice* (Oklahoma City, 1934).

the officers undertook to arrest Smith he resisted, seized a gun and was killed by the officers.[13] Captain Bonneville made another investigation and reported "about 750 men, women and children have fled beyond the limits of the nation for safety. Murder and strife continue. Light horse or police companies are assigned to each district—these companies are certainly very summary dealers in justice; tis indeed a deplorable state of things; they have good laws & if properly administered no people could be happier."[14] Farms on Beattie's Prairie within what is now Delaware County were abandoned; the owners took up their abode in Arkansas and made the hamlet of Evansville their headquarters. Arbuckle ordered these refugees fed at public expense and warned that the money would come out of the funds of the Cherokee Nation. It was charged that this indulgence was much abused to the prejudice of the country. The Indians were encouraged to come to Arkansas and live at the expense of the public. "Some who have a greater supply of provisions on hand than they want, sell first to the contractors, and then turn right around and receive regular issues out of the same for the subsistence of themselves and their families."[15] Instead of abating the belligerent force "on the line," the issuing of free rations to them encouraged the congregating of restless and lawless spirits whose activities discredited the peaceful Cherokee citizens collected there; Indians who had fled their haunts from fear excited by the deliberate misrepresentations of whites and half breeds who were engaged thus in a systematic effort to augment their following, to break down the established government, and create a division in the tribe that otherwise could not be accomplished.[16]

The people of Arkansas at last became tired of providing sanctuary for Cherokee criminals and the refugees, from supposed dangers in their own country. And the *Arkansas Intelligencer* demanded that the Starrs who had committed murders in the State be apprehended and delivered up to the proper authorities or driven from the State.[17] A

13   *Cherokee Advocate*, January 8, 1846, p. 3, col. 3.
14   Bonneville to quartermaster general, February 5, 1846, QMG, *Book 26*, No. 129.
15   *Cherokee Advocate*, December 25, 1845, p. 3, col. 1.
16   United States Senate *Document* No. 331, Twenty-ninth Congress, first session.
17   *Arkansas Advocate*, February 5, 1846, p. 3, col. 3.

meeting of citizens of Washington County adopted resolutions that were presented to Captain Boone requesting him to remove the encampment of refugee citizens from their county.[18]

A memorial to Governor Drew was addressed by citizens of Evansville and vicinity March 4, praying that steps be taken to remove from their neighborhood the Cherokee refugees; they charged that their visitors harbored criminals who committed murder and depredated on their property.[19] The Governor replied on the sixteenth that if General Arbuckle did not give them relief he would call out a force "to clear the line of these murderers and give peace and quiet to our citizens." But he thought relief would be found in bills pending in Congress providing for the division of the Cherokee Nation.[20]

It was now pretty well established and understood that the refugees were composed first of those interested in building up a following and fostering a division of the tribe; second, of those whose fears had been played upon and had been the innocent dupes of the first class; and a third was the criminal element some of whom finding their sanctuary in Arkansas about to be closed against them decamped for Texas. The Federal forces took possession of Fort Wayne and compelled Stand Watie and his followers to leave. Stand Watie soon afterward departed for Washington to join the delegation of his partisans there.

Maj. George Lowrey acting principal chief issued a call for a special session of the National Committee and National Council for February 3, 1846; the chief delivered a message representing that measures were on foot by the representatives of the Treaty Party "to affect materially the government and condition of the Cherokees." And with the consent of the legislative body he appointed Rev. Stephen Foreman, Clement V. McNair, member of the National Committee and John Thorn, judge of the circuit court additional members to proceed to Washington and join the delegation there for the purpose of protecting the integrity of the Cherokee Nation in its negotiation with the Federal government.[21] They bore with them a memorial signed by 1,676 male adult citizens addressed to the President. In it they surveyed briefly the recent lawlessness in the nation which they attributed to the

18 *Ibid.*, col. 2.
19 *Cherokee Advocate*, March 26, 1846, p. 3, col. 2.
20 *Ibid.*, April 2, 1846, p. 3, col. 2.
21 *Ibid.*, February 5, 1846, p. 3, col. 2.

bandits referred to by General Jones's commission; vouched for all that the delegation headed by John Ross represented and protested against any negotiations with private citizens—referring to Stand Watie, John Bell and others representing the Treaty Party.[22]

The resolute and dauntless principal chief of the tribe, John Ross, was in Washington where his talents were in greater need than at home. In his place at home was the venerable Maj. George Lowrey who was perhaps overwhelmed by the disorders surrounding him. Yielding to his emotions the chief issued a proclamation announcing that "in times of national calamity and difficulty and fear, it is peculiarly becoming that both rulers and people, should humble themselves before Almighty God, the sovereign disposer of all human events, and look to him for direction in their difficulties, deliverance from their calamities and fears, and the bestowment of needed blessings—such a time is the present with the Cherokee Nation."

He designated Friday, the 6th day of March next, as a day of fasting, humiliation and prayer, throughout the nation and asked the people to meet in their respective places of worship and offer up prayers for forgiveness of the transgressions of the Cherokee people, for the restoration of health throughout the nation; that scenes of violence and blood and other civil disorders be abated.[23]

Shortly after the delegation selected by the Treaty Party council had proceeded to Washington in the interest of the scheme to divide the tribe, another epidemic of murder and outrage broke out in the nation. On March 23, Agent McKissick reported to the Indian department the murder of Stand, a prominent member of the Ross party, by Wheeler Faught, at the instigation of the "Starr boys." This murder was committed in revenge for the killing of James Starr and others during the outbreak of the preceding November. It was followed by the murder of Cornsilk, another of Ross's adherents, by these same "Starr boys," and six days later the spirit of retaliation led to the killing of Turner, a member of the Treaty Party. On the twenty-fifth of the same month, Ellis, Dick, and Billy Starr were wounded by a band of Ross's Cherokee police, who chased them across the line of Arkansas in an attempt to arrest them for trial before the Cherokee tribunals for the murder of Too-noo-wee two days before. General Arbuckle took them under

22   United States Senate *Document* No. 331. Twenty-ninth Congress, first session.
23   *Cherokee Advocate*, February 5, 1846, p. 3, col. 1.

his protection, and refused to deliver them for trial to the Cherokee authorities until the latter should take proper steps to punish the police who killed James Starr. Subsequently, Baldridge and Sides, of the Ross party, were killed by Jim and Tom Starr, in revenge for which the light horse police company of the Ross government killed Billy Ryder of the Treaty Party. Early in April Ta-ka-to-ka, the head of the police was killed; for his participation in this murder Faught was executed by the Ross government.

In this manner the excitement was maintained and the outrages multiplied until, August 28, Agent McKissick reported that since the first of November preceding there had been an aggregate of thirty-three murders committed in the Cherokee Nation, nearly all of which were political in character.[24]

General Arbuckle and the governor of Arkansas both concurred in the conclusion reached at the council of the Old Settlers and Treaty Party and urged the authorities at Washington to carry into effect their scheme to divide the Cherokee Nation. Delegations were appointed to go to Washington and present their views; the Treaty Party delegation reached Washington early in April, 1846; it was composed of George W. Adair, John A. Bell, Joseph Lynch, Bryce Martin, and Ezekiel Starr.[25] Stand Watie joined the delegation later having remained at Fort Wayne in command of his followers fortified there until ordered by the army officers to disperse. Soon the Old Settlers and Ross faction or established government were also represented in Washington.[26]

24 Charles C. Royce, "The Cherokee Nation of Indians": *Report of the Bureau of American Ethnology* for 1887, p. 303.

25 Stand Watie remained at Fort Wayne where his service as commander probably impressed those who were acquainted with it and developed qualities of leadership that singled him out for high command in the Confederate army when the Civil War involved his tribe. George Starr a brother of James Starr was married to Nancy, daughter of John Bell and a sister of John A. Bell, March 5, 1840 (*Arkansas Gazette*, March 18, 1840, p. 3, col. 5).

26 While in Washington on this delegation, Capt. John Rogers died and his funeral was held from Mrs. Eugene A. Townley's boarding house June 13, 1846 (John Brown to Medill, June 13, 1846, OIA; *Arkansas Intelligencer*, July 4, 1846, p. 3, col. 1). Ezekiel Starr a member of the Treaty Party delegation also died in Washington (*ibid.*, May 2, 1846, p. 2, col. 1). Capt. John Looney died in Washington May 15, 1846, at the age of seventy years, and was buried in the Congressional Cemetery the next day. Though he was one of the Old Settlers, he was a member of the Ross delegation. He was a nephew of the celebrated chief Enolee or Black Fox. He fought under Jackson

The delegations presented their conflicting claims and views to the commissioner of Indian affairs and the President. The commissioner on March 13 submitted to the secretary of war an extended and carefully prepared report that represented the views of the administration. It justified the acts and grievances of the Treaty and Old Settler parties and recommended a division of the Cherokee tribe as prayed by these two factions. It placed all the blame for the situation on John Ross and "his extraordinary influence over his infatuated party." It pursued and relied on the fallacy that the act of union of 1839 was "not entitled to consideration, for that act cannot justly be regarded as valid or binding, because as has been stated, its stipulations and the inducements held out to the western Cherokees to enter into it have not been and never can be fulfilled. . . . . Thus commenced the dissensions between the parties, and several efforts to form a union between them entirely failed." History has exposed the error of these statements for the act of union thus attempted to be cast aside became the keystone in the arch upon which the Cherokee tribe flourished through the remainder of its tribal history. Notwithstanding the dictum of this mouthpiece of the administration, the tribe was in fact united under the act of union devised by John Ross and his followers and this document stands a monument to this most determined, patient, and patriotic Indian leader.

In line with the recommendation of the commissioner, President Polk on April 13, 1846, submitted a special message to Congress recommending legislation either dividing the Cherokee country between the opposing factions or providing a new home for one or the other of them,[27] so that they should be separated and live under governments as distinct tribes. "These measures," he said, "are the only means of arresting the horrid and inhuman massacres which have marked the history of the Cherokees for the last few years, and especially for the last few months. . . . . I am satisfied that there is no probability that the different bands or parties into which it is divided can ever again live

---

against the Creeks and at the battle of Talledega received a severe gunshot wound, for which he was allowed a pension for life (*ibid.*, June 26, 1846, p. 1, col. 4). Joel M. Bryan was a member of the Old Settler delegation and with the other delegates boarded at Mrs. Townley's boarding house for $8.00 a week. Bluford West who was a fugitive or refugee from the Cherokee Nation died in Washington of pneumonia on April 2, 1845.

27 James D. Richardson, *Messages of the Presidents*, IV, 429.

together in peace and harmony; and that the well-being of the whole requires that they should be separated and live under separate governments as distinct people."

After much discussion the House committee on Indian affairs on June 2 introduced a bill authorizing a division of the Cherokee Nation, one part to be occupied by the Old Settlers and Treaty Party, and the other by the "Ross Party." This was indeed a critical period in the history of the Cherokee Nation. Only a little more than a year before, the report had been made to the secretary of war by the president's commission. The veteran adjutant general of the army, the head of the commission was in no way connected with the factions in the tribe; the other two members Mason and Butler had served for years in the Cherokee country and had first-hand knowledge of what had transpired there. This, the only commission sent to the Cherokee country, made an exhaustive report based on a large mass of evidence heard by them.

Under the succeeding Polk administration the new secretary of war, William L. Marcy, ignored the report of the commission, espoused the claims and pretentions of the dissident factions; on their statements and without hearing evidence or pursuing any investigation the secretary assumed as true the charge by General Arbuckle, and maintained a truculent attitude towards John Ross and all he stood for. Ross and his delegation bitterly opposed the legislation presented by the administration and it is indeed a tribute to the indomitable and dogged persistence of this Cherokee statesman, as well as to his skill and powers of persuasion, that they were able to defeat the measure. In its place commissioners were appointed to hear and investigate the contentions of the conflicting factions and their findings were incorporated in a new treaty enacted August 6, 1846,[28] an achievement for which Ross had been contending ever since 1839. This treaty adjusted the whole field of unsettled claims and dissension. It undertook to settle all matters in controversy between the Cherokee tribe and the Government and between the factions of the tribe; and was probably all that saved the Indians from a much worse condition.

In the first place the treaty determined that the lands occupied by the tribe belonged to all the members, and that a patent for the same

28 Kappler, op. cit., II, 415.

should be issued to the tribe, and thus disposed of the contention of the Old Settlers that it belonged to them alone. Party distinctions were obliterated, a general amnesty was declared, and all offences and crimes against the Cherokee Nation and individuals thereof by citizens of the tribe were pardoned, this amnesty to extend to all who would return to the Cherokee Nation on or before December 1, 1846. All members of the tribe residing without the Nation were invited to return to their homes and live in peace. It was agreed that all factions would join in upholding and enforcing the laws of the Nation against all future offenders. Laws would be passed for the protection of all and authority given for any faction peaceably to assemble for the purpose of petitioning for the redress of grievances. All armed police, light horse, and other "military organizations" were to be abolished and the laws enforced by the civil authority alone, whatever that may have meant.

It was admitted that the Government had made large payments to individual claimants for spoliation, had paid other large sums for various purposes and had improperly charged them against the $5,-000,000 consideration agreed upon for their lands in the East. And for this it was agreed that the Government would make restitution. This was a vindication of the claims long urged by the Indians that had kept delegations at great expense in Washington seeking adjustment from administrations that had stubbornly resisted them. Per capita payments, long solicited by the Indians, were thus provided for and another contention was put at rest. An allowance was made to the Treaty Party for losses suffered by them including $5,000 to the heirs of Major Ridge, and equal amounts to the heirs of John Ridge and Elias Boudinot.

In all, a multitude of claims and points of controversy growing out of the Treaty of 1835 and arising since then, that had kept the Indians in a ferment of rancor and unrest with the Government and with each other, were adjusted, thus opening the way to a return to order and peace in the tribe.

The period of active political disturbances and civil disorders seemed now drawing to a close, and the tribe entered upon a new era of prosperity and tribal achievement. Little of substance remained of the old quarrels. But the smoldering heart burnings, bitter memories and jealousies cherished by the politically disappointed minority could not be so soon forgotten, and lived to burst into flame with the outbreak

of the Civil War, when the tribe was rent again along the line of cleavage produced by the ignoble artifice employed by the Government
agents who negotiated the fraudulent "treaty" of New Echota in 1835;
when the leaders of the Treaty Party among whom white blood predominated, were found on the side of the Confederacy.

A period in their unhappy political distractions having been achieved
by the Treaty of 1846, we may now consider other phases of Cherokee
history.

CHAPTER TWENTY-SIX / *Advancement*

THE Cherokee tribe was early noted for its pursuits of civiliza-tion and desire for education. The first mission where youths of that tribe were taught was established in December, 1801, by the Society of United Brethren for the Southern States, commonly called Moravian Brethren, at Spring-place three miles east of the Connesaga River, near the public road leading from Georgia to West Tennessee.[1] The school continued in operation for many years and boys and girls were taught reading, writing, arithmetic and some of them English, grammar, and geography. The girls were taught spinning, sewing, knitting and marking, so that they could make their own stockings and those of their families. The boys were taught agricultural labors and even to make their clothing.

Dr. Morse reported that as early as 1800 the Cherokee people under-stood the use of the wheel and card, with which they manufactured cot-ton cloth that in turn they made into clothing. They used the horse and plow, wagon roads were opened up by them and a number of natives owned and operated gristmills and saw-mills. Some of them manufac-tured spinning wheels and looms, and in certain neighborhoods the women wove coverlets and double twilled cloth, and others manu-factured sheets for family use. The venerable Charles Hicks, an intel-ligent chief of the Cherokee and one of the first to be baptized at the Moravian mission, wrote an interesting letter in 1819 for the informa-tion of Dr. Morse. He said that the "Cherokees had already with stimu-lus spirits, entered the manufacturing system in cotton clothing in 1800, which had taken rise in one Town in 1796 and 7, by the repeated recommendations of Silas Dinsmoore, Esq. which were given to the

1 Morse, *op. cit.*, 153.

Chiefs in Council."[2] Dr. Morse said that some of the Cherokee lived in very decent style. Two of them named Vann had built good brick houses.

When a delegation of Cherokee Indians visited Thomas Jefferson in May, 1806, he gave them some good advice on the subject of improving their condition. "I see, with my own eyes," he said, "that the endeavors we have been making to encourage and lead you on in the way of improving your situation have not been unsuccessful— it has been like grain sown in good ground producing abundantly. You are becoming farmers, learning the use of the plough and the hoe, enclosing your grounds and employing that labor in their cultivation which you formerly employed in hunting and in war; and I see handsome specimens of cotton cloth, raised, spun and wove by yourselves; you are also raising cattle and hogs for your food. . . . . You will find your next want to be mills to grind corn, which by relieving your women from the loss of time in beating it into meal, will enable them to spin and weave more.

"When a man has enclosed and improved his farm, built a good house on it, and raised plentiful stock of animals, he will wish when he dies, that these things should go to his wife and children, whom he loved more than he does his other relations, and for whom he will work with pleasure during his life. You will therefore find it necessary to establish laws for this. When a man has property earned by his own labors, he will not like to see another come and take it away from him, because he happens to be stronger, or else to defend it by spilling blood. You will find it necessary then to appoint good men judges, to decide contests between man and man according to reason and to the rules you shall establish."[3]

Return Jonathan Meigs, Cherokee agent, reported in 1801 that "There was thirty-two pieces of cloth wove in Dougle-Head's Town within 14 months past. There was about 600 yards wove the last year in one loom at Hiwassee. . . . . The Bold Hunter's family made this year, 90 yards of cotton cloth, raised the cotton, spun and wove the cloth. . . . . Hilderbrand the miller living on Highwassee says that he ground some wheat raised by the Indians the last summer, about 20

2   Letter from Charles Hicks to Dr. Jedidiah Morse, ibid., 167. Hicks was one of the first men in the Cherokee Nation who learned to read and write.
3   Cherokee Advocate, January 2, 1845, p. 3, col. 5.

or 30 bushels. That several families have some wheat this fall. Wheat is also raised by the half breeds at or near Crowtown; that wheat grows well in this country. . . . . Burgess's family raised hemp, flax, and cotton the last year. . . . . The Cherokees had salt peter caves where gun powder was made; 200 pounds of powder a year is paid by white men for use of the cave."[4]

Colonel Meigs said the Cherokee had "many thousand head of cattle & other domestic animals. They manufacture cotton cloth in every part of the nation for the cloathing of their families. In 1803 they consented to have a public school established, which commenced in the course of 1804. At that time there was a small private school. The President of the United States gave the particular superintendence of such schools as the Reverend Mr. Gideon Blackburn should be able to establish, to him. Mr. Blackburn established his first school on the river Highwassee & afterwards united the private school with it. The number of scholars in this school is now about 48. Since, Mr. Blackburn has established another school under another instructor; the large school has two instructors. In the two schools there are 73 scholars. These children are all Cherokees or children of white men by Cherokee women." Mr. Blackburn was a minister of the Presbyterian Church at Marysville, Tennessee. Dr. Morse says that he taught the school with great zeal, ingenuity, perseverance, and with great success for four or five years until his means were exhausted. He had at one time eighty pupils who were clothed, fed and taught at his expense.[5] Another early laborer in that field was the Reverend Evan Jones, who in 1805 left records of his work. For many years he served as a teacher among the Cherokee in their eastern home and after their removal west to Indian Territory.

The first establishment by the American Board of Commissioners for Foreign Missions among the Cherokee was that of Brainerd in 1817, on the west side of Chickamauga Creek in Tennessee and two miles from the Georgia line; among the early workers there were the Rev. D. S. Butrick and the Rev. S. A. Worcester. Dr. Morse gives the names of eight Cherokee boys and two Choctaw who were attending school in 1820 at Cornwall, Connecticut, also conducted by the American

4 "Indians" Return Jonathan Meigs, "Memorandum Book of Occurences, 1796-1807," Library of Congress, *Mansucript Division.*
5 Morse, *op. cit.,* 158.

Board of Commissioners for Foreign Missions; the Cherokee were Elias Boudinot or Kub-le-ga-nah, Leonard Hicks, Thomas Bassel or Taw-tchoo-o, David S. Taucheechy, or Taw-chee-chy, John Ridge, John Vann, James Fields, and David Brown or A-wih; the Choctaw were McKee Folsom and Israel Folsom. Several of these boys became prominent in the affairs of their tribes. Dr. Morse was impressed with "the calculation of the eclipse of August 2nd, 1833, very neatly projected and the results stated in the usual form by Elias Boudinot, a Cherokee of seventeen."[6]

In those early days the Cherokee Nation east of the Mississippi was governed by the acts of the national council which met annually. Written laws of the tribe had been recorded and preserved as far back as 1810[7] and included many wholesome measures devised to maintain an orderly course of conduct by the members of the tribe. The Cherokee people established their national council in 1817, which elected as president John Ross who served in that office for many years. The national council and national committee in 1820 laid off the Cherokee country into eight districts, appointed circuit judges, sheriffs, constables and justices of the peace, and laid a tax on the people to build a court-house in each district.[8]

June 1, 1827 the Cherokee people held an election for delegates to a convention that was to form a constitution for the nation. The names of the districts were Chickamaugre, Coosewatte, Amaoah, Challoogee, Hickory Log, Etowah, Tanquohee, and Aquahee. The delegates from the first district were John Ross, Richard Taylor, and John Bainbridge; for the second John Martin, Joseph Vann, and Kalachulee; from the third were Lewis Ross, Thomas Foreman and The Hare.[9] The convention met at New Echota July 26, 1827, and adopted a republican constitution.[10]

The population of the Cherokee country by the enumeration of their agent in 1809 was 12,395 Cherokee, half of whom were of mixed blood; besides 583 Negro slaves, and 341 white, making a total of 13,319. They had by 1820 increased to 14,500 souls. They had property

6 *Idem*, 278.
7 *Idem*, 172.
8 *Arkansas Gazette*, May 26, 1821, p. 2, col. 4.
9 *Ibid.*, August 7, 1827, p. 1, col. 5.
10 *Missouri Republican*, October 4, 1827.

in horses, cattle, sheep, ploughs, mills, etc., estimated at about $571,500. Their country included at that time sixty-five villages and towns.[11]

By 1825 their census showed a total population of 15,160, including 1,377 Negro slaves; they had 22,531 black cattle, 7,683 horses, 46,732 swine, 2,566 sheep, 330 goats, 762 looms, 2,486 spinning wheels, 172 wagons, 2,843 plows, 10 sawmills, 31 gristmills, one powder mill, 62 blacksmith shops, 8 cotton gins, 18 schools, two turnpikes, 18 ferries and 20 public roads.[12]

Further interesting statistics concerning the Cherokee people were compiled by Eugene A. Vail. He says that on their predatory excursions to the Carolinas they carried off slaves whom they used to work their lands, of whom 610 were males and 667 females. Their agricultural and industrial wealth consisted of thirty-three flour-mills, thirteen sawmills, sixty-nine forges, two tanneries, and other belongings of an industrious and progressive people.[13] It is not surprising that many of the whites of Georgia, less progressive than these Indians coveted their land and herds and other property.

With the removal of the Arkansas Cherokee to their western home Dwight Mission was also removed. The log buildings at the settlement of Nicksville,[14] on Sallisaw Creek, were purchased from Col Walter Webber and the school was opened here May 1, 1830.[15] Two other schools were begun by the missionaries, in the new Cherokee nation, one at Fairfield and one at the forks of the Illinois. The missionaries proceeded to erect a number of buildings for the mission at Dwight. A dining room and kitchen built of hewn logs was two stories high, twenty-four by fifty-four feet in size; it was chinked with stones and pointed with lime mortar and whitewashed, and had two fireplaces. Log houses for residences were built of two rooms with a passageway

11 Morse, op. cit., 152.
12 Census furnished by Elias Boudinot to *New York Observer*, copied in Edwards-ville (Ill.) *Spectator*, May 20, 1826, p. 3, col. 4.
13 Eugene A. Vail, *Sur Les Indiens de l'Amérique du Nord* (Paris, 1840), p. 67.
14 When the legislature of Arkansas created Lovely County in 1827 Nicksville was made the county seat (Foreman *Pioneer Days in the Early Southwest*, 65), and a post office was established there April 25, 1828 with John Dillard as postmaster; it was discontinued October 2, 1829. This location is near the present Marble City, Sequoyah County, Oklahoma.
15 Foreman, op. cit., 66; Washburn to Evarts, September 1, 1830, Andover-Harvard Library, *Missionary letters*, Vol, LXXIII, No. 2.

between, the whole under one roof, and verandas the full length front and back, and four of them a story and a half high; one was two stories; the dormitory for boys was also of logs two stories high with a gallery for each floor. Altogether, there were eleven log structures erected by September, 1830, beside a number of small outbuildings; the mission premises appeared as a considerable institution in the wilderness.

With the completion of the school at Dwight there were sixty-five pupils and for many years this institution maintained a reputation as the best school in all the Indian country. Boys and girls both were educated there and many of the graduates became teachers in this and other schools of the tribe.

Dwight assumed a position of considerable importance in the activities in the Cherokee country. It was the destination of Rev. S. A. Worcester, who arrived there with Mrs. Worcester May 29, 1835. They left Brainerd on April 8, and proceeded overland through Kentucky, Illinois, and Missouri to avoid swamps then impassable for wagons. They were detained a week in Hopkinsville, Kentucky, by the illness of Mrs. Worcester. They sustained a heavy loss in the sinking on the Arkansas River of the steamboat on which their household goods, table linen, bedding and clothing were being carried to the West; besides, there were Mr. Worcester's books and the printing paper for the press which also was on the sunken boat. They salvaged some of the property, but many of Mrs. Worcester's choicest possessions were stolen, including her best feather bed, much table linen, and eight blankets. Their greatest loss however, was in printing paper and books.[16] The printing press rescued from the river was delivered at Fort Gibson about the first of June and with the consent of the Cherokee council it was set up at Union Mission where Mr. Worcester operated it, the first printing press within what is now Oklahoma. In August they began printing the Cherokee alphabet and select passages of scripture.[17] Until Boudinot arrived from the East in 1837 Mr. Worcester had no Cherokee interpreter and the press was mainly employed in printing books and tracts prepared by others in the Choctaw language. The press was continued here until June, 1837 when it was

16 Worcester to Greene, June 1, 1835, *idem* LXXI, No. 64.

17 *Ibid.*, No. 67. Besides printing books and tracts in Cherokee and Creek they "also printed a book in the Osage tongue, with our letters" (Louis Richard Cortambert, *Journey to the Country of the Osages*, 41).

removed to Park Hill where Mr. Worcester had located December 2, 1836, having removed from Union Mission when his new home was ready for occupancy. Here he operated the press for many years.[13]

In 1837 it was said that the Cherokee were further advanced in agriculture than any other tribe. Those living in the western country had between 1,000 and 1,100 farms where they produced corn, oats, potatoes, beans, peas, pumpkins, and melons and raised horses, cattle and hogs; some of them had taken and filled contracts for the garrison at Fort Gibson and for subsisting immigrant Indians to the amount of $60,000.00[19] John Rogers, a native Cherokee was manufacturing eighty bushels of salt a day at the Grand Saline on Grand River, then considered one of the greatest assets of the Cherokee Nation.[20] Native traders were engaged in merchandising and transportation;[21] others operated gristmills and sawmills of great importance to the tribe. Native Cherokee traders, guided by Kichai Indians, were seen as far from home as the Forks of the Brazos River in Texas on their way to the Comanche Indians with powder and lead to exchange for horses and mules.[22]

The Cherokee were supporting their few schools and a number of native teachers were employed, including the famous Sequoyah, who was paid $400.00 a year for his invaluable service in teaching the use of his alphabet. "The Cherokees show a great deal of improvement," said the commissioner of Indian affairs, "and are still improving and bid fair at no distant date to rival their white brethren of the west in point of wealth, civilization and moral and intellectual improvement..... The greater part of the Cherokees are farmers, have good comfortable homes and live, many of them, as well and as genteel and in a pecuniary point of view will compare with the better class of farmers in the states."

The Committee and Council of the Cherokee Nation in General Council, June 7, 1835, directly after the arrival of Rev. Mr. Worcester

18 *Missionary Herald*, March 1837; *Report* of American Board of Commissioners for Foreign Missions for 1837.

19 *Report* of commissioner of Indian affairs for 1837.

20 In 1842 plans were made to enlarge the salt works here to permit of its manufacture on a large scale.

21 *Arkansas Intelligencer*, April 12, 1845, p. 2, col. 1.

22 *Telegraph and Texas Register*, December 23, 1837, p. 3, col. 1.

and his printing press, adopted a resolution declaring that no more missionary establishments could be located in the Nation until the General Council should enact laws to authorize and regulate all such establishments;[23] but provided that private teachers might continue to enter the nation and reside in the families of citizens for the education of their children.[24] The Cherokee council then met at Tolluntusky, at the mouth of the Illinois River. John Jolly, Joseph Vann and John Rogers were the principal chiefs, John Smith was president of the Committee and Glass president of the Council, William Shorey Goodey secretary *pro tempore* and William Thornton acting clerk.

The Moravian missionaries preached their last sermon to the Cherokee Indians before their enforced migration, on September 16, 1838. A party of three of them, Miles Vogler, Herman Ruede and John Renatus Schmidt, then set out for the western country; they traveled the route taken by the Indians, through Kentucky, Illinois, Missouri and Arkansas, on October 27 passing through Fayetteville and into the Indian Territory. They located first and began a station on the Barren Fork where most of the Indians who had been attending their church were settled. This place proved sickly and with the consent of the Cherokee council Mr. and Mrs. Vogler removed to Beattie's Prairie; the Indians did not follow in numbers sufficient to encourage them and the missionaries then removed to the head of Spring Creek and began a missionary station known as New Spring Place.[25] At first the Cherokee council was reluctant to permit the Moravian settlement here, but in 1842 they gave their consent. The Moravians were indefatigable and for many years maintained mission stations and schools at Barren Fork, Beattie's Prairie, and New Spring Place.[26]

After the removal of the eastern Cherokee to Indian Territory the tribe numbered about 18,000 persons, two thousand of whom professed

23 The Cherokee had "no public schools, and but two or three of any description [in the West before emigration]; when the emigration shall be completed it is to be expected that the number will be greatly increased" (Armstrong to Harris, October 31, 1838, OIA "Schools, Western Superintendency" A 402).

24 John Smith and other Cherokee to Vashon, June 7, 1835, OIA.

25 At a place now called Oaks.

26 *Report* of David Z. Smith, August 1, 1844 in commissioner of Indian affairs *Report* for 1844.

Christianity. While divided into two bitter political parties by the machinations of Schermerhorn, both factions were remarkable for their fidelity to the laws of the nation and strict observance of treaty obligations. Cause for bitter complaint, however, existed in the fact that the authorities of Arkansas persisted in entering the Cherokee nation and arresting members of that tribe for offenses committed upon white people wandering into their country but having no business there. This was a great hardship on the Indians, who were compelled to travel many miles to attend the trial of such cases in the courts of Arkansas.

The Cherokee people were favored with a rich and productive country divided into woodland and prairie, well watered and adapted to raising wheat, corn, oats, and vegetables. Many of the natives owned stocks of cattle, horses, hogs and sheep, and some had valuable fruit orchards. The more prosperous Indians possessed neat looking farms and houses and exhibited signs of wealth and intelligence; some of them owned fine residences and even the poorer members of the tribe had comfortable houses.

After the arrival of the great majority of the tribe from the East in 1839 the Cherokee people exhibited an increasing interest in education. John Ross took the lead in this movement. One of his first acts as chief after the establishment of the new government in September 1839 was a special message submitting to the Cherokee National Council communications from the Moravian missionaries Rev. Miles Vogler and Rev. Herman Ruede, the Baptist Rev. Evan Jones, and the Presbyterian Dr. Elizur Butler seeking permission to set up their mission churches and schools in the Nation.

Some of the Cherokee immigrants already had "full and well selected libraries. Thousands of them can speak and write the English language with fluency and comparative accuracy, and as many hundreds who draw up written contracts, deeds, and other instruments for the transfer of property."[27]

The Cherokee had intermarried more with white people than had any other tribe and by their associations had acquired many of the customs and much of the view point of the white race. Having a larger percentage of white blood than any other of the immigrant tribes, they

27 Butler to Crawford, ibid., for 1843.

justly boasted more outstanding individuals distinguished for intellect and leadership; so also did they possess more lawless characters; more bloodthirsty bandits; more merciless feuds than all the other immigrant tribes together.[28]

The Cherokee people suffered irreparable loss in the progress they should have achieved by the party strife, division and faction growing out of the old treaty. As time passed, political animosities and feuds existed in spite of the nominal adjustment of governmental differences; but regardless of this situation, the people continued to exhibit commendable zeal in the promotion of education, agriculture, domestic economy, and industry, which were reflected in the neatness and style in which they lived, and the possession of necessities and comforts of living enjoyed by them.[29] It was said that the wearing apparel manufactured from the raw material in the nation by the women with spinning wheel and loom[30] compared well with the products of private families of the same character in most of the States. By 1844 Dwight Mission that had contributed much to the advancement of the Cherokee people had been converted into a girl's school in connection with which there were ten teachers.[31]

28 The most desperate men in the history of these feuds were the Starrs. Besides the slaying of the Vores they were charged with the butchery of a family of the name of Wright, and of participation in the "Cane Hill Tragedy" some time before (Benson, *Life among the Choctaws*, 158). It is also a well known fact that many of the best people in the Cherokee Nation were and are of the Starr family; for integrity and good citizenship they are excelled by none.

29 "The Cherokees, you are aware, are more intelligent as a whole, and further advanced in civilization, than any other tribe within my jurisdiction. Many of them are men of decided talents and education" (Armstrong to Crawford, *Report* of commissioner of Indian affairs, 1843).

30 In 1845 Agent Butler reported that "there are 400 spinning wheels manufactured at the public expense and issued annually, one-half of which are made by a Cherokee and are of good workmanship (Butler, *report*, September, OIA, "Cherokee" B 2569). These were made by a Cherokee named Bullfrog for which he was promised by the United States Government $4 each, which four years later he was trying to secure (Brown to commissioner of Indian affairs, August 20, 1849, OIA, "Cherokee" file B 495).

31 The boys' school at Dwight burned in 1840 but was rebuilt and the school was opened again March 1, 1841 (American Board of Commissioners for Foreign Missions *Report* for 1841).

CHAPTER TWENTY-SEVEN / *Cherokee People at Home*

IN SPITE of bitter dissension in the tribe, the determination of
jealous minority leaders to prevent functioning of the government established by an overwhelming majority, the inexplicable
efforts of the administration at Washington and the military
authorities in Indian Territory to discredit the leadership striving to make it operative, the Cherokee government did function effectively and was able to lead the people in the direction of progress and
achievement.

Their constitution was founded on republican principles, and
created three departments of government. The legislative was composed of two bodies, the Committee and the Council. The Nation
was divided into eight districts: Delaware, Going Snake, Flint, Skin
Bayou, Illinois, Canadian, Tahlequah, and Saline. Each district elected
two members to the National Committee and three to the National
Council. These bodies met annually in the autumn for two or three
weeks and the members received $2.50 a day each during their at-
tendance. While the council was in session a public table was kept
at the expense of the Nation where all who wished could eat.[1] The laws
enacted were based upon equal rights and privileges and with the
constitution were printed in English and Cherokee and distributed
throughout the Nation.[2]

The executive department was headed by a principal chief with a
salary of $1,000 and his expenses and an assistant chief, both elected
every four years. Sheriffs, clerks, and other officers were designated to
execute the laws. Debts were collected in the usual way by execution.
The judiciary consisted of a supreme court of five members that sat

1 *Report* of commissioner of Indian affairs for 1843.
2 *Ibid.*, for 1842.

once a year; a circuit court of four members that convened in the spring and fall; and a district court for each of the eight districts that sat when-ever occasion required. Civil and criminal codes were adopted. Jury trials and pleadings were provided for. Administrators and executors were appointed to settle estates.

Many of their leaders were men of decided talents and education. The judges of their circuit and district courts were "appointed more for their probity and personal worth than their legal attainments, and will compare in point of moral worth with any similar body in the United States. They are rigid in the execution of their laws, generally impartial in the administration of justice, as yet necessarily in a rude state," reported their agent Pierce Butler. The first chief justice, John Martin, died October 17, 1840, and Rev. Jesse Bushyhead was elected in his place.[3]

"As a people they are very tenacious of the management and regula-tion of their internal affairs. There are believed to be about 2,000 professors of the Christian religion, consisting of Baptists, Methodists, and Presbyterians; the former comprise much the largest class, and may be considered the first class of Cherokees. For intelligence and general integrity, there are about 4,000 others who might be classed among the first. Much the largest class of the Cherokee are half-breeds, or what are known to be the middle class, who are ardent, and enterprising, and passionately fond of gaming. When not under the influence of ardent spirits, they are hospitable, and well disposed; but, when under such influence, their worst passions seem to be aroused. The evil of introducing spirits among them, invariably carried in by the lowest class of whites, I do not hesitate to say is the cause of all their troubles with the citizens of the United States. The Cherokees, as a people, are not disposed to labor; but within the last two years there is a manifest change in this particular, both from necessity and inclination. They are now engaged in agricultural pursuits. There is no game within 150 or 200 miles of their limits. Their country is well watered, and supplies abundantly all the products known to that latitude, such as corn, wheat, oats, tobacco, and hemp. Within the limits of the nation there are two abundant and valuable salt springs. One of them is leased to a Cherokee for an inconsiderable sum, but is not worked to much

3 Emmet Starr, *History of the Cherokee Indians*.

advantage either to him or the nation. Stone coal of the finest quality abounds in two sections, adjacent to each other in the nation.

"There is a small class, termed mountain Indians, who are ignorant, and but slightly progressed in moral and intellectual improvement; have few comforts, and plant barely sufficient for subsistence. Many of the Cherokees own slaves, and many may be called comfortable livers; all of them own stock cattle, yet make but little beyond their own consumption."

In his report for 1843 Butler noted that "immediately after their removal and settlement beyond the Mississippi, from causes incident to such a state of things, the Cherokees rather diminished than increased in population. They have devoted themselves with more steadiness and industry to the cultivation of the soil; which may be regarded as their national employment, and which affords an easy and abundant subsistence; from this as well as other causes, their numbers are rapidly increasing. In their houses, farms, and fixtures they have advanced in civilization. They generally live in double log cabins, and have about them the utensils and conveniences of such habitations. Though fond of relaxation and amusements, they are far from being improvident in their habits. This increasing disposition to provide for the future, instead of giving themselves up to the enjoyments of the present, strongly marks a tendency to raise themselves in the scale of intellectual and moral beings. . . . . In the ordinary transactions of life, especially in making bargains, they are shrewd and intelligent; frequently evincing a degree of craft and combination that strike the mind as remarkable."[4]

The far-sighted chief of the Cherokee Nation employed his active mind in planning movements for the good of his people. And directly after his return from Washington and under his influence the Cherokee National Council on December 16, 1841, enacted legislation setting up a common school system for the Nation. Eleven schools were provided for in the eight districts, supported by the interest on the national school fund. In these schools under the superintendency of Rev. Stephen Foreman a native Cherokee, reading, writing, arithmetic, bookkeeping, English grammar, geography, and history were taught. Nine of the teachers were white men, of whom one was an adopted citizen by

4 *Report* of Pierce M. Butler September 30, 1843, in *Report* of commissioner of Indian affairs, 1843.

marriage. And the other two were native Cherokee. There was provided for each teacher $535 for his pay and the purchase of school
books. The Cherokee council created a separate fund for the board,
clothing and education of the five to ten orphan children attending
each of the several public schools in the Nation. In 1843 there were
500 pupils in all the schools.

Besides these tribal institutions were the missionary establishments
embracing both churches and schools. The American Board of Commissioners for Foreign Missions was operating missions at Dwight,
Fairfield, Park Hill, and Mount Zion, together with a missionary school
at each place. John Huss, a native preacher, had a church on Honey
Creek. Dwight Mission under the superintendence of Rev. Jacob
Hitchcock had a school of fifty-five girls, including forty-five regular
boarding pupils; Mr. and Mrs. Nathaniel B. Dodge were the teachers,
The Fairfield Mission under the direction of the Rev. Elizur Butler.
included a school for boys and girls averaging about twenty-five in
number. It was located south of the site of the present Stilwell, Oklahoma. The seventy-two members of the church were nearly all Cherokee Indians. Mount Zion school was in charge of the Rev. Daniel S.
Butrick.

The mission at Park Hill was in charge of the Rev. Samuel A. Worcester and accommodated forty-seven pupils, all Cherokee but five.
Here Dr. Worcester operated the printing press removed from Union
Mission in 1837. On it he and his assistants published books and
pamphlets in Cherokee, Creek, and Choctaw. In 1843 he reported the
following publications from his press since it was first set up at Union
in 1835:

In the Cherokee Language

TITLE	No. of PAGES	SIZE	No. of COPIES
Child's Book	8	18 mo.	200
Cherokee Primer (two editions)	24	24 to.	4,500
Catechism (two editions)	8	24 to.	3,000
Select Passages of Scripture	24	24 to.	5,000
Cherokee Hymns	48	24 to.	5,000
Cherokee Hymns	68	24 to.	5,000

Title	No. of pages	Size	No. of copies
Cherokee Almanac for 1836	24	12 mo.	450
Cherokee Almanac for 1838	24	12 mo.	500
Cherokee Almanac for 1839	36	12 mo.	2,000
Cherokee Almanac for 1840	36	12 mo.	1,800
Cherokee Almanac for 1842	36	12 mo.	1,000
Cherokee Almanac for 1843	36	12 mo.	1,000
Tract on Marriage	12	12 mo.	1,500
Tract on Temperance	12	12 mo.	1,500
Gospel of John (two editions)	100	24 to.	6,500
Gospel of Matthew	120	24 to.	3,000
Epistles of John (two editions)	20	24 to.	8,000
Cherokee Laws	54	12 mo.	1,000
Methodist Discipline	45	24 to.	1,000
Address on Intoxicating Drink	8	24 to.	5,000
Message of Principal Chief (in Cherokee and English)	12	24 to.	1,000
Special Message of Principal Chief (in the Creek Language)	8	24 to.	1,000
Child's Guide	24	16 mo.	
Muscogee Teacher	54	18 mo.	

In Choctaw

Title	No. of pages	Size	No. of copies
Choctaw Friend	190	12 mo.	3,000
Choctaw Reader	126	12 mo.	2,000
Choctaw Constitution and Laws	..	12 mo.	
Methodist Discipline	48	24 to.	
Epistles of John	27	24 to.	1,000
Child's Book on the Soul	16	24 to.	400
Child's Book on the Creation	14	24 to.	400
Bible Stories	23	24 to.	350
Choctaw Almanac for 1836	16	24 to.	
Choctaw Almanac for 1837	24	24 to.	
Choctaw Almanac for 1839	24	24 to.	
Choctaw Almanac for 1843	44	24 to.	

From July 18, 1845 to August 18, 1846 they printed 276,000 pages of Cherokee school books and tracts, 386,000 in Choctaw and 18,000 in Creek; the largest was a Choctaw spelling book of 108 pages.[5]

The Methodist Society employed twenty-seven preachers in the nation, "of whom fifteen were local." Twelve labored as circuit preachers, including four natives. There were 1,400 communicants. There were also prosperous Sunday schools in many of the societies in which instruction was given both in English and Cherokee. The Baptist Association had 750 communicants and included two ordained preachers, Rev. Jesse Bushyhead and John Wykliffe, both natives; and five native licensed preachers, Lewis Downing, Peter, Tu-ne-no-lee, Potts, and T. Soowotscikee. "The Cherokee Baptist Mission formed themselves into an auxiliary missionary society to the mother board in Boston, and have two schools, supported by their joint efforts. One is entirely a school for females, and is taught by Miss Hibbard; the other is under the charge of Miss Ross, and is for the instruction of both boys and girls. Both of these are competent teachers and accomplished ladies. The first has thirty-five and the other forty-five pupils. They have a large brick school house, built by the Cherokees; and altogether, the schools are answering the most sanguine expectations of their friends."[6]

An event of outstanding importance in the history of the Cherokee Nation and of the whole Indian Territory was the great international Indian council held at Tahlequah in 1843. It began in June and lasted four weeks. It was called by the Cherokee chiefs and was attended by representatives of eighteen tribes. The delegates exchanged views on the problems facing them and agreed on certain mutual obligations of great importance to the tribes attempting to adjust themselves to new associations and responsibilities forced on them by the recent emigration from the East.[7]

An event of greater significance to the Indians was the beginning of their weekly national newspaper, *The Cherokee Advocate*, which made its appearance in September 1844. This paper was printed partly in the English language and partly in the characters invented by the immortal Sequoyah that could be read by nearly every Indian even though he could not read English. It took the place of the *Cherokee*

5 *Ibid.*
6 *Ibid.*
7 For an account of this council, see Foreman, *Advancing the Frontier.*

Phoenix that had been published in their eastern home until it was seized and destroyed in 1832 as part of the program of the Government to break the spirit and destroy the resources of the Indians in their indomitable struggle to resist the efforts to drive them from their homes. William P. Ross was the first editor of the *Advocate* and he issued a readable paper that flourished for many years and contributed much to the welfare and literacy of the Cherokee people.[8]

Cherokee Agent Butler was a conscientious observer of his charges. In his report for 1844 he gave some further interesting observations concerning them: "The Cherokees are a people fond of sports and social amusements. Many of them keep up the ancient custom of annual 'ball plays,' which usually take place after the crops are laid by. This is an amusement which, as a friend of their people, I would be far from discouraging or wishing discontinued, when not carried to an excess. It is above all others trying to their powers of endurance, and probably contributes largely to the development of their manly and athletic forms. It promotes social intercourse by drawing together, from all parts of the nation, the young men, when, with friendly rivalry, a contest of skill, strength, and endurance is often maintained for hours. . . . . Besides this sport, they pursue that of training and rearing the blood-horse;[9] are fond of dancing, and have an uncommon relish for music.

"The Cherokees are exceedingly fond of reading and have a very inquisitive mind. They seem to take great delight, too, at present, in the manual process of writing, and take every occasion to employ it in preference to oral communication—not so much among themselves, however, as with the whites and agents of the government. Many of them have a taste for, and some acquirements in, general literature. Much benefit may be expected from their printing-press, lately in

8 William P. Ross, a nephew of John Ross and Lewis Ross, was born in 1820 at the foot of Lookout Mountain. He was graduated from Princeton College in 1842. November 16, 1846, he was married to his cousin Mary Jane, the daughter of Lewis Ross. The *Advocate* was established by the act of the Cherokee Council of October 25, 1843.

9 Samuel Mayes, a Cherokee, purchased a famous racing stallion named Argyle, that had won many notable races in a number of states on the Atlantic coast. Mayes brought the horse to his plantation in Flint District, and in the *Cherokee Advocate* advertised his service. From this horse much good blood was introduced in the Nation (*Cherokee Advocate*, March 6, 1845, p. 3, col. 6).

operation. The more general diffusion of information will lead to further improvement. Although imaginative they have nothing that we can call poetry; but, as orators, they are conspicuous in some of the essential excellencies of the art. Bold, brief, and earnest, they adapt their ideas and expressions with uniform tact to the nature of their subject and the character of their hearers, and *stop when they have done.* Their candidates for council follow our example of 'taking the stump' upon all questions of public interest. They speak both in Cherokee and in English; the latter being necessary, from the large number of white men, who have been adopted by the nation. Although they are in some instances losing the native tongue, yet, as a written language, it has become in a measure fixed; and the tenacity with which they generally cling to it, as to many other of their national characteristics, renders it improbable that it will ever be entirely abandoned. Although not entirely ignorant of painting, they have had heretofore no scope for the development of any talent in that art, or in sculpture. In music they have a decided taste, and many of them perform well on different instruments."

The terms of the treaty with the Indians provided for eight public blacksmiths, six of whom were Indians; they were paid by the Government and worked without cost to the Indians. There were also two wheelwrights who manufactured 400 spinning wheels annually for the Indians, but Butler said that this supply did not equal one-third of the demand.

The council at Tahlequah in 1844, the first under the new set of officers chosen at the first popular election under their new constitution, was held in a setting of hope and optimism. "At present," said their national newspaper, "everything about our Town is life and animation. The number of persons called together by the annual sessions of the National Council, though not so great as on some similar occasions, is quite considerable. Besides the public officers—Councilmen, Judges, Clerks, Sheriffs, &c., there are many others in daily attendance, some of whom are called hither by business and others by a curiosity to see and hear what is occurring in the Nation.

"Tahlequah. . . . became the seat of Government of the Cherokee Nation in 1839 after the reunion of the Eastern and Western branches of the Cherokee family. The location of the town is central and beautiful and combines advantages of good health, excellent spring water, and a plentiful supply of timber for firewood and purposes of building. The surrounding country is in our opinion, of surpassing beauty, presenting a diversity of mountain, woodland, and prairie scenery. The prairie which extends within the town reservation, affords luxurious grass, which is a good substitute for hay, and as much land of productive quality as will be required in many years, for agricultural purposes by those wishing to live 'in Town.'

"After it became the seat of government, a number of log cabins were thrown up about the place, without, however, much regard to order, as they were destined for the temporary accommodation of those engaged in the transaction of public business. But a regular town having been laid off last winter, and a number of lots sold to citizens of the Nation, these cabins will be removed and others built, which will present a better appearance.[10] A few houses have, however, been already erected and others are in contemplation, of the 'join up' kind.

"The Supreme Court has just opened its annual session, in a new and commodious brick Court House.[11] which in point of neatness and durability is perhaps surpassed by no building of the kind in Arkansas. The contractor for doing this job is a Jersey carpenter, whose habits of industry secure him constant employment. The mason work was done by a 'little Yankee' all the way from Boston. Our house is also a spank new one, eighteen by forty feet, two stories high, ceiled, etc. Our country woman Mrs. Taylor, has also in forward state of erection, a new brick house, intended for a hotel, which will be, when completed, not only a great accommodation to the public, but also, an ornament to our Town."[12]

10   The appearance of these cabins in 1841 was described by Major Hitchcock: A Traveler in Indian Territory, 36. On January 8, 1845, a measure was enacted by the Cherokee council requiring all houses and other improvements "on the public square in the town of Tahlequah to be removed before the first of the next September" (Cherokee Advocate, January 23, 1845; Cherokee Laws, Edition of 1852 (Tahlequah) p. 117).

11   The Cherokee council in October, 1844, appropriated $2775.00 to pay the contractor, James A. Price, for constructing the building (Cherokee Advocate, October 26, 1844, p. 3, col. 1).

12   Mrs. Taylor's hotel was constructed by some Mormon artisans; they were part of a contingent who had broken off from the main body of Mormons on their way west, and started to Texas. When they arrived at Tahlequah they found there was work to be had in the busy little hamlet and tarried awhile; they were also engaged in proselyting for their church until through the influence of the missionaries the people compelled them to move on.

CHAPTER TWENTY-EIGHT / *Sequoyah and His Alphabet*

T HE influence that contributed more to the literacy and progress of the Cherokee people than any other was the invention of the Cherokee alphabet by Sequoyah or George Guess, a citizen of the tribe, who spoke no English. At an early day he realized that there was a magic in the written word that set apart from others the man who could read. Inspired by the desire to discover a set of characters that could be used to express the sense and sound of Cherokee language he set to work, and after years of discouraging labor and ridicule by his neighbors, he invented an alphabet of eighty-five characters that the people of his tribe could use. It was so simple that they were able to master it in a few days and soon a large part of the tribe employed the new alphabet in uses never known to them before.

Sequoyah joined the Cherokee in Arkansas in the early twenties, and after his departure the tribal council furnished the money with which the American Board of Commissioners for Foreign Missions had a font of type cast in the characters invented by this modern Cadmus, and a printing press was set up at New Echota, Georgia, on which was printed the *Cherokee Phoenix*, part in English and part in Cherokee. This paper contributed much to the literacy and advance of the tribe until it was seized by the Government as part of the plan to drive the Cherokee Indians to the west. Sequoyah was employed by the Cherokee in their western home as a school teacher, and the *Cherokee Advocate*, printed partly in Cherokee, carried on his great work of education and enlightenment.

Sequoyah did not take much part in public affairs in his nation, but in 1839, at the time of greatest need, he joined those patriots, who, in face of bitter opposition, were endeavoring to reunite the tribe under a government; and on the part of the Western Cherokee served as president of the convention that adopted their Act of Union to which his name is signed. In the summer of 1842, desiring to explore the western prairies and become acquainted with his red brethren who roamed and hunted there, Sequoyah, then about eighty years old, in company with a few other Cherokee, loaded several pack horses with goods and visited the Comanche Indians. After remaining with them for some time with his son and two or three other companions, he made his way into northern Mexico. Here he hoped to find and collect some scattered bands of Cherokee Indians with the intention of inducing them to return with him to the Cherokee Nation. However, his death in August, 1843, defeated his plans and he was buried in San Fernando in Mexico.[1]

The Cherokee people were appreciative of the great service of Sequoyah and sought to show their gratitude in a manner explained by Chief Ross: "Head of Coosa, Cherokee Nation, January 12, 1832. Mr. George Gist; My friend: The legislative Council of the Cherokee Nation in the year 1824 voted a medal to be presented to you, as a token of respect & admiration for your ingenuity in the invention of the Cherokee alphabetical characters; and in pursuance thereof, the late venerable chiefs, Path Killer & Charles R. Hicks, instructed a delegation of this nation, composed of Messrs George Lowrey, Senior, Elijah Hicks & myself to have one struck, which was completed in 1825. In the anticipation of your visit to this country, it was reserved for the purpose of honoring you with its presentment by the chiefs in General Council; but having so long been disappointed in this pleasing hope, I have thought it my duty no longer to delay, and therefore take upon myself the pleasure of delivering it through our friend Mr. Charles H. Vann who intends visiting his relatives in the country where you dwell. . . . John Ross." The medal, says John Howard Payne, was "made at Washington & of silver, to the value of Twenty Dollars. On one side was thus inscribed: 'Presented to George Gist by the General Council of the Cherokee Nation, for his ingenuity in The Invention of the Cherokee Alphabet, 1825.' Under the inscription were two pipes

1 Butler to Crawford August 6, 1845, OIA; *Report* of P. M. Butler: *Report of commissioner of Indian affairs for 1845.*

crossed; and an abridgement of the above on the reverse of the medal, encircled a head meant to represent George Gist himself.

"Gist still resides in Arkansas and the last that was heard from him, he had adapted his alphabet to the language of another of the Indian nations who had removed thither, the Choctaws, to whom he was teaching the use of it, with triumphant success. Gist is lame—was so, I believe, from infancy. . . . . he was troubled with a wife whose capacity was very limited and who did not enter into his ambitions. He built him a cabin apart from his family & there would study and contrive. His habits were always silent & contemplative . . . . . To this cabin he confined himself for a year, the whole charge of his farm and family devolving on his wife. When all his friends had remonstrated in vain, his wife went in and flung his whole apparatus of papers & books into the fire, & thus he lost his first labor. . . . after two more years of application completed his work. All speak highly of his drawing & of his silver work. . . . . He was about 40 when he began his work."[2]

2   John Howard Payne *Manuscripts*, Ayer Collection, Newberry Library. Payne collected this information during his visit with John Ross in Tennessee in 1835 (Foreman, *Indian Removal*, 266). This is part of the material he planned to use in writing a history of the Cherokee Indians. A slightly different version is that of Dr. Samuel George Morton, incorporated in a paper entitled "Origin and Characteristics of the American Aborigines," written by him and read at the annual meeting of the Boston Society of Natural History, April 27, 1842. Attached to the medical staff of the army, Doctor Morton spent two years with the Indians during their removal West. While serving with the Cherokee Indians in 1838 he came to know Sequoyah's son (probably Teesey Guess) who acted as "lingster" or interpreter and told him interesting things about his father and his work. The thoughts of Guess were first directed to the making of an alphabet, he said, "by observing his nephew, who had just returned from a distant school, spelling some words, whereupon he immediately exclaimed that he could effect the same in his vernacular tongue. . . . . Building a hut in a retired spot. . . . he devoted himself exclusively to this great labor. His fellow-countrymen grew suspicious of his object. . . . . Believing that he was engaged in some diabolical plan to blow up the nation, succeeded in drawing him from his hermitage, when they burned up his cabin, hieroglyphics and all. But. . . . returned to his supposed black art. . . . he was soon fortunate enough to exhibit to his people one of the greatest wonders of modern times.

"A newspaper in the Cherokee language was soon published. . . . and had not the Georgians, in a spirit of Vandalism, destroyed their printing establishment, the whole Bible for years past might have been read in the Cherokee language" (*The United States Magazine and Democratic Review*, XI, 614).

More than two years after Sequoyah departed for Mexico, and not knowing whether he still lived, the Cherokee National Council on December 24, 1844, voted a pension of $300 to him by the name of Guess; to be paid to him if living, or to his wife if he were dead.[3] In January, 1845 the commissioner of Indian affairs authorized the expenditure of $200 to defray the expense of a party to go in search of him.[4] Near the Red River this company met some of the companions of Sequoyah who told him that the venerable philosopher was dead, and they returned to Fort Gibson. The information was conveyed in a report to Cherokee Agent P. M. Butler:

"(*Translation*) P. M. Butler, Cherokee Agent, Sir; Having reached the Red River on my way, I met with the following Cherokees from Mexico:—Jesse, the leader of the party, The Worm, Gah-na-nes-kee, The Standing Man, and The Standing Rock. The last named, The Standing Rock, attended Sequoyah during his last sickness and also witnessed his death and Burial. Tsee-sa-le-tah, the son of Sequoyah, remains on Red River. He is very sorry that the remains of his Father are buried so far from his own country and remains where he is on this account. As Sequoyah was the object for which I had started in search

---

Elias Boudinot, the first editor of the *Cherokee Phoenix*, took a prominent part in securing from white people funds with which the type and press were purchased for the tribe. Boudinot was succeeded as editor by Elijah Hicks who served for two years. After the State of Georgia had confiscated many of the homes of the Cherokee people and forbade their holding national councils on their lands in Georgia, they met at Red Clay over the line in Tennessee. There in the spring of 1835 it was determined to publish their national paper in their new capital, and a wagon was sent to New Echota for the press and equipment. It was then learned that at the direction of Rev. John Schermerhorn and Benjamin F. Currey the press had been seized by the Georgia guard commanded by the notorious William N. Bishop, with the assistance of Stand Watie who claimed that as his brother Elias Boudinot had helped to raise the money for its purchase, he had a proprietary interest in it. The press was then employed in the interest of Georgia by publishing matter in the Cherokee and English type calculated to destroy the influence of the majority faction of the tribe opposed to the efforts of the Georgians. The Cherokee authorities endeavored in vain to recover their press (John Ross and others to Lewis Cass, April 22, 1836, OIA, "Cherokees East" C 4); the press was last known in the possession of Currey (Currey to Ross September 9, 1835, *ibid.*). Whatever became of this most interesting implement of culture the Author has been unable to learn.

3   *Cherokee Advocate*, January 16, 1845, p. 4, col. 2.
4   *Ibid.*, February 13, 1845, p. 3, col. 2.

and having learned the fact of his death, which I communicated to those who sent me, it will be useless for me to proceed any further. I will return toward home. He is dead without a doubt. His remaining family, Widow, two Daughters and a young man live some where in Skin Bayou District. Oo-no-leh. 15th May, 1845."[5]

The first Indian Mission Conference of the Methodist Episcopal Church was held at Riley's Chapel, the Methodist Church near Tahlequah on October 25, 1844.[6] The Conference was "bounded on the north by the Missouri River; on the east by Missouri and Arkansas states; on the south by Red River, embracing all the Indian Territory in its limits. In this Territory, we believe, there are about 90,000 Indians, many of whom are rapidly advancing in moral and intellectual improvement. They are far better supplied with good schools than their white neighbors."[7] The membership of the Indian Mission Conference was 3,210. "Of these 85 are whites; 2,992 Indians; and 133 colored. There are twenty-seven local preachers stationed—7 of whom are Indians—5 Cherokee and 2 Choctaws. There are 27 local preachers —22 of whom are Indians and 5 whites."[8]

The Cherokee Bible Society was organized in October, 1841. Its purpose as announced in the constitution, was "to disseminate the sacred Scriptures in the English and Cherokee languages among the people of the Cherokee Nation." It was non-sectarian in character and Christians of all denominations were invited to join. The first year little was accomplished, but interest increased in the succeeding years. In 1844 the annual meeting was held in the courthouse at Tahlequah on October 16 and reports were received from branches at Tahlequah, Muddy Spring, Honey Creek, Sallisaw, and Illinois. The society had just suffered a great loss in the death of Rev. Jesse Bushyhead and Richard Taylor was elected to succeed him. The officers were all Cherokee Indians except Rev. Thomas Bertholf, treasurer, and Rev. S. A. Worcester, one of the members of the executive committee.

The desire for education in the Cherokee nation was growing and in January, 1845, Fredrick William Lynde announced in the *Cherokee Advocate* that he would open a school at Park Hill. He would furnish

5 Butler to Crawford, August 6, 1845, OIA.
6 *Cherokee Advocate*, October 26, 1844, p. 3, col. 2.
7 *Ibid.*, November 2, 1844, p. 3, col. 4.
8 *Ibid*

the paper, ink, inkstands, quills, slates, pencils and knives for the students to "learn to make and mend their own pens." A debating society would be formed "by the young gentlemen of the school and the neighborhood, and weekly recitations, original and selected will be given by the Instructor and members of the Society. . . . . Board can be had for $1.25 per week in respectable families contiguous to the School."[9]

The next month Dwight W. Hitchcock opened a school at the mission house at Park Hill; the terms were seventy-five cents a month. Hitchcock, a recent graduate of Amherst College, was the son of Rev. Jacob Hitchcock of Dwight Mission. The next spring a public school was opened at Tahlequah with a Mr. Covel as teacher.

The Cherokee Female Seminary in connection with the Baptist Mission was advertised in the summer; it was to be under the superintendence of Miss Sarah Hale Hibbard. The design of the school, the notice said, was the "improvement, subsequent usefulness, and ultimate happiness of the young ladies of the Cherokee Nation," and it was believed they would find there as good facilities for an education as they could find in eastern schools.[10]

The orderly part of the Cherokee Nation, that of the great majority, was comporting itself much as any well established commonwealth. The regular election was held throughout the Nation Monday, August 4, 1845, and there was no strife. Sheriffs for the respective districts were elected and members of the National Committee and the Council. Notice was published in several issues of the *Advocate* that on August 16 a society for the promotion of agriculture and domestic arts would be organized and five premiums of silver cups, worth from three to ten dollars each, were offered by the Cherokee Agent Pierce M. Butler for the best specimens of homespun cloth, coverlets, belts and socks. An Arkansas paper cited this as an example to be followed by white people of that state.[11]

On the date advertised the society was organized with William Shorey Coodey president and several Cherokee vice presidents. Mrs. Rachel

9   *Ibid.*, January 16, 1845, p. 4, col. 4.
10   *Ibid.*, August 21, 1845, p. 3, col. 6.
11   *Arkansas Intelligencer*, July 12, 1845, p. 2, col. 1; *Cherokee Advocate*, August 7, 1845, p. 3, col. 6; January 22, 1846, p. 3, col. 1. The latter item contained also the information that Chief John Ross had been elected a member of the Pennsylvania Historical Society.

Report of mission sent to search for Sequoyah; translated reads as follows:

P.M. Butler, Cherokee Agent.

Sir:

Having reached Red River on my way, I met with the following Cherokees from Mexico,—Jesse, the leader of the party, The Worm, Gah-na-nes-kee, the Standing Man, and the Standing Rock. The last named, the Standing Rock, attended Sequoyah during his last sickness and also witnessed his Death and Burial. Tsee-sa-le-tah, the son of Sequoyah remains on Red River. He is very sorry that the remains of his Father are buried so far from his own country and remains where he is on this account.

As Sequoyah was the object for which I had started in search and having learned the fact of his death, which I communicate to those who sent me, it will be useless for me to proceed any further. I will return toward home. He is dead without a doubt. His remaining family, Widow, two Daughters and a young man live somewhere in Skin Bayou District.

OO-NO-LEH.

Bayou District,
15th May, 1845.

Cherokee Male Seminary

Orr, Mrs. Eliza Ross, and Mrs. Sarah Foreman were named a committee to award the prizes. "The meeting was then briefly addressed by Rev. Stephen Foreman who drew a contrast between the state of agriculture as it is *now* found among the Cherokees, and what it was comparatively a few years ago, when they planted their little crops of corn, beans, &c., by using the shoulder blade of the deer instead of the plough and hoe; and enumerated some of the advantages that would be likely to result to the people from the formation of an agricultural society, in the cultivation of the soil, in the management of their household affairs, in the rearing of stock and in the dissemination of useful information on a variety of subjects intimately associated with their present condition."

The committee on the premiums then awarded to Mrs. Nancy Adair of Flint District the silver cup for the best ten yards of home-made cloth; to Mrs. Jane Dougherty of Flint District a silver cup for the best coverlet; to Mrs. Jinny Wolf of Tahlequah District a silver cup for a beaded belt; to Miss Catherine Gunter of Tahlequah, a cup for the best cradle coverlet; and to Mrs. Martha Daniel, a cup for a pair of socks.[12]

The meeting then adjourned to Saturday, October 11, when a constitution drafted by the president, Mr. Coodey, was presented and adopted. Provision was made for meeting annually at Tahlequah to listen to a program, and for awarding premiums for excellence in domestic workmanship to be exhibited. The name adopted was "the Agricultural Society of the Cherokee Nation"; the object, the encouragement and improvement of agriculture, domestic manufacturing, and rearing of stock.[13]

There were a number of enterprising men in the Cherokee Nation who did much for the progress and comfort of the people while advancing their own interests. Several merchants at Fort Gibson, Park Hill, Tahlequah and Flint kept adequate stocks of goods which they sold for cash or exchanged with the Indians for beef, hides, tallow, deer skins, coon skins, fox skins, beeswax, wool, and other produce.[14]

Joseph Vann was an active member of the tribe who owned and ran a steamboat named the *Lucy Walker* on the Arkansas, Mississippi

12   *Cherokee Advocate*, August 21, p. 3, col. 1.
13   *Ibid.*, October 16, 1845, p. 3, col. 1.
14   *Ibid.*, September 2, 1851, p. 2, col. 1.

and Ohio rivers until the boilers exploded and the boat sank near New Albany, Indiana, about November 1, 1844. Many people were killed, including Mr. Vann and his son-in-law, Preston Mackey. James S. Vann purchased the steamboat *Franklin* of 150 tons burden for the Arkansas River trade in the spring of 1845.[15] In the autumn of 1844 the first cotton gin in the Cherokee Nation was erected by George W. Gunter on his place fifteen miles above Fort Smith on the Arkansas River. It had a capacity of four to five thousand pounds of cotton daily.

Next to the resolute, vigilant, and successful defense of their tribal government against the efforts of jealous and disappointed factionists to break it down, the manifestation of greatest significance in the Cherokee Nation was the temperance movement. Aside from the enforced removal of the Indians from their eastern homes, nothing had brought so much distress, misery, and apprehension to the Cherokee people as the introduction among them of whisky by white people. At the time they needed every facility and encouragement possible for the reconstruction of their homes and institutions and recovery of their morale, their faltering efforts were harrassed and nullified by this devastating curse. All the crimes in the calendar were committed under its influence. Indians neglected the building of their homes and cultivation of crops for their sustenance. Peaceable citizens were terrified in their homes and on the highways by drunken Indians, and hindered in the performance of their peaceful occupations necessary to a restoration of normal life in the country.

The Cherokee Temperance Society was organized by the western Cherokee September 12, 1836[16] and it grew as its need became more and more apparent. The emigrants who arrived in the winter and spring of 1839 had witnessed the debauchery caused by the introduction by white people of whisky into their late country and in the emigrating camps along their sad journey. With these scenes fresh in their minds, immediately on arrival in their new home they held temperance meetings to plan campaigns for rescuing their people from the

15   *Arkansas Intelligencer*, April 12, 1845, p. 2, col. 1. Lorenzo De Lano of Park Hill was a partner in the ownership and operation of the steamer *Santa Fe* that plied up and down the Arkansas River. While landing some Choctaw emigrants at Fort Coffee in January, 1849, a flue collapsed resulting in the death of one person and scalding of others (*Cherokee Advocate*, January 22, 1849, p. 2, col. 1).

16   *Ibid.*, November 5, 1849.

wretchedness caused by these white vultures, and to enable the immigrants better to meet the problems of readjustment. At the meeting of the temperance society in 1843 more than 2,000 members had been enrolled. Largely through the influence of this organization a rigid law for the suppression of the introduction and sale of liquor was enacted by the Cherokee council October 25, 1841. At the international Indian council held at Tahlequah in the summer of 1843 the sheriff seized and destroyed more than 1,700 gallons of whisky introduced within the premises occupied by the delegates, their families and other visitors.

The laws enacted by Congress were intended to prevent the introduction of whisky, but white men could ply their trade profitably without violating them. At Fort Smith, Evansville, Maysville, and other towns on the Arkansas and Missouri border, the principal industry was the retailing of whisky to Cherokee Indians, and there was scarce an issue of the *Cherokee Advocate* that did not contain an account of a murder of, or by, a drunken Indian. By resolution of the Cherokee council January 10, 1845 the governors of Arkansas and Missouri were solicited to aid in the suppression of this traffic, but in vain.

Another lawless section was that immediately surrounding the military reservation containing Fort Gibson. Here grog shops and brothels were established, usually by a low class of Cherokee citizens who catered to the sensual appetites of the soldiers at the post. In drunken brawls in March 1845, several soldiers were killed and their friends in reprisal burned the houses of some of the Cherokee participants. A military inquiry was instituted at Fort Gibson and when the Cherokee citizens were called to testify, on the objection of Colonel Mason the court held that the testimony of an Indian could not be received to contradict that of a white man; this was the law in Arkansas, the court held, and therefore would be the law in a military tribunal in the Indian Territory.

Much excitement resulted. The Cherokee people held a mass meeting in Tahlequah to express their indignation at the ruling of the military court and the scenes of dissipation and prostitution near the reservation. Resolutions couched in well chosen words were adopted, representing to the United States Government the great menace to the peace and order of the Cherokee Nation caused by the presence of Fort Gibson, and praying that it be abandoned.[17] The matter then reached the grand jury at Little Rock, that, with quaint naïvete, condemned the Cherokee Indians for maintaining grog shops near Fort Gibson, which, they said, should be suppressed by the potent arm of the United States. But this grand jury of white men from Arkansas had no words of condemnation for their own citizens who, in violation of the law, furnished the whisky and sent it into the Indian country, or retailed it on the border.

Repeated and disgraceful acts of disorder and lawlessness induced the *Cherokee Advocate* to offer an explanation that permits an interesting insight into conditions and their causes in the nation: "The increase of immorality among the Cherokees commenced several years back, and had its origin in the unfortunate circumstances that surrounded them prior to being removed from their eastern homes. Before the policy of removing to the west all the Indians indigenous to the east of the Mississippi River, had extended its iron hand to the Cherokees, their general condition was happy and promising. Their rights were generally well protected. They felt secure in their persons and possessions, and enjoyed peace and contentment. Availing themselves of this gracious state of affairs, so indispensible to the moral and intellectual advancement of all communities, whether white or red, they rapidly improved.

"Their condition was changing, as it were, by some magic influence. The domestic arts began to flourish. Industry secured with their frugal habits, abundance of the necessaries and comforts of life and even many of its luxuries. Schools received reasonable encouragement. The reduction of their language into a written one, enabled distant friends to communicate one with the other, while the weekly newspaper conveyed instruction and amusement to the inmates of the humblest log cabin. In short, their situation was happy—the light of Revelation had dawned upon them with its benign influences and the star of future prosperity glittered brightly in their firmament. . . . . When it was ascertained that the Cherokees were strongly, unconquerably adverse to removing West, a regular system of the most infernal vexations was concocted and put into operation by some of the States and private whites, to wear out their patience, to make their situation a

17 *Ibid.*, April 3, 1845, p. 3, col. 2.

bed of thorns and to 'grind them to the dust' or drive them from their homes.

"Treaties were disregarded,—States' laws were extended over them,—the ancient land marks broken down, and the Cherokees left the victims of those who fettered them with chains and cast into the same prison the missionary and the murderer—who converted churches into grog-shops—who flooded the country with whisky—tore down the government of the Indians as if it were a fabric of straw—punished innocent individuals and perpetrated other acts which we have not the time, much less the disposition, to enumerate.

"The great mass of the Cherokees remained uncorrupted and incorruptible. But some were changed by glittering silver, some became gamblers, some drunkards, some idlers, and others were seduced from the path of virtue and innocence. From among those last enumerated, may be found some of those depraved but unfortunate beings, who, while indulging the habits and vices imbibed from the whites, commit the crimes that are occurring in our country.

"Other sources of crime may be found also, in the traffic in ardent spirits on the frontier, and in the reckless, infractory spirit diffused among certain classes by the singular importance that is permitted abroad, to attach to the restless, mercenary factionists that creep into existence as the Chiefs, Head-men, &c, of this and that party among the Cherokees. The last mentioned, we consider indeed the most prolific of all other sources of crime amongst the Cherokees."[18]

The destructive floods of 1844 that washed away corn fields and the drought the next year brought many Cherokee people to a state of destitution, and the government of the tribe appropriated money to purchase food for as many as possible. For this purpose depots were established in the spring of 1845 in the different districts where corn was issued to the most needy; not sufficient, however, said the *Advocate*, to relieve the urgent wants of many. "Indeed, to supply all the poor, is a thing scarcely possible, as they are so numerous, and the obtaining of corn for bread and planting is attended with such great difficulties and expense. All however, will be done, we doubt not, that can be done; and it is to be hoped that our unfortunate men and women,

18   *Ibid.*, May 1, 1845, p. 3, col. 1.

and their helpless, hungry children, will be saved, at least, from the horrors of starvation."[19]

Contrasts among the Cherokee people were not unlike those among white people. Three weeks after the above account the *Advocate* carried a notice that fifty dollars reward would be paid for the capture and return of a slave, the coachman and butler of George M. Murrell, a merchant living at Park Hill who was married to Minerva, the daughter of Lewis Ross, and niece of the Chief. Spencer, the Negro, had driven his master to the residence of Capt. John Benge in Skin Bayou district, and while there made his escape. He was about forty years old and had been purchased by Mr. Murrell in New Orleans. When last heard of he was "clothed in a pair of Janes pants. . . . a brown Janes dress coat, three-fourths worn, a silk hat, brim lined with Bombazin. He took with him also a blue cloth frock coat, with velvet collar—also a black dress coat, and two blankets."[20]

Largely attended temperance meetings were held at Fairfield in Flint district just west of the Arkansas line near where large amounts of liquor were retailed to the Indians. The meetings were called by Walter S. Adair, president of the National Society. A large concourse attended in one of the school houses of Fairfield Mission and after a prayer in Cherokee an opening address was made by the president. A Cherokee hymn was sung, then a speech in English by a missionary from Dwight; an English hymn was followed by a speech in Cherokee by Maj. George Lowrey, and that, in turn, by a hymn in Cherokee. After Dr. Elizur Butler of Fairfield spoke, an English hymn, "Stalks Abroad a Direful Foe," was sung and then another speech in Cherokee was delivered. The meeting began at 11 o'clock and at 2 a recess was taken for refreshments. The meeting was then renewed and after a number of speeches and songs in English and Cherokee, the children sang "Come and Join Our Temp'rance Army," "Away With Melancholy, nor Doleful Changes Ring" and then the people were invited to come forward and sign the pledge. Seventy-four signed, among whom "were some veterans in King Alcohol's army." Similar meetings in this and other districts in the nation were held. It was time, thought the *Advocate*, "that the feelings of the people should be roused to the importance of

19 *Ibid.*, May 1, 1845, p. 3, col. 2.
20 *Ibid.*, May 22, 1845, p. 3, col. 6.

this subject, and every effort be made to impress it upon their minds. The ravages made by Whisky within a few months past, the murders and other crimes that it has caused to be perpetrated in our midst, to say nothing of the heavy tax thus imposed on our treasury, call upon every public spirited citizen to rise up against the common enemy, and to use every effort to drive him from the land."[21]

Seven hundred people attended another meeting at the same place in July. Addresses were made by George W. Adair and other Cherokee Indians, and the Flint District Auxiliary Temperance Society, with Cherokee officers was organized. "The congregation was at regular intervals entertained with the singing of some excellent Temperance songs, selected for the occasion, both in the English and Cherokee language. The band was composed of several gentlemen and ladies, the majority of whom were Cherokees. Dr. Elizur Butler "exhibited and lectured on Dr. Sewell's Plates. They contain a representation of the stomach of a man of health to that of the beastly drunkard. This is a new source of information to our people respecting deleterious effects of intoxicating drink, and one I think well calculated to make a deep impression upon the mind. The Doctor showed the uses of the stomach and the great importance of keeping it in a healthy state—and demonstrated satisfactorily that whisky in no form nor shape was needed for that purpose."

At 2 o'clock a recess was taken "for the purpose of partaking of a cold collation furnished by the neighborhood; this was made ready under some walnut and locust trees in Dr. Butler's door yard, on two long tables prepared for the occasion—one designed for the males and the other for the females. The provisions were such as the country affords; viz: beef, bacon, mutton, fowls, cheese, butter, corn and wheat bread, roasting ears, Irish potatoes, and sweet cold water, mixed with what our people call gr-wi-si-de. This makes an excellent and really palatable drink and one which every teetotaler will say is a good substitute for whiskey." After the program, about sixty more names were added to the roll of signers of the pledge of abstenance. The devotion of those present must have been real, as they sat patiently in a hot room to listen to the proceedings for about six hours, until late in the day before they departed.[22]

21 Ibid., May 29, 1845, p. 3, col. 1; ibid., June 5, 1845, p. 3, col. 1, account by D. D. Hitchcock.
22 Ibid., July 17, 1845, p. 3, cols. 4 and 5.

The Flint Auxiliary Temperance Society met at Muddy Spring on September 4 with four or five hundred present, and though the meeting was broken up by a storm forty-nine signed the pledge.[23]

As the temperance movement expanded, on October 2 a childrens' temperance meeting was held at Tahlequah. Discourses were delivered by the Indians and missionaries, and "the children accompanied by a couple of their number on violins, sung several Temperance songs with spirit and good taste. . . . . They were then formed into a procession under three or four neat banners with suitable devices, by Mr. J. F. Wheeler, and having marched about awhile were conducted to a table where they were well supplied with 'sweet cold water' and a collection of the substantials, as well as some of the delicacies of life. The program was then resumed and they listened to a reading of the regulations for the formation and control of a 'Cold Water Army'; to be composed of Temperance children in the nation under sixteen years of age, and officers were elected for the ensuing year."

The exercises were viewed with great interest by the editor of the *Advocate* "as they must have been by every other man who reflects upon the immense ruin brought on this people by whiskey and other spirituous liquors, and that the shortest and most effectual way of working a reformation among a people, is to begin with the rising generation among them."[24]

The Cherokee Temperance Society was now firmly established throughout the nation and the annual meeting was held at Tahlequah on October 16. William P. Ross, the secretary, made an interesting report from which it appeared that 585 new names had been added to the roll of the organization during the past year to bring their membership to 3,058. The cause of temperance, he showed, was advancing. With great good sense he stressed the significance of the organization and education of the children under the banner of temperance. "Commencing thus early in life, to march along the path of temperance, these youthful soldiers, now the beauty and hope of our country, and hereafter to become its mothers, fathers, laborers, law-givers and guides, must exercise an immense influence, and perhaps are those destined to consummate the great cause in which they have enlisted."[25]

23 *Ibid.*, September 18, 1845, p. 3, cols. 2 and 3.
24 *Ibid.*, October 9, 1845, p. 2, col. 1.
25 *Ibid.*, October 23, 1845, p. 3, col. 1.

CHAPTER TWENTY-NINE / The Cold Water Army

THE missionaries and leaders of the nation realized the seriousness of the whisky menace and proceeded by an intelligent campaign of education to combat it. Temperance meetings now were frequently held in all parts of the Cherokee Nation. Dr. Butler was always on hand to lecture on his "plates" and he traveled over the country exhibiting them to all who would listen. These looked with interest on the first pictures they had ever seen of the stomach and other internal organs, demonstrating to them the great harm resulting from the use of whisky.

These temperance meetings were earnest and solemn occasions, but the leaders endeavored to make them interesting as well as impressive. Accounts of them held a prominent position in the *Cherokee Advocate* from which one learns of the quaint features of the programs. For example, at a meeting of the Tahlequah District Temperance Society at Riley's Chapel, presided over by Rev. Stephen Foreman, the long program included the songs "The Drunkard's Wife," to the tune of "Ingleside"; "The Drunkard's Dying Wife," "The Penitent Rum Drinker," "and volunteer songs any one has to offer."

Mrs. Edith Walker of Fort Gibson, a granddaughter of the Rev. Samuel A. Worcester, recalls as one of her earliest recollections the rallying of the Cold Water Army at the convening of the National Council in November of each year; they would form a "march of allegiance around the Capitol square, carrying banners and singing temperance songs written and set to popular airs of the day by my grandfather, when we listened to temperance speeches by the most prominent men of the nation and members of the Cherokee council; and at the noon hour every body was served with barbecued meat, chicken, pie and cake, which the mothers, wives and sweet-hearts prepared. I can remember my mother as she stood over the furnace kettle in the old mission kitchen, and fried two bushels of doughnuts for one such occasion.

"My mother's eldest sister, Mrs. A. E. W. Robertson, accompanied her father on yearly visits to the different districts of the Nation to play the melodeon for the singing of the temperance songs at the gatherings for instruction and encouragement, until the fame of the Cherokee Cold Water Army spread far and wide, and a similar organization was asked for by the Choctaws and Creeks."

Mrs. Walker's mother also wrote her impressions of those interesting occasions.[1] "The Cherokee council in the early days of the temperance movement was held in a large shed in the centre of what is now Capitol Square. The annual meetings of the temperance society were always held during the session of the National council; and the officers of the society were, many of them, members of that body, as were also many of the speakers at the meetings. Some were both native preachers and members of the council. The only qualifications for membership in the Society, was to sign the Society pledge, as follows: 'We hereby solemnly pledge ourselves that we will neither use nor buy, nor sell, nor give, nor receive as a drink, any whisky, brandy, rum, gin, wine, fermented cider, strong beer, nor any kind of intoxicating liquor.'

"Between annual meetings there were other meetings held and auxiliary societies organized in all parts of the Nation. My father taught his children and all who came under his influence to help in the temperance work. All young men who at different times dwelt in his house (and there were usually more than two or three) learned that they could do something and that they were expected to do their part; some could sing, some speak, and some help to wait on the assembled people when dinner time came. We children knew that what we could do, we were bound to do with no word of objection. Our father took us with him to the meetings, and we all had our parts to perform. My brothers made music when they were hardly taller than their violins. One brother spoke the first 'speech' he ever made in public at the age of sixteen on temperance.

1 Mrs. Hannah Hitchcock, the daughter of Rev. S. A. Worcester, was the widow of Dr. Dwight H. Hitchcock.

"We went to many temperance meetings in different parts of the Nation; some in the woods on the banks of the beautiful clear-running streams, or near some of the fine springs so plentiful in our Nation. The people gathered from near and far; meat was barbecued; bread, cakes and pies provided, and no effort was spared to have an interesting and happy time for all. Through the courtesy of the Christian commander of Fort Gibson, Col. Gustavus Loomis, my father was permitted to have the attendance at some of his meetings of 'the finest band in the United States Army' then stationed at Fort Gibson; and once a choir of nineteen soldiers sang temperance songs, and more delightful singing I never heard in all my long life. Great was our consternation and grief when that fine band was ordered to march with the regiment to the Mexican War, and left Fort Gibson, never to return.

"At the request of Rev. R. M. Loughridge, missionary at Tullahassee mission, my father went to the Creek Nation to organize a Temperance society. He took with him his children and his 'seraphine'; a brush shed was constructed near the Old Agency, and there near the agency spring, the people gathered and a temperance society was organized. The 'seraphine' was played by my sister who afterwards became Mrs. A. E. W. Robertson, principal and superintendent of the Tullahassee manual labor mission school.

"My father, Dr. Worcester, wrote the songs for the Cherokee Cold Water Army; and taught the boys and girls to sing and march to them; he spent hours and days making for them banners of different devices. Many happy days we had, preparing for and attending the meetings. We sang 'Come and join our Temperance Army,' 'Water, Sweet Cold Water,' &c. The annual meeting of the Cold Water Army was held at Tahlequah. Some of us had to ride the five miles from Park Hill in the slow clumsy ox-wagon, with the boxes and baskets of provisions for the dinner; while the more fortunate ones went in a four-mule wagon sent through the kindness of a wealthy neighbor, Mr. George M. Murrell, with a Negro driver, to carry thirty or forty children gathered in from the neighborhood. Those who rode behind big plodding old Pete and Broad had to start earlier than the others, though all were up and stirring by daylight to get ready. We had to bear it as well as we could to see the other party go dashing by us, singing and shouting, with a streamer twenty feet long flying, and other banners waving. That last, last, meeting, before the Civil War put a stop to all such things, was on July 4, 1860, after the death of its founder.

"On that day 125 children marched in line around the public square in Tahlequah. Every child carried a little banner with a printed device; the girls' banners white, the boys' pink, besides the twenty foot streamer at the head of the line with 'Cold Water Army' in large letters painted on it and many other banners of different devices and mottoes. The years had passed until I was no longer a child; two of my children marched in that company, and a third one, too small to keep up, was carried by her father alongside."

Pierce M. Butler, who was born in South Carolina in 1798, served in the Seventh Infantry at Fort Smith and Fort Gibson. He was made first lieutenant in March, 1822, and captain in 1825. On May 26, 1826, he was married to Miss Miranda Julia du Val at the home of E. W. du Val in Crawford County, Arkansas. In 1829, while in recruiting service in South Carolina, he resigned from the army and was elected cashier of the branch bank of that state. He served as governor of his native state from 1836 to 1838, and on September 17, 1841, he was appointed agent to the Cherokee Indians, when he took up his residence at Fort Gibson. He was intensely loyal to the Cherokee Indians and took a vigorous part in their controversies with the troops stationed at Fort Gibson. He very much desired reappointment, but in the shiftings of politics it was denied him. He was of that small class of intelligent Indian agents who were not only able but made it part of their business to write interesting descriptions of the Indians and their progress in the scale of civilization. The student of these Indians is under great obligations to agents such as Butler, Logan, Stokes, and others for much of what we know of those periods of Indian history.

In the spring of 1846, upon the termination of his service as Cherokee agent, Butler made a final report to Maj. William Armstrong, acting superintendent for the Western Territory, which contains some interesting observations on the tribe. He was greatly impressed by the progress of the Cherokee people as evidenced by "their change of sentiments relative to females, and the now high and exalted estimate of female character, disclosed by the countenance and encouragement given to her cultivation, and the many opportunities afforded her of improvement; being regarded no longer as a slave—as personal property —but as a friend and companion. This change in the condition of the women manifests itself in their manners, dress and general deportment. Under this head I take great pleasure in making mention of a school taught at the seat of government by Miss Mary Hoyt, a native Cherokee, and which will bear comparison with any institution of like character west of the Mississippi river. Miss Hoyt is the grand daughter of the venerable Major Lowrey, second chief of the nation. In acquirement, lady-like deportment and capacity for government, she has few if any superiors. . . . and wish that the impress of her own character may be made on the minds of her pupils.

"Temperance. . . . has been a God-send to the Cherokee nation. Its progress has been marked by a successful suppression of vice, and a happy subjugation of the turbulent and depraved passions. The number of members is, as will be seen, about 2,700—a larger proportion of the whole people than can be found in any other of equal extent of population. Private associations among themselves, of a similar character, produce a like effect, working, perhaps a more lasting and permanent reformation, from the fact that they pride themselves on their undeviating adherance to a promise, and their fidelity to this pledge. The saving influence of this society shows itself not only in the voluntary abstinance from the use of spirits, but also in their manifest demonstration of an intention to prevent its importation into their country. From my observation and acquaintance with the Indian Tribes, I am decidedly of opinion that all restrictive laws or arbitrary action by superior power is productive of evil consequences. . . . . The effect of the present law is to introduce by stealth, liquors of a bad quality, and at exhorbitant prices, whilst the consumption is induced by frolics in a spirit and temper in proportion to the efforts made to restrain the inclination. The experiment is now being made of allowing the sutlers to sell to the garrison, which I approve of, and believe will result in a correction of this evil."

Butler referred again to the advance of the Cherokee farmers who had many of the luxuries of life, neat farms, abundance of cleared lands, a good system of cultivation; they displayed great care and rivalry in the improvement of their cattle, horses, hogs, and sheep. The soil of the country was productive and yielded an ample support at little cost from which they enjoyed all the comforts and necessities of life. Many of the Cherokee men displayed great mechanical skill, and most of the farmers were able to stock their plows, helve their hoes, and make gates and doors to their dwellings. But the women contributed as much to their common welfare as the men. "They are fond of spinning and weaving and manifest great ingenuity in the manufacture of domestic cloth. . . . . It is a pleasing spectacle and a subject of great congratulations to the friends of these people, to witness, on a Sabbath, the father, mother, and children clad in the products of their own labor; the material is well manufactured, and in the selection, variety, and arrangement of the colors, they exhibit great taste and skill."

Butler paid a tribute to the Cherokee printing press which had been "chiefly instrumental in placing the Cherokees one half a century in advance of their late condition; providing an easy and cheap mode of diffusing instruction among the people, and stimulating them to further exertion and improvement. . . . . It is an object that cannot fail to strike the heart of the philanthropist with peculiar emotion to be in the neighborhood of the press on the day the paper is struck off, and witness the eagerness with which it is sought after, particularly by the more ignorant class who neither speak nor read the English language, but who acquire their own alphabet in twenty-four hours. Two or three of the Cherokee columns are occupied with portions of Peter Parley's Travels, which they read and enjoy with much zest."[2]

Governor Butler was succeeded as agent in 1846 by James McKissick, of Fayetteville, Arkansas, formerly of Tennessee; Butler was then entrusted with negotiations of a delicate nature with the western Indians.

McKissick died suddenly, January 13, 1848, in his office at the Cherokee agency seven miles east of Fort Gibson. Colonel Loomis, commanding at Fort Gibson, acted as agent in the interval, and a large number of Cherokee people signed a petition for the appointment of Marcellus du Val to fill the vacancy, but the president appointed Richard C. S. Brown from near Fort Smith, who arrived at his post in March, 1848, and served until the next year when he was removed. When Brown assumed the duties of the office he reported that the improvements at the agency, then located at Manard Bayou, consisted of four log cabins much in need of repair, about 600 yards from a fine spring, and that there was a frame house near by that had been erected by

2 *Cherokee Advocate*, April 2, 1846, p. 2, col. 1.

Berthelet & Heald for a storehouse and was occupied by John Waitie, the interpreter. There was also a farm of eighty acres in connection with the agency. He asked for authority to build new houses or to locate the agency elsewhere.

Dr. William Butler, of Greenville, South Carolina, brother of Pierce M. Butler, was appointed Cherokee agent May 30, 1849. He reached the agency with his family on December 7, of that year, after a journey of two months overland, the rivers being too low for navigation. Dr. Butler served as agent until September 24, 1850, when, after an illness of five weeks at the agency, he died at the age of sixty-one. Dr. Butler was a native of South Carolina and in the war of 1812 had served as a surgeon in the army.

Brigadier-general W. G. Belknap in command of the infantry at Fort Gibson, then acted as Cherokee agent until the appointment of George Butler, son of Dr. Butler, October 31, 1850. On July 5, 1851, Butler reported that, in accordance with instructions, he had sold the agency buildings for $250 and had located the new agency three miles northwest of Tahlequah in a high and healthful country.

OLLOWING the execution of the treaty in Washington in the summer of 1846 the delegates returned home—all but three —Ezekiel Starr, Capt. John Looney, and Capt. John Rogers, who succumbed to Washington life and died in May and June. When the Cherokee council met in October Chief Ross and Assistant Chief Lowrey not having returned, William Shorey Coodey acted as chief. The Cherokee people felt that a great burden had been lifted from their shoulders by execution of the new treaty, which put at rest many disturbing contentions that for years had kept the nation in a turmoil. They could now look forward to peace and renewed industry and progress. The superintendent of schools, James M. Payne, gave notice that "eight teachers of unexceptional moral character, and competent qualifications, are wanted to take charge of the Public Schools of the Nation."[1]

The Western Cherokee faction met at Tahlontuskee November 16 to confer about the claims they were entitled to make under the recent treaty. Capt. William Dutch presided, and a committee of five was appointed to draft the necessary resolutions.[2] A new feature in the lives of the Cherokee people was the successful introduction into the Nation of flour from the mills of James A. Scott on Cowskin River in Southwest Missouri. The year before he had sent at one time four flatboats laden with flour down the Cowskin, Grand, and Arkansas rivers all the way to Fort Smith. A few months later Jordan Wheeler also was shipping flour down the rivers from Missouri to Lewis Ross at the Grand Saline, to Fort Gibson and other points on the rivers.[3]

1 *Cherokee Advocate*, August 13, 1846, p. 3, col. 1.
2 OIA, Southern Superintendency, *Cherokee file* B 271.
3 *Arkansas Intelligencer*, March 28, and June 26, 1846. These same boats brought in whisky to make trouble for the Indians.

Chief John Ross, always the leader in movements for the advancement of his people and alert to discover opportunities to render them
service, had observed the effect of five years of common schools on the
youth of the Nation. He believed the time was ripe for the inauguration
of schools offering more advanced courses of study. Accordingly in
October 1846 he submitted to the National Council a message recommending legislation providing for the establishment of a male and a
female seminary. The Council thereupon on November 26 passed a
bill reciting that "Whereas, the improvement of the moral and intellectual condition of our people is contemplated by the Constitution, and
whereas, we are now in possession of means sufficient to carry out, to a
further degree of maturity, the National system of education already
commenced"; and directed that "two Seminaries or High Schools be
established, one for males, and the other for females."

The next spring the chief and executive council selected sites,
adopted plans, made contracts and later superintended the construction of the buildings for the schools, the female seminary near Park Hill,
and the male near Tahlequah. Cornerstones containing books, documents, and papers—records of Cherokee history—were prepared;
that of the first on June 21, 1847 and of the male seminary October 28
were laid by Chief Ross with appropriate ceremonies in the presence
of large gatherings of Cherokee people who were justly proud of this
new evidence of their progress.

The people of the Nation grieved over the death of their friend
Gov. Pierce M. Butler, who, at the head of his South Carolina command, the Palmetto Regiment, was killed at the battle of Churubusco,
Mexico, August 20. At the residence of her mother in Illinois District,
occurred the death from consumption October 18, of Mrs. Eliza
Martin, wife of Gabriel Martin, and daughter of Walter Webber. The
people are outraged by the "notorious villain Mat Guerring and Gang"
who broke into a home of some free mulatto and mixed-Cherokee-blood
people at Fort Gibson and kidnaped two girls. "In the presence of the
mother they tied the girls while in bed and carried them off to the
States."[4] This was the same Mat Guerring who had committed many

4 *Cherokee Advocate*, October 7, 1847. The Cherokee council on November 27,
1847, appropriated $23.00 to reimburse Charles Landrum and Pigeon Halfbreed for
expenses incurred in recovering two girls, granddaughters of Shoeboot, kidnapped
September 27 from the residence of their mother in Delaware District to be sold
into slavery (*Laws of the Cherokee Nation* [Tahlequah, 1852] p. 156).

crimes on the eastern line of the Cherokee Nation and had so far escaped the punishment he so richly deserved. But Tom Starr was arrested at Evansville, Arkansas, by Deputy United States Marshal Latta and taken to Van Buren, charged with the murder of an old Negro man in Crawford County.[5] Lieut. Cave J. Couts of the First Dragoons, "who has long been at Fort Gibson departs to join his regiment under Gen. John E. Wool in Mexico. Lieutenant Couts has made many friends at Fort Gibson and among the Cherokee people at Tahlequah and Park Hill who see him leave with much regret," of which notice is taken by the *Advocate*.[6] Charles Landrum, sheriff of Delaware District, had pursued Guerring and at Warsaw, Missouri, captured the two kid-naped mulatto girls who has been left there for sale, and had them home in time for the *Advocate* to relate the account on November 11.

J. M. Bryan of Beattie's Prairie is advertising for "Rackoon, Fox, Wildcat, Otter, and Opossum skins" which must be "stretched perfectly square and every particle of grease taken off. . . . . Deerskins should be stretched in the same way." Bryan offers in exchange fall and winter goods.[7] Early in December a boat is seen ascending the Arkansas River with twelve barrels of whisky belonging to whisky dealers near Fort Gibson. Tatnall H. Post, sheriff for Illinois District, intercepted the boat, smashed in the barrels and poured the whisky in the river.[8]

The Cherokee agent had ridden all morning and he was hungry. He rode his horse into one of the streams of clear water that are so numerous in the Cherokee Nation. While the horse drank his fill the agent looked about him in search of a habitation that he felt must be near this beautiful stream. Only the sweet note of a titmouse, the strident call of a flicker and the noisy gurgle of his horse as he refreshed himself from the stream broke the silence. Then he heard in the distance a familiar sound that told him he was near food and refreshment. He guided his horse up the bank and through the woods where he saw a comfortable log house whence issued the sound he had heard—the hum of a spinning wheel and the smack of a loom. Mother and daughter were at home spinning and weaving. This audible evi-

5   *Cherokee Advocate*, November 4, 1847.
6   *Ibid.*
7   *Ibid.*, November 18, 1847.
8   *Ibid.*, December 9.

dence of industry was common throughout the Cherokee country. The Indians were "generally industrious," said the agent, "and very neat in their household affairs. You generally find them neatly and fashionably dressed in home-made clothes of their own manufacturing; in passing through the country, the wheel and loom are frequently the first sounds that greet the ear. On your arrival at their houses, the neatness and taste they display in the selection of colors, and the manufacturing of the cloth, is not to be surpassed in any part of the government." He said that the tribe was prospering in spite of the fact that the people had not yet forgotten the contention that had made so much trouble for them; and that they were as capable of managing their affairs as most people are in a new state or territorial government.[9]

Contracts for the construction of the seminaries have been let; carpenters' and joiners' work went to Brown and McCoy.[10] "Died at the residence of his son Mr. David Hilderbrand, near this place, on the 20th inst., at 11 P. M., Mr. John Hilderbrand, one of the oldest men in the nation. Mr. Hilderbrand was a native of Pennsylvania, of German extraction, and was born on the 12th of February, 1755, and was consequently, aged at the time of his death, 92 years, 10 months, and 8 days. He came among the Cherokees east of the Mississippi, more than fifty years ago, among whom he intermarried. He retained a remarkable degree of activity up to within a short time of his death. He left more than 100 lineal descendants, a majoriy of whom are residing among the Cherokees."[11]

Capt. Enoch Steen of the First Dragoons, has arrived at Fort Gibson. He is one of the heroes of Buena Vista and bears a serious wound from that engagement, from which he has not recovered.[12] The Old Settlers held a council in Skin Bayou District and selected Capt. William Dutch and John L. McCoy as delegates to Washington to secure the money due them under the recent treaty.[13] On December 14, at Beattie's Prairie, the Rev. Cephas Washburn married John A. Bell to Mrs.

9 Brown to Rutherford October 10, 1848: *Report* of commissioner of Indian affairs, 1848.
10 *Cherokee Advocate*, December 9, 1847.
11 Ibid., December 23, 1847, p. 2, col. 2.
12 *Fort Smith Herald*, December 29, 1847.
13 Ibid.

Sabra Buffington.[14] A Cherokee man who had been to Maysville, Arkansas, returning home, drunk, of course, froze to death on Beattie's Prairie.[15] The remains of the Cherokee agent, James McKissick, are to be taken to Fayetteville and laid beside those of Colonel Yell.[16]

W. P. Ross, editor of the *Advocate*, is away from his post in February and his place is taken by D. H. Ross. J. D. Willison is advertising for sale his improvements in the Cherokee Nation: 125 acres of land cleared and under good fence, with dwelling and other buildings on the "road leading from Fort Gibson to the Verdigris landing about three miles from the former and one mile from the latter place."[17] J. and W. T. Mackay and Company are advertising that they have purchased the saline operated by Daniel R. Coodey in Illinois District, and that they have on hand a large amount of salt that they will exchange at the rate of fifty cents a bushel for warrants or national tickets.[18] James M. Payne, agent of salines, advertises that he will lease four public salines; one operated by Lewis Rogers in Delaware District, one operated by David Vann near James McNair's, one operated by William Rogers, the two latter in Saline District, and one occupied by Akey Smith, generally known as Webber's Salt Works in Illinois District.[19] Bois d'arc seed is quoted at $20.00 a bushel in Fort Smith. Tom Starr has secured a change of venue from Van Buren to Johnson County, Arkansas.

Directly after his appointment as Cherokee agent, Richard C. S. Brown contracts with James A. Hart, of the Cherokee Nation, to make seventy-five spinning wheels for the Cherokee people for the sum of $300.00. Similar contracts were made with John Drew and Robert Rungon.[20] The editor of the *Advocate* saw a huge panther twelve miles from Tahlequah on the road to Fort Gibson.[21] Because of high waters in March and April the mail carrier was unable to reach Tahlequah for some weeks. John Meigs is erecting a neat hewed log store building in Tahlequah adjoining the *Advocate* printing office.[22] There

14 *Ibid.*
15 *Cherokee Advocate*, January 6, 1848, p. 2, col. 6.
16 *Ibid.*, January 17, 1848.
17 *Ibid.*, February 14, 1848.
18 *Ibid.*, January 24, 1848.
19 *Ibid.*, February 21, 1848.
20 OIA, Incoming letters.
21 *Cherokee Advocate*, April 3, 1848.
22 *Ibid.*

is much complaint of the introduction of whisky by boats coming from Cowskin River in Missouri down the Grand River.[23] Tom Starr and Michael Doolin broke jail in Clarksville and made their escape.[24] At last comes the welcome news that "Mat Guerrin, the notorious land pirate, was killed in Flint District, last Friday night.[25] He, Ellis Starr, and Washington Starr were killed by two United States deputy marshals, Smith and Latta, and a number of Cherokee while the latter were attempting to arrest them for a "number of atrocious murders, robberies and other crimes committed by them and others of their band."[26] "The Arkansas is now in fine boating order. Several boats have come up to Fort Gibson during the last few days."[27]

In July D. H. Ross retires as editor of the *Advocate* as W. P. Ross assumed charge.[28] The governor of Arkansas offers a reward of $400 for the arrest of Tom Starr and Michael Doolin.[29] Moses Daniel, a prominent Cherokee, is dead.[30] An enthusiastic meeting of the Cold Water Army at Tahlequah, and a Methodist camp meeting on Fourteen Mile Creek are noted in July. Foreman and Reese have just opened a new stock of goods in Tahlequah. A meeting has been called in Tahlequah to discuss the construction of a road from Fort Gibson and Tahlequah to the Arkansas line to interesect the Van Buren and Fayetteville stage line.[31]

At a horse race in Skin Bayou District, George W. Fields, former sheriff of Illinois District, was killed by Martin Benge on August 31.[32] It was thought the killing of Ellis and Washington Starr since the amnesty of 1846 was involved in the murder of Fields. Benge was tried in November and acquitted. Excitement caused by the Gold Rush enters much into public affairs and discussion at this time. Controversy over the subject of slavery and emancipation among the In-

23 *Ibid.*, 100 gallons of "cowskin whisky" was emptied from a boat by the sheriff of Saline District (*ibid.*, May 22) May 1.
24 *Ibid.*, May 29, 1848.
25 *Ibid.*, June 5, 1848.
26 *Ibid.*, June 12, 1848.
27 *Ibid.*, June 5, 1848.
28 *Ibid.*, July 10, 1848.
29 *Ibid.*, July 3, 1848.
30 *Ibid.*
31 *Ibid.*, July 31, 1848.
32 *Ibid.*, September 11, 1848.

dians engaged the attention of some of the missionaries and occupied considerable space in the newspapers. The Cherokee council and the supreme court began their sessions October 2. The council was opened by the message of Maj. George Lowrey, acting chief. Captain Dutch was reported too ill to attend. George W. Gunter of the Cherokee Nation has raised some excellent upland rice on his farm a few miles above Fort Smith.

"The little log cabins situated on the north and south sides of the Public square in which the council and Committee formerly held their sessions have been sold by order of the Committee and are about to be removed. The large shed in the center of the Square, which is not without its interesting associations as marking the spot where the Constitution of the Nation was adopted, and where the general council of the Indian tribes was held, has met with a similar fate and will soon be converted into fire wood, horse stables or some ignoble use."[33] The national council has granted a license, the first in its history, to Landrum and Blackstone of Beattie's Prairie to operate a lead mine for five years on Spavinaw Creek in Delaware District.[34]

Clement V. McNair and William P. Ross are appointed delegates to Washington. Ross resigns as editor of the *Advocate* and is succeeded by James S. Vann.[35] Capt. William Dutch died November 14 at his home on the Canadian River. He was a famous warrior against the Osage Indians. "During an interval of peace and amity, for some slight offense or natural disposition to rove, he left his home and country, and became for a number of years a resident among the Osages. Having taken a wife among them, he became identified with all their interests; joining in all their predatory excursions against the other tribes of the prairies.

"His Osage wife for some offense was put to death by her people; from that moment his feelings and ties of friendship for the Osages were broken, and turned into the most implacable hatred, and desire for revenge. It was during this time, when avenging his private wrongs, that some of his most daring feats of bravery were performed. The number of Osage that fell by his hand and scalps taken, were not precisely known, not even by himself." When asked "he held in his

33 *Ibid.*, November 6, 1848.
34 *Ibid.*
35 *Ibid.*, November 13, 1848.

hand an hair rope ten or twelve feet long, holding up and shaking the rope, intimated that the hair of the scalps taken would have made a rope like that. His name at that time was a very terror to the Osages. The report of a gun in their vicinity, would fill them with fear, and they would fly to their arms, crying,'Dutch! Dutch! Dutch!'

"At the time of his death he was a member of the Cherokee National Council and was, we believe, the most influential man among the 'western' or 'old settler' Cherokees. He had rendered them essential service in their councils, represented their interests as a delegate to Washington, and other important services, to the entire satisfaction of his countrymen. His martial deeds were the most brilliant portion of his life—his hawk-like and flashing eye seemed to bespeak his martial spirit."[36]

The Old Settlers or Western Cherokee met in council at the mouth of Illinois River December 4. It was extremely cold, but so important was their business that 200 were upon the ground. They met to promote some plan to secure from the Government the money promised by the treaty more than two years before, and of which the Indians are in great need. A committee of twenty-four was chosen by the people in attendance, and William Shorey Coodey and John Drew were selected as delegates to go to Washington in an effort to secure the money promised them. The delay was characteristic of the dealings of the Government with the Indians.

The intense cold made it possible to slaughter game birds in the country with little trouble. Flocks of thousands of grouse were seen near Tahlequah scarce able to fly for the cold. Schrimsher and Gunter netted 250 of these birds in two days time, and on another day caught 133. The continued cold delayed the departure of the delegates to Washington. The Arkansas and Grand rivers above Fort Gibson were still frozen in January so that horses could be taken across on the ice. Three Cherokee people were frozen to death. A Creek woman near Fort Gibson was delivered of twin girls with no one near but a blind sister.

36 Ibid., November 27, 1848. For further accounts of Dutch see Grant Foreman, Indians and Pioneers. Ten years before while the Mexicans were trying to involve the immigrant Indians in their intrigues, Dutch was invited to enlist in the war against Texas but he refused to have anything to do with it (Arbuckle to adjutant general May 11, 1838, AGO, ORD, headquarters Second Department, Western Division, Fort Gibson, Book 111).

The mother and one child perished with the cold, but the other child survived. Work on the seminaries was practically suspended by the weather.[37]

In spite of the cold, however, a meeting of the citizens was "held at the court house Tuesday evening, December 26th, at early candle light, to discuss building a Methodist church in Tahlequah."[38] "Our village is making rapid strides in improvement. Another store-house has just been completed and well filled with a handsome stock of goods by our enterprising townsman, Johnson Thompson. We have in the town of Tahlequah, five hotels, five stores, two smith shops, a tailor shop, and a fair prospect of an increase of the assortment."[39]

The gold fever was taking hold of a number of people in the Cherokee nation. Meetings were being held in Tahlequah where plans were discussed for organizing an emigrant party to California. J. S. Vann, editor of the *Advocate*, was one of the leaders of the movement. He and Daniel M. Gunter advertised the enterprise and invited others to join. R. J. Meigs advertised for sale his "valuable farm and residence at Park Hill."[40] Lewis Ross advertised for sale several hundred bushels of salt at the Grand Saline at fifty cents a bushel. Joseph Vann, agent for the Cherokee Nation, gave notice that on March 15 he would sell to the highest bidder the saline lately occupied by Lewis Ross.[41] Word was received of the death of Henrietta J. Coodey, daughter of William Shorey Coodey, at Ellicott's Mills, Maryland, January 28. She had just been to Washington to see her father who was ill.[42] Temperance society meetings were being held all over the Cherokee Nation.

Chief John Ross was going into the mercantile business. He had been so occupied with the public affairs of his nation that he had

37 *Cherokee Advocate*, December 18, 1848; *Fort Smith Herald*, January 3, 1849. Rev. S. A. Worcester's report is released, giving an account of the mission work in his charge. His printing press at Park Hill has printed 1,376,000 pages of books and tracts during the year. Six of these books in 24to editions of 4,000 each, were in Cherokee as was the thirty-six page 12 mo. *Cherokee Almanac* for 1848. A forty-eight page book of temperance songs in 24to numbering 3,500 and 300 copies of Cherokee laws 12mo and 107 pages were printed in English.

38 *Cherokee Advocate*, December 18, 1848.

39 *Ibid.*, January 8, 1849.

40 *Ibid.*, January 15, 1849.

41 *Ibid.*, February 19, 1849.

42 *Ibid.*, April 9, 1849.

neglected his personal fortunes. He purchased the store building of R. J. Meigs at Park Hill, and opened a well assorted stock of dry goods and groceries. Here, he said, he was prepared to furnish all the necessaries of life and California emigrants could secure many articles for their outfits.[43] The brick work on the Cherokee seminaries was completed the first of April. The contractor, Mr. Mahoney, had been paid, but he had neglected to pay the laborers who worked for him and there was much complaint.[44] The unwelcome news was received that Congress had appropriated $20,000 for the completion of Fort Gibson. The Cherokee people would much rather have seen the post abandoned.[45]

Mrs. Martin, widow of the late Judge John Martin, went to Fayetteville, Arkansas, to visit her youngest daughter and several grand daughters who were students at Miss Sophia Sawyer's seminary, so popular with the Cherokee people. News had just been received that while there she contracted pneumonia and after an illness of a week, died on March 14 at the age of 56.[46] The California fever was growing in interest. Word was received that more than 400 wagons bound for California had passed the Choctaw agency in a week.[47] James Vann, editor of the *Advocate* could not longer resist. He abandoned the paper and joined an emigrant party to California. David Carter took his place as editor.[48] An impromptu California emigrant was on the way. John Rollin Ridge was reported to have killed Judge D. Kell of Beattie's Prairie and escaped. He was said to have started to California.[49] Martin Benge and Cucumber Jack, who killed George Fields, surrendered.

Gloom rests on the land from the news just received that William Shorey Coodey is dead in Washington. This distinguished public servant of his nation died on Sunday, April 16, 1849, at the age of 43. It was he who wrote the act of union under which the factions of the tribe reorganized the government of the Cherokee Nation after their emigration. He was given a distinguished funeral in Washington; a

43 *Ibid.*, February 19, 1849, p. 2, col. 1.
44 *Ibid.*, April 2, 1849.
45 *Fort Smith Herald*, March 21, 1849.
46 *Ibid.*, March 28, p. 3, col. 2.
47 *Ibid.*, April 25, p. 2, col. 1.
48 *Ibid.*, May 23.
49 *Cherokee Advocate*, May 21, 1849.

procession headed by the United States Marine Band conducted his body to the Congressional cemetery. The local and eastern papers contain extended accounts of his life and work. A post office has just been established at Grand Saline, which will receive mail from Tahlequah once a week.[50] Another Cherokee veteran has passed away; George Fields died at his residence on April 14 at the age of more than eighty. During the Creek war he fought under Andrew Jackson and distinguished himself for bravery. He was wounded in one of the battles and received a pension from the United States.[51]

Maj. George M. Murrell has just received a large consignment of new goods for his store at Tahlequah. He advertises "a new supply of spring, summer, and fall goods—new and fashionable prints, callicoes, check Stripes, Ginghams, Muslins, robes, silks, etc. Neatest and best summer wear for Gents, blue, brown, black and gray summer cloth, suitable for pants, &c. A superb lot of Gents and Ladies saddles and bridles, boots, shoes, &c. And a great many other articles too tedious to mention. All adapted for the town and country."[52]

News has been received of a daring attempt to kill and rob the Cherokee agent, Richard S. C. Brown. Just before daylight on June 6 the robbers broke into his house and struck him with an axe, but neighbors came to his rescue and frightened the bandits away. The agent had in his possession $18,000 to be paid out to the Indians and that fact was doubtless known to the assailants. Two suspected Cherokee have been released as indications point to two discharged soldiers and a Negro now in custody.[53]

A significant event is that of the organization of the first Masonic lodge among an Indian tribe. The ceremony took place in the courthouse in Tahlequah July 12. The introductory prayer was delivered by Rev.

50 *Ibid.*, May 12, 1849.
51 *Fort Smith Herald*, May 23, 1849, p. 2, col. 1.
52 *Cherokee Advocate*, June 25, 1849, p. 2, col. 1.
53 *Ibid.* The next summer four Cherokee Indians boarded the steamboat *General Shields*, stranded on the Cherokee side of the Arkansas River about nine miles above Fort Smith, and, "after attempting to murder two men on board of the boat who fortunately escaped alive but severely wounded, they robbed the boat of almost every thing they could carry off conveniently, carrying off all the bedding, clothing, etc., and one rifle, brass mounted and new, and three carbines. They broke open a safe taking out some money and several trunks carrying off valuable clothing, good coats, etc." (AGO, ORD, Fort Smith *letter book* p. 9, August 27, 1850).!

Thomas Bertholf and the installation of officers was conducted by officials from Arkansas. The officers elected were W. S. Adair, W. M.; N. B. Dannenberg, S. W.; Joseph Coodey, J. W.; T. W. Emerson, S. D.; W. L. Holt, J. D.; David Carter, treasurer, and William P. Ross, secretary.[54] On October 30, 1852, the Cherokee council donated to the Cherokee Lodge of Masons and the division of the Sons of Temperance two lots in the town of Tahlequah on which to erect a lodge building within two years from that date.[55] Many of the Cherokee were Masons.

A correspondent for the *Fort Smith Herald* thinks our little village of Tahlequah "is a quiet and orderly place, though rather dull in the way of business. Here are four stores, one saddler's shop, a tailor's shop, three blacksmiths' shops, a shoemaker's shop, and three taverns. I am well pleased with the people, as they are moral, industrious, and given to hospitality. The editor (David Carter) is a fine specimen of an enlightened Cherokee gentleman. . . . about forty years old. He commenced life a poor orphan boy; he has a fine plantation two miles from here, black with darkies."[56] The people of Arkansas are trying to get our citizens interested in road building so as to facilitate our neighbors' emigration to California. A road meeting has just been held at the home of David Vann on Sallisaw Creek to plan the construction of a road from Van Buren by way of the North Fork of the Canadian River to Little River. It was resolved that citizens of Van Buren and of the Cherokee Nation unite in the constuction of this road and that the Creeks be invited to coöperate.[57] Another road enthusiast visits Tahlequah on August 3 and endeavors to interest the citizens in building a road from that place to the "line" or stage road north of Fort Smith.[58]

Cholera at Fort Gibson has caused some alarm. The captain of the steamboat *Swallow* reported that when his boat left the post there had been 100 cases and twelve deaths.[59] Fortunately, the cases have yielded to treatment and are subsiding.

54   *Cherokee Advocate*, July 16, 1849; *Fort Smith Herald*, August 22, 1849.
55   *Laws of the Cherokee Nation* (edition of 1868, St. Louis), p. 92.
56   *Fort Smith Herald*, July 18, 1849, p. 2, col. 3. He was grandfather of the late Charles Carter member of Congress from Oklahoma.
57   *Ibid.*
58   *Ibid.*, August 2, 1849.
59   *Ibid.*, August 6, 1849, p. 2, col. 1. Soon there were 172 cases in the Fifth Infantry at the post and seventeen deaths (*ibid.*, August 20, 1849, p. 2, col. 1).

Another indication of progress in the neighborhood is the establish-ment of a sawmill on Park Hill Creek near the entrance to Illinois River, by William P. and D. H. Ross. They are offering thirty-seven 1-2 cents each for 1,000 or more logs twenty inches in diameter delivered at the mill. They will also pay liberally for cherry and walnut logs.[60] The famous oil springs fifteen miles from Tahlequah are attracting attention. It is said they will cure liver complaint, gout, rheumatism, general debility and other ailments. Mrs. Susannah Ridge, widow of the slain Major Ridge, has died at the age of eighty years on Honey Creek September 1.[61] Fall sports are now in order. James Kell, proprietor of the Leon race course on Beattie's Prairie, is advertising a sweepstake race for three year olds past, on Tuesday, November 27; the entrance fee will be $100.

More serious matters are occupying the attention of the leading men of the Nation. The National council had adopted a resolution to call the whole Cherokee people together Monday, November 7, to decide upon a plan or adopt some measure to relieve the Cherokee Nation of its public debt.[62] In response to this resolution Chief Ross issued a proclamation calling the people together to consider and act on the subject.[63] The annual meeting of the Cherokee Temperance Society was well attended. Practically all the officers of the National govern-ment and most of the leading men of the Nation belong to it. Reports were made of many interesting meetings all over the Cherokee Nation, during the past year. Josiah Reese, sheriff of Canadian District, alone destroyed forty-eight barrels of whisky during the year.[64]

The new year of 1850 was ushered in with scenes of rioting and murder induced by the introduction of whisky. A number of persons went to the home of Jack Thompson in the Cherokee Nation about a mile from Fort Smith on Christmas night and killed Bluford Rider and Sam Brewer, and stabbed Wiley Thompson, brother of Jack, and Mrs. Thompson. Nah-che-yah, of Flint District, was killed. Randolph Rogers killed a Negro, and Partridge, of Flint District, was killed. Some mis-creant fired the residence of John Drew, three miles from Fort Gibson,

60 *Cherokee Advocate*, August 20, 1849, p. 3, col. 5.
61 *Ibid.*, September 3, 1849, p. 3, col. 4.
62 *Ibid.*, October 22, 1849, p. 2, col. 1.
63 *Ibid.*, October 29, p. 2, col. 2.
64 *Ibid.*, November 5, 1849.

and it was entirely consumed with everything in the house.[65] Eleven men were put on trial in Skin Bayou District January 15 for the killing of Rider and Brewer.

The fifth anniversary of the Flint District Auxiliary Temperance Society is fittingly observed at Fairfield Mission July 12; an interesting program is rendered.[66] Many people of the Cherokee Nation are grieving over the death of Miss Ellen Stetson at Dwight Mission; she served long years there and instructed many of the Cherokee people when they were children.[67] The examination of the pupils at the end of the term of school at Riley's Chapel on August 2 is largely attended by the parents and other friends of the students. The long and interesting program includes the reading of a newspaper in manuscript published by the pupils in imitation of the printed papers that had come into their hands.[68] William P. and D. H. Ross of Tahlequah have added to their sawmill equipment for making flour and they are now advertising for wheat. This promises to contribute to the comfort of the people of the nation and make a market for their wheat.

There has been another fight between some of the Cherokee across the river from Fort Smith, caused, as usual, by the use of Fort Smith whisky. Charles Tikaneesky killed Moses Vickory with a knife. On Sunday Richard Blackburn came in the neighborhood looking for some cattle. Columbus Vickory tried to kill him with a shotgun; Blackburn took it away from him; they closed with each other with their knives and Blackburn finally killed Vickory. The feud between the Thompsons and Vickorys has continued until there is not a male member of either family left.[69]

The Cherokee council opened October 9 and Chief John Ross, relieved of the duties that kept him so much of the time in Washington, is on hand to deliver his message. The assemblage was graced by General Belknap and lady and others of Fort Gibson, who were introduced to the council. General Belknap is now acting Cherokee agent to supply the vacancy caused by the death of Dr. William Butler.[70]

65 *Fort Smith Herald*, January 5, 1850, p. 2, col. 2; *Cherokee Advocate*, January 7, 1850, p. 2, col. 1.
66 *Cherokee Advocate*, July 30, 1850, p. 2, col. 2.
67 *Ibid.*
68 *Ibid.*, August 6, 1850, p. 2, col. 1.
69 *Fort Smith Herald*, July 20, 1850, p. 2, col. 3.
70 *Cherokee Advocate*, October 12, 1850, p. 2, col. 1.

It has been a dry summer and autumn and the streams have little water in them. A Cherokee came into town and said Grand River is so low that a duck could walk across it without getting its feet wet; that there is no water in the Arkansas. He has seen, so he said, the turtles dragging the catfish over the bars to the pools further down; the catfish lying on the bars with their mouths open gasping for water—the turtles thrust their tails into the mouths of the fish, which close on the tails, and they drag them into the water.[71]

Rev. Lewis Downing preached a sermon in Cherokee at the court-house in Tahlequah on January 12.[72] Dannenburg and Harnage are merchants at Flint. The firm of John Ross & Company is dissolved and the business will be continued by William P. and D. H. Ross.[73] Denkla and Woodward are advertising their clothing store at Flint; they will take beef hides, bees wax, tallow, corn, corn meal and produce generally. Murrell's cheap store at Tahlequah wishes to buy corn, dried beef, hides, deer, wolf, coon, fox, and wild cat hides, bees wax, tallow and pecans.[74] J. T. Mays is advertising that he will run his stallion, Bill Coodey, against any horse in the Cherokee Nation from one mile to four with equal riders on each, for $250 in cash.[75] John W. Stapler & Company are now established across the street from the *Advocate* office. S. Foreman & Company and Mr. Wells will open their stores soon. "We have eight stores in our little town and three others in embryo."[76] The dentists, Dr. W. J. Grant and Dr. R. S. C. Noel, are advertising in the *Advocate*, besides James S. Vann, attorney-at-law.[77] An innovation in the country has caused considerable interest: "post-office stamps" have been received here, and our merchants have offered to take them "at cash rates" in payment for goods, as currency is scarce.[78]

71 *Fort Smith Herald*, October 11, 1850, p. 2, col. 4.
72 *Cherokee Advocate*, January 14, 1851, p. 2, col. 1.
73 *Ibid.*, February 11, 1851, p. 3, col. 6.
74 *Ibid.*
75 *Ibid.*
76 *Ibid.*, July 29, 1851, p. 2, col. 1.
77 *Ibid.*
78 *Ibid.*, September 30, 1851, p. 2, col. 3.

CHAPTER THIRTY-ONE / *Approaching the Civil War*

T HERE was great rejoicing in the Cherokee Nation in the spring of 1852. Word had gone out for the citizens to assemble at Fort Gibson and receive the per capita payment of the moneys promised them by the Treaty of 1846 after nearly six years of procrastination characteristic of the Government's dealing with the Indians. John Drennan, superintendent of Indian affairs for the southern superintendency, had paid the Old Settlers in the preceding autumn and then went to New Orleans to secure funds for the eastern or emigrant Cherokee people. He was obliged to remain in the city several weeks waiting for the currency to be minted; a tedious journey, delayed by low water in the rivers, brought him to Van Buren in February and after the rolls[1] were completed he secured a force of troops to guard the money to Fort Gibson where the payment began on April 5. There were many Indians present, besides many merchants, hucksters, and purveyors of all sorts of pastries, sweets, and trifles to lure the Indians' money from them. It required a month to complete the payment to all who came to the post; under the protection of the troops there it was possible to prevent the introduction of whisky among those camped on the reservation.[2] There was a large amount of money now in circulation in the Cherokee Nation, but it was soon spent and only a small part of it did any permanent good. Abundant crops this year added to the opulence of the Cherokee people. Naturally the flow of whisky continued and the friends of temperance redoubled their efforts. The Sons of Temperance

1 The rolls showed a total of 17,530 Cherokee living in the west.
2 *Report* of commissioner of Indian affairs for 1852.

held a largely attended meeting at Tahlequah, where speeches were made by members in English and Cherokee.

The time had now come when it was proper and necessary to give the growing town of Tahlequah corporate capacity. It had been laid off into town lots by authority of an act of the Cherokee council of October 28, 1843; on October 30, 1852, a measure was enacted incorporating the inhabitants therein under the name of the "Alderman and Town Council of the Town of Tahlequah," with the ordinary powers and duties of a municipality. The construction of a jail at Tahlequah was being agitated against much opposition. Prisoners were held in the custody of guards who were paid fifty cents a day for their services; as there were many so employed to detain the numerous prisoners in the Nation, they and their friends who enjoyed the prosperity that accrued from this system had been able to defeat the construction of the jail for a long time. The enforcement of the criminal laws had nearly bankrupted the nation; one recent trial alone had cost more than $2,000.

The great ambition of the progressive Cherokee people after long delay was realized in the opening of their two advanced schools. These two large brick and stone buildings represented an investment of tribal funds of about $80,000. It was planned to open them in October, 1850, but as the buildings were unfinished at that time and the furniture had not been delivered, it was impossible to do so. Finally on May 6, 1851, the exercises attending the opening of the Male Seminary were held; they were of absorbing interest and were attended by a large concourse of proud Cherokee people. Twenty-seven students were admitted on the opening of the school for the regular four-year course, and in February next, twenty-five more. The studies taught there included geography, history, arithmetic, algebra, English grammar, composition, elocution, and French, Latin, and Greek languages.

To make the season full to overflowing with proud Indian achievement, the Female Seminary was opened the next day with similar pomp and ceremony. William P. Ross and David Vann, then members of the Cherokee delegation in Washington, had been authorized to proceed to New England and employ teachers for the schools. They went to Mount Holyoke College, whence came many teachers of the Indians; there they employed Miss Ellen R. Whitmore and Miss

Sarah Worcester, graduates of the school who became principal and assistant respectively of the new Female Seminary. They engaged also Rev. Thomas B. Van Horne of the Theological Seminary at Newton near Boston, and from the senior class of Yale College employed Mr. O. L. Woodford of Connecticut. They then accompanied the two Mount Holyoke graduates on the long hazardous journey to the Indian country. Sarah Worcester was a daughter of Rev. S. A. Worcester of Park Hill. Rev. Dr. Elizur Butler was the first steward or manager of the Female Seminary. These two schools were governed by a board composed of Chief John Ross, ex-officio president, David Vann, William Shorey Coodey, James M. Payne, and William P. Ross. Later as vacancies occurred on the board, H. D. Reese, John Thorn, David Carter, and Riley Keys were appointed and confirmed by the National Committee, later called the Senate. Each school was planned to accommodate 50 pupils.

"The school opened with twenty-five young ladies, the Flower of the Cherokee Nation as pupils," related the venerable Hannah Hitchcock many years later of the Female Seminary. "Ever after, the seventh of May was celebrated in commemoration of that happy day. One anniversary which I particularly remember—the large hall and the Parlor were beautifully decorated; and fragrant with perfume from great bunches of the lovely wild Pink Azalea or Bush Honeysuckle. The Military Band from Fort Gibson was on hand that day through the courtesy of General Belknap, post commander at that time. The exercises of the day included a most entertaining performance—the crowning a May Queen, Miss Josephine Dannenberg, who will be remembered by some as Mrs. Remus who died in Tahlequah not many years ago. It was a beautiful ceremony: distant music was heard, and as the sound came near a troop of young ladies appeared all in lovely light dresses, escorting their queen, singing as they marched and gathered round the throne—a bower of vines and flowers; and the maid of honor placed the crown of lovely roses on her head. In the afternoon when the exercises in the house were over, the band stationed themselves out in the shady Blackjack woods back of the building, and the company, ladies and gentlemen in pairs, promenaded round and round to the music of the Band to their hearts content." Besides primary English branches, history, botany, algebra and Latin were taught in the girls' school. Vocal music received much attention also. There were fifty pupils in attendance the second year; thus both schools were filled to the capacity fixed by law.

The people were proud of their schools and school system, and the number of uneducated was rapidly diminishing. The Cherokee Nation had a better common school system than either Arkansas or Missouri. At this time there were 1,100 pupils attending twenty-one common schools,[3] of whom 677 were boys and 423 girls. There were, in addition, 114 orphans who were cared for out of the orphan fund, but who attended the common schools. Later, a separate school was established for the orphans. Of those attending the common schools, 149 were "A-B-C-darians," 435 studied reading and spelling exclusively, 149 geography, 163 geography and atlas, 272 oral arithmetic, 192 written arithmetic, 225 English grammar, and 345 writing.[4]

This was a happy and prosperous year for the Cherokee, though there was a good deal of sickness caused by a wet spring and summer; during the preceding winter the Nation had been ravaged by smallpox that carried off many people. There were numbers of deaths from pneumonia, and chills and fever took their toll of strength and energy. "Many of the full-blood Cherokees yet have great aversion to the medicine of the regular faculty, and prefer the roots and herbs of their own native doctors. The more enlightened portion are fast losing that prejudice, and always call in a regular physician when one can be had; and it affords me much pleasure to be able to state that they have among them several physicians of high reputation in their profession, both whites and natives.

"The Cherokees have great reason to be thankful for the abundant yield with which the earth has repaid the labor of the husbandman. The common people are making slow but steady advances in the science of agriculture; the more enlightened and intelligent portion who have means live much in the same style of the southern gentleman of easy circumstances. Many of the dwellings of that class are large, comfortable, and handsome buildings; their fields, too, are well en-

3 The schools were held in substantial hewn log houses, with glass windows, fireplaces or stoves. They were neat and comfortable, provided with desks, benches, and black-boards. The teachers, many of whom were natives, were paid $33.33 a month.

4 *Report* of commissioner of Indian affairs for 1852, *Report* of superintendent of schools.

closed with good rail fences, and their yards and gardens are hand-somely paled in, and the grounds tastefully laid off and ornamented with rare and beautiful shrubbery. The moral influence which is being brought to bear upon the youth of the country, through the indefatigable efforts of the principal chief, and other intelligent and leading men of the nation, in the great cause of education, must tell powerfully upon the rising generation.

"The common schools of the nation were never in a more prosperous condition, and the exercises of the past year in the male and female seminaries have given entire satisfaction to the parents of the students and to the friends of education throughout the nation. Many of the Cherokee women are neat and industrious housewives, and have acquired many of the finer accomplishments of the whites. Some of them are accomplished needle women; their taste and skill in embroidery may be seen at the Crystal Palace in New York, where has been sent for exhibition a full Indian suit of dressed buckskin, beautifully embroidered with silk. This beautiful piece of work was designed and executed by the ladies in the family of Mr. J. M. Payne. The art of manufacturing cloth, both wool and cotton, is carried on to a considerable extent in some families. Some specimens which I have seen from the looms of Mrs. W. A. Adair would hold strong competition for prizes at any of the agricultural fairs of the States."[5]

The responsible men of the Cherokee Nation were becoming greatly concerned about the public debt. Many of them, including the editor of the *Advocate*, favored laying a tax on the people and a bill for that purpose was introduced in the National council, but defeated. The average citizen was opposed to it and advocated the sale of their "neutral lands" of 800,000 acres in Kansas Territory, which they believed would raise sufficient funds to pay all the debts and would finance their public enterprises that up to now were paid for out of the annuities due from the Government. The people were worried also by agitation in Congress to establish the "Territory of Nebraska," which would incorporate some of their lands.[6] The cause of temperance was now promoted by three organizations, The Sons of Temperance with five divisions, numbering 302 members, the Cherokee Cold Water

5 George Butler, Cherokee agent, to Thomas S. Drew, September 13, 1853: *Report* of commissioner of Indian affairs for 1853.
6 *Ibid.*

Army with 150 members, and the Cherokee Temperance Society with more than 2,000.

In addition to the schools belonging to the Cherokee Nation there were many under the supervision of the missions of the various church organizations. The Moravians, Baptists, Methodists, and Presbyterians each conducted a number of schools. The latter at Park Hill continued to operate a printing press where every year was produced a large output of material for the education and elevation of the Cherokee people. In 1854 Dr. S. A. Worcester reported that during the year his press had printed 756,000 pages; consisting of part of the *Book of Exodus,* the *Cherokee Almanac* for 1854, and a new edition of the *Cherokee Primer, Cherokee Hymn-Book,* and a part of the *Gospel of John,* all in the Cherokee language, but half of the *Almanac* was in English. He reported also the completion of a church at Park Hill, constructed of brick, fifty by fifty feet with a portico of ten feet, and a seating capacity of 400. The Presbyterians had five branches, at Dwight, Fairfield, Park Hill, Honey Creek, and Lees Creek. The Methodists had six missions with a membership of 1,379. The Baptists maintained at their mission near the Arkansas line a press on which in 1854 were printed a large number of extracts from the Scriptures, translated from the English into Cherokee by John Butrick Jones. The Baptists had six churches and four branches with 1,200 members, mostly full-bloods; there were five hewn log meeting-houses erected by the Indians, varying from thirty feet square to seventy by thirty feet, and five smaller ones for neighborhood meetings.[7] Some of the missionaries, however, were exasperating the slave-holding Indians by their discussions of the subject of emancipation.

The year 1854 was marked by a drought that resulted in an almost total crop failure throughout the immigrant tribes, which brought much suffering but spurred the people to renewed industry the next year. Their agent reported that despite the embarrassment caused by their national debt and other difficulties they had to contend with, the Cherokee people continued to improve in many respects. There had been little crime in the past twelve months, their laws were rigidly enforced, and there was more harmony among them than there had been for many years. Agent Butler particularly urged the abandonment

7 *Report* of commissioner of Indian affairs for 1854.

Spring House on site of Old Cherokee Orphan Asylum, Salina, Oklahoma, formerly the home of Lewis Ross

*Rectory of the Moravian Mission at Oaks, Cherokee Nation,
constructed about 1844*

of Fort Gibson; the Cherokee people resented the presence of an army post on their land; but more than that they desired to be put in possession of the garrison site where they could use the only good boat landing in the country. Here they looked forward to securing the commercial advantages such a river port would provide, around which they hoped an important town would grow.

A delegation that had been sent to Washington during the session of Congress failed to secure the sale of the "neutral lands" to relieve them of their oppressive national debts. Abolitionist missionaries continued to cause complaint of their meddling with local affairs. The Cherokee were complaining bitterly of the grievous oppression exercised by the court sitting at Van Buren, Arkansas. The Nation having set up its own machinery for the detection and punishment of crime within its limits, was incensed that authorities connected with the United States court insisted on invading the Cherokee country, arresting members of the tribe and taking them to Van Buren to be tried for offenses alleged to have been committed in the Nation. Members of the Cherokee tribe were seized, carried to Van Buren and thrown into prison where, for lack of information of procedure in the white man's court, they often lay for months without remedy or redress. This conflict of authority led to much unhappiness and unrest. It was only as late as 1847 that Indians were made competent witnesses in the white man's court.[8]

This year produced an astonishing report from Dr. Worcester's press; "The printing at Park Hill since my last report, has amounted to 1,025,000 pages, consisting of a further portion of Exodus, and four editions of the Gospel of John in Cherokee, an Almanac for 1855, in Cherokee and English, and a portion of the Gospel of Matthew in the Muskogee or Creek language."[9] In this year the membership in the Methodist mission had increased to 1,450 members, whites and Indians, besides 150 Negroes. There were employed in these missions six white and eight Indian missionaries. Besides these there was one Moravian Mission.[10] The difficulties with which schools were obliged

8 Butler to Dean, August 11, 1855: Report of commissioner of Indian affairs for 1855.
9 Worcester to Butler July 27, 1855: Report of commissioner of Indian affairs for 1850.
10 Report of commissioner of Indian affairs for 1855.

to contend is indicated by the fact that they had been embarrassed by the delay of books on the way, which had been held up by low water on the Arkansas River for ten months.

The Male Seminary in this year saw its first graduating class of five members who entered with its opening in 1851. They were graduated in February and twenty-three new students were admitted in March. The attendance during the spring session was 46. Daily exercises had been had in declamation and frequent exercises in English composition. The five members of the first class studied geometry, Latin, intellectual philosophy, and rhetoric; the six of the second class, Latin, geometry, and natural philosophy; eleven in the third, elements of history, algebra, physiography, book-keeping and Latin; and 21 in the fourth class, Green's analysis of the English language, arithmetic, geography reading, elocution, and penmanship. In the Female Seminary there had been at times as many as sixty students in attendance. The first graduating class, numbering twelve, left the school in the spring of 1855. Pupils were permitted to enter at the age of fourteen if they had the necessary qualifications, usually acquired in the Cherokee common schools. At this time the third and fourth classes studied arithmetic, mental and written, geography, botany, and Latin; the second class, algebra, physiology, Watts on Improvement of the Mind, and Latin; the first class, geometry, history of Greece, Natural Theology, and intellectual philosophy. Pauline Avery was principal, assisted by Charlotte E. Raymond, and E. Jane Ross. For years many of the teachers in this and other tribal schools were graduates of Mt. Holyoke College, but the Cherokee authorities sought to qualify members of the tribe as teachers to take charge of all the schools; in time there were very few teachers from outside the Nation.

Peace at length seemed to have settled over the Cherokee country; Agent George Butler, in his report for 1856, found little cause of anxiety except that the educational facilities of the nation seemed to be in jeopardy; the large surplus of school funds on which the tribe had been drawing was exhausted. The Male and Female seminaries closed in the autumn of that year not to reopen for ten years after the devastation caused by the Civil War had been in a measure repaired.

The health of the country, Butler said, was good; it was fairly well supplied with physicians, and a number of young Cherokee were preparing themselves for the medical profession by placing themselves under the instruction of established physicians in their country and completing their studies at an eastern medical college. Everywhere was a demand for more schools, but A. W. Duncan, the new superintendent, having no funds for the purpose, took the novel stand that the twenty-one schools were as many as they had need for and that the country would be better off if more of the youth devoted themselves to farming and mechanical pursuits instead of aspiring to qualifications that would relieve them from manual labor. "Our lands are uncultivated," he said; "shops are vacant, or never have started; we must buy machinery, furniture, produce, stock and goods, all at foreign markets, or else hire them made at home by white men. The nation cant live without money or its equivalent. There is everything to take it out. There is nothing made—all is bought. When we take into the account that all these purchases are to be made too, out of the meager currency put into circulation as the proceeds of our invested funds, which does not amount to more than scarcely half a share of some minor New York firm, the picture is still more alarming."[11]

At the opening of the 1857 session of the Cherokee council Chief John Ross, on October 5, delivered his customary message which is worthy of note for its patriotic and statesman-like utterances: ". . . . I visited in person during the past summer, the different districts to inform myself of the general condition of the country. The evidence of progress by the Cherokee people furnished by this tour was of the most cheering kind, and contrasts favorably with their condition fifty years ago. Well cultivated farms, which have yielded abundant crops of grain, and thus affording a full supply for the wants of the people; well filled public schools, large and orderly assemblies, and quiet neighborhoods, which were seen in all the districts, showed marked improvement, and furnish a sure indication of the susceptibility of all classes among the Cherokee people for a thorough civilization. To accomplish this work, upon which depends such great interests, it becomes the duty of the national council to sustain and strenghten our institutions within our own limits, and to guard against every untoward encroachment.

"The surest safeguard for the government of the nation must be found in the respect and confidence of the people; and these can be

11   *Ibid.*, for 1856.

secured only by its affording that protection to life and property for which it was instituted. Its form is eminently adapted to produce these ends, and if it fails of such results it must be because the laws are not wisely and impartially administered. It is, therefore, the clearest dictate of duty that, so far as depends upon your action in selecting those who are to dispense justice by the enforcement and exposition of the constitution and laws, you should discard every other consideration, and seek only for the largest measure of ability, integrity, and patriotism. If our rights of soil and self-government, of free homes and self-chosen institutions, are worth the toils and struggles of the past, they are worth present defense and continuation upon the most permanent footing. Years of trial and of anxiety, of danger and struggle, have alone maintained the existence of the Cherokee people as a distinct community; and such must continue to be the case, if we would live as men ourselves, and discharge the debt we owe to posterity."[12]

The ruthless intention of the surrounding white population to seize the lands of the Indians and trample under foot the rights guaranteed by treaty was called to their attention by the astute Chief: "As intimately concerned with this subject, you cannot fail to be seriously impressed with the change of policy shown by the United States government in her dealing with the Indian tribes in the Territory of Kansas and Nebraska. And, as an evidence of the dangers with which we ourselves are threatened, I need but refer to the language and sentiments expressed in this regard by the present governor of Kansas (Robert J. Walker, former United States senator from Mississippi) in his inaugural address. Coming from the distinguished source they do, they cannot but admonish us that the renewal may be at hand of those measures of agitation which but so recently forced us from the homes of our fathers. That you may fully understand the sentiments of the governor, who, if I mistake not, was in the Senate of the United States when the removal of all the Indians from the east to the west side of the Mississippi River was the policy of the government, and when the treaty was made which declares that the country we now occupy shall be a home for ourselves and our descendants forever, and never be embraced within the limits of any State or Territory without our consent, I make the following extract from that address:

12   *Ibid.*, for 1857.

" 'Upon the south Kansas is bounded by the great south western Indian Territory. This is one of the most salubrious and fertile portions of this continent. It is a great cotton growing region, admirably adapted, by soil and climate, for the products of the south; embracing the valley of the Arkansas and Red rivers; adjoining Texas on the south and west, and Arkansas on the east; and it ought speedily to become a State of the American Union. The Indian treaties will constitute no obstacle, any more than precisely similar treaties did in Kansas; for their lands, valueless to them, not now for sale, but which sold with their consent and for their benefit, like the Indian lands of Kansas, would make them a most wealthy and prosperous people, and their consent on these terms would be most cheerfully given. This territory contains double the area of the State of Indiana, and, if necessary, an adequate portion of the western and more elevated part could be set apart exclusively for these tribes, and the eastern and larger portion be formed into a State, and its land sold for the benefit of these tribes (like the Indian lands of Kansas), thus greatly promoting all their interest.' "[13]

Education and temperance continued to be of paramount importance in the public mind. The growth of sorghum cane and the making of molasses were first noted among the immigrant tribes in the report of 1858, where George Butler, Cherokee agent, says that two of his neighbors, M. M. Schrimsher and D. M. Hunter, presented him with a sample of the molasses which he pronounced very fine. The Cherokee who produced it had extemporized a mill, and were planning to make enough the next year to sell quantities of it. Much sickness and mortality was caused that year by malarial fever and many prominent citizens had died; but the nation was well supplied with physicians, many of whom were Cherokee graduates of the best medical schools of the country.

After the formal abandonment of Fort Gibson in September, 1857, and the removal therefrom of ammunition and supplies, the reservation was placed in the hands of Daniel R. Coodey for the tribe, and the Cherokee Council passed an act on November 5, 1857, creating within what had been the reservation, the town of Kee-too-whah,[14] and providing for laying it off into town lots; from the sale of these lots exclusively to citizens of the Cherokee Nation about $20,000 was realized. Sub-

13   *Ibid.*
14   Grant Foreman, *Advancing the Frontier*, 74.

sequently the council passed an act removing the capitol from Tahle-quah to Kee-too-whah, but it was vetoed by the chief. While the Cher-okee at the time were satisfied with the removal of the garrison from Fort Gibson the Creeks and Indian officials regretted that this aban-donment of the post and "the growing up of a vicious little town there, have given unusual activity to the whisky trade in that region of the Cherokee country and in the Creek country adjoining."[15]

The superintendent of public schools for the Cherokee Nation visited all parts of the nation twice in 1858 and found "quite a change for the better since 1855. More acres are in cultivation; there is an improvement in buildings; much more attention is being given to the rearing of stock of all kinds; there are fewer cases on the criminal calendar; the schools are well attended, and are in a prosperous con-dition; and every thing wears a cheering aspect to every lover of his people."[16]

Cherokee Agent Butler in 1859 reported a marked improvement in agricultural pursuits. "This is evidenced by enlarged farms, more thorough tillage, the largest yield of wheat ever harvested in this nation, the application of machinery in farming, such as reapers, mowers, threshers, &c., more comfortable houses erected and improvement of those already built. And in almost every instance, is to be found a good vegetable garden, and, wherever it is practicable, spring houses for the preservation of milk, butter and cheese, are to be found." Imitating the example of their neighbors in Arkansas, they had been accustomed to allow their cows and calves to run together instead of saving the milk for butter and cheese, and used "con-na-ha-ney" or hominy as a substitute for milk. A large number of cattle had been sold at remunerative prices by residents of the nation; the raising of cattle had become a leading industry in the tribe. But lack of adequate transportation had prevented the Cherokee people from marketing corn, bacon, butter, cheese, hogs, and sheep sufficiently to give them proper encouragement to produce them in greater quantities. In August the Cherokee elected their principal and second chiefs, mem-bers of the council and sheriffs.[17]

There were reported 21,000 Cherokee, 4,000 voters, 1,000 whites

15 Rector to Greenwood: *Report* of commissioner of Indian affairs, 1859.
16 *Ibid.*, for 1858.
17 *Ibid.*, 1859.

and 4,000 Negroes; 102,500 acres in cultivation, 240,000 head of cattle, 20,000 horses and mules, 16,000 hogs and 5,000 sheep; an average of thirty-five bushels of corn produced to the acre, thirty of oats and twelve of wheat.[18] There were thirty schools attended by 1,500 pupils; and of the teachers all but two were Cherokee.[19]

As the country was noticeably drifting into the Civil War the officials in the Indian service looked about them to take their bearings and adjust their fortunes and loyalties to the impending event. Elias Rector, who was to side with the South, had more than once declared that the Indians must yield their lands to the irresistible pressure of white settlement. "I have already spoke, in a previous report," he said, "of the certainty that this fine country must ultimately, and at no distant day, be formed into States. Not only the remorseless flow of our population, but stern *political* necessities, make this decree as fixed as fate.

"Heretofore, from the time when Washington and the Senate solemnly guaranteed to the Creeks *forever* the possession of *all* their lands that had not then been ceded by them, down to the time when a like solemn pledge was given by our commissioners to the Choctaws, and thence on to this day, our policy has been to meet present necessity by pushing back the Indian tribes from part of the lands guaranteed to them; effecting this by cajolery or force, and violating our faith, previously pledged, to pledge it again, that we may, when necessity presses, violate it anew; giving a new guarantee, to be in like manner broken in its turn.

"It will not be worthy a great, generous, or Christian people, thus to deal with its solemn treaties, promises, and engagements, in regard to the country in question; nor will it be wise to continue any policy, or adopt any measure, to answer only a temporary purpose, leaving the stern exigencies to press upon us anew, at some not very remote day." And Rector strongly urged that the Indians be encouraged to sell part of their lands to white people so that the country could be settled by the whites. His shrewd argument was obviously directed to strengthening the South in the Indian country.[20]

The next year Rector advanced grounds for immediate military

18 Butler to Rector, September 10, 1859, *ibid.*, 1859.
19 *Ibid.*
20 Rector to Greenwood, September 20, 1859, *ibid.*

occupation of the Indian Territory. Overnight, it seemed from his account, the Cherokee people had become an unruly and lawless people. "There has been much disturbance among them during the past year, and great strife and contention; hostile parties have been organized, and, it is said, an extensive secret association formed among the full-bloods." This reference was to a society of Indians who were endeavoring to hold their tribe loyal to the Union. "Murders are continually committed, and other outrages perpetrated. Great excitement now exists, and violence—is believed to be the intermeddling by the missionaries among them, headed by Evan and John Jones, with the institution of slavery.

"The crops have almost wholly failed the present year in a large portion of the nation, and the Indians must suffer much for want of bread. The Cherokees are not improving in morals, nor is the cultivation of the soil increasing among them. There are many lawless and vicious men among them, and much gambling and dissipation prevails; there will be no improvement until peace and order are restored, and that will not be until a military post is established in or on the edge of their country, with a sufficient force stationed there to keep down violence, suppress outrages, and make the agent something more than a man of straw. I have already, over and over again, urged the establishment of such a post at Frozen Rock, on the Arkansas River. It is useless for me to repeat what I have already said on the subject, and I can add nothing to it." Further along in his report the superintendent, exasperated that his recommendation had been ingored by a harassed government, added: "If it is considered at all important that the authority of the United States should be maintained, and peace and order inforced in the Cherokee country, a military post should at once be established at Frozen Rock. If that is not done, the agent should be withdrawn, and disorder left to take its course.[21]

21 Rector to Greenwood, September 24, 1860, *ibid.*, for 1860. Two years before, Albert Pike at Fort Smith had strongly endorsed Rector's urgent appeal for the establishment of a fort at Frozen Rock. He added that it was "of great importance to the South that the tribes west of Arkansas should be induced as soon as possible to open up their country to settlement, and fitted as speedily as possible to become citizens of the United States" (Pike to secretary of war, September 28, 1858, AGO, OFD, 243 P 58).

CHAPTER THIRTY-TWO / *Reconstruction Achieved*

AND now the Indians stood at another crisis in their lives. The brief interval of peace was drawing to a close. Happily the sorrow and desolation immediately ahead was not revealed to them. The portent of current events was lost upon a people who desired nothing more ardently than complete isolation from the policies and disputes of their white neighbors.

They could look about and meditate upon their surroundings with much satisfaction. Three decades had passed since Jackson's Removal Bill[1] decreed the surrender of their beloved homeland. The forbidding countenance of a strange western country had softened until it too became invested with the qualities and sentiment of home. This with patience and perseverance had been achieved at a cost it has been the lot of few peoples to experience. They not only survived the tragedy of eviction from their own country and transfer to a far-off land under the most desolating conditions; but after they recovered from the shock of removal and devastating mortality, they had improved their condition to a state far in advance of that enjoyed by them in the East. Governments were now functioning, public schools were in operation, education had become a passion, agriculture and industry were progressing, all in a degree never before known to them; they had advanced far on the road to civilization.

This achievement was made possible primarily by the intelligence, character, and fortitude of the Indians. But in a measure that can never be adequately appraised, the missionaries were responsible by reviving

1 For an account of this legislation and the removal of the Indians see Foreman, *Indian Removal, op. cit.*

the morale, hope, and resolution of these harried people. Removal to a country where the white man ceased from his efforts to take their land contributed much, for it gave the Indians courage and opportunity to improve their condition.

Next to meeting the demands for food and shelter for themselves and their dependents the occupation that engaged their attention more than any other was the pursuit of education. This suddenly developing interest in a primitive people was a phenomenon of more than common interest which had its genesis in recent conditions in which they were involved. Before their removal from the South when they began to realize the menace of the white man's aggressions, some of the leading members of the tribes sensed a method of arming their people for defense. With the aid of the missionaries they shrewdly strove to imitate the white man by educating their people and taking a more secure hold on their homeland through the medium of constitutional governments. By approximating a stabilized social order and availing themselves of the white man's knowledge of letters and methods of thinking and acting, they equipped themselves to defend their rights. This development resulted in some remarkable demonstrations of sagacity and clear thinking by the leaders among the Indians. The threat of intelligent resistance provoked and was soon met by more powerful aggressions of the whites and state and Federal governments, that quickly turned the tide against the weaker red people who were driven before it to the West. But the seed of education sown by the missionaries had taken root and survived to flourish after the desolation of removal.[2]

The Choctaw people were the first to be located after emigration and they were the first to send their children to the schools made possible by their annuities and the help of the missionaries. But it was the Cherokee who set the example of a national school system. The early settlers of this tribe had a few schools but they were almost entirely dependent on the missionaries for such education as their children received. It was not until after the arrival of the large body of emigrants and the inauguration of the new government under Chief John Ross, that a national school system was established in December, 1841. Eleven months later the Choctaw Nation followed this example

2   Robert Sparks Walker, *Torchlights to the Cherokees*: Grant Foreman, *Indians and Pioneers*.

and made similar provision. From this time there was friendly rivalry that placed these two nations far to the front in the field of education.

The leading men of the tribes exercised a paternal influence over the "common people" that contributed to their welfare and progress. The laws enacted in their legislative councils bear the marks of these men who were responsible for them. The great majority of the people did not think in terms of conventional laws or rules of conduct. They understood the tribal customs and clan rules handed down from parent to child and revealed by their old men and they were content to let their chiefs and counsellors make all other laws. This is illustrated by the numerous laws relating to their slaves. The great majority of the people had no slaves; it was only the comparatively few rich Indians who enjoyed this luxury.

Exercising the power they possessed the leaders of the tribes would have been more than human if they had not derived financial profit from their opportunities. Yet they labored for the good of their people and in the main were trusted by them. That some of the signers of Indian treaties surrendering their lands in the East received substantial bribes for their acts was notorious and fully established by the records. It became a sort of custom in some of the tribes that the station of chief carried with it as a perquisite the right to receive from the Government financial rewards for which they were not expected to account to their people. This developed from the policy of the Government of so treating the members who were in a position to bind the tribes; it was a species of bribery employed by the Government to accomplish its ends and was known to the "common people" as something they were powerless to prevent and therefore a necessary evil, though not condoned by them.

Much has been said about the Cherokee "false treaty" of 1835; but there is no evidence that the signers received financial rewards for their acts. Nor is there any evidence that Chief John Ross profited to the extent of a dollar through the opportunity presented by the large amount of money employed in the removal of his people. To this day there persist stories that Ross did make money out of that business; stories based upon nothing more than tradition handed down these many years. The Author has pursued every available source of information and has reached the conclusion that these stories originated at that time in the heated discussions and feuds growing out of the

MAP OF INDIAN TERRITORY

~1842~

Map of Indian Territory, showing tribal boundaries
at the time covered by *The Five Civilized Tribes*

DE

NOR

CEDAR OR LI

WALNUT CREEK

FORT HOLM
Chouteau's
Trading H

WASHITA RIVER

RUSH CREEK

CHICKASA

BEAVER CREEK

WILDHORSE CREEK

MUD

Shawnee Delaware and Kickapoo Trail

WALNUT CREEK

RED RIVER

CREEK

Compiled by Grant Foreman
Traced by Will Blake

WARREN'S
TRADING POST

From *A Traveler in Indian Territory*, edited by Grant Foreman

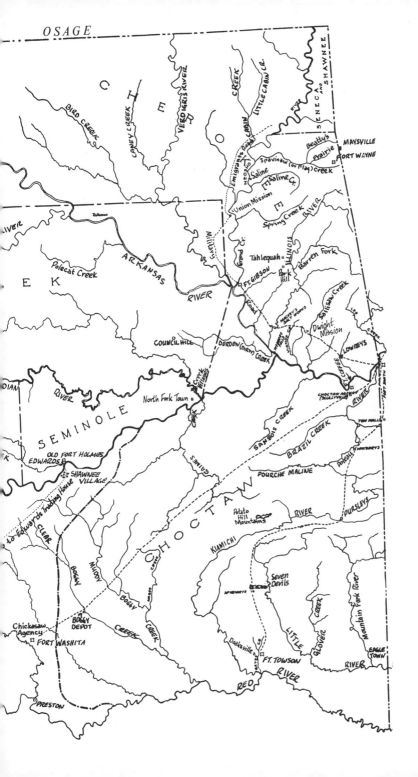

jealousies and heart burnings of the minority faction. One of Ross's bitterest critics, Benjamin F. Curry, commissioner for Cherokee removal, leveled the charge against him that he "did the thinking" for his great following.[3] It was probably true in a measure; they trusted Ross and through this trust his personality dominated the great majority of the tribe and accounted for his long tenure as chief. It was his successful sway over the Cherokee Nation that embittered the minority faction against him. Colonel Hitchcock's exoneration of Ross would seem to be conclusive on the point.

Wonder at the achievements of the Indians in the field of reconstruction and advancement is increased when one considers the difficulties deliberately created by the Government. It was concerned first with the removal of the Indians by any means available; all other considerations yielded to this; if it was necessary to employ bribery, so be it. The Government early adopted the policy of dealing with a minority of a tribe and then pretending that the whole tribe was bound. This it did when it bribed William McIntosh to sign the Creek Treaty of 1825[4] which initiated a feud and division of the tribe that lasted for sixty years and greatly retarded its recovery and reconstruction after removal. A period of almost civil way prevailed in the Cherokee Nation from the feud growing out of inducing a handful of unauthorized men of the tribe to sign the "Treaty" of 1835 and then going through the fraud of ratification by the United States Senate of what was called a treaty, but which notoriously was not a treaty.[5]

The fatuous effort to compel the Creeks and Seminole Indians to amalgamate and an equally foolish and futile attempt to force a similar union of the Choctaw and Chickasaw Indians were only slightly less mischievous. These four outstanding instances of injustice and ineptitude by the Government interposed such tremendous difficulties to normal recovery that their success and progress in spite of them were remarkable. Much of what they accomplished is to be attributed to the loyalty, good sense, and patience of some of the Indian agents for which some of them—not all—were notable. The missionaries again deserve a generous share of the credit.

3 *Indian Removal*, 246.
4 Kappler, *op. cit.*, 151.
5 *Ibid.*, 324.

The Government clearly did not know what to do with these immi-grant Indians and had no definite policy for dealing with them and promoting their welfare. Its legislation and administration were there-fore often expedient, ill-advised and inadequate. Having but a vague knowledge of the character, condition, and needs of the Indians, there was the added difficulty of the great distance between their homes in the Indian Territory and the seat of government in Washington where the Administration was engaged in making laws and regulations for a people it had never seen.

In some ways this isolation was an advantage to the Indians for in spite of the inefficiency of the administration of their affairs by the Government, when left much to their own resources they made amazing progress in adjusting themselves to their new surroundings; a progress that developed at a more rapid pace than in any period since the Civil War when initiative and self-reliance were supplanted by government paternalism. The Government at times actively interfered with the aspirations and natural progress of these people. They had been promised in their treaties that they should be allowed to govern themselves and that they should never be made part of a state of the Union. But to the great exasperation and anxiety of the Indians the Government for years in violation of its promises pursued them with plans approaching co-ercion, to unite them in a confederacy of civilized and wild Indians;[6] a policy that left the Indians in a state of uncertainty and unrest and interfered seriously with their normal recovery. However when released from this interference the resilient spirit of the tribes caught step again with the tempo of their interrupted progress.

Streams and settlements, council grounds and geographic divisions were given cherished names brought from their old nation. Time aided the older people to forget the grief over the loss of their old homes, and to substitute the new in their affections. Younger generations having no recollection of any other, had no regrets to live down, and contributed with greater facility and in a large measure to reconstruc-tion and readjustment.

It is undeniable that the Government did greatly aid the Indians by providing a home for them then far removed from the devastating influence of the white man. Relieving them from the hopeless struggle

6 For an extended treatment of this subject see Grant Foreman, *Advancing the Frontier*, 185.

against the whites who were determined to have their land, the hopes and aspirations of these red people found an atmosphere in which they could expand; in which they could assert the manhood and freedom they cherished and could live in their own normal way. In this atmosphere, in sincere pride of their race and conscious of a state of independence, they organized their governments and other institutions of an orderly people and pursued a course that earned for them the name of The Five Civilized Tribes.

BIBLIOGRAPHY

AFTER the emigration of the Indians described in this book an agent was appointed to reside with each of the tribes. He was required to counsel with them concerning the performance of treaty obligations and all problems arising in their new environ- ment and to report annually to the department of Indian affairs on their condition and progress. The agent in turn received reports from the missionaries, teachers, and others having duties of a public nature to perform in the Indian country. These activities resulted in a vast accumulation of mansucript material in the department of Indian affairs and the war department. Some of the most important of this was included in the annual reports of the commissioner of Indian affairs. These reports were usually printed as exhibits to the annual messages of the presidents that appeared as executive congressional documents and thus became the most extensive and valuable contempo- rary printed accounts of the Indians. The great mass of this correspondence and reports concerning the Indians in their western home however, was never published and remains in the files of these departments. This, in the main, hitherto unpublished material, furnished the principal source from which this book was written. In addition the author has extracted from many printed congressional documents important and detailed accounts of the Indians from other sources the originals of which were deposited in the war department or the Indian office; and others made directly to Congress, such as memorials, investigations, committee reports, and official reports to Congress. From these much essential information was obtained. Contemporary newspapers also contributed greatly to this work.

Reference herein to the material in the office of Indian affairs is abbreviated OIA In the war department material the references are shortened as follows:

Adjutant general's office, old files division: AGO, OFD.

Adjutant general's office, old records division: AGO, ORD.

Adjutant general's office, old records division, war department files: AGO. ORD. WDF.

Quartermaster general's old files at Fort Myer: QMG.

Other primary sources drawn upon for the contents of this book are the mis- sionary letters recently in the custody of the American Board of Commissioners for Foreign Missions at Boston and now deposited in the Harvard-Andover Theological library; United States Senate files; manuscript division of the Library of Congress; Draper Manuscript collection in the State Historical Society of Wisconsin; Byington letters in the library of the Oklahoma Historical Society; manuscript collection in the library of the Author.

An authority frequently referred to in this book is United States Senate *Document* No. 512, Twenty-third Congress, first session, "Indian Removal." Because of the length of the name, for brevity the title is shortened in the references to "Document," followed by the volume number.

Printed Works Consulted

American State Papers. *Documents, legislative and executive of the Congress of the United States,* Class V, "Military Affairs," Vols. VI, VII.

Rev. Henry C. Benson, *Life among the Choctaw Indians* (Cincinnati, 1860).

Thomas Valentine Parker, *The Cherokee Indians, with Special Reference to their Relations with the United States Government* (New York, 1907).

George Catlin, *Letters and Notes on the Manners, Customs, and Condition of the North American Indians,* Vols. I-II (Philadelphia, 1857, and various editions).

Commissioner of Indian affairs, *Annual Reports.*

Elliott Coues (ed.), *Expeditions of Zebulon Montgomery Pike* (New York, 1895), Vols. I, II, III.

H. B. Cushman, *History of the Choctaw, Chickasaw, and Natchez Indians* (Greenville, Texas, 1899).

Abbe Emannuel Domenech, *Seven Years Residence in the Great Deserts of North America* (London, 1860).

Rachel Caroline Eaton, *John Ross and the Cherokee Indians* (Chicago).

Grant Foreman, *Pioneer Days in the Early Southwest,* (Cedar Rapids, 1926).

———, *Indians and Pioneers,* (New Haven, 1930).

———, *A Traveler in Indian Territory* (Cedar Rapids, 1930).

———, *Indian Removal* (Norman, 1932).

———, *Advancing the Frontier* (Norman, 1833).

———, *Indian Justice* (Oklahoma City, 1934).

Adelaide L. Fries, *The Moravian Church* (Raleigh, 1926).

Joshua R. Giddings, *The Exiles of Florida* (Columbus, 1858).

[Dr.] R[odney] Glisan, *Journal of Army Life* (San Francisco, 1874).

William H. Goode, *Outposts of Zion* (Cincinnati, 1863).

Josiah Gregg, *Commerce of the Prairies: or the Journal of a Santa Fé Trader,* Vols. I, II (New York, 1844 and various editions).

Frederick W. Hodge (ed.), *Handbook of American Indians North of Mexico* (Bulletin No. 30, Bureau of American Ethnology, Washington, 1912).

Charles J. Kappler (ed.) *Indian Affairs "Laws and Treaties"* (United States Senate *Document No. 452,* Fifth-seventh Congress, first session, Washington, 1903).

J. D. Lang and Samuel Taylor, *Report on the Indian tribes west of the Mississippi River* (Providence, 1843).

Laws of the Cherokee Nation (Tahlequah, 1852; St. Louis, 1868, and various editions).

Constitution, Laws, and Treaties of the Chickasaws (Tishomingo City, 1860).

Constitution and Laws of the Choctaw Nation (New York, 1869; Dallas, 1894, and various editions).

[Augustus W. Loomis] *Scenes in the Indian Country* (Philadelphia, 1859).

Isaac McCoy, *History of Baptist Indian Missions* (New York, 1840).

————, *Annual Register of Indian Affairs within the Indian (or Western) Territory 1837* (printed at Shawnee Baptist Mission House Indian Territory, 1837).

Thomas L. McKenney and James Hall, *History of the Indian Tribes of North America*, Vols I, II, III (Philadelphia, 1854, and various editions).

Capt. R. B. Marcy, *Thirty Years of Army Life on the Border* (New York, 1866).

James Mooney, *Myths of the Cherokee* (Nineteenth Report, Bureau of American Ethnology, part 1, Washington, 1900).

Rev. Jedidiah Morse, *A Report to the Secretary of War of the United States, on Indian Affairs, Comprising a Narrative of a Tour Performed in the Summer of 1820* (New Haven, 1822).

Narcissa Owen, *Memoirs of Narcissa Owen, 1831-1907* (Washington, 1907).

W. B. Parker, *Notes taken during the Expedition commanded by Capt. R. B. Marcy through unexplored Texas in the summer and fall of 1854* (Philadelphia, 1856).

J. C. Pilling, *Bibliography of the Muskhogean languages* (Bulletin No. 9, Bureau of American Ethnology, Washington, 1889).

James Richardson, *Messages of the Presidents* (Washington, 1903 Vols. I-X).

Mrs. William P. Ross, *The Life and Times of William P. Ross* (Fort Smith, 1893).

Charles C. Royce, *The Cherokee Nation of Indians* (Fifth Report, Bureau of American Ethnology, Washington, 1887).

Rev. Edmund Schwarze, *History of the Moravian Missions among the Southern Indian Tribes of the United States* (Bethlehem, 1923).

George G. Smith, *The Life and Times of George Foster Pierce D.D., LL.D.* (Nashville, 1888).

Capt. John T. Sprague, *The Origin, Progress, and Conclusion of the Florida War* (New York, 1848).

Emmet Starr, *History of the Cherokee Indians* (Oklahoma City, 1921).

Dr. John R. Swanton, *Early History of the Creek Indians and their Neighbors* (Smithsonian Institution, Bureau of American Ethnology, Bulletin No. 73, 1822).

————, *Source Material for the Social and Ceremonial Life of the Choctaw Indians* (Smithsonian Institution, Bureau of American Ethnology, Bulletin No. 103, Washington, 1931).

Joseph B. Thoburn and Muriel H. Wright, *Oklahoma, a History of the State and its People* (New York, 1929).

United States Statutes at Large, Vol. V (Boston, 1850); VII, "List of treaties between the United States and the Indian Tribes" with names of Indian signers (Boston, 1846).

United States Senate *Document No. 1*, Twenty-third Congress, first session.

————, *Executive Document No. 512*, Twenty-third Congress, first session, vol. I, II, III, IV, V, "Indian Removal."

————, *Executive Document No. 3*, Twenty-fifth Congress, second session.

————, *Document No. 298*, Twenty-eighth Congress, first session.

————, *Document No. 24*, Twenty-eighth Congress, second session.

————, *Document No. 138*, Twenty-eighth Congress, second session.

————, *Document No. 140*, Twenty-eighth Congress, second session.

——, *Document No. 301*, Twenty-ninth Congress, first session.
——, *Document No. 331*, Twenty-ninth Congress, first session.
——, *Document No. 439*, Twenty-ninth Congress, first session.
——, *Executive Document No. 1*, Thirty-first Congress, first session.
United States House of Representatives, *Executive Document No. 2*, Twenty-fourth Congress, first session.
——, *Document No. 129*, Twenty-sixth Congress, first session.
——, *Document No. 162*, Twenty-sixth Congress, first session.
——, *Document No. 188*, Twenty-sixth Congress, first session.
——, *Document No. 222* Twenty-sixth, Congress, first session.
——, *Executive Document No. 219*, Twenty-seventh Congress, third session (Hitchcock Report).
——, *Document No. 234*, Twenty-eighth Congress, first session.
——, *Executive Document No. 4*, Twenty-ninth Congress, second session.
——, *Executive Document No. 42*, Thirty-sixth Congress, first session.
Eugene A. Vail, *Sur Les Indiens de l'Amerique du Nord* (Paris, 1840).
Cephas Washburn, *Reminiscences of the Indians* (Richmond, 1869).
Lieut. A. W. Whipple and Lieut. J. C. Ives, *Report of Explorations for a Railway Route near the Thirty-fifth Parallel of North Latitude, from the Mississippi to the Pacific Ocean* (Washington, 1853-4).

Newspapers and Journals

Arkansas Advocate (Little Rock).
The Arkansas Gazette (Little Rock).
Arkansas Intelligencer (Van Buren).
The Army and Navy Chronicle (Washington, D. C.).
Boston Alliance and Visitor.
Cherokee Advocate (Tahlequah).
Cherokee Phoenix (New Echota, Georgia).
Choctaw Telegraph (Doaksville, Indian Territory).
Chronicles of Oklahoma (Oklahoma City).
Constitutional Journal (Helena, Arkansas).
Daily National Intelligencer (Washington, D. C).
Dallas (Texas) *Herald.*
Edwardsville (Illinois) *Spectator.*
The Foreign Missionary Chronicle.
Fort Smith (Arkansas) *Herald.*
The Indian Advocate (Louisville, Kentucky).
Jackson (Missouri) *Advertiser.*
The Jackson (Tennessee) *Gazette.*
Knoxville (Tennessee) *Register.*
Louisville (Kentucky) *Public Advertiser.*
Louisville (Kentucky) *Weekly Journal.*
Memphis (Tennessee) *World.*

Missionary Herald.
The Missouri Republican.
Missouri Saturday News.
Natchitoches (Louisiana) *Herald.*
National Banner and Nashville Whig.
The New Orleans Bee.
New York Evangelist.
The New York Journal of Commerce.
New York Observer.
The New York Recorder.
New York Sun.
New York Tribune.
Niles' Weekly Register (Baltimore).
The Northern Standard (Clarksville, Texas).
Pittsburg Recorder.
Public Advertiser.
Religious Intelligencer.
Telegraph and Texas Register.
The United States Gazette (Philadelphia).
The United States Magazine and Democratic Review.
Western Citizen (Paris, Kentucky).
Wheeling (West Virginia) *Gazette.*

INDEX

Boggy Depot (Indian Territory): 88, 112, 114; Chickasaw rations issued at, 100, 101; destroyed, 89.

Boggy River: 100, 112.

Boiling Springs: at Fort Washita, 109, 121, 122, 123, 139.

Boktuklo: 46, 56.

Boluxies (Biloxi) (Indians): annoy Chickasaw, 122.

Bonneville, Maj. B. L. E.: investigates Cherokee disorders, 341, 344.

Boone, Capt. Nathan: 341.

Boudinot, Elias: 292; attends school at Cornwall, 355; first editor of Cherokee Phoenix, 384; rumor concerning, 289; signed treaty of 1835, 296; unpopular with Western Cherokee, 297; valuable interpreter, 297; killed 292, 293, 317; claims of heirs adjusted, 350.

Bowlegs, Billy (Seminole chief): 248, 261, 263, 273; described, 249, 254; visits Washington and New York, 254; emigrates west, 274.

Bowlegs, Jim (Seminole chief): 248

Bowman, Lieut. G. N.: 166.

Border tribes: depredate on immigrants, 187.

Brainerd Mission, Cherokee Nation: 354.

Brazos River: 138, 139, 337.

Brewer, James: 46.

Brewer, Sam: 404.

Bridges built in Indian Territory: 92; remains of, 93.

Broken Arrow: 208.

Brooks, Maj. W. T. H.: 251.

Brown, A. V.: 116.

Brown and McCoy: 395.

Brown, David: at Cornwall, 355.

Brown, John (Cherokee chief): 291, 292, 295, 299, 302, 304.

Brown, John M.: 343.

Brown, P. P.: 60, 70.

Brown, Richard C. S. (Cherokee agent): 390, 402.

Browning, Wesley: 114, 118.

Brushy Creek: 114.

Bryan, J. M.: 394.

Buckner, Rev. H. F.: 205; describes Creeks, 206; religious work among, 208.

Butler, Rev. D. S.: 354.

Butler, Rev. Elizur: 360, 382, 383, 385, 409.

Butler, George (Cherokee agent): 412, 414, 418.

Butler, Pierce M. (Cherokee agent): 107, 227, 328, 330, 374, 376, 391; describes Cherokee people, 368, 369, 388 ff.; investigates Cherokee troubles, 322 ff.; relates Cherokee grievances, 325; treaty expedition to Texas, 244; death of, 393.

Butler, Dr. William (Cherokee agent) 391, 405.

Buffaloes in Indian Territory: 43.

Buffington, David: 327.

Buffington, Joshua: 307.

Buffington, Sabra: 396.

Burnham, Anna: 46.

Bushyhead, Isaac (Cherokee official): killed, 327.

Bushyhead, Rev. Jesse (Cherokee official): 285, 286, 321, 367, 375.

Byington, Rev. Cyrus: 18, 19, 20, 21, 35, 42, 46, 55, 63; joins Choctaw in West, 64; description of home, 46; trials of, 42; described Indians, 47, 48, 49, 52, 82, 84; translates Scriptures into Choctaw, 55, 84.

Caddo (Indians): depredate on Chickasaw, 104, 119, 122, 128, 129, 143; fight with Wichita, 119; some welcomed to Chickasaw home, 123; protect frontier, 187; removed to "Leased District," 144.

Caffrey, John: 33.

California road through Seminole country, 276.

Camp Arbuckle: 123, 135, 151, 265.

Camp Mason: 153.

Campbell, Archibald: 303, 308, 313.

Campbell, John: 148.
Canadian River: 112, 113, 128, 134, 153, 171, 192, 223, 245, 268, 270.
Canard, Motey (Creek chief): 216.
Canby, Lieut. E. R. S.: 225.
"Cane Hill Tragedy": 361.
Captives from Texas: in Chickasaw country, 107.
Carey, James: 308, 329.
Carney, Ellen: 46.
Carr, Rev. John H.: 66.
Carr, Paddy: 174.
Carr, Richard; 209.
Carr, Thomas C.: 209.
Carr, Tom: 263.
Carter, Colbert: 116.
Carter, David: 307, 403, 409.
Casey, Capt. J. C: 253, 254.
Catawba (Indians): ask for admittance in Chickasaw tribe, 122; admitted to Choctaw, 76.
Cattle: driven to California, 81; from Texas driven through the Chickasaw country in 1854, 141.
Caudle, Captain: 107.
Cedar Keys (Florida): 247.
Cedar timber in Indian country: 92.
Center College: 209.
Charity Hall (Chickasaw school): 99.
Checote, Samuel (Creek chief): 181.
The Cherokee Advocate: 367, 368, 371, 375, 378, 379, 382, 385, 394, 396, 400, 401, 406.
Cherokee Female Seminary: 393, 395; completed, 401; opened, 408; description of, 409, 414; first graduating class, 414.
Cherokee (Indians): advised by President Jefferson, 353; emigration of, 281, 316, 356; mortality of immigrants, 281, 282; destitution of, 155, 282; description of, 283; building new homes, 288; slanderous reports concerning, 288; fight against whisky by, 288; industry described, 353, 354; as slave holders, 356, 364, 397, 398, 420; as agriculturalists,

193, 356, 360, 363, 368, 389, 407, 411, 417, 418; artisans, 352, 356, 371, 389, 411; use of spinning wheels, 283, 352, 353, 361, 376, 377, 394, 395, 411; merchants, 358, 377, 394; millers, 358, 404, 405; steamboat owners, 377, 378; description of, 363 ff., 368, 380, 394, 414; by Piece M. Butler, 368, ff., 388, ff.; by Rector, 420; sell provisions to Fort Gibson, 163; wealthy citizens, 164; industries, 283; production of salt, 363, 396; lead mines, 398; first cotton gin, 378, whisky consumed, 363; progress of, 17, 360, 361, 362, 388, 418; Sequoyah and his alphabet, 371; pension for, 374; controversy with Creeks, 147; depredations on Chickasaw, 104, 112, 113, 122; destitution of, 382; made competent witnesses in state courts, 413; condition before Civil War, 421.
Cherokee Male Seminary: 393, 395; completed, 401; opened, 408; description of, 409, 414; graduating class, 414.
Cherokee (Nation): laws and government, 291, 305 ff., 310, 313, 314, 326, 355, 259, 369 ff.; Treaty of 1835, 296; meeting of factions at Takatokah, 291; meeting at Illinois Camp Ground, 298; intemperate actions, 300; Act of Union, 299, 300, 305, 306, 314, 348, 372;
"Western Cherokee" or "Old Settlers" meeting, 289, 332; misunderstood by army officers, 289; prepare for hostilities, 290; reorganize government, 291; Dragoons dispatched, 302; alarm groundless, 302;
Effort to unite factions, 291, 292; Boudinot and the Ridges killed, 292, 293; "Western Cherokee" contention, 305; government of, 359; meeting, 332; and "Treaty Party" union of 298, 307; sends delegation to Washington, 308, 329; meeting at Fort Gibson, 295.
Cherokee (Nation): Convention at Tahlequah, 303; at Tahlontuskey, 298, 299;

factional differences and disorder, 321, 324; council described by Major Hitchcock, 321; delegations to Washington, 308, 309, 322, 329, 336, 347; negotiate with secretary of war, 329, 330, 331, 348; letter from President Tyler, 321; negotiations with Governor Stokes, 307; interference by secretary of war, 309, 310, 311, 312; annuities withheld, 312; new treaty recommended by John Howard Payne, 318, 319; investigation, 323, 332 ff.; elections, 326, 376; disorder at polls, 327; disorders renewed, 338, 346, 404, 405; explained, 339; statistics on murders, 347; exaggerated reports, 340; demands of General Arbuckle, 341; threatened with military intervention, 336; factionists flee to Arkansas, 341, 344; seek home in Mexico, 336; disorders instigated by whites, 342; reprisals, 343; division of tribe proposed, 304, 336, 347; recommended by President, 348, 349; defeated by Chief John Ross, 349; commission to consider conditions, 349; new treaty of 1846 negotiated, 349; factional differences adjusted, 350, 351;

Population of, 323; grievances against Arkansas, 325, 413; host to Seminole immigrants, 226, 232; relations to Seminole, 233; efforts to remove, 234; public debt, 411; taxation proposed, 411; printing, 365, 390, 412; international Indian council at Tahlequah, 367; handling of prisoners, 408; emancipation of women, 388; missionaries and missionary establishments, 359, 364, 365, 367; Cherokee Bible Society, 375; Temperance movement, 288, 378, 405; The Cherokee Temperance Society, 378, 384, 412; Cold Water Army, 384, 411; Sons of Temperance, 411; meetings described, 383 ff.; benefits of, 389; Gold Rush through, 397, 400 ff.; Masonic lodge organized, 402; roads planned, 403; statistics concerning, 355, 356, 375; districts of, 255, 362; agricultural society, 377; territorial aggressions against proposed, 416, 417; change of policy recommended, 419, 420.

The Cherokee Phoenix: 292, 368, 371; destruction of, 374.

Cherokee schools: 359, 375, 376, 389, 392, 410, 411, 415, 417, 418; early education, 352, 354; missionary schools, 412; advanced schools proposed by John Ross, 393; authorized by Cherokee council, 393; cornerstones laid, 393; seminaries established, 393, 395; schools after emigration, 360; school system, 364, 422.

Cheyenne (Indians): 132; menace Seminole, 278.

Chiaha (Creek) town: 175.

Chickamauga Creek (Tennessee): 354.

Chickasaw and Choctaw Herald: 144.

Chickasaw (Indians): 97, 98, 99; habitat, 97; contact with whites, 17; emigration, 99; demoralization from removal, 100, 117, 128; immigrants purchase improvements from Choctaw, 100; suffer from smallpox, 101; destitution of, 155; condition of, 117; progress, 144; description of, 97; customs, 106, 110; funeral customs, 103; medicine men, 142, 143; homes described, 142; annuities payable to, 127; complain of Kickapoo, 75, 129; as agriculturalists, 97, 98, 101, 104, 106, 111, 112, 128; cotton growers, 106, 111; operate mills, 106; use of spinning wheels, 111; as artisans, 98, 111; supply travelers with provisions, 111; furnish supplies for Fort Washita, 113, 129; Fort Arbuckle, 136; destroy army whisky, 139; imprisoned by officers, 140; Chickasaw and Choctaw Herald, 144.

Chickasaw Nation: laws of, 92, 98, 106, 197; constitution adopted, 121, 131;

Chickasaw Nation, 131; union with Chickasaw dissolved, 89; admit Catawba Indians, 76.

Choctaw schools: 30, 33, 35, 36, 42, 44, 45, 47, 57; enumerated, 77; attendance at, 47, 48; houses erected, 30; location of, 46, 61, 62, 68; school system planned, 58, 61, 422; closed by sickness, 77, 80; destroyed by storm, 63; studies in, 78; examinations in, 79; "Saturday and Sunday schools," 77; "Neighborhood schools," 77; school exercises, 65; facilities enlarged, 70; teachers graduates of eastern schools, 85; attendance of boys in state schools, 58; disadvantages of, 59.

Choctaw Telegraph: 70.

Cholera: among Choctaw, 81; in army, 138; at Fort Gibson, 150, 403; among Creeks, 150, 175.

Chouteau, Col. A. P.: 147, 148, 149, 165; trading house flooded, 23; sells buildings for Creek Agency, 183.

Chuala Female Seminary: 63, 77, 85; girls make clothing, 85.

Clark, Gen. William: 148.

Clear Creek: 39.

Clegg, Austin: 105.

Clermont (Osage chief): death of, 165.

Clough, Miss Eunice: 39, 40, 42, 46, 65.

Coacoochee (Seminole chief): see Wild Cat.

Co-cha-my (Coachman) Ward: frees, 65; Creeks from bondage, 175.

Cochnaner, N.: 69.

Coffee's Trading Post: 27, 112, 337.

Cogswell, J.: 46.

Colbert, Dougherty: 110.

Colbert, George: death and sketch of, 101, 102.

Colbert, Holmes: 116, 131.

Colbert Institute (Chickasaw Nation): 126.

Colbert, Joseph: 107.

Cobert, Levi: 110.

Cobert, Pitman: 79, 108, 109, 116, 123.

Colbert, Winchester: 107, 114, 122.

Colbert, Zach: 116.

Cold Water Army: 384, 385, 387, 397.

Cole, Col. Robert: 50.

Coleman "The Widow,": 47.

Collins, Rev. W. D.: 181.

Colson, Daniel: 301.

Comanche (Indians): 27, 120, 132, 133; depredate on Texans, 104, on Chickasaw land, 128; council with Creeks, 203; at Grand Council, 204; trade with Seminole, 245; massacre Seminole Negroes, 265; menace Seminole Indians, 278.

Concha (Choctaw Indians): 40.

Concharte Micco (Seminole Chief): 225.

Conway, Gov. James S.: 159, 161.

Coodey, Daniel R.: 328, 396, 417.

Coodey, Henrietta J.: 400.

Coodey, Joseph: 403.

Coodey, William Shorey: 307, 316, 341, 359, 376, 392, 409; writes Cherokee Act of Union, 300.

Cooper, Douglas H.: Choctaw-Chickasaw agent, 76, 82, 85, 88, 92, 129; recommends new army post, 132.

Copeland, Henry K.: 44.

Cornelius, Rev. Elias: 19.

Cornwall (Connecticut): school attended by Indian boys, 354.

Cotton Gin Port: 99.

Council, international, at Tahlequah: 188, 190, 203, 367.

Council Hill (Oklahoma): 192.

Couts, Lieut. Cave: 394.

Creek (Indians): 17; contact with whites, 17; emigration of, 147, 152, 159, 174, 175; settlements of immigrants, 151, 182, 186; suffering of, 152; sickness and mortality of, 150, 178, 211; harassed by Osage, 152, 164, 165; suffer from drought, 205, 210; from floods, 182; destitution of, 155, 161; whisky introduced, 168, 191, 217; demoralization of immigrants, 154, 162, 163; land claimed

agriculturalists, 196; at Grand Council, 204; depredate on Chickasaw, 143; on Creeks, 152; sell game to Fort Gibson, 163; invited to Cherokee council, 298.
Denkla and Woodward: 406.
Denney, J. J.: 196.
Dent, Capt. Frederick T.: 262.
Denton, J. B.: 45.
Derringer: fire-arms for Indians, 28.
Derrisaw, Jacob: 216.
Dillard, John: 356.
Doaksville (Choctaw Nation): 25, 26, 46, 60, 63, 70, 82, 88, 122, 129; Arkansas synod meets at, 82.
Dona Ana (Tex.): 138.
Doak and Tims (traders): 53.
Doolin, Michael: 397.
Doublehead, Bird: 301.
Dougherty, Mrs. Jane: 377.
Douglas, Rev. Orson: 239 ff.
Dow, Neal: 78.
Downing, Lewis: 367, 406.
Dragoons: to Cherokee Nation, 302.
Drennan, John: Indian superintendent, 74, 407.
Drew, John: 307, 399, 404.
Drew, Leroy: 175.
Drew, Richard: 263
Drew, Thomas S.: governor of Arkansas, 85, 345.
Drought: afflicts Indians, 94, 205, 210, 406, 412, 420.
Duncan, A. W.: 415.
Duncan, Rev. E. B.: 114.
Durant, Ben: 175.
Durant, Lachlan: 175.
Dutch, Capt. John: 304, 306, 308, 392, 395; sketch of, 398; death of, 398.
Du Val, E. W.: 388.
Du Val, Gabriel: 263.
Du Val, Marcellus: Seminole agent, 244, 248, 251, 261, 262, 264, 390; interest in Seminole slaves, 259.
Du Val, Miranda Julia: marries Pierce M. Butler, 388.

Du Val, William J.: 259.
Dwight Mission: 46, 376, 405, 412; removed from Arkansas, 356; description of, 356, 357; importance of, 357, 361; burned, 361.
Dwight, Jonathan E.: 60, 66, 67.
Dwight, J. R.: 70.

Eagletown (Choctaw settlement): 43, 44, 46, 48, 52, 63, 82.
Eaton, John H.: secretary of war, 150.
E bah ma tubby: 107.
Eaken, Rev. David W.: 194.
Echo Harjo (Creek chief): 203, 216.
Econchatti Micco (Seminole chief): 239.
Edwards, H. B.: builds bridges in Indian country, 92.
Edwards' Trading Settlement: 93.
Egmont Key (Fla.): 274.
Elk Creek: 237.
Elliot Mission: 99.
Emigrants: to Texas through Indian country, 111; to California, 112, 120, 134, 138.
Emerson, T. W.: 403.
Emory, Maj. W. H.: 144.
Eneah Micco (Creek chief): death of, 166.
Evansville (Ark.): 336, 342, 379.
Everglades (Fla.): 274.
Eufaula (Okla.): 62, 112, 224.

Factor, Jim: 253.
Fairfield Mission: 356, 382, 405, 412.
Farquehar, George C.: 60.
Fayetteville, (Ark.): 302.
Fields, George W.: 397, 401, 402.
Fields, James: 355.
Fields, Richard: 231.
Fields, Turtle: 307.
Fifth Infantry: 134, 138.
Fisher, Silas: 33, 67.
Fleming, Rev. John: 46, 148.
Fletcher, James (Choctaw chief): 57.
Flint District: 341.
Flint settlement: 406.
Floods damage Indians in 1833: 22, 24;

in 1844 damage Chickasaw, 107; Creeks, 182; Seminole, 237; Cherokee, 381.

Florida: war ended, 247, 273; motives of people in keeping hostilities alive, 247, 273, 274.

Florida: legislates against Seminole, 253.

Folsom, Daniel: 70, 88.

Folsom, Capt. David: 27, 35, 40, 41, 68; operates salt works, 48, 52.

Folsom, Henry: 88.

Folsom, Isaac: 57.

Folsom, Israel: 33, 41.

Folsom, I. P.: 80.

Folsom, Nathaniel: 65.

Folsom, Noah: 88.

Folsom, Peter: 89.

Folsom, Sampson: 110.

Folsom, Simpson: 88.

Folsom "The Widow": 47.

Foos Hadjo: 274.

Foreman, Alexander: 308.

Foreman, James: killed by Stand Watie, 325.

Foreman, Mrs. Sarah: 377.

Foreman, Rev. Stephen: 341, 345, 377, 385.

Foreman, S. and Company: 406.

Foreman, Thomas: 355.

Forks of the Illinois Mission: 356.

Fort Arbuckle (Indian Territory): 106, 135, 137, 144; built on site of Kickapoo village, 266; supplants Fort Washita, 124; road to, 137; encourages Chicka-saw settlement, 123; Chickasaw agency located at, 89; corn furnished by Chickasaw, 136; abandoned, 90.

Fort Arbuckle (Fla.): 250.

Fort Clinch (Fla.): 250.

Fort Cobb: established, 132.

Fort Coffee: 45, 61, 100, 378.

Fort Coffee Academy: 61, 62, 77, 85, 242; sickness in, 80; closed by measles, 94.

Fort Gibson: 130, 138, 152, 159, 237, 302, 407.

Fort Gibson: 130, 138, 152, 159, 237, 302, 407; flooded in 1833, 24, 112; troops go to relief of Chickasaw, 104; protect Creeks, 151; Creek emigrants located at, 152; Seminole camped at, 226; Seminole slaves claim protection from, 256; camped at, 278; provisions stored at, 156, 157; afflicted by smallpox and cholera, 150, 403; difficulty with Cherokee, 379; abandonment urged by Cherokee, 413; proposal alarms Creeks, 210; troops leave, 139; abandoned, 417; abandonment permits sale of whisky, 217; Cherokee council at, 295, 309; Indians denied market at, 163.

Fort Leavenworth: 302.

Fort Myers (Fla.): 273.

Fort Smith: 28, 29, 112, 138, 225, 268, 331, 379, 405; market for Indians, 105; troops leave for Fort Cobb, 132; Seminole emigrants arrive at, 251; abandoned, 90, 139.

Fort Sill: 132.

Fort Towson: 26, 39, 46, 60, 63, 65, 70, 114, 337; supplied by Choctaw Indians, 47, 53; abandoned, 44, 85, 86; used for Indian agency, 87, 88, 89; Choctaw council meets at, 88.

Fort Washita: 70, 107, 117, 120, 122, 138, 139, 337, 342, 343; established to protect Chickasaw, 105, 112, 133, 134; Chickasaw agency at, 89, 127; provisioned by Chickasaw, 113, 129; center of activity, 140; headquarters Seventh Military Department, 140; described, 142; Chickasaw gathering, 109; troops leave for Fort Cobb, 132; abandoned, 90.

Fort Wayne: 286, 288, 302, 342, 347; whisky introduced at, 322; occupied by Stand Watie, 342; Cherokee re-moved from, 345.

Fountain Church (Creek Nation): 195.

Fourche Maline: 114, 122.

Fourteen Mile Creek: 397.

Frauds by contractors: on Creek immi-

grants, 156 ff., 286; on Cherokee immigrants, 285 ff.; described by Major Hitchcock, 286, 287, 323.
Frazier, Jackson: 113, 123.
Frontier, new plans to protect: 140.
Frozen Rock, fort recommended at: 420.
Fushhatche Micco (Creek chief): 155.
Fushutchee Emarthla: 274.

Gah-na-nes-kee: 374.
Gaines, Gen. E. P.: Alarmed about Takatokah council, 289.
Gaines, George S.: 75.
Gamble, James: 107.
Gardner, James (Choctaw chief): 57.
Garland, Colonel: 46, 56.
Garrett, W. H.: Creek agent: 207, 210, 251, 273.
Gibbons, Lieut. John: 253.
Gildast, W. E.: 88.
Glasgow, Harrison and Company: 157, 161, 285, 286.
Glass, The: 359.
Glover's Fork River: 46.
Gold Rush: emigration through Chickasaw Nation, 112, 120, 134, 138; through Cherokee country, 397, 400, 401.
Goode, Rev. William H.: 53, 62.
Gooding, George C.: 87.
Gooding, Mrs. Esther: 87.
Goodland (Choctaw Nation): 93.
Good Spring: 122, 131.
Goodwater: 63.
Gopher John: 226, 228, 231, 258.
Goshen (Choctaw Nation): 21.
Governor's Island (N.Y.): 254.
Grand (Neosho) River: 153; in flood, 24.
Grand Council: 203, 204.
Grand Saline (later Salina, post office): 331, 402.
Grant, Dr. W. J.: 406.
Great Raft in Red River: 48.
Great Wahoo Swamp (Fla.): 236.
Greenwood, Dr. A. E.: 88.

Guerring, Mat.: 393, 397.
Guess, George (see Sequoyah).
Guess, Tessee (Tsee-sa-le-tah): 336, 373, 374.
Gunter, Catherine: 377.
Gunter, Daniel M.: 400.
Gunter, Edward: 303, 308.
Gunter, George W.: 398; first cotton gin, 378.
Guy, William R.; 106, 117.

Hainai (Ironeyes) (Indians): 122, 143.
Hair, James: 301.
Hair, Jefferson: 301.
Halahtochee (Seminole chief): 224.
Halfbreed, Pigeon: 393.
Halleck Tustenuggee (Seminole chief): 236, 237, 245, 247; returns to Florida, 248, 253.
Hardage, Siah: 263.
Hargrove, K. W.: 294.
Harkins, George W. (Choctaw chief): 33, 66, 67, 89; description by, 64.
Harjo Echo (Creek chief): 120.
Harley Institute: 126.
Harley, Joshua: 120.
Harnage, Ambrose: 293.
Harnage, John: 336.
Harper, Kenton: 119.
Harrald's Bluff (Swallow Rock): 24.
Harrell, Rev. John: 62, 80.
Harris, Cyrus (Chickasaw governor): 123, 131, 143.
Harrison, Peter: 181.
Hatch, Charles G.: 45.
Hawkins, Napoleon B.: 189.
Hay, Rev. Americus L.: 195; described Creek people, 196.
Hays, Jack: 24.
Hays, Thomas: 34.
Heart, Betsy: 76.
Henderson, Thomas: 36.
Henry (McHenry) Jim: 197.
Hibbard, Sarah Hale: 367, 376.
Hicks, Charles R.: 352, 372.
Hicks, Eli: 294.

Hicks, Elijah: 303, 308, 313, 327, 372; editor *Cherokee Phoenix*, 374.
Hicks, George: 286, 308, 341.
Hicks, Henderson: 294.
Hicks, Leonard: 355.
Hill, Seaborne: killed by Captain Dawson, 173.
Hilderbrand, David: 395.
Hilderbrand, John: 395.
Hills, Olivia D.: 179.
Hitchcock, Dwight W.: 376, 386.
Hitchcock, Maj. Ethan Allen: investigates frauds on Creek Indians, 158 ff.; on Cherokee, 285 ff.; report to secretary of war, 323, 324; advice to secretary, 168; describes frauds, 286, 287; describes Creeks, 177; Cherokee, 321, 370; estimate of John Ross, 322.
Hitchcock, Mrs. Hannah: 386.
Hitchcock, Rev. Jacob: 376.
Hitchiti (Indians): 184.
Holmes, Maj. T. H.: 139, 141, 251.
Holt, William: 308.
Holt, W. L. 403.
Honey Creek: 284, 285, 292, 375, 404, 412.
Honey Springs: 112.
Hoolatahooma (Redfort, Choctaw chief): 20.
Horse Prairie (Choctaw Nation): 26.
Hotchkin, Rev. Ebenezer: 39, 40, 46, 55, 63, 78, 83.
House of Representatives: demands Hitchcock's report, 324.
Howell, Calvin H.: 52.
Hudson, George: 46, 67.
Hunter, D. M.: 417.
Hunter, Capt. R. L.: 130.
Humes, Samuel: 141.
Huss (Hauss) John: 304, 308.

Illinois Camp Ground: Cherokee council, 298.
Illinois River: 139, 158, 228, 285, 331, 332, 375.
Indian Mission Conference: 375.

Indians imposed on by whites: 74, 75.
Ironeyes (Kainai) (Indians): annoy Chickasaw: 122.
Iron Bridge (Choctaw Nation): 93.
Irwinton (Ala.): 175.
Ish to ho to pa (Chickasaw king): 110, 111.
Ish hit tata: 107.
Imihl-hla-tubbe: 139.
Island Bayou: 130.
Islands, Rev. Joseph: 195.
Islands, Rev. William: 195
I-yan-nubbe (Ayanabi) Mission: 77.

Jack's Fork River: 114.
Jacobs, Eli: 158.
Jasper County (Miss.): 75.
Jefferson College: Choctaw youths attend, 58.
Jefferson, Thomas, advises Cherokee, 353.
Jesup, Gen. Thomas S.: 226, 243; promise to Seminole, 243, 255; in Seminole War, 268.
Johnson, Lieut. A. R.: 342.
Johnson, Col. Jack: 74.
Johnson, Col. Richard M.: 35.
Johnson, Senator Robert W.: 82.
Jolly, John (Cherokee chief): 289, 332, 359; death of, 291.
Jones, A. H.: 132.
Jones, Evan: 317, 360, 420.
Jones, John: 48.
Jones, John Butrick: 412, 420.
Jones, Robert M.: 48, 53, 65, 79.
Jones, Gen. Roger: 332.
Jones, Sam (Abiaca) (Seminole chief): 248, 253.
Judge, Thomas L.: Seminole agent, 228; describes Seminole, 229, 237, 238.
Jumper, Jim (Seminole chief): 252, 253, 260.
Jumper, John (Seminole chief): 260.

Ka-li-tish-ka: 139.
Kearny, Col. S. W.: 302.

McCall, Capt. George A.: 288.
McClellan, Maj. William L. (Choctaw agent): 22, 24.
McCoy, John L.: 395.
McCurtain County (Okla): 40.
McCurtain, Kennedy: 89.
McGee, Arch: 122.
McGillivray, Alexander: 175.
McGilvery's Company: 110.
McIntosh, Chilly: 149, 195, 198; sells improvements for Creek agency, 182; described, 198; offers to remove Seminole from Florida, 253.
McIntosh, Jane: 189.
McIntosh, Lizzie: 208.
McIntosh, Nunin: 263.
McIntosh, Roley: 147, 149, 152, 155, 177, 179, 184, 209, 216, 262; wealth of, 187; attempts Wild Cat's capture, 264; succeeds Eneah Micco as chief, 166.
McIntosh, William: 149, 195, 198.
McKavett, Lieut. Henry: 228; removes Seminole Indians, 228.
McKenney, Johnson (Choctaw chief): 57.
McKenney, Thompson (Choctaw interpreter): 44, 60, 67, 79.
McKinney, Rev. Edmund: 180.
McKissick, A. H. (Wichita agent): 143.
McKissick, James (Cherokee agent): 341. 346, 396; death of, 390.
McLaughlin, Benjamin: 116.
McLaughlin, James (Chickasaw chief): 114.
McLean's Bottoms: 71.
McLean's Ferry: 92.
McNair, Clement V.: 345, 398.
McNair, James: 396.
Mackey, J.: 396.
Mackey, Preston: 378.
Mackey, Samuel: 158.
Mackey, W. T.: 396.
Mail: to western army posts, 139.
Major, Daniel G.: 132.
Manard Bayou: Cherokee agency, 390.
Marble City (Okla.): 356.

Marcy, Capt. R. B.: 134, 203, 265; establishes Camp Arbuckle, 135; Fort Arbuckle, 137; lays out road to Fort Arbuckle, 137; on expedition in 1854, 140, 143.
Marcy, William M. (secretary of war): 335; threatens Ross faction, 336; ignores report of commission, 349.
Marriage institution: among Choctaw, 47.
Marshall, Benjamin: 158, 159, 189, 190, 215.
Marshall, Thomas: 194.
Martin, Brice: 347.
Martin, Eliza: 393.
Martin, Gabriel: 393.
Martin, John: 355, 401.
Martin, Mrs. John: 401.
Mason, Col. R. B.: 237; misunderstands Cherokee council, 289; investigates Cherokee troubles, 332 ff.
Mayes, J. T.: 406.
Mayes, Samuel: 368.
Mayfield, Jess: 336.
Maysville (Ark.): 379.
Meek, I.: 290.
Meigs, John: 396.
Meigs, Return Jonathan (Cherokee agent): describes Cherokee industry, 353.
Meigs, Return Jonathan (Cherokee): 400, 401; attempt to kill, 338.
Merrill, Elizabeth: 46.
Methodist Episcopal Church South: 77.
Methodist Mission: 413; schools, 412; missionary work, 80, 181, 188, 194.
Mexican emissaries: intermeddle with Choctaw, 50.
Mexican War: troops return to Fort Washita, 133, 134, 140.
Mexico, mules brought from, 134; Seminole desire to remove to, 261; Cherokee seek home in, 336, 337.
Miami (Indians): protect frontier, 187.
Mikanopy (Seminole chief): 224, 230, 231, 232, 246, 260; death of, 257.
Mikasuki (Sam Jones, or Abiaca, Seminole band): 274.

Miles, Col. Dixon S.: 134, 135.
Military influence: on Chickasaw, 133.
Military road: 126, 130, 137, 138, 140, 141.
Miller County (Choctaw Nation): 40.
Mills operated by Indians:.101, 107, 129.
Missionaries to Indians: 18-22, 35,.36, 37, 38, 39, 46, 57, 97, 179, 365, 367.'
Mississippi: 82; laws extended over Chickasaw Nation, 99.
Missouri: 281; governor called on for aid, 302.
Mogolushas (Mugulasha) (Indians): 72, 73.
Money Taker: 301.
Monroe (Chickasaw school): 99.
Moore, Lyman: 209.
Moore, Matthew: 336.
Moravian Brethren: 352, 359; mission, 413; schools, 412.
Mormons: at Tahlequah, 370.
Morrison, Sarah Jane, 76.
Morrison, Thomas, 76.
Morrison, William, 76.
Morse, Rev. Jedidiah: 352.
Morton, Dr. Samuel George: 373.
Moulton, Samuel: 46.
Mount Clover (Mex.): 337.
Mountain Fork River: Choctaw settlement on, 38, 39, 42, 46, 63, 82.
Mount Holyoke College: 408, 409, 414.
Muddy Spring (Cherokee Nation): 375, 384.
Mules from Mexico, 134.
Murrell, George M.: 382, 387, 402, 406.
Mushulatubbe (Choctaw chief): 26, 36; opposes education, 36: dies, sketch of, 49; his four sons, 50.
Mushulatubbe (District, Choctaw Nation): 26, 35, 44, 70, 79; emigrants settle in, 75.

Nannubee, Bill: 119.
Nah nubby, Capt. Chickasaw: 107.
Nail, Joel H.: 33, 47, 106.
Natchez (Indians): 184.

Natchitoches (La.): 22.
Navigation: 48, 71, 101, 135, 392, 394; specifications of keel boat, 136; stimulated by Indian emigration, 155; of Arkansas and Verdigris Rivers, 155.
Ned, Jim: 119.
Negroes: kidnapping of, 393.
Neighborhood schools: 77.
Neighbors, Robert S.: 144; killing of, 144.
Neosho (see Grand) River.
Neshoba County (Miss.): 72.
Neugin, Rebecca: describes Cherokee immigrants, 283.
New Echota (Ga.): 293. 355.
New Hope Academy: 62, 77, 80, 85; closed by whooping cough, 94.
New Orleans: 228; provisions shipped from, 156, 157.
New Spring Place: 359.
Newton County (Miss.): 75.
Nicholson, Braxton: 343.
Ninety-eighth Meridian: survey of, 132.
Nitakechi (Choctaw chief): 25, 26, 27, 40; in Mexican intrigue, 50; death of, 72.
Nocose Emathla (Seminole chief): 274.
Nocose Yohola (Seminole chief): 159, 248.
Nocus Harjo: 273, 274.
Noble, George: 253.
Noel, Dr. R. S. C.: 406.
Nonih Hacha (Mountain) River: 38, 41.
Norfolk school: 63.
North Fork River: 196, 223, 245, 263, 268, 270.
North Fork Town: 112, 162, 195, 205, 248, 261; site of Asbury Mission, 196.
Norwalk Male Seminary: 77, 81.
Nunih Waiwa: 140.

Oaktahasars Harjo: 216.
Oaklafaliah (Red Fork) District: 45.
Oak Ridge Mission: 277.
O'Connor, Lieut. Edgar: 272.
Ohiahulway: proposed Creek capitol, 183, 192.

Price, John L.: 33.
Price, Looney: 303, 307, 308.
Price's Prairie: 304.
Primitive customs: 18, 19.
Printing in Indian Territory: 56, 373, 390, 400; first press, sunk in river, 357; set up at Union Mission, 357; removed to Park Hill, 358; output, 365, 400, 412, 413; at Baptist Mission, 412.
Provisions, waste of: 156.
Pugh, Dr. Francis: 88.
Pushmataha (District, Choctaw Nation): 25, 32, 63, 122.

Quesenbury, W.: 336.
Quapaw (Indians): annoy Chickasaw, 122; few permitted on Chickasaw land, 123; supplies sunk in river, 150; protect Creeks, 187; attend council at Takatokah, 289; invited to Illinois Camp Grounds, 298.

Raiford, Phillip H.: 205; describes Creeks, 205.
Railroad: through Indian country projected, 86, 92.
Raines, Austin J.: 157 ff.
Ramsey, Rev. James B.: 60, 66, 67.
Rations: issue of, 285.
Raymond, Charlotte E.: 414.
Reconstruction and readjustment: 421; difficulties encountered by Indians, 424.
Rector, Elias: 93, 94; recommends sale of Choctaw land, 93; explores "Leased District," 143; deplores abandonment of Fort Gibson, 217; goes to Florida, 272; returns with Seminole, 274; description of Cherokee, 419, 420; recommendations, 419.
Red Clay (Tennessee): 374.
Redhead, Molly: 76.
Red River: 45, 48, 72, 100, 106, 114, 129, 337, 374.

Red River (Apuckshunnubbee or Oaklafaliah) District: 26, 33, 45.
Reece, Charles: 336.
Reed, George: 46.
Reese, H. D.: 409.
Reese, Josiah: 404.
Reude, Herman: 359, 360.
Riddle, John: 47.
Rider, Billy: 347.
Rider, Bluford, 404.
Rider, Suel: 338.
Ridge, John: 284, 285; rumor concerning, 289; signing Treaty of 1835, 296; killed, 202, 293, 317; claims of heirs, 350.
Ridge, John Rollin: 401.
Ridge, Major: killed, 202, 293, 328, 404; claims of heirs adjusted, 350.
Riley's Chapel: 375, 385, 405; temperance meeting, 385.
Rind, H. G.: 45.
Robertson, Mrs. A. E. W.: 387.
Robertson, Alice M.: 213.
Robertson, W. S.: 213.
Robinson, Rev. J. C.: 125.
Rogers, Granville: killed, 343.
Rogers, John (Cherokee chief): 291, 295, 299, 302, 304, 329, 332, 343, 359; goes to Mexico, 310; loses salt works, 331; dies in Washington, 347, 392.
Rogers, John (Fort Smith merchant): 23.
Rogers, Lewis: 396.
Rogers, Randolph: 404.
Rogers, Thomas L.: 329.
Rogers, Will: 304, 308, 396.
Ross, John (Cherokee chief): 227, 288, 336, 405, 406, 409, 423; and Cherokee emigration, 281; describes frauds on Indians, 286; effort to unite factions, 291, 292; elected chief, 303, 307, 326; delegate to Washington, 303, 308; blamed for killing of Boudinot and Ridge, 294; treatment by Gen. Arbuckle, 295, 299, 301; by secretary of war, 303, 306, 309, 310, 316; returns from Washington, 313; addresses Cher-

okee council, 314 ff.; annual message to council, 415; defeats bill to divide nation, 349; friendship for Seminole, 230; married to second wife, 331; early public duties, 355; recommends advanced schools, 393, 422; estimate by Hitchcock, 322, 368, 424.

Ross, R. H.: 396, 404, 405, 406.

Ross, E. Jane: 414.

Ross, Mrs. Eliza: 377.

Ross, Lewis: 306, 313, 355, 369, 382, 392, 400.

Ross, Minerva: 382.

Ross, William P.: 368, 384, 396, 398, 403 ff., 408, 409.

Ruble, Rev. Thomas B.: 197, 209.

Ruggles, Major Daniel: 140.

Rugglesville (at Fort Washita): 140.

Running Water: 122.

Rush Creek: 106.

Rush Springs (Okla.): 106.

Rutherford, Samuel M.: helps remove Seminole from Florida, 272, 274; urges compliance with promises to Seminole, 276.

"Saturday and Sunday schools": 77.

Saffarans & Lewis (traders): 101.

Sackett, Capt. D. B.: 132.

Sanders, Arch: 327.

Sauk (Indians): at Takatokah council, 289.

Sawyer, Miss Sophia seminary: 401.

Salina (Okla.): 331; Grand Saline, 402.

Salt, manufactured by Indians: Choctaw, 45, 48, 52; in Cherokee Nation, 358, 363, 396, 400; Cherokee legislation affecting, 331.

Salt Plains: 203, 204.

San Fernando (Mexico): 372.

Sallisaw (Salisor) Creek: 139, 375, 403.

Schermerhorn, Rev. John: 296, 318, 374.

Schmidt, John Renatus: 359.

Schrimsher, M. M.: 417.

Schrimsher and Gunter: 399.

Scale, Capt. A.: 175.

Scott, James A.: 392.

Seeley's (Thomas) Company: 110.

Seminole (Indians) customs: 268, 277; divisions into towns, 244; six chiefs, 246; emigration of 224, 225, 228, 248, 251; land occupied by Creeks, 224, 284, 285; located at Fort Gibson, 278; statistics, 224, 225; census, 239, 276; slaves among, 231, 232, 242, 255; customs as to slaves, 243, 255, 263; separate villages for slaves, 243, 259; living in Cherokee Nation, 226, 230; friendship for Cherokee, 230; kill stock of hosts, 227; Cherokee effort to remove, 234; removing to own land, 232.

Seminole (Indians): last battle in Florida, 236; captured by General Worth, 236; Florida "War," 273; kept alive by whites, 275; hostilities ended, 247; resumed, 248; surrender to General Twigs, 249, 250, 251; inducements to surrender, 250; negotiations, 251, 252, 253; threat to shoot negotiators, 252; delegations to Florida, 248, 252, 253, 254, 261, 272, 275; surrender, 255, 256.

Seminole (Indians): described, 229, 231, 234, 244, 246; as agriculturalists, 237, 238, 246; rice growers, 237, 246; as traders, 245, 260; kill their interpreter, 228; attend council at Takatokah, 289; consumption of whisky, 230, 231; failure to keep promises with, 226, 236, 276; farm implements not provided, 228; annuities unpaid, 243; promises to made by Generals Taylor and Jesup; attempt to merge them with Creeks, 223, 268; Creeks seek to govern, 242, 244; difficulty with Creeks over slaves, 242, 243; slaves promised to Creeks, 256; returned to Seminole owners, 257, 258; capture attempted by Creeks and whites, 262, 263; Seminole request separation from Creeks, 269; separation achieved, 270; education not considered, 246; schools solicited, 276, 277; schools by Bemo and Lilly, 277; government of, considered, 277; agency building erected, 276; prey to hostile Indians, 278; Negroes attacked by Comanche Indians, 264, 265; country described, 270; California road through, 276; effect of Civil War on, 278; introduced whisky, 119; annoy Chickasaw, 129; protect surveyors, 132; destitution of, 155.

Seneca (Indians): attend councils at Takatokah and Illinois, 289, 298.

Seventh Military Department: headquarters at Fort Washita, 139, 140.

Seventh Infantry: 138; ordered to Florida, 248.

"Dr. Sewell's Plates": intemperance movement, 383.

Secretary of war William Wilkins: negotiations with Cherokee, 329.

Sequoyah: 292, 298, 299, 301; sketch of, 371, 372; salt works of, 331; alphabet, great value of, 371; pension voted by Cherokee council, 374; searching party makes report, 374.

Shawnee Town: 44, 45.

Shawnee (Indians): 27, 104, 143; as agriculturalists, 196; annoy Chickasaw, 122, 143; in Grand Council, 204; council at Takatokah, 289; invited by Cherokee, 298; band to join Creeks, 176.

Shuk-hu-nat-chee (Sukinatchi) (Indians): 72, 73.

Sittewakie (Cherokee): 286.

Six Towns (Choctaw) (Indians): 20, 33, 50, 72; description of, 73.

Sizemore's Woodyard (Alabama River): 175.

Skin Bayou District: 375.

Skullyville (Choctaw Nation): 140; Choctaw constitution adopted at, 89, 90, 91; description of, 89.

Slavery among Indians: Choctaw, 54; Creeks, 171, 174; discussion by missionaries, 54, 83, 413, 420.

Smedley, Rev. Joseph: 44.

Smith, A. J. (Chickasaw agent): 119.

Smith, Akey: 396.

Smith, Archilla: 343.

Smith, Charles. 343.

Smith, I. M.: 263.

Smith, Joe: 263.

Smith, Moses: 308.

Smith, Samuel: 159.

Smallpox: among Choctaw, 49; Creeks, 150, 155; Cherokee and Seminole, 155; Chickasaw, 101.

Sodom (Creek Nation): 166.

Soft Shell Turtle: 301.

Sons of Temperance, The: 411.

Southern Superintendency: 93.

Spavinaw Creek: 398.

Spaniards: emigrated with Seminole, 176.

Spear, Archibald: 301.

Spear, James: 301.

Spear, John: 301.

Spears, Joseph: 301, 336.

Spencer Academy: 58, 66, 67, 77, 180; location of, 60; description, 60, 67; exercises at, 66; sickness in, 78.

Spencer, John C., secretary of war: 60, 323.

Spiro (Okla.): 93.

Sprague, Capt. John T.: 248; friendship for Seminole, 254.

Springplace (Ga.): 352.

Springston, Anderson: killed, 324.

Springston, Isaac: 328.

The Standing Rock: 374.

The Standing Man: 374.

Stand Watie: 293, 304, 342, 346, 347, 374; sketch of, 294; accuses John Ross, 303; delegate in Washington, 306; kills Foreman, 325; evacuates Fort Wayne, 342; leaves for Washington, 345.

Stanley, Lieut. D. S.: 144.

Stapler, John W.: 406.

Stapler, Mary B: marries John Ross, 331.

Stark, Oliver P.: 60, 93.

Starr, Bean: 327, 328, 343.

Starr, Billy: 346.

Starr, Dick: 346.

Starr, Ellis: 327, 328, 338, 346, 397.

Starr, Ezekiel: 329, 332, 336, 347; dies in Washington, 347, 392.

"Starr Gang": 112, 327, 328, 338, 339, 346, 361.

Starr, George: 347.

Starr, James: 304, 336.

Starr, Thomas: 327, 328, 338, 346, 397.

Starr, Tom: 347, 394, 396, 397.

Starr, Washington: 338, 397.

Starr, William: 338.

Steamboats: *Alert*, 74; *Arkansas*, 274; *Caspian*, 156; *Cocchuma*, 156; *Cottonplant*, 251; *Fashion*, 251; *Franklin*, 378; *General Shields*, 402; *Grey Cloud*, 274; *J. B. Gordon*, 251; *Lucy Walker*, 377; *Magnolia*, 275; *New Hampshire*, 71; *Privateer*, 156; *Quapaw*, 274; *Santa Fe*, 378; *Swan*, 225.

Steen, Capt. Enoch: 342, 395.

Stephenson, Capt. James R.: 157, 158, 159.

Stetson, Miss Ellen: 405.

Stilwell (Okla.): 285.

Stokes, Gov. Montfort: 42, 284, 295, 301, 306, 308; describes Creek Indians: 154, 163; Osage, 165; attends council at Takatokah, 290; negotiations with Cherokee, 307; office suspended, 308.

Stone Fork Creek, 337.

Stuart, Capt. John: 289.

Stuart, William P.: 110.

Sulphur Fork (La.): 22.

Surveys: 132.

Swallow Rock (Harrald's Bluff): 45.

Tafala (Choctaw hominy): 19.

Tahlequah (Cherokee Nation): Cherokee convention at, 303, 326, 342, 375, 384, 385, 387, 388, 402; Cherokee capitol, 332, 369, 370; description of, 400, 403; incorporated, 408; Methodist church proposed, 400.

Tahlontuskey council house: 298, 299, 331, 332, 333, 392.

Takatoka (Double Springs): 289; meeting at, 291, 305.

Talley, Rev. Alexander: 37, 44.

Tampa Bay (Fla.): 176, 236, 248, 249, 253.

Tawakoni (Indians): join Wild Cat, 264.

Taylor, Mrs. (hotel at Tahlequah): 370.

Taylor, Richard: 286, 336, 355, 375.

Taylor, Samuel, Jr.: describes Creeks, 171.

Taylor, Thomas: 307.

Taylor, Gen. Zachary: 225, 328, 330, 338; investigates Cherokee disorders, 327; consideration for Seminole, 227; warfare with, 245; promises to, 256; recommends fort for Chickasaw, 133.

Temperance movement: by Cherokee, 288, 378, 382, 383, 386, 389, 405, 408, 411; meeting described, 382.

Territorial government proposed: 82.

Texas emigration: 111, 112.

Texas Indians: removed to "Leased District": 131, 144.

Texan-Mexican controversy: involved Choctaw Indians, 50.

Texas Road: 111, 112.

Texas settlers: measures to protest, 138; cattle and mustangs driven through Chickasaw country, 141, 143; whisky sent into Chickasaw country, 143.

Thlathlo Hadjo: 248.

Thomas, Maj. George H.: 144.

Thompson, Benjamin F.: 285.

Thompson, Dr. J. L.: 336.

Thompson, Jack: 404.

Thompson, Johnson: 400.

Thompson, Miss Nancy: 181.

Thompson, Wiley: 404.

Thorn, John: 341, 345, 409.

Thornton, William: 359.

Three Forks, The: 148.

Thumb, Thomas: 307.

Tikaneesky, Charles: 405.

Walking Wolf: 41.

Wall, Maj. Thomas: 79.

Warren's Trading Post: 112.

Washburne, J. W. (Seminole agent): 269; describes Seminole, 269.

Washburn, Rev. Cephas: 395.

Washington Monument: Chickasaw place stone in, 123.

Washita River: 43, 106, 112, 117, 129, 130, 135, 144, 328.

Watie, John: 391.

Webber's Falls: 328; Indians carry corn from, 160; Seminole arrive at, 225, 228.

Webber's Salt Works: 396.

Webber, Walter: 285; sells buildings for Dwight Mission, 356.

Weed, Dr. George L.: 150.

Webster and Reed: 196.

West, Bluford: 307, 332; dies in Washington, 348.

West, Ellis: 338.

West, Jacob: kills Bushyhead, 327.

Wewoka: Seminole Negro settlement, 258, 263.

Wheat: early growth in Creek country, 148.

Wheeler, John F.: 252, 384.

Wheeler, Jordan: 392.

Wheelock (Choctaw Mission): 39, 46, 56, 63, 77, 78, 81; school enlarged, 58, 59.

Whipple, Lieut. A. W.: 92.

Whisky sold to Indians by whites: 43, 47, 48, 64, 74, 78, 83, 87, 127, 143, 171, 173, 322, 378, 379, 380, 381, 394, 396; introduced in Creek Nation, 154, 162, 168, 207, 387; in Cherokee Nation fight against, 288, 404; by Seminole Indians, 119, 143, 268; in army posts, 135, 139, 140.

White, P. H.: 263.

White settlers abandon improvements: 38.

Whitmore, Miss Ellen R.: 408.

Wichita (Indians): on Chickasaw land, 106, 107, 128, 133, 143; annoy Chickasaw, 122; create disturbance, 119;

flee from Caddo, 119; new home of, 131.

Wichita Mountains: 128, 132, 203.

Wild Cat (Seminole leader): 224, 226, 229, 230, 231, 244, 246; and Alligator go to Washington, 237, 241; on trading expedition, 245; on treaty expedition, 244; difficulty with Creeks, 259, 260, 264; description of, 260; schemes of, 261, 262, 263; council with Seminole, 264; takes colony to Mexico, 262, 264; attracts attention of Government, 266.

Wild Horse Creek: 135.

Wild Indians: fear of by immigrants, 51, 106.

Wilkins, William (secretary of war): recommends commission to investigate Cherokee complaints, 332.

Wilkinson, Lieut. James B.: 24.

Williams, Rev. Loring S.: 37, 41, 42; made postmaster of Eagletown, 43.

Williams, Louisa M.: 46.

Willison, J. D.: 396.

Wilson, Col. Henry: 139.

Wilson, William: 60.

Witchcraft: believed in by Indians, 20, 33.

Wolf, James: 107.

Wolf, Jinny: 377.

Wolf, Young: 307.

Woodford, O. L.: 409.

Worcester, Rev. S. A.: 21, 56, 375, 400, 409; and Mrs. Worcester arrive at Brainerd Mission, 354; at Dwight Mission, 357; translator of Gospel, 293; conducts Park Hill press, 56; regrets Boudinot's action, 297; leads temperance movement, 385.

Worcester, Sarah: 409.

Worm, The: 374.

Worth, Gen. William J.: 236, 247.

Wright, Rev. Alfred: 21, 40, 58, 59; joins Choctaw in West, 37; translates Scriptures into Choctaw, 37, 56, 84; starts Wheelock Mission, 39; enlarge-